ROUTLEDGE LIBRARY EDITIONS:
TURKEY

Volume 4

NEW APPROACHES TO STATE AND PEASANT IN OTTOMAN HISTORY

NEW APPROACHES TO STATE AND PEASANT IN OTTOMAN HISTORY

Edited by
HALIL BERKTAY AND SURAIYA FAROQHI

LONDON AND NEW YORK

First published in 1992 by Frank Cass

This edition first published in 2016
by Routledge
2 Park Square, Milton Park, Abingdon, Oxon OX14 4RN

and by Routledge
711 Third Avenue, New York, NY 10017

Routledge is an imprint of the Taylor & Francis Group, an informa business

© 1992 Frank Cass & Co. Ltd

All rights reserved. No part of this book may be reprinted or reproduced or utilised in any form or by any electronic, mechanical, or other means, now known or hereafter invented, including photocopying and recording, or in any information storage or retrieval system, without permission in writing from the publishers.

Trademark notice: Product or corporate names may be trademarks or registered trademarks, and are used only for identification and explanation without intent to infringe.

British Library Cataloguing in Publication Data
A catalogue record for this book is available from the British Library

ISBN: 978-1-138-19429-8 (Set)
ISBN: 978-1-315-62621-5 (Set) (ebk)
ISBN: 978-1-138-19493-9 (Volume 4) (hbk)
ISBN: 978-1-315-62859-2 (Volume 4) (ebk)

Publisher's Note
The publisher has gone to great lengths to ensure the quality of this reprint but points out that some imperfections in the original copies may be apparent.

Disclaimer
The publisher has made every effort to trace copyright holders and would welcome correspondence from those they have been unable to trace.

Chronology*

486–751	Merovingian rule on Gallo-Roman soil.
about 498	Baptism of the Merovingian Chlodwig (Clovis). He adopts the Catholic faith.
751–880	Carolingian rule in continental western Europe.
11th century	Christianisation of Norway, royal domination established.
early 11th century	Mahmud of Ghazna establishes a state in India, Khurasan and Transoxania.
976–1025	Reign of Basil II, Byzantine Emperor.
1071	Battle of Malazgird. Defeat of Byzantines, Turkish migration into Asia Minor.
1081 – late 12th century	The Komneni emperors rule Byzantium.
1077–1243	Seljuk rule over most of Anatolia. (The dynasty did not officially disappear until 1302.)
1220	Mongols devastate Transoxania and Khurasan.
1243	Mongols defeat Anatolian Seljuks at Kösedağ; Mongol suzerainty over much of Anatolia.
1258	Mongols conquer Baghdad, kill caliph.
1259–1294	Qublai Khan rule in China.
1260	Mamluk rulers, recently established in Egypt and Syria, turn back a Mongol army.
1261–1310	Foundation of the Menteşe, Aydın,

---

* This chronology includes only events referred to in the various articles, which explains its heterogenous appearance.

early 14th century	Saruhan, Karesi and Ottoman principalities in western Anatolia. Civil service examinations and Imperial Academy restored in China.
1332–1406	Ibn Khaldun, historian and social theorist, *maître à penser* of many educated Ottomans.
1326	Death of Osman Gazi, eponymous founder of the Ottoman dynasty, succeeded by Sultan Orhan.
1361	Ottoman conquest of Edirne (Adrianopel).
1368	Mings expel Mongol dynasty from Peking.
1389–1402	Bayezid I Ottoman Sultan.
1402	Timur defeats Bayezid I in the battle of Ankara.
1405	Death of Timur, rapid disintegration of his empire.
1451–1481	Reign of the Ottoman Sultan Mehmed II, 'the Conqueror'.
1453	Ottoman conquest of İstanbul (Constantinople).
1481–1512	Reign of the Ottoman Sultan Bayezid II.
1512–1520	Reign of the Ottoman Sultan Selim I 'the Grim'.
1520–1566	Reign of the Ottoman Süleyman I 'the Magnificent'.
1521	Defeat of the Comuneros revolt in Spain.
1526	Conquest of northern India by Babur. The Mughal dynasty begins to rule.
1526–1699	Struggles between the Ottomans and the Habsburgs for control of Hungary.
1528–1589	Architectural activity of Mimar Sinan.
1533	Hayreddin Barbarossa, Grand Admiral of the Ottoman fleet, conquers Tunis for the Ottomans.

CHRONOLOGY

1551	Ottoman conquest of Tripolis.
1557	Inauguration of the Süleymaniye mosque in İstanbul.
1555–1562	Visit of Ogier G. de Busbeck, Habsburg ambassador to Sultan Süleyman, to İstanbul and Anatolia.
1580–1620	Military rebellions in Anatolia, known as the Celali rebellions.
1611–1684/5	Evliya Çelebi, author of a ten-volume travelogue describing the Ottoman Empire.
1618–1648	The Thirty Years War in central Europe.
1628	Fall of the Huguenot fortress of La Rochelle to Louis XII.
1645–1669	War of Crete, eclipse of Venice as a Mediterranean power.
1650–1830	Ascendancy of local dynasties (*ayan, derebey*) in many parts of the Ottoman Empire.
1695	Institution of life-time tax farms (*malikâne*).
1700	Death of Carlos II, the last Spanish Habsburg.
1700–1760	Economic revival in many regions of the Ottoman Empire.
1707	Death of the Mughal ruler Awrangzib.
1730	Rebellion of Patrona Halil in İstanbul, ends the roccoco-inspired 'Tulip era' in Ottoman palace culture.
1730–1790	French ascendancy in Mediterranean trade.
1789–1807	Reign of the Ottoman Sultan Selim III.
1790–1818	Ottoman, later Ottoman-Egyptian wars against the Wahabis.
1808–1839	Reign of the Ottoman Sultan Mahmud II.

1838	'Rescript of the Rose Chamber' inaugurating the Tanzimat period.
1838–1876	Tanzimat period.
1858	Ottoman land law, considerably facilitates the acquisition of all-but-freehold property rights.

Editors' Introduction

The central theme of this double special issue of *The Journal of Peasant Studies* is that of state and peasant in Ottoman history. We present it at an exciting time in Ottoman historiography, when the orthodoxy and rigidity of the past are being forcefully challenged, on a wide variety of fronts. Those fronts are identified in Suraiya Faroqhi's article, 'In Search of Ottoman History'.

That orthodoxy, which continues to hold sway among Turkish historians, is, in the formulation of one of our contributors, characterised by the twin weaknesses of document-fetishism and state-fetishism. The challenge is here made both in general terms and with the problematic of state and peasant clearly seen as of central significance. It is obviously essential that the general challenge be made, and we think it important that the problematic of state and peasant is here presented as part of that general challenge. Naturally, however, it is state and peasant that attracts the major part of our attention.

Suraiya Faroqhi, in her Introduction, places these new approaches to the state and peasant in Ottoman history in the general context of developments in the historiography of the Ottoman Empire and highlights the major themes of each article. That we need not duplicate. But there are some aspects of this special issue which we may draw to the attention of the reader.

The first is that it is essentially about *context*: the material context in which the Ottoman peasant existed; the real (as opposed to the idealised) context of the relationship between peasant and Ottoman state; and the ideological context within which Ottoman historiography has conceptualised and approached the peasantry, as well as other issues. In setting these contexts, it provides a research agenda, rather than a set of finished results: a series of new questions, rather than a statement of conclusions.

The special issue is a passionate and powerful cry for a decisive break in the way that the issues in question are approached by historians; which demands a complete departure from Turkish nationalist historiography. We do clearly see what the outlines of the outcome of such a break and such a departure might be. But what we have is more a manifesto for action – a call to historians of the Ottoman Empire – than the finished outcome. The fuller, more nuanced, outcome will be the product of ongoing and future scholarship. Here are stated the questions and issues that such scholarship must confront.

In Ottoman history, peasantry and state are dialectically intertwined. Treatment of the peasantry in the Ottoman empire requires that the state be addressed head-on: that the nature of the Ottoman state be identified adequately. The Ottoman state needs to be demystified. This is an urgent priority. It is also a demanding task. Apart from anything else, the great bulk of documentation available to historian emanates from the Ottoman state. That documentation needs to be decoded and read with the greatest of care.

A feature of the studies published here is the strong comparative dimension which they possess: a dimension powerfully absent in nationalist historiography. As is pointed out, the illumination of a genuinely comparative approach derives, in part, from the expansion in the range of questions which historians of individual instances take to their material. For Haldon and Berktay, these are questions which derive from Marxism and from Western European historiography; for Suraiya Faroqhi from Western and Russian historiography; for Isenbike Togan from a study of Chinese history (comparing the state founded by the Mongols in thirteenth- and fourteenth-century China with the Ottoman state). This proves at once liberating and illuminating, both for Ottoman history and for the sources of comparison. If, as Suraiya Faroqhi suggests, Ottoman history has become more cosmopolitan in its continuing encounter with 'other histories', at the same time other histories are enriched in the process of comparison.

In addition, the contributions by Haldon and by Berktay have a strong theoretical underpinning, informed by historical materialism; but never at the expense of a properly and rigorously empirical approach. Halil Berktay rejects emphatically the 'unreconstructed empiricism' that has blighted Ottoman historiography in the past (and, of course, other historiographies) and which has prevented, and continues to prevent, recognition of the 'reality of peasant life' – the life of the *raiyyet*, the Ottoman dependent cultivator. In that, he is joined by John Haldon. He makes a forceful plea, however, for concrete empirical research. For Berktay, the writing of history is a process of 'mental *tâtonnement*', in which 'what is knowable becomes knowable not in itself, but by going back and forth in successive iterations between evidence, theory and ideology, by scrupulously checking History and Historiography against each other'. That is a principle which the editors of *The Journal of Peasant Studies* endorse most strongly.

T.J.B. for EDITORS, *The Journal of Peasant Studies*

Introduction

SURAIYA FAROQHI

In the 1960s and 1970s, the Turkish debate concerning the place of the Ottoman Empire in world history was vibrant, and conducted largely in Marxist terms. Researchers, who in certain cases had participated in the incipient socialist debates of the 1920s and 1930s, argued in favour of regarding Ottoman state and society as an instance of feudalism.[1] Moreover, Mehmet Fuat Köprülü, who may be regarded as the 'founding father' of modern-style Turkish studies and by no means a radical, also saw a Turco-Mongol feudalism functioning in the Middle Ages [Köprülü, 1941; Berktay, 1983]. However, feudalism often meant different things to different people. Many participants in the Turkish discussion were not particularly interested in the details of the feudalism debate going on in Europe, and probably were but marginally aware of the two major definitions of feudalism. As a result, the 'political economy' definition emphasising lords, serfs and peasant family enterprises, as well as the extraction of surplus by non-economic means, was rarely distinguished from the 'juridical' definition, which stresses inter-personal ties of dependence of men to lords and a developed fief system.[2] Several misunderstandings in later debates were to ensue from this confusion.

Views of the Ottoman Empire as a feudal system implied that the Ottomans possessed characteristics in common with a great many pre-industrial societies the world over, or if a narrower definition of feudalism is adopted, at least with pre-industrial Europe and Japan. However, the years which followed the crash of 1929 were quite unpropituous to universalistic claims of this sort. Economically speaking, this was an extremely difficult period, and the government responded by a policy of autarky, which soon had an impact on intellectual life as well. Ties to the outside world were difficult to maintain, and were widely regarded as dangerous, were seen even as a source of subversion. A casual remark by Ahmed Refik, influential historian and journalist, today remembered mainly as an editor of Ottoman documents, illustrates the tension this situation generated in

---

Suraiya Faroqhi is at Ludwig Maximilians Universität, Munich, Federal Republic of Germany. The author thanks Christoph Neumann for his comments and suggestions.

perceptive intellectuals. When discussing the biography of the architect Sinan, he devotes a few lines to the glories of the Renaissance, in which people threw off the bonds of superstition and rediscovered the glorious paganism of antiquity.[3] 'Totally separate from this humanist activity which encompassed the whole world, the Turks created a civilisation inspired only by Iranian influence.' While greatly exaggerating the geographical area in which the Renaissance unfolded, Ahmed Refik postulated that the Turks remained total strangers to this civilisation. By contrast, recent historians of art and culture such as Aptullah Kuran, Gülru Necipoğlu or Cemal Kafadar probably would not deny that a distance existed but view it in much less absolute terms.[4] Ahmed Refik does not in any way denigrate the 'happy age of mankind' inaugurated by the Renaissance, and through explicit reference to 'Iranian influence' he qualifies the isolation he postulates. The author does not refer to the 'Arabic' component in the Ottoman civilisation, probably because of his secularist outlook, and as an educated Istanbullu, he apparently was not much inspired by the history of the early medieval Turks of Central Asia.[5]

In the course of the Second World War, during which Turkey maintained an armed neutrality, isolationist tendencies gained yet further ground. Autarky was no longer a stop-gap solution advocated *faute de mieux*, but became a positive virtue, while the past was ransacked for campaigns and conquests to be exalted. Ömer Lütfi Barkan's studies of Ottoman colonisation, which involved the banishment of large numbers of people to remote areas, stressed perpetual preparedness for war [Barkan, 1949–50; 1951–52; 1953–54]. The low standard of living which prevailed during the war years, and the limitations of scholarly contacts all strengthened the isolationist strand in Turkish historical thinking during that period.[6]

While the economic conjuncture visibly improved after 1950, historiographical trends were slow to respond. In part, this slowness admittedly is an optical illusion. Many studies written during the war years could only be published in the 1950s, and reflect not so much the temper of the times, but that of preceding decades. Moreover, Barkan, the major figure in Turkish historiography during these years, was born in the early 1900s and had formed his ideas in the 1920s and 1930s.[7] But political factors equally slowed down the obsolescence of World War paradigms: Stalin's demands for Turkish territory at the end of the Second World War had ended the comparably relaxed relations between Turkey and the Soviet Union which had prevailed in the 1930s. Anti-Turkish agitation appeared in the Soviet media, and in the nervous atmosphere ensuing, anti-communist reactions of the McCarthyite variety became widespread in Turkey.[8]

A division of opinion within the Turkish intellectual community which became apparent from the late 1930s onward also affected historiography. Until the immediate pre-war years, Turkish intellectuals' support for the Kemalist movement had been broadly-based, and intellectuals critical of the state were limited in number. Even some oppositionists, in so far as they did not choose to emigrate, were on occasion willing to cooperate with the government and accept official appointments [Karaosmanoğlu, 1955: 8–9]. However, from the late 1930s onward, the régime became much less willing to tolerate public criticism, and quite a few intellectuals were gaoled and kept in prison for the duration of the war and even beyond.[9] This conflict led to a permanent division between those intellectuals willing to accept the 'official line' and those who saw themselves as oppositionists. Within the universities, a critical stance became all but impossible to maintain; and only journalism or *belles- lettres* were open to those with historical interests and unwilling to renounce open expression of their critical views.[10] As a result, 1950s historiography presents an extraordinarily conformist picture.

From the mid-1960s onward, the situation began to change. One factor was the increase in civil liberties provided by the constitution of 1961. From about 1965 on, the range of reading matter available to an intellectual dependant upon publications in Turkish vastly increased, as pressure on translators and publishers relaxed. Moreover, among European intellectuals, the denunciation of Stalin at the Twentieth Party Congress (1956), and the rebellions in Poland and Hungary during the same year encouraged re-examination of historical schemata current during the Stalinist period. Feudalism was one of the first concepts to be challenged. A universal category of feudalism was now regarded as the negation of the history of individual peoples, as part of a Stalinist attempt to impose monotonous regularity upon pre-capitalist history.

In this context, historians who considered themselves Marxists without subscribing to any party line rediscovered the concept of the Asiatic mode of production, with which Marx had briefly experimented but which he had not elaborated in any serious way [Anderson, 1979: 484ff]. In 1971 Sencer Divitçioğlu inaugurated the Turkish discussion with an essay in which he attempted to demonstrate that the Ottoman Empire was a representative of the Asiatic Mode, with a free peasantry in villages largely isolated from the market, cultivating lands belonging to the state. Several discussions of this issue in Turkey were, however, motivated more by political than by scholarly considerations. Thus, if Ottoman society was feudal, and feudalism not totally abolished with the founding of the Turkish Republic, then it made sense for 'revolutionary' elements to seek bourgeois allies in the struggle to complete the destruction of feudalism. But this strategy would have made little sense if the Turkish bourgeoisie of the 1960s and 1970s was not an autochthonous growth, but an extraneous accretion to a system which by definition could not have generated a bourgeoisie.[11]

The Kemalist movement advocated economic, political and cultural changes imposed from above, and thus regarded itself as a successor to the Tanzimat régime (1839–76), which profoundly transformed Ottoman state structures by administrative fiat.[12] However, certain sections of the 1960s' New Left were deeply hostile to the Tanzimat and all it stood for. The Tanzimat was now regarded as the main reason for the alienation of the state from the people it governed [Çavdar, 1970: 5]. The proponents of this view, however, while lyrically praising a state 'close to the people', did not draw the obvious conclusion, namely that such a state involved a return to religion, both in its *şeriat*-minded and its *sufi* versions. Thus the novelist Kemal Tahir, who combined 'Anatolian' patriotism with an exaltation of the early Ottoman state, yet played down the role of religion [Kemal Tahir, 1967].

Historians for the most part hesitated to involve themselves in the debate concerning the Asiatic Mode of Production, which was therefore mainly conducted by economists, political scientists and literary men. Yet certain proponents of the Asiatic Mode of Production felt an obvious affinity to Ömer Lütfi Barkan, whose works they used as source material. The common denominator was the exaltation of the state as a guarantor of 'peasant freedom', which kept the inroads of capitalism at bay.[13] Moreover Barkan shared with many proponents of the Asiatic Mode of Production, Ottoman-style, the vision of a state in which the public role of religion was much reduced. Mosques, soup kitchens and dervish convents interested Barkan as the institutional core of developing villages and cities, as the source of data on price history and as the providers of credit at controlled rates, but not as religious phenomena [Barkan, 1962–63, 1966, 1975b].

Barkan's vision of the Ottoman state allowed merchants only a reduced role, he seems to have regarded them with a good deal of scepticism. However, in the 1960s Halil İnalcık squarely placed the merchants on the Empire's political and economic map [İnalcık, 1969]. When in an important article published in 1977, Huri İslamoğlu and Çağlar Keyder renewed the case for the Asiatic Mode of Production in the Ottoman realm, their image of the underlying society was vastly different from that envisaged by Barkan [İslamoğlu and Keyder, 1977]. While Barkan had regarded this society as essentially passive, İslamoğlu and Keyder based their work on İnalcık's vision of a vigorous, capital accumulating merchant class. At a later stage, İslamoğlu entirely abandoned the Asiatic Mode of Production; but even in 1977 the two authors saw state–society tensions of a kind that older proponents of this view had not envisaged [*İslamoğlu*, 1987: 1–26].

Adherents of the view that the Ottoman Empire was a social formation dominated by the feudal mode of production were less visible in Turkish academic life. Yet Barkan polemicised against the idea in writing, while mostly avoiding public arguments with representatives of the Asiatic Mode of Production view [*Barkan*, 1956, 1975a]. This probably was due to the realisation that if the Ottoman Empire was classed as feudal, it was placed in the same category as the states of medieval Europe. This, however, was considered objectionable from at least two points of view. On the one hand, societies in which the central power was weak and administration decentralised – and this was the prevailing view concerning medieval feudal states – were regarded as something primitive, while the reason for exalting the Ottoman state was exactly the fact that it appeared as 'strong' and centralised. On the other hand, during the 1960s and 1970s many Turkish intellectuals, and specifically Barkan, saw themselves as belonging to the Third World and regarded European intervention as the source of all evil [*Barkan*, 1975b: 4–8]. The two motifs could be connected: Turkey was a Third World country, exposed to aggressive intervention on the part of the European-dominated world economy, but if incorporation had not led to outright colonisation, this was due to the strongly built structure of the Ottoman Empire. This view of things also explains why the 'world economy' thesis in its Wallersteinian shape continues to attract Turkish historians and social scientists.[14]

The adoption of a Third World identity should have encouraged Turkish researchers to undertake comparative studies with Iran, India, China or even Inner Asia; but this did not in fact happen with any frequency. Language barriers, lack of the necessary library holdings and a limited number of employment possibilities all acted as deterrents. In the 1950s comparisons between the Ottoman Empire and Japan at one point had been in vogue; but this interest was initiated by American rather than by Turkish scholars, and had few repercussions in the Turkish academic environment [*Ward and Rustow*, 1964]. This is quite comprehensible, given the, for a Turkish scholar, especially unattractive problématique. Within the modernisation paradigm, Meiji Japan came out as a success and the Ottoman Empire as a failure; and as the modernisation paradigm was more and more discredited, the comparison project also was dropped.

It has sometimes been suggested that social science or history professors in Europe or the United States, when training graduate students from Third World countries, encourage the latter to write theses on their respective societies, since this is a way to obtain access to primary materials not otherwise available [*Tekeli*, 1977: 41]. This factor has certainly contributed its share toward discouraging comparative studies, as Turkish graduate students failed to acquire the necessary expertise. But at least as important is a factor endogenous to the Turkish academic environment. When a graduate student selects a thesis topic on an issue not immediatly relevant to Turkey, he/she is put under fairly strong pressure to show 'what that has to do with us'. Students may even be told that Turkish society is not wealthy enough to finance research of little direct relevance, and many Ph.D. candidates easily internalise this pressure. Even within the Wallersteinian 'world systems' framework, which involves a European core and peripheries of different cultural and political backgrounds, comparisons involving the Ottoman Empire have been launched only quite recently, namely in 1990.[15] Of course if one rejects the 'world economy' framework, it is easy to find an explanation for this omission. Pressures coming from the core area according to this model are constructed as so overpowering that the reactions of local societies to European penetration are insignificant, and it is therefore unnecessary to study them. But I believe that this criticism is unfair, and that pressures toward 'isolationism' coming from the academic environment are much more significant.

In the recent past, comparative studies have however appeared on the academic agenda, both within and outside the 'world systems' framework. I would suggest that non-academic factors have been more important than dynamics within Ottoman historiography in bringing about this change. In the early 1980s a sizeable number of top-level Turkish historians and social scientists emigrated, and gifted graduate students often elected to stay abroad after completing their degrees. However, these expatriates maintained close ties to the Turkish academic environment, to which some of them ultimately returned. As a result, Turkish history and social science became more cosmopolitan, a tendency which gained ground due to the official policy of seeking membership in the European Economic Community. A scholar with a determined orientation toward Europe now became an asset, since he or she could establish lines of communication not otherwise available.

Equally significant, in the long run, was probably the opening of frontiers as a result of the 1989 political changes in Eastern Europe. To begin with, this event has increased the number of participants in the debate on Ottoman history, which has normally been somewhat claustrophobic. Moreover, the notion of feudalism belongs to the intellectual baggage of all persons who have been trained in Eastern European or Soviet universities. It is still too early to determine what consequences this factor will have for our debate; complete rejection of the feudalism concept is certainly 'on the cards' if the latter were once again to be identified with Marxism of the 'official line' variety. But it is also possible that this concept will resurface, albeit in a new shape. In the short run, it is probably more important that old borders have fallen, that places hitherto inaccessible have become less so, and that international dialogue has broadened; all these factors should encourage a broader comparative approach to Ottoman history, with or without feudalism.

On a more academic level, comparative studies have also resulted from increased debate among Marxists and non-Marxists grappling with the problem of state formation. In the 1970s and 1980s there was a notable reaction against the study of economic conjunctures, demographic structures and popular mentalities, which had dominated European historiography in the previous decades, and the attempt to 'bring the state back in' still continues [*Evans, Rueschemeyer and Skocpol*, 1985].

The most sophisticated researchers do not advocate a simple return to old-style political history, but call for re-examination of the state in the light of socio-economic and cultural studies.[16] Debate has focused on the question of to what extent cultural and political phenomena develop autonomously from the 'underlying' socio-economic structure. For many researchers the metaphor of 'underlying' structures and political or cultural superstructures has itself become anathema. When dealing with the state, scholars confront the problem to what extent the persons who make up the state apparatus act 'autonomously', that is, independently, of the needs and desires of the social class from which they had been recruited.[17] Some scholars, in my view mistakenly, have regarded the Ottoman Empire as a classical example of such an 'autonomous' ruling class; they have been led astray by Ottomanist historians themselves, who have greatly exaggerated the degree to which young boys recruited into the Ottoman administration through the 'child levy' (*devşirme*) were cut off from their previous social environments. In my view the 'state fetishism' of Ottomanist historians is the very old-fashioned base upon which rest some of the more recent views on Ottoman 'despotism'.[18]

This discussion is likely to continue unabated in the near future, since one of the more solid bases of state fetishism in the twentieth century has been undermined, and the 'bureaucratic socialism' or state capitalism of the Soviet Union rapidly is being transformed. The events of 1989, and the social and ecological devastation they revealed, have shown a state constructed as a 'perfect war machine' to generate anything but a good life for its subjects. In the long run, such a state will even endanger its own survival. This insight has confirmed the idea Niels Steensgaard suggested in 1978, namely that the crisis of seventeenth-century Europe, whose disparate timing from country to country has roused so much debate, can be explained by the excessive cost of absolutism, war and preparation for war [Steensgaard, 1978]. Mehmet Genç's attempt to explain the Ottoman economic crisis of the late eighteenth century as an outcome of war financing may be regarded as basically the same vision, transported into an Ottoman environment [Genç, 1984].

This view of the state as a Moloch, as an organisation which threatens the lives of ordinary citizens, involves an anti-centralist view shared at present by many historians; after all, even the super-centralist historiography of France has paid tribute to Flandres and the Langue d'oc regions.[19] In the Ottoman context, the cautious 'rehabilitation' of local notables (ayan), whom earlier nationalistic historiography had execrated, may be viewed in the same context: Necdet Sakaoğlu, Günsel Renda and Ayda Arel have presented these families as the upholders of the interests of their respective *petits pays* and as bearers of a provincial culture, which was receptive to Istanbul motifs but assimilated them into regional traditions [Sakaoğlu, 1984; Renda, 1989; Arel, 1986]. Scepticism vis-à-vis the central state as an institution, as opposed to individual governments, is voiced less easily in Turkey than in many other countries, and one almost needs to be a prince to openly advocate decentralisation.[20] Therefore, it is all the more remarkable that a 'decentralising' strain has appeared in Ottomanist historiography.[21]

Through this sceptical reappraisal of the centralising state, Ottomanist historiography may also pick up a theme which it has so far refused, namely the investigation of border areas between history and anthropology. Norbert Elias, an early representative of this genre, has aroused a degree of interest among Turkish intellectuals; yet his attempt to link the most private spheres of human life, such as personal hygiene and table manners, to the formation of the central state has not induced Ottomanist historians to take up this line of work [Elias, 1969]. Much the same thing can be said about empirical research on the formation of African states which has interested certain historians of early medieval Europe. But researchers dealing with the pre-Ottoman (beylik) period of Anatolian history, or with the settlement of nomads, have but rarely availed themselves of the possibilities for formulating new questions which this material allows.[22] Nor has the study of *mentalités* fared much better. The attempt to decipher the attitudes of people who have left few written traces has been perceived as a challenge only in the case of women's history. And even women's history is still a marginal field to most Ottoman historians, though recently it has been developing a wider appeal. This reticence on the part of Ottomanist historians vis-à-vis the 'interface' between history and anthropology is remarkable, particularly since studies in historical anthropology were pioneered by historians forming part of the *Annales* group, such as Emmanuel Le Roy Ladurie, Michel Vovelle, Robert Muchembled and in the Byzantine sector, Evelyne Patlagean [*Le Roy Ladurie*, 1975; *Vovelle*, 1982; *Muchembled*, 1978; *Patlagean*, 1977]. By contrast, the economic and social studies of an earlier period, associated with the names of Fernand Braudel, Emmanuel Le Roy Ladurie or Guy Bois had been a source of inspiration to Ottomanist historians [*Braudel*, 1966; *Le Roy Ladurie*, 1969/1974; *Bois*, 1976]. It seems that the latter, both Turks and non-Turks, have internalised state-centred paradigms to such an extent that the genesis of the state in historical times has become a kind of tabu. States precede history, almost like Platonic ideas or the word of God in the gospel of St. John. Moreover, the private lives of people are not regarded as a serious topic for research. The latter is limited no longer quite to kings and battles, but includes industries, bullion transfers and incorporation, phenomena which even if they do not form part of traditional political history, directly affect the lives of states. It remains to be seen whether the new concern for women's history will be strong enough to 'crack' this paradigm.

The studies presented here take issue with various of the paradigm's weak points. To begin with, they are all comparative in approach. John Haldon as a Byzantinist and a student of Marxist political theory examines the Ottoman Empire; while his expertise as a medieval historian functions as a backdrop, he concerns himself with the degree and the limits of autonomous action on the part of the Ottoman ruling group.[23] Within a broad view of feudalism, which he regards as the dominant mode of prroduction for human societies ever since the neolithic revolution was completed, he emphasises the role of the Turkish aristocracy throughout the period of Ottoman expansion. This is a reaction against the standard Ottomanist view that Ottoman society could not have been feudal because it did not possess a hereditary nobility. This point certainly makes sense within the definition of feudalism Haldon has adopted. But in my view, more significant is his argument that the institution of the 'levy of boys' (*devşirme*) by the Sultans from the late fifteenth century onward constituted not only a measure designed to increase the ruler's political control at the expense of the Turkish aristocracy, but also an element within a struggle over economic resources. If this competition was a significant element of the struggle between *devşirme* recruits and the older Turkish aristocracy, there remains little reason to insist that the Ottoman ruling class was entirely political in origin, totally owed its genesis to the central state and should therefore be placed in a category apart from 'typical' feudal societies. In turn, this interpretation greatly reduces the need to postulate some variant of the Asiatic Mode of Production or else claim that the Ottoman Empire was a polity *sui generis*, incommensurable with other known states and societies.

Haldon's article constitutes an effort to defend Marxist state theory by entering into a sustained debate with non-Marxists, at a time when political, intellectual and moral challenges to socialism are more serious than they have been for a long time. His attempts to seek common ground with his opponents are apparent at every turn; he studiously avoids the temptation to withdraw into a dream world, a reaction found not infrequently among Stalinists and Maoists. While salvaging the 'first principles' of historical materialism he proposes variety and flexibility in historical work, thereby continuing the tradition of E. J. Hobsbawm and Rodney Hilton.

Halil Berktay shares with Haldon a commitment to historical materialism and modes of production as central categories of analysis. For him the concept of feudalism is even more central than it is to Haldon, and in his entire published work he has defended the idea that (in the political economy and not in the juridical meaning of the term) the Ottoman social formation was feudal [*Berktay*, 1987, 1990]. In his analysis, it is decisive that Ottoman primary producers were small peasants with direct access to land, ploughs and animals, that is, the means of production. Surplus value in the shape of taxes and dues therefore could be collected from them only by political coercion, not through the work process itself, as is usual under capitalist systems. Whether dues are collected by individual lords or a centralised state in this perspective becomes a secondary matter.

Berktay is concerned with the early stages of state formation; he compares the Ottoman experience with early medieval Europe, that is, with the Merovingian and Carolingian periods and even with Iceland. Thereby implicitly he de-mythologises the early Ottoman state. The latter no longer springs ready-made from the head of some Central Asian Pallas Athene, but comes into being in the concrete environment of medieval Anatolia and Rumelia, which incidentally is much more open to historical investigation than Dark Ages France, Iceland or Central Asia. His contribution lies in his thorough familiarity with the ins and outs of the European debate on feudalism, ass it has been conducted in both in Marxist and non-Marxist circles. If the debate on

Ottoman feudalism is to be revived, his work will constitute a starting point.

Isenbike Togan comes from quite a different historiographical tradition. As a student of China and Central Asia, she applies categories current in these disciplines to Ottoman history, with unexpected results. Even her problématique would not have occurred to a 'straight' Ottoman historian. In China whenever there occurred a major social or political crisis, the result was a change of dynasty. When the Mongol (Yuan) dynasty was no longer able to handle the tension between assimilation of Chinese political patterns at the centre and autonomous action by Mongol princes at the periphery, it fell from power. But the Ottoman dynasty survived conflicts which would have caused 'the mandate of Heaven' to be withdrawn from the Yuan, or any other Chinese dynasty for that matter. Moreover, while the Ottoman and Yuan dynasties went through a sequence of comparable phases, these phases were much longer in the Ottoman case than in that of the Yuan Empire – in the latter instance most phases were limited to a very few years. What was the secret of Ottoman longevity?

Togan's article is built on the premise that the Mongol Empire in China and the Ottoman Empire in Anatolia and the Balkans shared a common fate, because they originated in the domination of a conquering elite over a sedentary population. This situation made necessary a complex adjustment of relations between the central government and the outlying provinces. Her basic categories are 'centralisation of power resources', which she calls '*accumulation*' and its opposite, namely, 'power sharing'; both policies can operate in the political and in the economic arenas; Togan shows no inclination to regard political ideology as primary, a tendency which has become part of the 'received wisdom' of present-day Ottomanist historiography.[24]

Suraiya Faroqhi's article is again concerned with Ottoman–European comparison, but with the early modern rather than with the medieval period. In consequence, her contribution focuses not on the Ottoman state's period of genesis, but on the time during which it was fully functioning and, due to the mass of documentation which it generated, readily observable. The main point of the article is that the Ottoman state of the sixteenth and seventeenth centuries belongs in the same category as the centralised, late feudal states of contemporary Europe, and is most readily comparable with France and Spain.[25] In this perspective, the admittedly significant differences between the rule of the Sultans and the absolutism of the larger European states mask even more significant similarities. Tax farming, the 'grandee mentality' of seventeenth-century high officials, the operation of political patronage and the activity of guilds are all pertinent examples. Thus one can read this contribution as an argument that the Ottoman state was of the late-feudal, centralising variety. Yet the question whether the Ottoman state was feudal is not central to the argument. Rather the article argues the existence of historical change inside Ottoman state and society, generated by internal dynamics and not merely a reaction and adaptation to challenges from a rapidly changing Europe.

Apart from Togan, the contributors deal with Ottoman and European history. In a sense that is a weakness, and as Togan has shown, possibly it is easier to try and make sense of Ottoman history with categories derived from Chinese, or for that matter, from Indian history. If only one of the contributors has attempted such a thing, this is due to the gaps in our historical education. Comparisons only work out if the researcher undertaking them is thoroughly familiar with the two societies to be compared, and for the Ottoman historian, this point of reference in most cases is Europe. But many researchers believe that this gap in our education can and should be filled, and to document the first steps in this direction, we have included a report by Halil Berktay on present, and as yet very tentative and preparatory, discussions between historians of India, Iran and the Ottoman Empire.

NOTES

1. Berktay [1990] discusses both the scholarly and the political implications of this debate.
2. The literature is too numerous to be listed here. For two classical works, see Bloch [1931/1966] and Bloch [1940/1966].
3. Ahmed Refik [1980: 1]. This edition has been linguistically modernised by Vahit Çabuk. I was unable to consult the original edition.
4. For relationships between Renaissance and contemporary Ottoman art compare Kuran [1987: 244 ff.]; Necipoğlu [1989]. Kafadar [1989] discusses first-person narrative and autobiographic writing, a genre often regarded as alien to the Islamic tradition, and is therefore also germane to our topic.
5. Compare the list of publications in Ahmed Refik [1980: XIII–XXIV]. Ahmed Refik concentrated on the Ottoman classical period, but also studied Ottoman relations with Europe.
6 The German and Austrian émigrés who found refuge in Turkey during the 1930s and 1940s did not change this picture, at least not with respect to historical studies.
7. The present authors are also subject to certain common influences. We were all born in the 1940s and received our formative experiences during the 1960s and 1970s. Our turn to be regarded as the product of our times is surely imminent.
8. As an amazing specimen of Stalinist anti-Turkish propaganda, compare the Second World War film 'The Third Blow' (Igor Savtchenko, 1948, Soviet Union). The caricature of a Kemalist diplomat has been inserted into a rather monotonous battle epos.
9. The most distinguished of them were the writers Kemal Tahir and Nazim Hikmet.

INTRODUCTION

10. On the manner in which the historian Niyazi Berkes was forced to leave Ankara University compare an oral communication by Martin Strohmeier at the German Congress of Orientalists (Munich, 1991).
11. For the argument that even the late Ottoman state placed severe limits on the activities of the bourgeoisie, compare Keyder [1987: 76–7].
12. A major anthology of studies on the Tanzimat was put together for the centenary of the Tanzimat in 1939 [*Anon.*, 1940]. This collective volume was dedicated to President Ismet Inönü and published under the auspices of Hasan Ali Yücel, Minister of Education.
13. 'Really, since land questions possess a special quality that imparts to them a persistent tendency toward degeneration, the state has always needed to intervene in an adjusting and an organizing capacity' [*Barkan*, 1940: 420].
14. The journal *Review*, published by Fernand Braudel Center, SUNY, Binghamton, frequently carries articles on the Ottoman Empire, largely written by Turkish scholars.
15. A conference on Ottoman manufacturing, held at the Fernand Braudel Center in November 1990, brought together historians of India, China, Europe, the United States and the Ottoman Empire. The papers will hopefully be published (editor: Donald Quataert).
16. Pierre Chaunu, who has probably gone furthest in postulating economic and demographic reasons for seemingly remote political and cultural phenomena, has yet produced a penetrating analysis of the early modern French state [Chaunu, 1977].
17. This issue also will be taken up by Rifa'at Abou-El-Haj, whose work on 'The Nature of the Ottoman State' is soon to be published by SUNY Press.
18. The state-centredness of Ottomanist historians probably explains why Anderson [1979. 484 ff.] has so much trouble disengaging himself from the Asiatic Mode of Production where the Ottoman Empire is concerned, even though on a theoretical level, he rejects the concept. On the problem as a whole, compare Islamoğlu [1987]. I owe a debt to Rifa'at Abou-El-Haj for allowing me to see his unpublished work and discussing these issues with me.
19. This is reflected in the structure of the *Histoire économique et sociale de la France*, particularly in the chapter on peasant life in the late medieval and early modern periods [*Le Roy Ladurie*, 1977].
20. In the late Ottoman period, the Ottoman prince Sabaheddin, in opposition to the Committee for Union and Progress, proposed decentralisation.
21. İlber Ortaylı has published a variety of studies on the administration of cities since the Tanzimat, which deal with yet another aspect of decentralisation and responsiveness to the concerns of urban dwellers [*Ortaylı*, 1985].
22. Lindner [1983] constitutes the exception which proves the rule.
23. Haldon has recently dealt with the state–society relationship in an early medieval setting [*Haldon*, 1990].
24. For an explication of ideological continuity between the different variants of the Near Eastern state (Sassanid, Abbasid, Ottoman) compare İnalcık [1969: 97–102].
25. This view implies that until the second half of the eighteenth century, similarities between the Ottoman Empire and the continental European states outweighed the differences. Only from about 1760 onward do we encounter rapid divergence, leading to incorporation into the European world system in the early nineteenth century.

REFERENCES

Abou-El-Haj, Rifa'at, unpublished, 'The Nature of the Ottoman State'.
Ahmed Refik, 1980, *Alimler ve Sanatkârlar* (Scholars and Artists), (edited by Vahit Çabuk), Ankara: Ministry of Culture.
Anderson, Perry, 1979, *Lineages of the Absolutist State*, London: Verso.

Anon., 1940, *Tanzimat I*, İstanbul: Maarif Vekâleti.

Arel, Ayda 1986, 'Image architecturale et image urbaine dans une série de bas- reliefs Ottomans dans la région égéenné, *Turcica* XVIII.

Barkan, Ömer Lütfi, 1940, 'Türk Toprak Hukuku Tarihinde Tanzimat ve 1274 (1858) Tarihli Arazi Kanunnamesi' (The Tanzimat and the Landholding Code of 1274/1858 in Turkish legal history), in Anon. (ed.), *Tanzimat I*, İstanbul: Maarif Vekâleti, pp.321–421.

Barkan, Ömer Lütfi, 1949–50, 1951–52, 1953–54, 'Osmanlı İmparatorluğunda bir İskân ve Kolonizasyon Metodu Olarak Sürgünler' (Deportations as a Means of Settlement and Colonization in the Ottoman Empire), *İstanbul Üniversitesi İktisat Fakültesi Mecmuası* (Journal of the Faculty of Economics, İstanbul University) XI, 1–4; XIII, 1–4; XV, 1–4.

Barkan, Ömer Lütfi, 1956, 'Türkiye' de 'Servaj' Var mıydı?' (Was there Serfdom in Turkey?), *Belletin* (Bulletin), XX, 78.

Barkan, Ömer Lütfi, 1962–63, 'Şehirlerin Teşekkül ve İnkişafı Tarihi Bakımından Osmanlı İmparatorluğunda İmaret Sitelerinin Kuruluş ve İşleyiş Tarzına Ait Araştırmalar' (Researches concerning the manner of establishment and functioning of major foundation complexes in the Ottoman Empire, as a question of urban organisation and historical development), *İ.Ü İktisat Fakültesi Mecmuası* (Journal of the Faculty of Economics, İstanbul University), 23, 1–2.

Barkan, Ömer Lütfi, 1966, 'Edirne Askeri Kassamı'na Ait Tereke Defterleri (1545–1659)' (Estate Inventories of the Official in Charge of *askeri* Estates), *Belgeler* (Documents), III, 5–6.

Barkan, Ömer Lütfi, 1975a, 'Feodal Düzen ve Osmanlı Tımarı' (The feudal order and the Ottoman *tımar*), in Okyar, Osman and Ünal Nalbantoğlu (eds.), *Türkiye İktisat Tarihi Seminei, Metinler, Tartışmalar* . . . (Seminar on Turkish economic history, texts and discussions), Ankara: Hacettepe Üniversitesi, pp.1–32.

Barkan, Ömer Lütfi, 1975b, 'The Price Revolution of the Sixteenth Century: A Turning Point in the Economic History of the Near East' (translated by Justin McCarthy), *International Journal of Middle East Studies*, 6.

Berktay, Halil, 1983, *Cumhuriyet İdeolojisi ve Fuat Köprülü* (Republican Ideology and Fuat Köprülü), İstanbul: Kaynak Yayınları.

Berktay, Halil, 1987, 'The Feudalism Debate: The Turkish End – Is "Tax-vs.-Rent" Necessarily the Product and Sign of Modal Difference?', *The Journal of Peasant Studies*, Vol.14, No.3.

Berktay, Halil, 1990, *The 'Other' Feudalism* (unpublished Ph.D. dissertation, University of Birmingham).

Bloch, Marc, 1931/1966, *French Rural History: An Essay on its Basic Characteristics* (translated by Janet Sondheimer), Berkeley, CA: University of California Press (original printing in 1931).

Bloch, Marc, 1940/1966, *Feudal Society* (translated by L.A. Manyon), 2 vols., Chicago, IL: University of Chicago Press (original printing in 1940).

Bois, Guy, 1976, *Crise du féodalisme, Economie rurale et démographie du début du 14ᵉ siècle au milieu du 16ᵉ siècle*, Paris: Editions de l'Ecole des Hautes Etudes en Sciences Sociales.

Braudel, Fernand, 1949/1966, *La Méditerranée et le monde méditerranéen à l'époque Philippe II*, 2 vols, 2nd, revised edition, Paris: Armand Colin (first published in 1949).

Çavdar, Tevfik, 1970, *Osmanlıların Yarı Sömürge Oluşu* (How the Ottoman Became a Semi-colony), İstanbul: Ant Yayınları.

Chaunu, Pierre, 1977, 'L'état', in F. Braudel and E. Labrousse (eds.), *Histoire économique et sociale de la France*, 7 vols., Paris: Presses Universitaires de France, Vol.1, 1, pp.9–230.

Divitçioğlu, Sencer, 1971, *Asya Üretim Tarzı ve Osmanlı Toplumu* (The Asiatic Mode of Production and Ottoman society), Istanbul: Köz Yayınları.

Elias, Norbert, 1969, *Über den Prozess der Zivilisation, soziogenetische und psychogenetische Untersuchungen*, 2nd edition, Bern: Francke AG.

Evans, Peter, Rueschemeyer, Dietrich and Theda Skocpol (eds.), 1985, *Bringing the State Back In*, Cambridge: Cambridge University Press.
Genç, Mehmet, 1984, 'Osmanlı Ekonomisi ve Savaş' (The Ottoman economy and war), *Yapıt* (Work), Vol.49, No.4; Vol.50, No.5.
Haldon, John, 1990, *Byzantium in the Seventh Century. The Transformation of a Culture*, Cambridge: Cambridge University Press.
İnalcik, Halil, 1969, 'Capital Formation in the Ottoman Empire', *The Journal of Economic History*, XXIX.
İslamoğlu, Huri and Çağlar Keyder, 1977, 'Agenda for Ottoman History', *Review*, Vol.I, No.1.
İslamoğlu, Huri, 1987, '"Oriental Despotism" in World System Perspective', in Huri İslamoğlu (ed.), *The Ottoman Empire and the World Economy*, Cambridge: Cambridge University Press and Maison des Sciences de l'Homme, pp.1–26.
Kafadar, Cemal, 1989, 'Self and Others: The Diary of a Dervish in Seventeenth Century Istanbul and First-person Narratives in Ottoman Literature', *Studia Islamica*, 69.
Karaosmanoğlu, Yakup K., 1955, *Zoraki Diplomat (Hatıra ve Müşahede)* (The Involuntary Diplomat, Memories and Observations), Istanbul: İnkılap Kitabevi.
Kemal Tahir, 1967, *Devlet Ana* (Mother Devlet), 2 vols., Ankara: Bilgi Yayınevi.
Keyder, Çağlar, 1987, *State and Class in Turkey. A Study in Capitalist Development*, London, New York: Verso.
Köprülü, Mehmet Fuat, 1941, 'Ortazaman Türk-İslâm Feodalizmi' (Turkish–Islamic Feudalism of the Middle Ages), *Belleten* (Bulletin), 19.
Kuran, Aptullah, 1987, *Sinan, The Grand Old Master of Ottoman Architecture*, Washington, Istanbul: Institute of Turkish Studies and Ada Press Publishers.
Le Roy Ladurie, Emmanuel, 1969/1974, *The Peasants of Languedoc* (translated by John Day), Urbana, Chicago . . . : University of Illinois Press (original printing in 1969).
Le Roy Ladurie, Emmanuel, 1975, *Montaillou, village occitan de 1294 à 1324*, Paris: Gallimard.
Le Roy Ladurie, Emmanuel, 1977, 'Les masses profondes: La paysannerie', in F. Braudel and E. Labrousse (eds.), *Histoire économique et sociale de la France*, 7 vols., Paris: Presses Universitaires de France, Vol.1, 2, pp.483–65.
Lindner, Rudi Paul, 1983, *Nomads and Ottomans in Medieval Anatolia*, Bloomington, IN: Research Institute for Inner Asian Studies.
Muchembled, Robert, 1978, *Culture populaire et culture des élites*, Paris: Flammarion.
Necipoğlu, Gülru, 1989, 'Süleyman the Magnificient and the Representation of Power in the Context of Ottoman–Hapsburg–Papal Rivalry', *The Art Bulletin*, LXXI, 3.
Ortaylı, Ilber, 1985, *Tanzimattan Cumhuriyete Yerel Yönetim Geleneği* (Traditions of Local Government from the Tanzimat to the Republic), Istanbul: Hil Yayın.
Patlagean, Evelyne, 1977, *Pauvreté économique et pauvreté sociale à Byzance, 4ᵉ–7ᵉ siècles*, Paris, The Hague: Mouton.
Renda, Günsel, 1989, 'Die traditionelle Malerei und das Einsetzen der westlichen Einflüsse', in Asher, M. et al., *Die Geschichte der türkischen Malerei*, Istanbul: Palasar SA, pp.15–86.
Sakaoğlu, Necdet, 1984, *Anadolu Derebeyi Ocaklarından Köse Paşa Hanedanı* (The Dynasty of Köse Paşa, an Anatolian Magnate Household), Ankara: Yurt Yayıncılık.
Steensgaard, Niels, 1978, 'The Seventeenth-century Crisis', in Geoffrey Parker and Lesley Smith (eds.), *The General Crisis of the Seventeenth Century*, London: Routledge & Kegan Paul, pp.26–56.
Tekeli, Ilhan 1977, 'Çevre Ülkelerinde Toplumsal Bilimlerin İdeolojik Sorunları' (Ideological problems of the Social Sciences in the Peripheral Countries), in Seyli Karabaş and Yaşar Yeşilçay (eds.), *Türkiye'de Toplumsal Bilim Araştırmalarında Yaklaşımlar ve Yöntemler* (Approaches and Methods in Social Science Research in Turkey), Ankara: Orta Doğu Teknik Üniversitesi, pp.31–54.
Vovelle, Michel, 1982, *Idéologies et mentalités*, Paris: François Maspéro.
Ward, Robert and Dankwart A. Rustow (eds.), 1964, *Political Modernization in Japan and Turkey*, Princeton, NJ: Princeton University Press.

The Ottoman State and the Question of State Autonomy: Comparative Perspectives

JOHN HALDON

I. STATE THEORY AND STATE AUTONOMY: THE PROBLEM

The Ottoman state has frequently been cited in works of comparative history or sociology as a particularly clear example of a centralised, bureaucratic state standing over a social formation which, in its essential economic relationships, exemplifies the 'Asiatic' mode of production. In this contribution, I want to examine these assumptions in respect of both the actual functioning of the Ottoman state and its apparatuses, on the one hand; and, on the other, of the concepts through which it might best be understood. In the process, I will suggest that Ottoman society can be approached most profitably in terms of feudal production relations (understood in the political economy sense, therefore, rather than the non-Marxist legalistic–political usage). I will then go on to suggest that, contrary to some recent 'state theorist' interpretations, states cannot act entirely autonomously from the relations of production on which they are founded, and that the Ottoman state (which supposedly counts as one of the most successful in this respect, since it has been assumed that it was able – through the *devşirme* – to create a state elite divorced from the rest of society) is no exception to this. The Ottoman state elite was no more divorced from the social relations underlying the state than any other social group.

All of this is predicated upon an essentially historical materialist perspective, however; and in order to demonstrate these points, I shall begin by taking up some recent challenges from state theorist analyses to a Marxist approach. This will entail a digression on the degree and nature of the explanatory and causal force we are to ascribe to 'the economic' in historical materialist analysis, that is to say, what role the relations of production and the forces of production play in the overall configuration and historical trajectory of state and social formation. My discussion of the Ottoman case will follow.

John Haldon is at the Centre for Byzantine, Ottoman and Modern Greek Studies, University of Birmingham, PO Box 363, Birmingham B15 2TT.

As mentioned already, recent comparative historical work has stimulated a great deal of interest in states and state formations, and in setting out to challenge what, from the point of view of 'state theory', are seen as traditional and flawed approaches, writers working from this perspective have taken up the question of the underlying causal relationships leading to the wide range of political structures and forms of the distribution of power within human society. Most have been concerned with modern industrial or industrialising societies, and there have appeared in the last year or so a number of excellent and penetrating critiques of some of these works, and so I will not address these here.

But two books have appeared recently which deal with pre-capitalist state formations and society, and these present major challenges to both traditional Weberian as well as Marxist approaches to the state and to the role of the economic, although they in their turn clearly derive much of their impetus and explanatory input from the two older traditions.

The books in question are Michael Mann's *The Sources of Social Power*, and W.G. Runciman's *A Treatise on Social Theory* (in particular Volume Two, which offers a wide range of specific analyses).[1] These two books present a challenge because both are clearly based on what are essentially materialist epistemological premises (although diverging from what each of them sees as many of the elements of 'traditional' views), and because both usefully propose new ways of conceiving of and then analysing social relations (whether in the economic, political-ideological or social-structural sense). Specifically, both form part of a developing tradition of analysis in which the key motif is the relationship between human agency and social structure. They challenge the tendency to ignore individual subjectivities in their structure-constituting role, which they argue is inherent to Marxist discussion and theories of agency and causation; and they attempt to rehabilitate in various guises what might be seen as a methodological individualism, a perspective which immediately poses problems and a challenge to a historical materialist history or sociology. Most importantly of all, they represent one aspect of a growing trend towards macro-historical sociology, the analysis of long-term historical and societal evolution through the interrogation of micro-historical analyses.

Crucial to Mann's work, for example, is the notion of social power, which – to summarise a complex and well-argued case rather crudely – can be seen as fundamental to the actual configuration of different networks of social relations and to the state formations which develop out of them. Equally important is his conceptualisation of the state as constituting itself as an autonomous actor in the evolution of social-economic and power relations.[2] Neither of these assumptions is, in itself, inimical to a Marxist analysis, of course (the framework within which I wish to make my own remarks), although I will argue that they need to be qualified in certain key respects.

Runciman's book, in contrast, is both more broadly comparativistic and addresses the issue of social-structural evolution and selection as a generic problem of human societal existence. Where Mann is concerned to explain, in effect, the reasons and processes behind the dominance of the West on the world-historical scene, Runciman is interested in the micro-structural elements and the process of selection and survival of social practices which make change in social relations possible, and which lead to the development or blocking of certain modes of the distribution of power. Both books, however, and several others which have appeared in the last few years,[3] have provided a great deal of food for thought for those concerned with trying to understand the reasons why states develop and evolve in the contexts and the ways in which they do, and how, why and if they do or do not transform the social relations within which they were embedded and upon which they were based.

In view of this continuing and important debate, therefore, and of the fact that there is a long and important Marxist tradition of interest in state formation which has produced several alternative ways of looking at them and their relationships with social formations,[4] I want in the present study to look at one particular problem: what is the relationship between state structures, their personnel (state elites) and the relations of production in pre-capitalist social formations? In other words, how 'autonomous' can such states become, and under what conditions? But since this question immediately raises the problem of the role of the economic in determining or not the ways in which this relationship functions and evolves, I will look also at this problem, and again in the specific context of pre-capitalist state formations.

For Marxist historians this has become particularly important. A great deal of criticism, both explicit and implicit, has been directed at Marxist writings on the state, and the related question of class and economic relations, as well as the (much misunderstood and misused) concept of class struggle. A symptomatic example is the fairly recent book edited by J.A. Hall, entitled *States in History*, which appeared in 1986,[5] and in which the majority of the contributors evince either a clear suspicion of or, in some cases, hostility to a historical materialist approach. Yet all the contributions are stimulating, constructive and valuable. And given the obvious failings of some traditional Marxist writing, both empirical and theoretical, in respect of the problem of the state, this attitude is hardly surprising, the more so since, in response to non-Marxist challenges in respect of the apparent autonomy of historically-researched political and ideological practices from the economic 'base', post-Althusserian and other versions of Marxist theory have not always been able to mount a particularly coherent counter-offensive. Such a response has been based primarily around the idea, found in Engels, for example, of the 'relative autonomy' of the political or other levels or instances of the social formation, an idea according to which a careful distinction is drawn between, determination, on the one hand, and dominance, on the other. Thus Poulantzas, following Althusser, argued that, while the economy (the relations of production and reproduction of a social formation) is always determinant 'in the last instance', it does not necessarily play the dominant role: this may be carried by certain 'superstructural' levels – ideology, for example – although the possibilities for this dominance are inscribed within the structure of the economic sphere. Hence elements which, according to the classical model, belong to the superstructure, can possess a 'relative autonomy'.[6] But this approach still remains open to criticism from those who argue that it allows no space for the autonomous effects of the political – as well as from those critics (not necessarily the same!) who find the Marxist theory of class and class struggle unacceptable. Quite apart from this, of course, there have been strong criticisms of this formulation from within Marxism. As I will imply, the continued use (or abuse) of the 'base-superstructure' metaphor underlies much of what is wrong with the Althusserian project. One purpose of this article, therefore, will be to suggest that such criticism (where it is based on more than straightforward political hostility) reflects a fundamental misunderstanding of how class and class struggle are to be invoked in historical explanation.

In fact, of course, Marxist historians (or some representatives of Marxist history-writing) are by no means alone in being accused of reductionist tendencies. The Annales school itself (if 'school' is the right word for such a broad set of tendencies and research programmes), as embodied in, for example, the work of Braudel, and the notion of the *longue durée*, could also be shown to represent in some ways a reductionist approach to politics, in which structures – natural, climatic, geo-political 'givens' and so forth – overwhelm the human, individual moments of social evolution and change. And so one is led to the conclusion that these challenges to Marxism, in particular, represent one of two basic approaches: either they are a response to the success of Marxist interpretations in both setting up problems and suggesting practicable hypotheses for their resolution; or they reflect a certain political-ideological hostility to Marxism which is, at least to a degree, and even if unconsciously so, partly a reflection of the current political-ideological situation (since the early 1980s) in Western Europe and North America especially.

A second set of criticisms related to the same question revolves around the problem of Marx's society-orientated humanism. The philosophical anthropology which underlies much of his writings and clearly informed his socialist ideals, undoubtedly represented an evolutionary and moral vision in which human history would culminate in the 'withering away' of states and the re-assertion of the essentially good and non-conflictual qualities of humankind. In accepting this perspective, of course, Marxists have been condemned also for accepting the subordinate and effectively non-causal value of the state (for example) which becomes merely an appendage (albeit a necessary one) to class society. This point has been made both in respect of Marxist approaches to the state and state formations as well as to Marxist attempts to explain historical processes in which war plays a major role. As Ernest Gellner has suggested, the central premise of Marx's approach seems to be that the root source of conflict, evil and maladjustment in society is class exploitation; and that consequently political coercion has no ontological foundation: it is merely a reflection of class struggle within the institutionalised structures of the state.[7] This is only one, rather narrow reading of the writings of Marx or Engels and many later Marxists, however. Historical materialism, as a coherent intellectual and political project, however pluralistically we may define and employ its paradigmatic theorems, is bound neither by a biblical loyalty to Marx's writings nor to the cultural-ideological discourses within which Marx the individual lived.

II. SOME REFLECTIONS ON HISTORICAL MATERIALISM

Before I address the state itself, therefore, I will suggest a partial response to some of these fundamental criticisms, beginning with the whole question of the philosophical underpinnings of the Marxist project. And here, I would make two crucial points.

In the first place, it seems to me that Marxists have traditionally been constrained by the ideological demands of the various historical conjunctures through which they have fought their political struggles, whether at a predominantly intellectual level or not, to place excessive emphasis, explicitly and implicitly, on their 'marxological' inheritance, too little on the structure of a historical materialism.[8] It is generally recognised that Marx's writings on history embody three major strands, whose original development and elaboration were mutually contingent, but the existence of each of which may not necessarily demand the others as its precondition. These three strands have been characterised as, first of all, a general philosophy of history, entailing, as I have said, a notion of progress and evolution, a moral vision which entails a process of human self-realisation through conflict and the resolution of contradictions in the structure of the process of production and distribution of wealth. Marx himself was not always clear about the effects of this visonary, if not quite inevitabilist, tendency in his thinking, a tendency clearly derived from Hegel – but it is clear enough in his political writings and to a degree in his more analytical work.

Secondly, there is a general theory of historical causation and change depending upon arguments for the primacy of productive forces. Developed, later modified and then rejected by Cohen, taken up again by others,[9] this approach has received a great deal of criticism from within Marxism, for its supposed determinism on the one hand, and the fact that 'productive forces' seem to vary in respect of their definition from historian to historian. As McLennan has pointed out, the questions raised by productive forces arguments can be resolved only at the most abstract and formalistic level. The teleology which can be implicit in their deployment as fundamental causes of social change and evolution ('progress') makes them both unsustainable as formal categories and inadequate to the demands of any detailed analysis of actual historical processes and the data which these have generated.[10]

Thirdly, there exists the analytic strand, concerning the concepts of modes of production, their historical sequence, and the relationship between actual social formations in all their complexity and the set of heuristic concepts through which they can be approached. Recent arguments have tended to concentrate on this last strand, and it is at this level in particular that problems of relative determination or causal autonomy have had to be confronted in terms of theoretically-informed empirical research.

I cannot enter these complex debates here. But it is only recently, I think, that Marxists have begun seriously to break away from Marx's own specific views in order to construct a *contemporary*, epistemologically *realist* and *historical materialist* account of social change. Marx and Engels laid out a vast range of materials informed by a number of key principles of analysis, principles which run through all their later writings and from which – in spite of gaps and sometimes contradictions and slippages – the broad outlines of a coherent materialist theory of history can be drawn. But they never formalised their ideas, and the debates which have fired proponents of one view or another have been fuelled by this gap. I would argue that, while Marx and Engels were certainly the original stimuli behind the development of a materialist conception of history as it is understood today, it is one which need no longer be affected by the Hegelian influences which, it has been argued, underlie much of Marx's own thinking.[11] Such a theory must be able to respond flexibly both to the demands of detailed, on-the-ground empirical research, as well as to those of a higher order metatheory of human social development and the causal principles underlying change and transformation. As Marx and Engels themselves insisted, the key elements for a heuristically useful conceptualisation of human society need to be extracted from the detailed study of actual historical cases, not derived *ex nihilo* on the basis of implicit or un-thought-through teleological assumptions.

I can do no better here than to paraphrase the discussion of McLennan,[12] who has argued that a realist epistemology provides the framework within which a number of different historiographical and sociological tendencies can be accommodated, and in which their residual antagonisms can be overcome, not by reducing them to the same common denominator, but rather by conceding their different functional intentions and coverage. For McLennan, realism embodies a conception of history as a structured process, complex but unitary. It posits also – and importantly for our purposes – a correspondence theory of truth in history.[13] Thus the idea that rival research programmes are necessarily incommensurate is rejected. It goes against epistemological pluralism, but permits pluralism of historiographical debate; and it insists upon the complex and interrelated structure of causal processes. But historical materialism, which is a realism, and which can, I would argue, take adequate account of other competing realist interpretative positions (feminist theory, the Annales tradition, state-formation theory) is nominally superior to them because its general model of long-term and short-term structural change claims to be able to handle both synchronic and diachronic elements; its theory of modes of production represents a holistic way of conceptualising the relations of cause and function across the long term, and of establishing a fruitful way of determining general tendencies. And, as I shall argue, its fundamental categories themselves constitute the premise for alternative trans-historical explanation based on, for example, the analysis of power and power relations. As Ellen Meiksins Wood has noted, Marx left – apart from the general principles of a (realist) materialist approach to the study of society – two important starting-points:

a point of entry into historical processes . . . a means of discovering a logic of process in history, by means of his general principles concerning the centrality of productive activity in human social organisation, the proposition that the 'innermost secret' of the social structure is the specific form in which 'surplus labour is pumped out of the direct producers', . . . And he provided a monumentally detailed and fruitful specific application of these general principles to the analysis of capitalism.[14]

Note that a logic of process is neither a logic of *progress* nor a logic of *inevitability*.

But a second point needs to be made. Such a reappraisal does not entail abandoning a socialist project to realise the emancipatory conditions under which exploitation and oppression will disappear (even if the traditional form of that project needs to be revised, perhaps drastically, in many respects), nor does it mean jettisoning the need to grant economic relationships a degree of analytic and explanatory priority in respect of both the structure and the possibilities for change, transformation or extinction of social formations; and hence explanatory of the actual course of human history, the reasons for particular historical developments and specific progressive 'leaps forward'.

In the first place, all historical analysis is informed by theory determined by cultural context and antecedents and hence imbued also with a general philosophy of human development (even if a negative, or indeterminate and anti-teleological one). It seems to me no bad thing to espouse a somewhat more positive approach to the problems of the world, even if a more agnostic reading of future possibilities and trajectories is advisable than has sometimes been the case in socialist politics. But apart from this, human history as a whole has been, in both a quantitative and a qualitative sense, the history of the expansion of resource-use and of the creation of wealth, even if it has also been the history of increasingly complex divisions of labour, and modes of surplus appropriation and distribution, both at a local and an international level. It has also been the history, on occasion, of conscious efforts to improve society for the good of all, even if we also feel that these attempts have, on balance, been less than successful in many respects (partly because, perhaps, many of the micro-structural facets of precisely such aspects of human and social relationships of power have received no or only very little attention from those involved in such events). And it is the study of history which can (or should be able to) explain why and how this process occurs in some areas but not others, and in particular ways, and what the effects might be upon those regions where it is not primary –

this is surely the burden of both Cohen's efforts to theorise the causal effects of the forces of production in the movement of human history and of what Gellner, followed more recently by Elster and others, called the 'torch-relay' metaphor of social development.[15] Because it is built upon the determining effects of economic relationships, as I will argue, Marxism, or historical materialism, cannot break its ties with the socialist project and become one option among many competing historiographical or sociological discourses, since the possibilities for a socialist future depend very much on questions of wealth production and distribution in the primary sense (for I will argue that although political control and geopolitical competition may determine the distribution of wealth, these elements are themselves determined in the first place by access to the control and distribution of the means of production – as I will show in the example of the Ottoman state and its elite).

In the second place, the connection between historical evolution and economic relationships sets a broad agenda, but must not necessarily dictate either the methodologies employed or indeed the purpose (and therefore function) of specific historical or sociological analyses. It leaves plenty of room for the increased incidence of comparative and awkward questioning which has been the form taken by one of the major challenges to historical materialism (from comparative sociology and anthropology); and it is not undermined by a decrease in the 'guiding' role of any general and programmatic theory which follows. Such a connection certainly does not prevent a detailed micro-analysis of specific moments in the history of specific social formations; nor does it condemn us blindly to accept categories or causal relationships without first examining them for their explanatory power and analytic adequacy. This was a point made very clearly by, for example, Plekhanov in the 1890s, when writing about the role of individuals in historical interpretation and causality, a context in which he also warned against precisely the sort of reductionism of which Marxists are supposedly guilty. But it has been argued just as forcefully more recently.[16]

Marxism is at its most exposed, however, in precisely this area of the connection between the general, macro-theoretical model of social-economic evolution and the micro-level of specific social formations, their internal articulation and structuration, and the ideological/motivational 'interests' they embody. Much of the blame may be placed, perhaps, on the fact that interest has tended to concentrate around the problems of general theory and metatheory, rather than on specific empirical research. Is a model which operates at such a high level of abstraction as that of mode of production actually able to *explain* the specific features of the societies it is applied to? Or are its general categories so all-embracing as to be explanatorily useless? My own view is that this is a question which is best resolved by demonstration. Historical materialist premises provide a heuristic framework through which the particular forms of macro-level structures can be located at the micro-level and articulated with the trajectories of development in a given social formation. It does not predict the form structures take, but it does provide an analytical and functional model for their limiting, constraining or dynamic results. Only through detailed empirical analysis can this be obtained, however, and only through such work can the multiplicity of social, economic and political agencies be causally related within a properly holistic analysis. And it is perhaps in this respect that both Marxists and their critics have on occasion asked or expected too much of their framework. Of course, we do not expect societal changes and the forms through which the social relations of production are expressed in each different culture, to reflect *directly* the demands of 'economic' factors. It was indeed the fundamentally mistaken nature of criticism based on this misapprehension which thinkers like Plekhanov took time to answer and to expose. And this simplistic approach unfortunately has typified much of the reductionist and determinist social science of the formerly communist states of Europe and the Soviet Union.

For except in the broadest sense, the political economy of any given set of relations of production will be masked by forms of cultural praxis and role-formation peculiar to each specific cultural area. It is just this 'unmasking' that constitutes a crucial area of Marxist research. Marx's *Capital* is the classic statement of the method in its *specific* and *applied* form. And Marxists who have in the past tried too hard to tie the micro-structural level too rigidly to the macro-structural context within which it is to be understood, as though the former were merely a reflection of the latter, have rightly formed the target for both Marxist as well as non-Marxist critics.

From one point of view, therefore, historical materialism, while firmly embedded within the philosophical terrain of a realist materialist epistemology, is less a philosophy itself than it is an empirical theory. It rests not on abstract dogmas derived philosophically, but, as has been argued, on premises that can be verified by empirical analysis. The debate over whether such premises are so derived, or represent merely a set of a priori statements, goes on; but it is only its ability to provide a viable research programme that will vindicate its claims. In the last analysis, therefore, my own preference for a theory of history and social structural change which awards priority to the determinant effects of the economic is founded on its heuristic superiority: in spite of the teleologies and reductionisms of some Marxist history-writing, in spite of its omissions and gaps, it still seems to me to present the best opportunity for providing a holistic account of historical change without losing any of the dialectical complexity of history as 'power relations' or the complexities of human psychology and the field of motivation, intention and identity which has been so important in recent theoretical debate – the work of Elster, and especially of John Roemer (epitomised as 'rational choice Marxism') which has done a great deal recently to re-orientate post-Althusserian Marxist theory and to reassess the effects of the 'structuralist moment'.[17] Crucially, Marxism claims to be able to account for power-relations, state formations and forms of conflict and oppression, within the framework of the forces and relations of production – that these have not until recently been on the agenda or have been only very inadequately theorised does not in itself, as some have implied, invalidate the Marxist project. It does set up a range of challenges, however, which Marxists are beginning to take up. This is especially true within what Anderson has dubbed the 'Anglo-Marxist' tradition.[18]

The above represents a rather weak formulation of the relationship between Marxism and socialism, of course, and it may be that in attempting to escape or avoid a determinism, I have proposed an overly pluralist approach by default. If this is so, I do not consider it an insurmountable objection. The socialist project is bound, in its very nature, to emphasise the economics of human social organisation as fundamental, whatever the nature and structure of the individual choices and selection of practices that are made. Historical materialism, which takes the material conditions of the existence and reproduction of human cultures (a category which must be understood to include social praxis itself if it is to have any validity) as determinant, must continue to provide the conceptual apparatus for a socialist politics. The task is to demonstrate why this conceptual apparatus need be neither economically determinist, nor functionalist, nor again unilinear in its mode of explanation. Dialectical explanation does not entail eclectic pluralism, any more than economic determination entails the loss of the political, emotional or psychological as crucial causal stimuli.

What I do not wish to do in this article is to try to rescue traditional propositions and beliefs of Marxist social theory which may seem already to have met justifiable rejection, merely by asserting their superiority or validity, or to claim that they have been improperly applied or understood by critics (although this has certainly occurred in many instances). I think this would be both time-wasting as well as intellectually and politically pointless. But it does seem to me to be the case that many criticisms levelled at Marxism depend on the specific version and interpretation of a particular tradition of Marxist history-writing, from which generalised points of disagreement can then be elaborated. And in point of fact, I would want to argue that Marxist historical-sociological analysis is in general much more sophisticated and much more open-minded than some of the cruder dismissals would have us believe. More importantly, many recent attacks on aspects of Marxist theory – especially in respect of state formations, for example, or the question of power-relations – have been unwilling to see the different functional intentions and coverage of the work they have in their sights, or have launched their critique from a level of analysis which is incommensurate with that of the work under review.

Hall's objection that Marxism cannot handle the causes of wars without resulting in an economic reductionism, for example, reflects both a generalisation from one particular version of Marxist/Leninist thinking on the one hand, and a reductionist notion of how the 'economic' is to be understood on the other. There is no reason why, from a historical materialist perspective, imperialism should not have been 'in fact the result of geopolitical rivalry rather than of economic necessity'.[19] But what are the causal features which make geopolitical rivalry what it is? Surely, the struggle over resource control and exploitation, and consequently the struggle over the particular forms of production relations in the societies in question, play a key role here. We must of course note that these interests are represented for the actors in question in a variety of ideological terms – national pride, military tradition and so on – yet this does not for all that alter the fact that state elites do not go to war for ideas alone. Would anyone seriously argue that the USA committed itself to a war in Vietnam, or the USSR to a war in Afghanistan, as a result of ideological imperatives, which had no roots in the societies which produced them, alone? Unless we are to hypostasise ideologies and deny them any foundation in the structure of social praxis and state formation, such an argument would be manifestly absurd. And if we reject (to a degree, reasonably enough) the idea that there was any potential direct or indirect economic gain from Indo-China for the USA (although everywhere is a market, potentially, and constantly expanding markets are essential to the demands of capitalist production) we still have to explain the context within which 'ideological imperatives' are generated. And it is surely beyond doubt that that context is one of political and therefore economic competition between state systems. And within states, there exists competition between politico-economic factions and vested interests, whose position may itself be best maintained by either promoting or opposing investment in military technologies or war itself. Both sides, whether we are speaking of states or political factions, present arguments in an ideological form, but the reality is, in the end, control of resources and the preservation, strengthening and extension of one or another set of political-economic relationships. Where states do appear to go to war for ideological reasons alone (such as treaty obligations, for example), we can be sure that something lies behind those ideas: it may not be a one-to-one link, or reflection, of any clear set of interests. But it would be a foolish historian or social analyst indeed who accepted what the sources appear to say at face value! Ideas are formed in a context, even where they clearly react back on that context, and such ideas represent interests in respect of power. And power is about means to ends, that is to say, about the control of resources, both human and material, in order to achieve or attain a specific goal or set of goals: usually, the maintenance, reproduction and, where (physically and ideologically) a *perceived* possibility, the extension of a given set of institutions – systems of power relations themselves and, therefore – and unavoidably – relations of production. Even where power is sought for its own sake (where, for example, the motivating force behind a particular political conflict is at least on the face of it the expression of a given psychology or programme), the effects of that conflict and its resolution must take the form of the maintenance or disruption of specific sets of practices, which are themselves constitutive of the relations of production and reproduction of the social formation.

Of course, no-one would seriously wish to link the causes of the First World War to direct economic necessity, although this is what Hall claims Marxist theory is *bound* to do. But that war is 'the characteristic product of a multipolar state system' is hardly an adequate refutation of the determining role of those states' vested or perceived economic interests on the one hand (external factor) and the relations of power within those states in respect of the dominant relations of production as expressed through the contingent local political ideologies (internal factor).

Similarly, Hall's objection that Marx's theory of class is flawed because the various national working classes failed to unite in a transnational anti-capitalist movement is itself odd. The collapse of proletarian internationalism is an interesting and important example of the defeat of one political credo by another emotionally and politically much more powerful and deep-rooted one, whatever the contradictions it may have demonstrated. The fact that economic relationships can be overdetermined by ideologies for very considerable periods of time is no argument that the former may not be transnational. The differential relationship of the English, French and German working class to the means of production are systemically the same, although the political and institutional forms through which this relationship was expressed varied. And capitalists the world over tend to respond in much the same ways when confronted by perceived threats to their livelihoods. Just as French capitalists chose to invest in imperial Russia, where greater profits were to be had than in their own country or its colonies, so English investment capital has traditionally flowed away from the United Kingdom to areas where labour is cheap, the workforce easily controlled, the rate of exploitation higher and investment returns quicker.[20] The fact that economic classes in the world capitalist system are determined also in respect of political activity and ideologies by national and intranational identities does not alter their common economic condition. Neither does it exclude the possibility that, sometime in the future, a transnational class politics will come into existence. To a degree, this already holds for international capital and corporate investors. The approach of '1992' and the debate over the European social charter has already highlighted some possibilities in this respect.

But Hall's comments nevertheless embody very real and serious criticisms of some actual Marxist historical and sociological writings, and it remains to demonstrate how a coherent theory of the state, for example, framed within a materialist paradigm, can escape them. I will return to the question of the economic frequently in the following sections.

III: THE NATURE OF THE STATE

In order to elaborate these arguments, I want to pursue the question raised in my introduction concerning a historical materialist approach to the state, state elites, the relative or absolute autonomy of state structures and practices, and the role of the economic in Marxist historical interpretation.

To begin with: what is a state? This is, in itself, something of a problem, since there is no formal consensus (not surprisingly) on what defines a state generally in use among all historians and sociologists. A wide range of definitions has been employed, reflecting the particular intellectual and political backgrounds of those who have worked on the problem. In what follows, I will adopt as a descriptive starting-point the general definition which has been evolved by recent commentators, notably Skalník and Claessen, Krader and most recently, Mann.[21] That is, that the state represents a set of institutions and personnel, concentrated spatially at a single point, and exerting authority over a territorially distinct area. As Mann notes[22] this description combines both institutional and functional elements, pertaining to the appearance of the state's apparatuses as well as to their functions and effects. But in addition, I would qualify the definition by adding that the central point at which state power is nominally located may be mobile; that authority is in principle normative and binding, and relies ultimately on coercion; and that the effectiveness of such authority will depend upon a series of contextual factors: geographical extent of the state, institutional forms through which power is actually exercised (for example, through a centralised and supervised central bureaucracy or through a dispersed provincial ruling elite). And while, with Radcliffe Brown, we can agree that the state is the product of social and economic relations and must, therefore, not be reified or personified in the process of analysis, it is important to stress that the state does have an identity as a field of action, as a role-constituting site of power and practices which can be independent, under certain preconditions, of the economic and political interests of those who dominate it. As a general point, this consideration has been expressed frequently in both Marxist and non-Marxist history and sociology in recent years, of course. But, as the criticisms of Marxist analyses outlined above should have made clear, it has not always been put into practice in the actual examination and interpretation of states.[23]

Finally, it is worth stressing that, in a purely functional way, all states (and indeed all similar, institutionalised structures) have an autonomy of *practice*, in so far as they represent a nexus of specialised roles and practices divorced from the routines of day-to-day social and cultural reproduction. Their personnel occupy and act out institutionalised and behaviour-determining roles specific to the symbolic and the functional demands of their allocated tasks. But this is not what is meant in the debate under review here. Rather, we are concerned with the organisational imperatives of the state apparatuses and the degree of their independence from the basic structural constraints of the social formation in which they exist.

In contrast to Mann, or Hall, or Skocpol, therefore, I want to argue that a Marxist theory of the state is by no means class reductionist. That is to say, Marxist theory is not bound to see the state *merely* as a tool of the ruling class. Certainly, Marxists have tended to see the state as a set of institutions which underwrite the maintenance and reproduction of exploitative class relations – in my view quite correctly. But this does not mean that it must be a simplistic and reductionist view; nor that we must adopt a functionalist argument and maintain that states come into being in order to achieve this end. But it is certainly one of the effects of their existence. The crude functionalism of much reductionist Marxist thinking (especially of the 1930s–50s) has been highlighted and criticised by Giddens. But some critics of Marxist theory still find it more convenient to attack this easy target than to look at more recent Marxist historians. Thus Marxist approaches to the state, which in recent years have tried to relate social relations of production as a whole to the state structures within which they exist but with which they have a dialectically constitutive relationship, have been dismissed by Mann, for example, as follows:

> most general theories of the state have been false because they have been reductionist. They have reduced the state to the pre-existing structures of civil society. This is obviously true of the Marxist, the liberal and the functionalist traditions of state theory, each of which has seen the state predominantly as a place, an arena, in which the struggle of classes, interest groups and individuals are expressed and institutionalised. . . .[24]

Such a broad generalisation seems to me unjustified (although one perceives the rhetorical logic of the statement). For both Marx and Engels attributed to the state a great deal of autonomy – the problem has lain partly in the appropriation of limited elements of their work and its application to specific problems by later writers working within a particular political-intellectual moment. And it has also, of course, lain in the particular priorities of Marxist political analysts of the state who, like everyone else, work within specific conjunctural constraints and demands. On the other hand, it is certainly true that Marxism has traditionally ignored the social-psychology of individual or group power-seeking, personal self-interest and (culturally-situated) greed – not surprisingly, since its emphasis has been on the broader relations pertaining between groups. But this does not mean that it cannot handle such phenomena.[25] What recent critiques have achieved is to point out the gaps and the consequent inadequacy of empirical work based on general theories which do ignore these elements, and to make it imperative for Marxists to take account of the socially-constitutive nature of these aspects of human society.

In fact, in dealing with various aspects of state history – notably of the nineteenth-century French state, for example – Marx was fully aware of the interests and purposes which a state machinery might develop, independent of the interests of the dominant class as a whole.[26] And while neither Marx nor Engels wrote in detail on pre-capitalist states (hence leading to the inevitable inconsistencies and contradictions of later elaborations on this theme), even in Engels' *Origin of the Family*,

Private Property and the State there is an awareness of the potential autonomy of state structures (albeit expressed in what has been seen as a class-reductionist formulation): 'periods occur in which the warring classes balance each other so nearly that the state power . . . acquires . . . a certain degree of independence from both'.[27]

Whether or not we accept Marxist and non-Marxist criticism of ideas such as relative autonomy, on the one hand, or – from a Marxist perspective – that there exists a 'partnership' between the dominant economic class and the state elite,[28] it does seem that, while a Marxist theory of the state which retains all the flexibility demanded by recent critiques of traditional historical materialist views is perfectly possible, it still has to be adequately theorised. The influence of Gramsci, of course, has been considerable in this respect – for example, the notion that the domination of the ruling class is elicited by consent as well as coercion, and that the state plays a key role in the process of legitimating a given social order and establishing a hegemonic cultural-political framework. This has been developed in the context of mainly modern, twentieth-century states; but it has important consequences for an understanding of the crucial relationships between ideology and the political–economic relations within a social formation, on the one hand, and the role and actions of state elites on the other.[29]

That the state thus has the potential to exercise authority and coercive force on behalf of interests which may respond more to the imperatives of a specific political ideology than to those of the interests of the dominant social and economic class is, therefore, not to be denied. Yet at the same time, from a Marxist perspective, this autonomy must by definition be circumscribed since, as I will argue below, the state is also embedded in the social formation from which it draws its personnel and its legitimate further existence. The question, therefore, of 'autonomy from what?' becomes crucial at this point.

As we have seen, the traditional approach attributed to Marxists has been the argument that, because they develop out of the growth of private property, a social division of labour and the growth of antagonistic class relations between rulers and ruled, dominant and subordinate groups, states must necessarily function in the interests of the ruling class, through the medium of whose particular class interests they develop. Put in such a functionalist and reductionist way, this is obviously too simplistic, even if not entirely wrong. But this is not the only necessary reading of either Marx or Engels on the state, nor of the potential of a historical materialist reading generally. On the contrary, it seems to me essential to argue within the framework of a general model of 'class struggle as the motor of history' for a model of the state as both a *de facto* instrument of class oppression and arena for class struggle, on the one hand; and as an institutional nexus of power relations on the other which generates its own practices independent of the specificities of that class struggle. But – and this is important for a historical materialist approach – this independence is always relative: however much a bureaucracy or state elite, which has been freed, or partially freed, from its social, economic and cultural roots through state service, might identify itself with, or re-interpret in its own institutional interests, the perceived interests and functions of the state in respect of the prevailing political ideological forms, and consequent political activities and policies, two key factors continue to operate: in the first place, a dominant social class is always able to exploit the existence of the state to maintain or enhance its position, and the state (or its leaders) can only survive if it retains the allegiance of this class (however antagonistic the latter might be in political terms to the specific policies or individual rulers of that state). In the second place, the state is itself always inscribed within exploitative relations of production and must of necessity constitute an arena which facilitates the promotion of the interests of the dominant class, or at the very least, does not intervene in a way contrary to the interests of the dominant class. In the context of capitalism, this point has been made clearly by Miliband. And the fact that this may only rarely be a conscious and rational intention of state leaderships or elites is irrelevant.[30]

We can thus reassert, albeit in a more nuanced form, Engels' original and much criticised formulation: since states develop in the context of class antagonisms, they rarely fail to provide conditions favourable to the interests of the economically dominant class, which by its means functions also as the politically dominant class and is through it able to ensure the reproduction of the prevailing relations of exploitation and subordination. But this in no way denies the possibility that state elites might themselves constitute the dominant class, or act in the short term in ways which may run counter to the interests of a dominant class. Neither does it exclude the possibility that such elites may over the longer term act in ways which are 'class neutral', when a balance exists between the vested interests of both state elites and dominant classes. But in the last case, the state is still part of the exploitative relations which maintain the two interest groups in their shared dominance of economic and political power. On the other hand, and as we shall see, the dominant class and its supporters generally are able to negate hostile actions – either by seizing the state itself, or by forcing a modification of state policies by non-co-operation, open rebellion, or in the capitalist context, by the withdrawal of capital and other forms of economic and fiscal 'sabotage'. And finally, it must be remembered that such relative autonomy of state apparatuses or policies and practices must always be understood within the context of specific ideological discourses: the rationales invoked by different factions and interests, and which may promote one course of action as opposed to another, are the key elements for an understanding of why, and under what conditions, state elites, or factions within them, exploit the relative autonomy of the apparatuses they staff.

A Marxist theory of the state, then, must be based upon the assumption of social stratification in the economic sense, that is to say, the existence of economic classes, in objective terms, bearing differential and contradictory relations to the means of production and, therefore, politically antagonistic; the existence of an economically dominant class with whose interests in both economic (that is, class) terms and political/ideological terms (factions, interest-groups and so on, determined by conjunctural political-ideological orientations) the state elite may or may not be in contradiction; the potential relative autonomy of the state under the direction of a ruler and dependent or less dependent state elite (or a faction thereof); the limitation of this relative autonomy in respect of the relations of production within which all members of the society and the apparatuses and institutions they constitute are inscribed, a limitation which operates both structurally and temporally. Such a theory must also take account of the structuring role of ideology and the symbolic universe within which the culture in question is constituted, and hence also the power of symbolic systems and beliefs to overdetermine economic relationships. In particular, it must take into account and be able to account for the fact that the existence of antagonistic classes in pre-capitalist societies does not mean that the latter were not also divided institutionally and ideologically along other, non-economic lines: the estates of medieval Europe, for example, or the tripartite political division of the eastern Christian world by political philosophers into producers, defenders and spiritual protectors. Such divisions are part of the relations of production, however, as we shall also see below; and on both theoretical and empirical grounds I would argue that economic (class) relations have always determined the parameters within which such other relationships develop and function.[31]

Such a theory must also have, of course, an evolutionary aspect as well as a descriptive one – synchrony must be complemented by diachrony. Structures are never fixed and stable over time, since institutions, whatever their nature, are always effectively structures of social reproduction, that is to say, there is a process inherent in their very existence. History must be incorporated into any structural analysis, not left out as an ingredient which can be added at the appropriate moment to account for that otherwise awkward phenomenon, change.

And so a theory of the state must also be compatible with an integrated theory of state formation and the origins of the state. I do not wish to carry my argument further than this, however – partly because it seems to me that recent work on state theory by non-Marxists has provided a great deal of stimulus to the construction of such a theory which is not in itself incompatible with historical materialist approaches, in spite of the differences noted above.

In particular, the typology of states and social formations (for both are represented) developed by Runciman[32] founded on both Weber and Marx, is compatible with this approach; although, as I have argued above, it addresses a different level of theory and analysis, a different degree of specificity, from that normally elaborated from within historical materialist programmes. In other words, it has different functional intentions and consequently a different degree of coverage of certain problems.

Runciman distinguishes four crucial stages, tracks of evolution which may or may not lead from one to another, but in which the degree of social stratification, social division of labour and development of contradictory relations of production play a fundamental role. These are articulated together to form modes of the distribution of power, in which the forms of economic, ideological and coercive power, distributed among differently-located roles, gives each social structure its particular form and content.[33]

First, there are social formations with either 'dissipated power' or 'shared power' – hunter-gatherer groups, for example, or in social-anthropological terms, small societies characterised by segmentary lineage organisation (that is, where 'stratification' exists as a vertical line between kin-groups and attributed functions within the society, rather than horizontally between groups with different economic power), among other pre-class systems. Second, there are semi-states, usually temporary extensions of the power of a single chieftain as a result of warfare or internal conflict. Third, and involving a greater elaboration of both coercion and a more explicitly political ideology, there are proto-states which develop, to quote Runciman 'from the existence of specialised political roles which fall short of an effective monopoly of the means of coercion to the existence of potentially permanent institutions of government properly so-called'.[34] Runciman goes on to elaborate five basic categories of state according to what he terms their 'distribution of power'. But before we go any further, it will be appropriate to take up one fundamental point about which I have already made a brief comment

– the role of the 'economic' as the key determining element in Marxist analyses of human societies.

IV: THE ECONOMIC: PRAXIS, AGENCY, STRUCTURE

As will by now have become clear, critics of Marxist approaches to the state have founded their disagreement on the question of whether or not states represent, or function on behalf of, the economically dominant class in a given social formation, and whether or not this embodies an unavoidably functionalist approach. This is, in its turn, a reaction to the emphasis placed by Marxists on the 'economic' and the role of class struggle. It is necessary at this point, therefore, to make clear how this aspect of social structure is to be understood and invoked in analysis.

An examination of the debate both within Marxist writing and among its critics reveals a great flexibility in the application of terminology. On the one hand, critics of Marxist approaches have regularly and almost programmatically misconstrued the direction of some Marxist work, and on the basis of a sometimes sloppy use of notions such as 'economic base' among Marxists themselves have been able to brand much Marxist writing as economistic on the grounds that primacy in both the structure and function of social and ideological institutions has been attributed to economic relations, without due consideration for other elements: politics and ideology, institutional stasis, warfare and so on. On the other hand, and while much of this criticism has actually come from Marxists themselves, there has been a great deal of Marxist writing which was guilty of an over-deterministic and economistic interpretation of social relations and institutions, so that such attacks have often been well-founded. Particularly problematic has been the tendency of economic reductionism to ignore the epistemologically fundamental dialectical nature of social praxis, and hence produce a form of functionalist logic which describes rather than explains.

Marx was, of course, primarily interested in the actual workings of capitalist relations of production. His comments and analyses of pre-capitalist social formations, and even more so of pre-capitalist modes of production, were sketchy to say the least. But a basic framework for the analysis of such historical societies can be developed from his and Engels' work on the subject and within a contemporary historical materialist framework.

What do we mean, therefore, by 'economic base', 'the economic', 'economic relations' and so forth? First, and crucially, these terms do not refer to a partial or discrete institution or set of material conditions. What is meant is the sum total of production relations or, in other words, the class relations of society as a whole. The famous passage from the Introduction to the *Contribution to the Critique of Political Economy* in which this is made clear, is reinforced in many places in Marx's work. In Vol. III of Capital, for example, Marx notes that

> it is always the direct relation of the owners of the conditions of production to the direct producers – a relation always naturally corresponding to a definite stage in the development of the methods of labour and thereby its social productivity – which reveals the innermost secret, the hidden basis of the entire social structure, and with it the political forms of the relations of sovereignty and dependence, in short, the corresponding specific form of the state.[35]

In the second place, the spatial metaphor of economic base and superstructure can be, and has often been, misconstrued. Both Marx and Engels were clearly aware of this danger. Marx was keen to emphasise the relationship between the two as historical and contingent, corresponding to, that is, compatible with, the institutional, organisational and ideological givens of the society, to which he attributed also an effectivity. As Marx says himself, the fact that it is the relationship between owners of the means of production and direct producers which 'reveals . . . the hidden basis of the entire social structure', does not

> prevent the same economic basis – the same from the standpoint of its main conditions – due to innumerable different economic circumstances, natural environment, racial relations, external historical influences, etc., from showing infinite variations and gradations in appearance, which can be ascertained only by analysis of the empirically given circumstances.[36]

This is emphasised by his answer to the criticism that the economic determination of social institutions is a specifically capitalist phenomenon and cannot apply to, say, medieval society, where ideology and politics (religion) play the key role. Marx noted that 'the middle ages could not live on Catholicism, nor the ancient world on politics': but these are the forms through which economic relations were in part expressed, rationalised and lived out.[37] Engels himself used the notion of 'ultimate determination' by the economy as a way of pointing to these social relations of production as providing the framework within which other aspects of social life are inscribed, but where at the same time a dialectical process exists, through which 'secondary structures' can also determine the form and development of economic relations.[38]

The point about all this, of course, is that Marx and Engels were constrained by a model – the base-superstructure model – which was designed specifically to highlight the inadequacies of classical political economic ideas about how societies work from an economic perspective, on the one hand; and traditional ideas about the nature of the state, ideology and so on, on the other. Unhappy formulations such as 'secondary structures' inevitably give a false idea of what is meant to modern thinkers. When it came to the point, both realised the inadequacies of this particular heuristic for a wider-ranging analysis, and tried to escape from its apparent determinism by the sorts of comments referred to above. 'We have all neglected (this aspect) more than it deserves. It is the old story: form is always neglected at first for content.'[39] And it is understandable that this spatial model of base and superstructure which, while being more than just a metaphor, was never intended to provide more than a general guide to the way in which economic and social relationships should be thought, has been frequently both misused and misunderstood.[40] It tends to give the impression of a static and undialectical social structure, so that the dynamic aspects of social change and the interplay of power-relationships are played down. And it tends also to a functionalist and descriptive account rather than an explanatorily motivated dynamic analysis.

In order to avoid this, and yet retain and justify the notion of the totality of social relations of production (the economic) as being fundamental to the ways in which any given social formation can function – as being determinant in the sense that they frame the possibilities of institutional and cultural forms and set limits to the exploitation of social power – two related points need to be made. In the first place, and as Godelier has argued,[41] those dimensions of the social structure which appear to dominate very many non-capitalist societies, but which are equally, in appearance, non-economic dimensions, regulate nevertheless the reproduction of specific sets of social relations.

As examples, the dominance of religion in many social formations (in medieval Europe, for example), or of kinship structures in Australian Aboriginal societies, or yet again of politics in the classical world, have all been used as rods with which to beat Marxist approaches for their ostensible economic reductionism. But as Marx had already noted, and as Godelier reaffirmed, these supposedly entirely non-economic 'superstructural' dimensions fulfilled also the *function* of relations of production; for all societies consist of structures which function to maintain and reproduce the sets of social relations of production of which they are composed. *Dominant* non-economic structures function also in this direction. This formulation is not in the least to *reduce* all reality to economics, nor the various dimensions of social structure to whatever aspect happens to be dominant. Structures are always multifunctional; but they remain *both* autonomous institutionally *and* structurally integral to the reproduction of the social relations of production. Descent, marriage and inheritance are regulated in all societies by kinship (whether or not this is represented through a particular religious-ideological institution); the relationship of human beings to the supernatural is regulated in all societies by religion of a greater or lesser degree of theoretical sophistication. Yet not all societies are dominated by either religion or kinship structures; and the explicit function of these regulatory systems alone, where they are dominant, cannot in itself explain this pre-eminence: another function must be in play. And this function must be that of a social relation (or set of relations) of production. In other words, the fundamental point to bear in mind is not what social relations appear to be – politics, kinship, religion – but what their role is.

It is the historian's task to locate the nature of the dominance of a particular dimension; and to find out why it has evolved also as the representative form of the relations of production. But this is not, I would argue, to fall into a functionalist mode of argumentation. 'Function' and 'necessity' can be used in both the weak and the strong sense. The contingent effects of social reproductive practices amount, amongst other emergent consequences and practices, to the maintenance of particular structures, chiefly relations of production. In this sense, we may speak of the *function* of a particular combination of practices insofar as their combination has certain *effects*. And it is precisely because the intentions of human actors are constrained within the cultural possibilities opened to them by the totality of practices in their society, that their unintentional effects causally contribute to the reproduction of those culturally limiting or delimiting sets of relationships and practices. Where major transformations or shifts in relationships occur, we can expect also to find breakdowns in the effectiveness of cultural constraints on the relevant practices; and the site of such ruptures is likely also to be the site of contradictory relations of production.

In the second place, human beings in social contexts occupy a multiplicity of roles – as Roy Bhaskar has emphasised – and the institutions which such roles constitute are also multifunctional, in so far as they bear a dialectical relationship with other institutions, roles and individuals. This is a point stressed also in both the work of Mann and Runciman as well as of much post-structuralist writing, albeit with very different emphases and intentions. The 'economic' is therefore to be understood in its wider sense, the 'production and reproduction of everyday life', a point made by Engels himself in his attempt to stem the development of more reductionist applications of Marxist theory.[42]

Now crucially, it is human practice that actually constitutes both economic and other activities in the totality of social life. Economic relations are thus also multi-faceted – practices which have an 'economic' aspect in one context or field of action have also, and inescapably, cultural and social effectivities. Equally, social practice in general is normally commensurate with social reproductive practice, and hence with the reproduction and maintenance of a particular set of production relations – economic relations. Without the fact of surplus production, which permits social formations to change, there can be no quantitative movements in the accumulation and expression of power, and no qualitative shifts in economic relations. In this respect it seems to me both logical and necessary to see economic relations as determining and delimiting the possibilities for change, advance or regression in human societies.

As I have already intimated, this is not a position which is congenial to either Mann or Runciman, who adduce three (or four) mutually interdependent but non-reducible dimensions of social power. Runciman, for example, argues that to suggest that one dimension is determinant of all the others in any way, except when merely the effect of a specific historical conjuncture, is both untestable and an aprioristic preemption of analysis. The difficulty with this, it seems to me, is that it defines the level at which analysis should take place – that at which economic, ideological and coercive power interact to effect changes in, or the direction of, practices – also on an aprioristic basis. For as I will suggest, both Mann's and Runciman's micro-analytical frameworks are actually aimed at (and effective at) a level of analysis which is itself emergent, and must first be situated within a primary framework or dynamic structure.

It could also be argued that the three basic modes of the distribution of power set out by Runciman tend to operate as descriptive and evaluative categories, but not as explanatory of causal relationships. As Runciman himself admits, the valuable notion of the 'competitive selection of practices' which he elaborates in his opening argument is valid at a descriptive level – but it does not answer the question *how* does this selection come about.

In fact, the answers it provides are of a functional type: certain practices were competitively selected because they must have been, for a specific historical and cultural context, functionally among the most suitable to meet the specific demands of social structural reproduction.

Runciman shows very well how this schema works also for paths of social evolution which turned out to be either dead ends, or to lead to major transformations. Yet this seems to be much the same as the formulation of Godelier in its implications. For it appears to me that, contrary to his assertion, all Runciman's examples rest upon what are, in the end, essentially economic criteria: threats to, shifts in, and realignments of the social relations of production, albeit *expressed* through different cultural-ideological means and represented by different institutional responses in different societies.

The difference between Runciman and Mann, on the one hand, and the historical materialist position I have adopted here, thus seems to me to lie in the types of social praxis one identifies as autonomous, and the degree of structural and causal primacy one wishes to attribute to them. In particular, it depends upon the context within which one wishes to employ them in the posing of specific questions. Obviously, the framework within which questions are posed and the nature of the answers one seeks has a basic functional relevance for the types of questions which can be asked. A Marxist approach will take social relations of production – along with the forces of production – as primary because, as Mann's book has suggested, using different criteria, human history taken as a whole has demonstrated a *qualitative* evolution in both wealth and power, and because this has been based upon the gradual but increasingly intensive production, exploitation and distribution of economic resources, even if this has occurred in a partial and sporadic way. But this, of course, tells us little or nothing about the location, probability, rapidity, extent or frequency of such developmental change.[43] It is in this context precisely that class struggle between groups with different and opposed relationships to the means of production becomes important (whether or not it is mediated through political-ideological institutions or through violence); and it is for this reason that Marx was quite right when he averred that human history has been the history of class struggle.

A more agnostic approach to the problem of determination, as adopted by Mann and Runciman, prefers a plurality of interrelated causal elements which determine and overdetermine one another according to context – time, place, structure. This pluralism in itself constitutes a rejection of a key element of Marxist social and historical theory. But the *taxonomy* of analysis employed (as opposed to the degree of causal autonomy attributed to specific elements within it) is not necessarily incompatible with a historical materialist framework: the dialectical relationships between institutions, roles and practices is a taken-for-granted of Marxist analysis. The task for Marxists, it seems to me (and as Godelier in particular has emphasised) is to demonstrate how and why apparently non-economic relationships can be effective as relations of production.

Finally, Runciman, in particular, directs his level of analysis and explanation at the specific and conjunctural interstices of the societies he examines. But this represents a level which has already moved away from, and taken for granted, the fundamental delimiting structure of economic relationships, a point I have raised already. It deals with the phenomenal forms, as they have evolved in each culture-specific and tradition-bound case. His three dimensions of social power are therefore already inscribed within their limiting (economic) frame of reference and possibility. His analysis revolves around the micro- and meso-structural elements of social practice, and seeks to elucidate the multifactorial and emergent characteristics of their interaction. But this is, in itself, no challenge to a heuristic approach which sees economic terms of reference as ultimately determinant, since it is perfectly clear – and again, as any practising Marxist historian would emphasise – that at this level the 'economic' plays only very rarely a direct or visible role in the movement of social forces, the social-psychological 'interests' (that is, perceptions) and intentional activities of social actors, the structuring of state policies and the *forms* which the social relations of production actually assume in the process of their reproduction. In this sense, of course, and as Miliband has also noted, the work of Skocpol, Mann and Runciman is more a challenge to Marxists to actually apply their theories on the ground through detailed empirical work than it is to the premises of a historical materialist conception as such.

The argument has been made pointedly by Norman Geras. In replying to the remarks of Mouzelis (that all versions of Marxism embody a reductionist tendency, subtly 'downgrading' the political, even when it is attributed with a relative autonomy, to the level of agency and conjuncture, without granting it the weight required for its different forms or institutional structures to be theorised in their own right), Geras notes that what this actually represents is the noticeable underdevelopment of the political within Marxist thinking. In fact, of course, and as Hall has noted, this 'underdevelopment' is by no means confined to Marxist research. In practice, Marxists have rejected notions of absolute autonomy of the political because, in the historical materialist perspective, the competing influences, limits and pressures imposed by economic relations (structures of exploitation and class) carry more causal weight. But relative autonomy is no less *real*, as Geras insists, because it is relative: 'the judgement they (Marxists) make here, concerning the explanatory primacy of relations of production and class' is not 'an a priori truth: it is an empirical hypothesis, albeit of long historical range'.⁴⁴

It is worth adding that, as I will suggest, while the economic is determinant, it is no more autonomous than any other relation or level or field within a social formation. How could it be, if it is taken as a set of functions rather than of social institutions? Relations of production no more float free than political, ideological, coercive or any other structures of a social formation. This is precisely what gives different social formations rooted in the same basic mode of production (or combination of such) their uniqueness and distinctive *modus operandi*. This is what makes different developments and forms of organisation possible within the same basic system of economic relations – as understood from the political economy point of view.

It is these other sets of relations which can overdetermine and react back upon production relations to bring on crises and even overcome them by opening the way to transformations at all levels, even though the solutions to such crises are also and in turn constrained by the totality of the social relations of production: that is, by the limits set up by the multiple combination of elements which make up the 'economic structure' of society in Marx's formulation. This is precisely what historians and historical sociologists are concerned with. But it does not mean, for all that, that the economic is only one element in a group of equivalent values – a point I will emphasise in section VII below.

What we have to deal with, in fact, are the numerous differential values or effectivities of social praxis in respect of the reproduction of daily life. Each individual member of a social formation occupies a range of different positions on the grid of social praxis. In other words, each combination of social practices has a different effect. Such positions all possess two qualities: they contribute causally to the maintenance and reproduction of a number of sets of relationships with other members of the society; and they furnish the bearer with a set of perceptions of self and, therefore, of the world. Different cultural formations will highlight or prioritise different roles or positions according to their symbolic universe and the political ideologies which are refined out of that symbolic universe. But it is the modern analyst who has to decide which combinations of social relations causally contribute towards the breakdown or transformation of certain social and cultural reproductive practices, and how new practices (and where possible, why particular practices only) evolve. It seems to me that it is ruptures within the pattern of social reproductive practice – within the social relations of production and distribution of surpluses – rather than in the extension or contraction of power relations or shifts in patterns of belief (which are themselves constrained by, but may determine the phenomenal form of, the relations of production, the degree of surplus appropriation and the nature of its distribution, as I will argue) which are determinant.

This is not to deny that human praxis is both dialectical, and constitutive of, as well as being patterned or constituted by, the pre-existing structures of practice into which each member of a society is born. On the contrary, this multi-factorial and dialectical model of human social relations is crucial to a properly materialist understanding of society. In the subjective experience of daily life most activities are granted an equivalent value in the social whole of existence. Only when specific questions or problems arise are some given a specific, and explanatorily functional, significance. Thus it is with historical and sociological explanation. In order to arrive at an understanding not just of the fact of change, but of its trajectory, we need to locate a dynamic or motor, we need to highlight for functional reasons of explanation and clarification specific relationships, which can then be related back to the actual causal sequences and structures which affect the societies in question. The historian, in attempting to determine the factors lying behind change, however limited in scope, will be drawn back to those elements which constrain, limit, promote or dissolve economic, political, legal and cultural forms and practices. Those factors are, I would argue, always to be found in the functional realm of the economic.

V: STATE FORMATION, SOCIAL FORMATION

Let us return once more to the typology of state formations. That proposed by Runciman defines them, as I have said, on the basis of their different modes of the distribution of power. Among the basic pre-industrial categories are listed those in which there is a fundamental distinction between citizens and non-citizens; between warriors and subjects; between a bureaucracy serving a ruler and the body of citizens or subjects; the feudal type, where power is decentralised and in the hands of a magnate class; and the bourgeois type, where the dominant group is actually located in the 'middle', between the mass of citizens or subjects and an absolutist ruler.[45]

This typology both cuts obliquely across political-ideological as well as economic relationships; and addresses an already evolved set of social practices. It will be readily seen that all the definitions represent political organisational structural forms, rather than directly economic ones. As a general typology, it also cuts across the Marxist framework of modes of production (ideal types of sets of social relations of production) and social formations (actual historical examples of these ideal types, generally in combination). Runciman's schema is also one of ideal types, as he admits; although there is an interesting tension here, so that he feels compelled to give special treatment to 'hybrids' (such as ancient Babylonia and Anglo–Saxon England in the tenth–eleventh centuries).[46]

But this tension actually reveals a major problem. For Runciman elaborates his schema in terms of actual historical societies, extrapolating the major modes from them. Assuming we accept this choice of types, he is still clearly unhappy about societies that cannot be made to fit the models neatly. Now, a set of ideal types is meant to describe not just an appropriate set of variants on actually existing systems, but a set of cohering structures and relationships which are conceptually necessary to the construction of a causal explanation of such systems, on the basis of certain common denominators. Of course, there are always examples which do not fit neatly into any schema. Indeed, given the infinite degree of variation between actual social formations, most societies demonstrate inconsistencies or awkward elements.

There seems little point in trying to explain all hybrids as such, and thus placing them outside the schema, since the result is to nullify the theoretical value of having a schema in the first place. The same problem arose with Balibar's notorious 'transitional' mode of production. Either we take the conceptual framework as adequate, and within the bounds of which all variables can be explained; or we abandon it, and treat each historical society as an *ad hoc* variant on the theme 'distribution of social power'. For the former, of course, we need to generate a conceptual framework which is both sophisticated and flexible enough to do this convincingly. In practice, Runciman uses his schema merely as a useful sorting-code: on the basis of certain descriptive traits in respect of the distribution of power and political organisation, societies can be grouped in five modes. Those that do not fit the pattern are dealt with as 'hybrids'. And this does not seem to me to provide us with any sort of *generative, explanatory* model.

The ideal types thus tend to be concretely exemplified in actual historical terms, contrasting, therefore, with the concept of mode of production, which represents a specifically theoretical space within which, heuristically, various social formations can be thought.

From the historical materialist perspective, the framework of modes of production (leaving aside for the moment the question of which modes can be conceptually established and whether or not there is an historically necessary order of evolution) is primarily a way of examining societies from the point of view of their political economy, but nevertheless holistically. Social formations are thus seen as totalities, including reciprocal relations with, and effects upon, adjacent cultures and economic systems, with overlaps and continuities at different levels or dimensions – although this is actually put into effect in Marxist theoretical work much less than in Marxist empirical research. But the main difference between Runciman's pluralist model and a Marxist approach is that the former represents its various modes of the distribution of power chiefly from the point of view of political structures. Both ancient and feudal societies are thus described from the point of view of the dominant forms of political organisation, for example, which is seen as the sum of a range of practices and roles, in turn the expression of the distribution of power.

As a descriptive and evaluative procedure, this is useful; and since the three modes of production, coercion and persuasion are granted equivalent causal values, shifts within and between them in respect of the practices from which they are constituted are enough to motivate an adequate explanation of the origins and results of change.[47] Social practice is not ignored – on the contrary, it is given a great deal of prominence. Thus individuals are enabled only by the flexibility of practices (which they embody) to adapt to changes in environment, and hence to mutate or recombine practice in order to retain the economic, ideological or coercive power attached to their roles. There is nothing un-Marxist about such an approach.[48] But for Runciman, history appears to be essentially the sum of a series of ever-widening and mutually-intersecting 'pools' of ideological, economic and coercive power, in which competition for power is the underlying motive and dynamic.

At this point, definitions of 'power' are crucial. In the discussion to which I have referred so far, power is generally understood as social power, as a generalised means to specific ends. Power is thus control over a variety of types of resource (wealth, people, knowledge), these resources then depending upon the areas of social life in which such ends are to be attained. Power can thus be exercised at a variety of levels – from the most personal (the exercise of power by one individual over another based on resources such as knowledge or the possibility of physical coercion) to the most public (political-military power exercised through authority over armies, police forces, food supplies and so on). But in all these contexts, the exercise of power tends towards an end (even if, in the example of personal physical coercion, bullying, that end is psychological gratification).

From a Marxist viewpoint, power is the political and psychological expression of economic dominance (since resources are, in the end, an essentially economic category), although this element may not necessarily be obvious either to the modern commentator nor clearly be conceptualised as such by those who wielded it. For as we have seen, social relations of production and hence control over key areas thereof, are generally represented in an ideological form which has no obvious single economic point of reference. Power is a product of the combination and articulation of human psychology, cultural forms and economic context. And while, as I have said, it is exercised in a relative autonomy from other structures in respect of its immediate *effects*, it does not spring out of nothing. Power, coercion and ideology are forms or expressions of *praxis*. They are modes through which particular sets of relationships can be maintained and reproduced. Power may indeed be central to social theory. But the struggle for, attainment and exercise of power is about resources, and must by definition be understood within the limits and possibilities set by the existing forces and relations of production.[49]

The general validity of a Marxist theory of modes of production determined, in the first instance, by the fundamental differences between contradictory systems of political economy can now be reaffirmed. Within this set of categories there is, of course, plenty of room for a second-level taxonomy of political and power structures, such as that elaborated on the basis of practices and roles by Runciman. It is thus possible partly to agree with him when he states:

> study of societies is the study of people in roles, and the study of people in roles the study of the institutional allocation of power; and since power is of three irreducible but interdependent kinds, societies can be modelled as catchment areas of three-dimensional space in which roles are vectors whose relative location is determined by the rules of the institutions made up of them

– but in which power (in its three irreducible forms) is understood as both a real product of social praxis and as a function of social reproduction.

The value of the Marxist approach lies in its economic specificity. Broadly-defined modes of production enable the historian to suggest for different social formations positions on a grid of social relations of production, in respect of both the general dynamic of the social formation, and the ways in which economic relations are expressed institutionally, through praxis. It also places limits on the types of state formations, for example, which may develop under the conditions of specific relations of production, and provides thereby a second causal explanatory framework for understanding how change occurs and why. In the next section, I will examine a particular medieval state formation within the framework of the feudal mode of production – defined in terms of the fundamental economic relationships which differentiate it from other modes, rather than through a description of its institutional forms.

The concept of the feudal mode of production has, of course, like all the modes in this general schema, been the subject of heated debates within Marxism, and of criticism from without.[50] The criticism from non-Marxists has generally taken the form of disagreement over the supposed economic reductionism of the concept, or from historians in particular, its lack of historical specificity and institutional continuity across cultures. I do not wish to enter into these debates again, since the first point has already been taken up at a general level in the foregoing discussion; and the second is also part of the intra-Marxist debate. This has concerned itself chiefly with whether or not the concept of the feudal mode should be extended to cover a wider range of social formations than those whose phenomenal forms and institutional structures resemble or approximate those of the two most widely-recognised feudal societies par excellence, medieval western Europe from the ninth century, and medieval Japan from the eleventh century. In this context, it needs to be remembered that the history of the concept 'feudalism' has in large part been the history of European historians attempting to understand the essence of European culture.

With this in mind, it is surely time that historians made the leap from a descriptive methodology whose roots lie in eighteenth-century humanist empiricism, to a broader and more analytic approach. A re-working of concepts such as feudalism, in which Europe no longer figures as the empirical focus and the measure of other social systems, but in which sets of social and economic relationships which have a value for the analysis of other societies and histories, has been one of the obvious results of the expansion of European historical awareness to non-European social formations. It has also been one of the most valuable contributions to practical historical research as well as theory made by Marxists. I have argued elsewhere for a broad application of the concept,[51] since it is within the general framework of sets of production relations organised along feudal lines that the appropriate pre-capitalist social formations can be discussed, rather than within a plethora of cross-cutting sub-categories (potentially one of the results of the method invoked by both Mann and Runciman).

Feudalism should be seen as the basic and universal pre-capitalist mode of production in class societies. It coexists with other modes, of course, but the set of economic relationships which marks it out has tended historically to be dominant. And it is worth recalling two important points. First, Marx never evolved a single, coherent theory of feudalism. On the contrary (and according to the purpose of his particular argument) he varied between a descriptive and empirical Eurocentrist approach, in which the specific characteristics of European feudal social formations dominates, and a much broader theoretical exposition of feudal relations of production. Second, he arrived at his modes via theoretical abstraction from empirical data ('historical facts') collected from each historical social formation as a whole according to the level of its productive forces, in order to be able to make such broad generalisations.

These feudal economic relationships consist in the following key, differentiating propositions: (1) that the extraction of rent, in the political economy sense of Feudal Rent, under whatever institutional or organisational guise it appears (whether tax, rent or tribute) is fundamental; (2) that the extraction of Feudal Rent as the general form of exploitation of pre-capitalist autarkic peasantries does not depend on those peasantries being tenants of a landlord in a legalistic sense, but that non-economic coercion is the basis for appropriation of a surplus by a ruling class or its agents; and (3) that the relationship between rulers and ruled is exploitative and contradictory in respect of control over the means of production. Now, as Halil Berktay has forcefully reminded us, this fundamental class structure 'corresponds to and is determined by that level of productive forces which roughly speaking emerged with the Neolithic revolution, and comprises field cultivation based on organic energy plus hand implements, capable of sustained surplus production as well as reproduction of the peasant family'. In its historical specificities, the feudal mode is represented in social formations where these conditions and production relations dominate. But at the same time, of course, each society develops its own particular institutional practices and ideological forms through which those relations are lived, founded on pre-given cultural tradition; and the states which arise, or are imposed upon, parts or all of such cultural formations will be correspondingly different in their forms and in their ideological and legitimating practice.

It is worth adding that my account of the feudal mode corresponds more or less with Amin's tribute-paying mode, which he uses to cover both those economic relationships which used to be thought typical of the 'Asiatic' mode, as well as those of the feudal mode. In Amin's schema, the feudal mode represents a peripheral and developed form of the tributary mode. But in principle he does not claim any difference in the mode of surplus appropriation or the ways in which the direct producers are combined with the means of production between these two modal structures. For the purpose of the present study, therefore,

I will continue to use 'feudal', even though I believe 'tributary' would be an adequate and, possibly – in view of the semantic squabbles to which Marxist and non-Marxist usages have given rise – a more advantageous term.

It is in terms of the feudal mode, therefore, that I will begin my discussion of the Ottoman state formation referred to at the beginning of this article. My intention is to demonstrate two main points. In the first place, whatever the degree of autonomy a state structure and the elite personnel which staff it may appear to show, however extended their institutionalised power may be, both in ideological terms and in real terms, its historical development and its potential for transformation are determined by economic relations, by the social relations of production which breathe life into it.

But the constraints which operate in feudal states are different from those which affect the autonomy of capitalist state structures or government elites. In the latter, states must promote the interests of capital because the creation of relative surplus value is essential to their existence. States are maintained ultimately not through their power to tax alone, but through the maintenance of the relations of production which guarantee this, with which they normally have only a managerial contact at best. Tax in capitalist states represents a key mode of surplus *redistribution*, since the process of surplus appropriation through the creation of relative surplus value, and that of primary surplus distribution, has already produced the 'resources' from which tax can be drawn.

In feudal societies, in contrast, the state always occupies a contradictory position with regard to other social-economic groups in relation to surplus wealth, which – in order to ensure their survival – they must appropriate directly from the producers themselves, as tax (in all its numerous possible forms), or indirectly as services rendered to them by the direct consumers of the surplus, usually represented by a state administrative-military class or an economically independent or semi-independent aristocracy of birth or service. The power of states to appropriate surplus as tax or tribute in the form of feudal rent depends upon their power to curtail or control the economic and political power of (implicit) rivals such as these. Feudal states and rulers compete indirectly for control over the means of production insofar as they must struggle to maintain control over the means of distribution, and thus the material preconditions for their autonomy. This might on occasion produce conflicts in which one side actually attempts to destroy the other. Most importantly, the very existence of the state in social formations dominated by feudal production relations means that relations of surplus distribution are inherently antagonistic. This is quite simply a reflection of the unavoidable contradiction inscribed in the institutional arrangements for surplus distribution and consumption – between the state, and the agents it must necessarily employ as intermediaries.

The struggle for such control is seen most clearly at the political level, of course, but the shifts and changes in the fortunes of either side entail no transformation of the mode of appropriation of surplus and the fundamental relations of production. What do change are the political relations of surplus distribution as between the two contradictory poles of the ruling class and the institutional means of the state. The limitations imposed upon the possible autonomy of feudal states, therefore, are constituted by both the mode of surplus appropriation and the relations of production, at the most abstract and general level; and by the relations of surplus distribution and their institutional forms. Only an analysis of the historically specific *forms* which express these fundamental relationships – together with the infinity of possible conjunctural and incidental factors present (including ecological and geographical constraints) can show how these different elements actually evolved in particular state or social formations.

In the second place, certain conclusions can be drawn from these considerations. States can only act autonomously from the ruling class of their social formation(s) for a limited period, and under certain ideological preconditions. When they oppose the interests of an economically powerful class, a political and structural crisis may result; where they are successful in promoting an independent policy which is antagonistic to the interests of the ruling class, the result is usually the collapse or fragmentation of the state. Even where the state or the rulers are able to constitute an effective ruling class themselves, the maintenance, reproduction and – crucially – the continued *dependence* (upon the ruler or state) of such an elite has been determined by the possibilities inscribed within the relations of distribution of the particular feudal social formation in question.[52]

VI: THE OTTOMAN STATE AND ITS RULING ELITE

The Ottoman state provides an excellent illustration of these questions. It has received a good deal of comparativist treatment in recent years, to a large extent because it has seemed to represent one of the better examples of a society and state which could be fitted on to the 'Asiatic' mode. But, as mentioned earlier, this concept has little heuristic value. In respect of its economic structure, which is, to emphasise the point, its relations of production and especially the way in which surplus was appropriated and distributed, the Ottoman state and social formations can be more usefully approached through the feudal mode and feudal production relations. It is interesting to note, incidentally, that until the Asiatic mode was imported into the historiography of the Ottoman state by Turkish critics of the traditional, positivist historiography of scholars such as Barkan, earlier, and still valuable, discussions of Ottoman state and society, exemplified in the work of Köprülü and Lybyer had taken its feudal nature absolutely for granted.[53]

Our chief concern here, however, is the relationship between the state, its apparatus, and those who staffed it, on the one hand, and the ruling class or dominant elite of the Ottoman world on the other. And we are immediately confronted by some of the legalistic myths of Ottoman historical studies: namely, that there was no stable, hereditary nobility within the Ottoman empire, and that consequently, the state was the ruling class;[54] and that the absence of private property in land, together with the importance of state slavery and the *devşirme*, or child levy,[55] meant that there could be no intermediate magnate class between the *re'āyā* (subject) peasantry and the state – in other words, that the state extracted surplus directly through its own agents.[56] How then did the Ottoman state function?

The seat of empire was, of course, the residence of the Sultan which, from the time of Mehmed II (1451–81) was at Constantinople (İstanbul, from the medieval Greek *eis tin polin*, 'in the City'). Here, in the palace, were the chief palatine administrative bureaux, military and naval headquarters, along with the Sultan's residence and the harem. The territories of the state were divided for fiscal and military purposes in to a number of *sancaks*, or 'banners', under the command of *sancakbeyis*, in turn making up a number of provinces, under *beylerbeyis*.[57] Each *sancak*, or district, was in turn divided into *kazas*, or sub-districts. The *sancak* commander held both civil and military authority; and a provincial administrative staff made up from the 'ruling class', an Ottoman technical term to which I will return in a moment, dealt with fiscal and military registers, revenues and expenditures, justice (under the *kadi*, or judge) and police (under the *subaşı*, chief of police).[58]

The Ottoman state had a class structure similar to that of all feudal states. In law and theory, its population was divided into two groups or estates, representing in effect the economically dominant class and its dependents, a military class with a monopoly of the right to bear arms and receive revenues and allocations of lands; and an exploited and producing class, a hereditary and permanent tenancy of (predominantly) peasants and farmers. From the time of Mehmed II (1451–81) the 'ruling class' was known simply as 'Ottomans', but also as warriors, military men – *askerī* – which effectively described their original duties and their origins. For it is important to remember that it was the latter aspect which was primary. Only with the final successes of Mehmed II in firmly establishing the *devşirme* (see below) class on an equal footing with the old Turkish nobility was the notion of the ruling class ideologically reconstituted – as 'Ottomans' – only then was the list of qualifications for admission to that class (as opposed to membership of the traditional, and tribal, older Turkish nobility, a warrior elite) elaborated; and only then was the term *'askerī* applied to all the members of this new, imperial ruling elite, even though many were not, of course, soldiers at all. But admission to this class qualified a person to bear arms and to hold a *tımār*, a grant of revenues and the lands from which they were drawn; and the close connection between the elaboration of a state structure on the one hand and the process of class formation or consolidation becomes very clear.

The chief general qualifications for entry into this class now became acceptance of Islam (although this was less important than it has often been assumed), loyalty to the Sultan and the state, and knowledge of the 'Ottoman way', that is, the practices, customs and language of the ruling dynasty and the state. This was, therefore, a limited meritocracy, although patronage and clientage were built into it in respect of the selection and the training of recruits. The 'ruling class' thus included all state servants and officers from the highest palatine official to the lowliest Muslim soldier. While the term describes a political-theological estate, with differential economic and power implications internally, rather than a ruling class *tout court*, it is also clear that it marks out a clear difference in respect of basic relationships to the means of production and distribution of surpluses between it, and the subject populations, the *re'āyā*.

The latter term signified 'protected flock', and comprised the majority population of the state, regardless of religion, and was made up mostly of subsistence peasant communities and pastoral nomads, with a small but important group of urban merchants and artisans. The nomads occupied an anomalous position, in so far as their military potential might be conscripted for short-term campaigns. On the other hand, the state consistently tried to fragment tribal groups and to convert them into dependent peasantries, since they represented a fundamentally ill-fitting element in this otherwise straightforward relationship of exploitation. Similarly, many *re'āyā* peoples, especially the subject Christian populations of the Balkans, provided allied or auxiliary troops for the Sultan's forces, although this never brought them 'ruling class' status.[59]

The revenues of the state were collected under two main headings, religious taxes and customary taxes, the former mentioned in and authorised by Islamic law (the *Shar'ia*, Turkish *şeriat*). These included the *iöşür* (tithe – although amounting to as much as a quarter or a fifth of cereal crops in some regions), the *cizye* or *harac* (poll tax) on non-Muslims, and a range of lesser levies. The Ottoman *öşür*, although originating as a contribution to the Islamic community from the faithful, and inscribed in Holy Law, was no longer a religious levy in practice: it represented the basic land or produce tax, and therefore the bulk of the state's revenue. Its ancient origin in the *şeriat* functioned as a fiction through which it was legitimated; and since there was no Muslim organisation in the sense of the Christian institutionalised Church, its revenues went to the state.

The customary taxes (*adat*) or 'sovereign right taxes' (*rüsum-ı-örfiyye*) were based on pre-existing levies in the conquered territories as well as dues introduced by the Ottoman state itself. They included additional, minor land taxes, pasturage dues, customs dues and so on. The main difference between these *örfi* taxes and the 'religious' dues lies in the fact that the former represented the ruler's authority as war-leader and conqueror, not delimited, therefore, by holy law, and representing an additional and legitimate source of income for the state independent of Islamic tradition and the authority of the *ulema*, the doctors and theologians of Islam. I will return to this below.

A third category of 'extraordinary' taxes, the *avarız*, or 'war-chest', eventually became regularised, but was levied separately from the other normal dues, collected by salaried state agents rather than by *tımar*-holders based in the provinces, as was the case with most revenues.

These revenues were distributed in various ways. All sources of revenue were organised in units called *mukataa* or allocations, which were in turn grouped according to whether the holder of the *mukataa* kept the revenue or returned it to the treasury, receiving instead a treasury stipend. The latter were usual on the whole only in the larger urban centres – administrative units covering markets and petty commodity production, or the collection of customs dues. The former were more numerous and more usual. The commonest was the *tımar*, an allocation of revenue in kind or in cash from the land, in which all or most of the said revenue was retained by the *tımar* holder in order to support a service for the Sultan. It was the *tımar* which formed the basis of the regular provincial cavalry of the Ottoman state until the later sixteenth century. As well as the *tımar*, revenues and lands could also be assigned to *mültezim* or tax-farmers who, in the usual way with tax-farmers, paid a variable annual sum to the treasury, but were permitted to retain for themselves any revenues above those required by the state. As we will see, this system gradually erodes the *timar* system, and comes to replace it almost entirely, generating at the same time the development of vast landed estates or *çiftliks* farmed by a depressed peasantry of sharecroppers and tenants. And it is important to note that, institutionally, the tension between these two forms of surplus appropriation reflects their common structural character. In effect, they operated at the same level, penetrated each other, and could quite easily (in one direction, for example, by a process of commutation of military service) be transformed into each other.

The right to collect taxes was expressed through Ottoman-Islamic law as an attribute of the Sultan alone, won by right of conquest and force of arms. All sources of revenue belonged in theory to the ruler, as his 'eminent domain'. In that sense, all land in the empire was at his disposal: in accordance with Islamic legal authority and practice, conquered lands became state property (*miri*), granted out as secure holdings to its peasant cultivators. Such notions of 'eminent rights' are not, of course, confined to the Islamic world alone. This was a formal attribute of many conquerors, or of rulers whose position was legitimated by conquest in theory, in many different societies at different times. William I of England claimed such rights after the conquest of 1066. But these political concepts representing aspects of specific historical ideologies of power and rulership, must not be taken at face value – the crucial point is to determine to what extent, and *why*, some rulers were able to turn these rights at times into a political reality. The practices and economic relationships through which these claims could be realised (and the nature of the power resources of the ruler – military technologies, for example, communications systems, and so on) are central.

In practice, of course, these territories could only be administered through the medium of agents or representatives of one sort or another. And it is worth recalling that until the time of Murad II (1421–51) and Mehmed II (1451–81) the rulers had held a relatively weak position, acknowledged as absolute rulers in secular terms, yet with only a precarious hold over the Turkish clans and nobility which still dominated the provinces and led the army and which, under the military leadership of the Ottoman dynasty, had brought the Ottoman state into being. It was precisely the promise of conquest and the winning of new lands for themselves which gave the clans and their leaders a rationale for supporting and promoting the Ottoman dynasty in its expansionist endeavours, a rationale which was represented and legitimated ideologically through the notion of the *Jihad*, the Ghazi war against the infidel. These clan leaders made up the *beys* who governed the conquered lands for the Ottoman rulers; and it is to them that the creation of the Ottoman state is to be credited.

Murad I (1360–89) and Bayezid I (1389–1402) had both attempted to limit the power of this older nobility by promoting the 'slaves of the Porte' (*kapıkulları*)[60] chosen from their *pençik*, one fifth of the booty taken in war. They had tried to develop a new military force, the *yeni çeri*, or 'new guard', recruited from such sources, more dependable than both the older *müsellem* cavalry and *yaya* (infantry) troops, which had represented in effect a rotational levy owed by the Turkish warriors and clansmen of Anatolia, who had received lands in the process of conquest, and who were bound to serve in the ruler's campaigns; and the predominantly Türkmen nomad cavalry who had formed the bulk of the Ottoman forces until the time of Orhan Ghazi (1324–59), father of Murad I. The rotational levy was itself a relatively ancient institution, developed in Seljuk times during the reign of the Sultan Malik Shah (1072–92), and representing to a degree a half-way development between tribal warrior structures and a disarmed and de-tribalised peasantry.

But the system of promoting slaves suffered a set-back after the battle of Ankara in 1402 (at which the Ottomans were utterly defeated by the army of Timur). Indeed, two clearly discernible factions had already developed at the Ottoman court under Murat I, with the Turkish nobles, in particular the marcher *beys*, who still led the armies and headed the conquest of new territories, who held these territories, granted to them in return for their military support, as *tımars*, fiefs, and which represented in effect vast clan territories or estates (and whose soldiers were loyal to their lords and war-leaders), in opposition to the Christian vassal rulers of the European and Balkan lands, who advised halting the advance against the Christians of the Balkans and turning against Muslim foes in Anatolia.[61] Such a policy favoured the interests of the Ottoman dynasty and the central state, of course, in contrast to those of the semi-independent Turkish elite; for the conquests in Europe also favoured the latter, who received vast tracts as extended benefices, as we have seen, gaining in their own power and authority and representing thereby a potential threat to the Sultan's centralised authority. Anatolia, in contrast, represented both a source of political opposition – independent tribal confederations existed outside the Ottoman state – and it was not organised in extensive clan or chieftaincy *tımars* in the same way as the Balkans, much more recent conquests; its absorption into the state would have promoted the interests of the rulers.

After the collapse of 1402 there followed an interregnum which lasted until the accession of Mehmed I, an accession secured only because Mehmed himself, in order to win the old Turkish nobility to his side, agreed to disband the slave guards regiments and to dismantle the *kapıkulları* system. Only under his son, Murad II, was this revived and built up once more, so much so that the still dominant faction of Turkish nobles began to favour a policy of peace and consolidation in order to limit the possibilities for further strengthening the slave element at court and in the army. The factionalism within the elite was now represented by the *devşirme*, or slave element, promoted by the Sultan, on the one hand, and the clan nobles and their kin on the other.

These factions took on an increasingly ideological guise as the stakes rose. *Örfi* law by definition favoured the ruler (since it was through this channel that he could expand his power) and the *devşirme*, and for this reason the old Turkish nobility turned increasingly to the *şeriat* (and its interpreters, the members of the *ulema*) in its attempts both to halt the further development of the *devşirme* as well as to demand the re-affirmation of the traditional, tribally-rooted relationship between clans/tribes and Sultan. Under Mehmed II, the conflict came to a head. The older nobility pressed for peace on the European front, a case strongly represented by the grand Vizir, Çandarlı Halil, and a member of the traditional clan elite. But the campaign against Constantinople – a major propaganda move, but of little military significance – went ahead. It was an ideological and symbolic gesture designed to strengthen his own authority in Islam, and the position of the *devşirme* and *kapıkulları*.[62] After his victory, Mehmed felt powerful enough to move decisively against the old clan elite. Çandarlı Halil was dismissed and executed, and there took place a wide-ranging purge of the older nobility: exile, execution, confiscations of *tımar* estates and provinces, the latter awarded to new men of the *devşirme*. By the 1460s, Mehmed had achieved the system generally referred to as the 'Ottoman state' in the discussions above. The Janissaries (*yeni çeri*, the 'new guard' mentioned already) were reformed, re-equipped, and had slave officers imposed instead of the older officer elite; the *devşirme* system was massively expanded and, with the support of the Janissaries, the new slave units, and a loyal body of trusted slave administrators (including the Grand Vizir, now likewise a member of the *kapıkulları*, and the Sultan's representative) Mehmed was able to impose his will in a radical re-affirmation of his own absolute authority.

Yet, in a second series of confiscations, in the 1460s and 1470s, forced upon him partly by a shortage of resources and of soldiers, he seized the properties of both religious foundations (*vakfs*) and secular landholders and, having returned them to *mırı* (state land) status, used them as the basis for an expansion of the provincial cavalry, the *sipahis*. This policy was itself a consequence of the new-found position and power of the *devşirme* elite, whom Mehmed now had to rein back in order to safeguard his key position as arbitrator between the poles of the *uç bey* (marcher lord) elite and the *devşirme* and its clients.

This was a crucial element in his policies. It is important to note that he did try to strike a balance between the new establishment and the old, for this was the guarantee of his own absolute authority – and that of his successors. A number of the older and more prestigious nobles were left with some of their *timars* intact, as well as their positions: and while he reduced the power of the frontier *beys* in command of the Türkmen and other troops directed at the enemies of Islam, by increasing their number and reducing the size of their commands, he could not afford to replace them entirely, for they represented the front line in the *Jihad*, both in the Islamic popular vision as well as in terms of military reality.

The Sultan's role was, therefore, the key. And the balance that was achieved depended very much on the character and ability of individual rulers. Mehmed II removed the aristocratic Çandarlı Halil, and replaced him with a line of *devşirme* vizirs, men who had no connection with the older establishment. Even so, his policies failed to resolve the factionalism: his actions were not unopposed, either from the vested interests of the *ulema* faction, or the Turkish Muslim nobility itself. In opposing the absolute authority of the ruler as reflected in *iörfi* law, preferring instead the older relationship of lords to war-leader which had epitomised the early period of Ottoman expansion, the Turkish nobility inevitably found itself in alliance with the representatives of the *şeriat*, the Holy Law of Islam, which in itself represented an alternative, and antagonistic, set of values and system of authority.

On Mehmed's death in 1481, there took place a serious reaction and partial reversal of his policies, accompanied by civil war. And in the struggle for the succession which followed, between the brothers Bayezid and Cem, ostensibly a political faction fight between two individuals, the problematic nature of the 'balance' reached by Mehmed II, and the antagonism between the vested interests of the *devşirme* and the Turkish aristocracy, became very clear. In order to counteract the increasing influence of the *devşirme*, for example, Mehmed II had in his last years appointed as his Grand Vizir Karamani Nişancı Mehmed Pasha, a member of the older Turkish elite, not of the *devşirme*, unlike all his predecessors since the unfortunate Çandarlı Halil. Mehmed Pasha's policies (which also favoured the *ulema*) were resented by the *devşirme*. So that on Mehmed II's death, a plot led by leading *devşirme* men, and with Bayezid as claimant to the throne, was able to win over the Janissaries and the *devşirme* leader of the Albanian campaign army, and defeat Cem, who fled to Rhodes. The Grand Vizir was killed by the Janissaries. In return for this support, however, and advised by his closest confidants, Bayezid promised to relax his father's policies and return much of the *vakıf* and other confiscated property which had been seized from the *devşirme* and its clients. In effect, the now powerful *devşirme* elite had become – in contrast to the period before the conquest of Constantinople under Mehmed II – the real conservatives, and sought to promote the position they occupied. At the same time, Bayezid himself was greatly influenced by the conservative *ulema*, and the alliance between old Turkish aristocracy and *ulema* was now replaced by an alliance between the latter and the *devşirme*: both parties now had a joint interest in limiting the Sultan's power, based on the exercise of *örfi* law, in favour of a more traditional approach. The problem for the 'autonomous' state, in the sense of a 'state for itself' (strong foreign policy, firm control over resource extraction, allocation and distribution, independence of state interests in this respect from those of any dominant elite with sources of power outside such interests) was now expressed precisely through the ideological tension between *örf* and *şeriat*, between Sultan's authority and Holy Law.

The structures, both ideological and administrative, which were established under Mehmed II provided the framework within which and through which these tensions and contradictions were to work themselves out.

The backbone of the army was now constituted by the Janissary corps, along with the central elite cavalry and artillery divisions, on the one hand, and the *sipahi* cavalry of the provinces on the other. The former were directly supported by the treasury, the latter by *timar* holdings. Since these holdings have been the subject of a great deal of discussion (and a degree of misinformation) with regard to the supposed absence of any 'hereditary nobility', it will be worth devoting a few lines to them here.

In essence, the *timar* holder was granted the right to collect the revenues of the district allotted to him as a living in return for performing state services – usually, but not always, military. *Timars* were divided into five groups, from the lowest, which provided an income of approximately 2,000 *akçes*, or silver aspers, per annum, to the highest grade, producing as much as 40,000 *akçes*. Such holdings, or rather allocations, provided for the basic income of most of the imperial officials, civil and military, from simple *sipahi* cavalry soldiers to the *sancakbeyi*s, or governors. Allocations of revenue were also given in return for outstanding service, great devotion to the Sultan, and as rewards for military prowess. A not inconsiderable number of *tımars* were also granted to religious functionaries or urban officials. But the vast mass of small *tımars* consisted in grants to *sipahi* soldiers intended to maintain the soldiers and their retainers.

Now, in spite of the authority of the Sultan in respect of the withdrawal of a *tımar*, or of the regular or occasional rotation of the larger *tımars* (*hass*es or *ze'amet*s) in particular, an authority which never entirely lapsed or fell into disuse, there was always a very great degree of continuity of occupancy. The central portion of a grant (the *ibtida* or 'beginning') generally passed to a son on his father's death, and on application. In most cases, permission to continue in occupancy was granted. Only those revenues which the father had accumulated as a result of rewards for good service could not be passed on. Retired *tımar* holders often kept the basic portion of their holding as a pension, the remainder going to their son or to another *sipahi* if there were no male offspring. The right to apply for and to hold a *tımar*, indeed, was hereditary within the *askeri* class.

From the time of Selim I (1512–20), furthermore, there is some evidence to suggest that a remnant of the old Turkish aristocracy of Anatolia and the Balkans was able to regain some of their ancestral holdings as *tımar* grants, thus reasserting their economic position; a process which had been inaugurated under Bayezid II who was obliged by political and ideological pressure to restore many of the privileges of both the Muslim Turkish nobility and the *devşirme* elite which had brought him to power, as we have seen.[63] At the same time, some of the indigenous nobles in the Balkans kept their lands and served the Sultan as *tımar* holders even after their defeat, although they were generally quickly absorbed into the Ottoman ruling class, thus losing any cultural particularism.

Some *tımar* holders had also a small plot of land or 'reserve' for private use, cultivated by day-labourers or share-croppers, which was entirely at their disposal. But this was more usual among the powerful holders of the much bigger *ze'amet* or *hass tımar*s, in which huge demesnes farmed by a substratum of the peasantry were often built up. And they were, in addition, also responsible for the collection of the land-tax, the periodic re-distributions of peasant holdings which might be ordained in the event of a plot becoming uncultivated or deserted, as well as the maintenance of civil order. Through the collection of fines and the receipt of customary prestations of labour, fodder, wood and so on, the *tımar* holder could thus build up a considerable income or reserve in both cash and kind. Thus, in spite of his ultimate dependence on the state for possession of his *tımar*, the timariot and his family were often able to maintain themselves relatively independently once an initial grant or allocation had been made. They were certainly an integral part of the local economy, not simply an imposition upon it, for they exercised on behalf of the state (and their own interests) a continuous supervision over and intervention in its affairs. They represented a crucial aspect of state control over the agrarian economy of the empire: the Ottoman land-codes show that peasant cultivators could do very little to change either their methods of production and their crops, or the rate of exploitation without state (that is, timariot) permission. And while the state also supervised thereby the timariots themselves, this had less to do with 'protecting' or 'defending the rights of' the peasantry – a popular interpretation among conservative historians of the Ottoman state – than with assuring an average rate of exploitation of peasant labour and the securing of the necessary surplus required by state interests as opposed to those of any third party.[64]

The *tımar* system has rightly been seen as the basis of Ottoman state power during the period from Meḥmed II to the death of Süleyman in 1566. And we can immediately make two important observations. First, that although *tımar* holders, and particularly the *sipahis*, were allotted revenues rather than lands – like the Byzantine *pronoia* which I will discuss below – they nevertheless constituted the state in one of its most important surplus-consuming forms. They represented the legal fiction of a medium through which surpluses were transferred to the state; and this medium was in itself, and regardless of any internal rotation among *tımar* holders, intended to prevent the alienation of the state's revenues to private sources, a permanent feature of the relations of production and surplus appropriation of the Ottoman state. While there was no hereditary aristocracy with permanently held *family* property, therefore, there did exist a hereditary ruling class, internally differentiated as we have seen, which reproduced itself both by birth and by recruitment of new *devşirme* elements. The fact that this class as a whole supposedly had no particularistic familial and class identities, and that formally service under the Sultan brought with it slave status, does not mean that it was not a class in the economic sense or that it did not reproduce itself in this form: that is, that it appropriated, consumed and thereby 'passed on' to the state (that is, it retained *as* the state) surpluses from the producing population in the name of the Sultan. It thus represented structurally a potentially antagonistic force which, without the political control made possible by successful warfare, territorial expansion and internal equilibrium, could (and did, of course) challenge the central authority over the distribution of resources and surpluses.

In this respect, the Ottoman state clearly rested upon the same fundamental structural principles common to all feudal social formations, where an intermediate class represents the state to the producers, consuming a large portion of the surpluses it extracts in the name of a central authority and an appropriate legitimating political ideology; and it contains the same structural contradictions in respect of control over the distribution of surpluses. The cyclical nature of the antagonistic relationship between central control and local consumption, centralising demands and centrifugal tendencies, between the 'public' and the 'private' aspects of pre-industrial state administrative demands, a cycle which depends then upon the complex, local combination of political, ideological and economic factors for its form and expression, is thus equally a part of the history of the rise and decline of the Ottoman state.[65]

That the state intervened at the ideological level through customary and state law, and the Sultan's 'protection' to prevent over-exploitation by *tımar* holders of the producers, in Ottoman political theory at least (as well as the theory of a whole generation of Ottomanists), does not alter this. Indeed, the state law (*örf*), in contrast to religious law (*şeriat*), represented precisely the ruler's right to legislate on the basis of *custom* (as we have said), so that while it represented in different parts of the empire the juridically-fixed form of the way the producing populations had been exploited for centuries, it was also a crucial medium of control over both the peasantry and the timariots, re-inforcing and consolidating the power-relationships and the relations of exploitation which had evolved out of the original conquest (or absorption) and which depended ultimately upon coercion. This is especially obvious in respect of the mass of the *reaya* population to the provincial governors and their officials and soldiers, representatives and symbolic of this 'state' law, who appear from the later sixteenth century (but possibly before – the evidence is somewhat sparse before this time) to have been particularly feared and hated for their exploitative and extortionate rule, and who were compared unfavourably with the representatives of the religious law, the *kadis* and jurists.

Neither does the fact that there existed a degree of social mobility alter the economic class nature of Ottoman society. In practice, the (hereditary) subject peasantries provided only through the *devşirme* an element of the ruling class, whose members had in any case, and regardless of origin, thoroughly to internalise and assimilate the ideology of the Ottoman establishment.

Furthermore, the policies of the rulers in actually moulding the formation of this ruling class – by weakening the traditional tribal and clan nobilities in favour of their own *devşirme* recruits, and through the institutionalised slavery that imperial service always brought with it – must be understood at more than just the political-ideological level at which it was, and often still is, represented: it embodied the struggle for power over and control of economic resources required to promote a particular ideology and the dynasty that proclaimed it (that is, the *Jihad* [Holy War] and *Ghaza* [raid]), and more specifically, a struggle over the *relations of surplus distribution* within the ruling military class of the expanding Ottoman state. For it must be clear that control over surplus distribution meant control over the resources of the state and hence political control as such. Yet in spite of its efforts and desires, the central authority never entirely removed the hereditary frontier nobility from its powerful position. Only in the later sixteenth century was it successful in lessening the power of this group; by which time the contradictions within the new system were already becoming apparent.[66] But what this means for state theory, of course, is that states can and do, under the appropriate conditions, influence the later moulding of economic classes. The inference from this, however, is not that they are supra-class structures themselves, or indeed autonomous of the social formation in which they stand. On the contrary, it shows how integrally determined states, and their political and economic strategies, are by the conditions within which the appropriation and distribution of surpluses takes place.

The second observation concerns the relationships within this broad ruling class, both between its provincial representatives and those at court, and between different factions at court: in particular, the rivalries which developed between those of *devşirme* origin and non-*devşirme* groups. Once again, the structural contradictions of surplus distribution within the dominant elite provides a dynamic element underlying Ottoman political and military decline, rather than the ideological forms through which these contradictions were expressed.

The story of these developments has been summarised by several historians, and is long and complex.[67] The primary contradiction lay in the structure of the ruling class itself, a class which depended for its economic well-being and its ideological unity on a continued policy of military and economic expansion. Once expansion ceased – as the state came up against a firmer European opposition north of the Balkans, and the Safavid Persian state in the East in the second half of the sixteenth century, and as it attained what represented its maximum viable extent in respect of both military and political control (crystallised in terms of communications and logistics) – these contradictions became apparent as the structure of Ottoman society and political organisation were radically transformed by the effects of its initial successes.

The sixteenth century witnessed a number of concurrent developments, which coalesced in the 1570s and 1580s. Particularly significantly, there took place a breakdown of rural order which has traditionally been ascribed to a demographic upswing, especially in Anatolia, in turn seen as resulting in a dearth of land. At the same time, an inflation caused by an influx of cheap Spanish silver reduced the values of the fixed incomes of the *timar* holders, especially the *sipahis* of Asia Minor. More recently, however, the degree and the supposed effects of this demographic expansion have been questioned, as have those of the import of silver and consequent inflation. In the first place, population expansion cannot convincingly be generalised to the whole of the empire, although there was an increase in many regions, such as the western Anatolian coast, especially the hinterlands of large urban and commercial centres, such as Izmir. In the second place, the movement of large numbers of *reaya* peasants from the land took two forms: on the one hand, it was promoted, at least initially, by the state itself, in its efforts to recruit ever greater numbers of mercenary soldiers with firearms into its service. On the other hand, many peasants fled to cities and defended towns in order to escape the endemic brigandage of the last years of the sixteenth century caused by the fighting between *celali* bands and renegade *levend* (mercenary) soldiers, and the state's *kul* or slave soldiers. For the shift in international military technology towards infantry and firearms had left both the elite janissary regiments and the traditionally-armed *sipahi* cavalry at a considerable disadvantage in their confrontation with European, especially Austrian, armies. Thus from the 1540s and 1550s especially the state began both massively to increase the size of the janissary corps (which İnalcık has estimated rose from only 10,000–12,000 in the 1450s to well over 30,000 in the period from 1590 to 1630), and to recruit ever greater numbers of mercenary soldiers with firearms from the *reaya* populations. The demand for such soldiers became especially pressing during the war with Austria from 1593 to 1606. These *sekban* units, however, were recruited largely at the expense of the traditional *sipahi* cavalry. For in order to maintain the new units, the state needed the revenues consumed by the increasingly marginalised provincial horsemen. Some of these revenues were thus transferred to the central fisc to finance the recruitment of more Janissary and *sekban* units. Provincial governors – *beylerbeyis* or *valis* – received greater power as the control or supervision of revenue collection and assessment came increasingly into their hands. The state needed cash; yet the silver inflation only exacerbated the situation; and the *sekban* units themselves – recruited from the rural peasantry – tended to be hired for the duration of a campaign, rather than be supported, like the *sipahis*, on the basis of a permanent arrangement.

The state had, on the whole, no arrangements for supporting such units in peacetime, however. The result was that, when it attempted to disband them or proved unable to provide lands or other means of support, many of them turned to brigandage and extortion, terrorising the localities they inhabited or passed through into providing for them. These bands were soon a major threat to Ottoman state power, representing both a source of disruption to established patterns of administration in the provinces, as well as to agricultural production and the state's ability to appropriate and distribute revenues according to its requirements. Peasant flight to fortified centres and the abandonment of land was one result. Devastating warfare between the ever-increasing numbers of janissary units based permanently in the provinces to check these *celali*, and the letter, was another. This expansion of the *kapıkulları* or slave units across the cities and provinces of the whole empire was of particular importance to the patterns of power distribution and control over the means of distribution of surplus wealth in the ensuing years. Finally, the *levend* or mercenary units, once raised, and then returned from the theatre for which they had originally been recruited, often remained together under their leaders, hiring out their services to the highest bidder. This was particularly the case after the military defeat of the *celali* at the hands of government forces in 1608, for having failed to win access to the *kapıkulları* and thereby achieve their political aims, such mercenaries turned increasingly over the course of the seventeenth century to service in the retinues of provincial governors and similar patrons, giving an independence of political action to such officials which they had only rarely possessed before. For they could now be independent of both the *sipahi* elite of the countryside, who had a vested interest in the maintenance and enforcement of central authority in respect of their *tımars*, and the janissaries and other slaves of the Porte established away from Istanbul.[68]

The fiscal problems which the state had to confront in attempting to support the vast number of mercenary and slave soldiers contributed in addition to a crisis of the *tımar* system as a whole, since the smaller allocations could no longer support the cost of the regular campaigns demanded of them. Confiscations of *tımars* for failure to appear at musters were ignored or circumvented, while many *sipahis* joined the *celali* brigands. As the *tımar* system became increasingly marginal to the state's immediate military requirements, and as the demands of the central government as well as those of provincial authorities and governors for cash grew, so tax-farming increasingly became the chief means for the state to raise reliably the sums it needed. Tax-farming had always been present, of course, but it now dominated the methods by which the state appropriated surplus.

One of the long-term results of these developments, however, was the very opposite of what the state and the rulers of the later fifteenth and earlier sixteenth centuries had intended. For it found itself now unable to prevent the gradual evolution, more rapidly in some areas than in others, of provincial officers and rural notables with estates (originating among both greater and lesser *tımar* holders as well as tax-farmers, themselves often officers within the administrative elite or their dependents and agents) who, apart from attracting economically depressed peasants to their properties, were able to exploit regular landlord-tenant relationships, primarily by virtue of the conversion of state revenues into farmed taxes collected at all levels by agents, both for the central fisc, as well as on behalf of local governors and other officials. The imprecision of the revenue registers from this time – the last years of the sixteenth century – which was an integral part of this process (and which reflected the difficulties inherent in adequately assessing revenues in a period of inflation) facilitated the formation of what were, in effect, estates and properties which remained, in theory, of *miri* status, but which became increasingly difficult to control from the centre. The process had already begun, but with the support of the rulers, during the middle of the sixteenth century, when a number of officers of the military-administrative elite were granted what were termed 'estate-like' revenues on a permanent basis from the normal state taxes. While the lands which went with these grants of revenue were not private property, they do seem nevertheless to have represented an important element in the building up of personal possessions in land and income among such elements of the state elite in the provinces, and in the conditions of the later sixteenth and seventeenth century described already they marked an important stage in the breakdown of the traditional system of revenue assignments proportional to state posts and under strict central control. The effective alienation of state revenues to the private consumption of members of the *askeri* class meant also, of course, a weakening of state control over the land and the basic relations of production.

The same process occurred in respect of *vakıf* estates (in theory corporate religious foundations endowed by the pious – including the Sultan – whose property was also derived from *miri* land) which also grew in extent and number. For they represented a legal and age-old way of circumventing both Koranic prescriptions on inheritance and, more importantly, a mode of subtracting lands and revenues from the state. Under their administrating families or organisations, such estates tended to become their private and hereditary property, a phenomenon which repeats itself in all Islamic societies.[69] But in the Ottoman context of the later sixteenth century and after, it had particular repercussions. And as this phenomenon of estate formation and revenue expropriation was general throughout the ruling class, from the most powerful down, the net result was a decline in state revenues and state power, as its resources were progressively alienated to the nascent landholding elite.

As the *timar* system declined, so the state relied increasingly, as we have seen, on the slave regiments and the *sekban* mercenary units, between whom there existed a fierce hostility. The janissaries, now spread throughout the empire, consolidated their position and economic independence in the towns in which they were based by allying themselves with, working for, and sometimes becoming members of the new landholding elite. The result was an increasing ineffectiveness of the *timar* system and its piecemeal transformation into an extended system of tax-farming (*iltizam*), partly influenced also by the Arab tradition as the Middle East and Egypt were incorporated into the empire during the sixteenth century. The vested interests of both court and provincial elites were embedded in this process. The state was left with its extraordinary levies, the *avariz*, over which it retained much greater direct authority, along with a range of similar extraordinary impositions, most of which tended over time, and as a response to the state's need for cash, to be raised as regular taxes. Over the same period – that is, from the later sixteenth to the end of the seventeenth century – the position of the peasantry seems also to have worsened: the brief century and a half of state supervision and regulation, whatever its real nature, and as it is reflected in the land-laws or *kanunnames*, was over, and the oppression of the rural population by a self-interested landlord class, fragmented though it was in respect of its varied origins and political affiliations, became the norm.

Civil wars, and the consequent widespread economic and demographic disruption in Anatolia in the late sixteenth and seventeenth century were at the root of many of these developments, as must by now be clear. Such wars were both symptoms of the problems facing the state, its inability to respond to them at a structural level, and acted at the same time as further stimuli to the changes in the older establishment. And although attempts at reform did occur – based chiefly on efforts to re-establish a 'golden age' of Süleyman and the mid-sixteenth century – they could not succeed. The function of Ottoman state ideology and political theory is in this respect crucial, for it presented a systemic rationale which both legitimated social relations and the state as these were refracted through it, yet was incapable of taking account of major shifts in its conditions of existence. While taking shifts of a local nature (both geographically and temporally) into consideration, as contemporary works of statecraft testify, it could offer no solutions, except to present itself as the only model upon which a secure state and a harmonious social order could be founded.

The *tımar* system continued to operate at varying levels of efficiency throughout the empire until its final abolition in the nineteenth century reforms, and until the very end there is ample evidence that the state never conceded the struggle to retain control over *mirī* land and the holdings of its *sipāhīs*. But the decline of the *devşirme* system due to demographic collapse in the seventeenth century, and the recruitment of Muslims and *reaya* directly into the Janissaries and the court establishment which occurred from the middle of the seventeenth century on, now meant that there was no longer a significant institutional difference between the Sultan's erstwhile loyal slaves and non-slave Muslims. The court was polarised around ambitious individual leaders and their clients, depending in turn on the continued support of powerful provincial interests. Three dominant factions can be distinguished in the palatine establishment: the Janissaries and provincial commanders, who used their troops to promote their political and economic interests; the administrative bureaucracy; and the religious leadership and intellectuals, the *ulema*, fiercely opposed to reform, which would have brought with it the re-establishment and promotion of *örfi* law and the legal authority of the state at the expense of Islamic tradition. In spite of periodic efforts to confiscate and return to the fisc the provincial private estates that had evolved, the government could no longer prevent the establishment and consolidation of a provincial and hereditary aristocratic elite which, while existing within the fiction of the Sultan's absolute authority, nevertheless maintained its lands and its power until the nineteenth century.

The role of the *ulema* or class of learned men was ideologically vital in this respect, for it was responsible for organising, propagating and defending Islam, interpreting and applying Islamic Holy Law, and training younger theologians and intellectuals. As a group, they were divided internally according to their specific functions; but they represented a deeply conservative element in the ruling elite – especially those concerned with the interpretation of Islamic law, the Koranic tradition and the state traditions of Islam. They dominated education and the judiciary and, of course, gained financially from their control over *vakıfs*. Together with popular religious orders, such as the Bektaşı dervishes, they provided one of the pillars of the opposition to the reforms of Selim III and of Mahmud II in the later eighteenth and early nineteenth century, reforms aimed initially at modernising the army and reorganising older corps, but in so doing threatened the position of the *ulema*, who relied on the Janissaries for support. They constituted a reserve of fundamentalist and anti-reformist sentiment that could mobilise the Janissaries (that other pool of conservatism and vested interest), and block any attempt to introduce structural change in the balance of power between this elite, in its various forms, and the central authority. Of course, the Sultans were still able to take action against individuals who, once isolated, could be successfully removed, but the power of this new elite as a class was never seriously challenged. By the later eighteenth century the *ayan* (provincial notables) and the *derebey* nobles of Anatolia had established tax-concessions based around landed estates or *çiftliks* which deprived the state of vast revenues, lands which were, in effect hereditary. The growth in the power and influence of the *ayan* families can be detected as early as the later sixteenth century. The central authority needed to employ local leaders, whatever their origin (many were of *kul* or slave origin, for example, established as Janissaries in provincial towns and with well-established vested interests in local affairs) to organise and lead the popular militias raised from the *reaya* to oppose the depredations of both the *celali* and *sekban* mercenaries, as well as the Janissaries who exploited the peasants and imposed irregular levies and other demands upon them in both cash and kind. At the same time, such local notables also operated as tax-farmers for the central government, using their positions to build up their own wealth and, especially significantly, acting as representatives of local interests to the central government. Such developments, which considerably weakened the state's fiscal as well as its administrative control over provincial affairs, began to have an effect clearly from the 1630s. But while the *ayan* rarely cherished any ambitions for political independence, the Anatolian *derebeys* ruled many regions as semi-independent lords with their own administrative apparatus – imitative of the Sultan's court and bureaucracy – so that the parcellisation of sovereignty constituted a major threat to the very existence of the centralised state. The threat to state authority was emphasised by the fact that many provincial governors employed their own private retinues, often recruited from brigand or mercenary bands, as I have said, hence attaining a greater degree of local independence.

It is important to note a difference, however, between these later examples of provincial independence, in respect of their significance for the authority and effectiveness of central government, and the many examples of the state deliberately delegating authority to local elites after the conquest of a particular region. Thus not all cases of 'regional autonomy' should be seen as necessarily contrary to the state's interests, at least not in their original contexts. After its final annexation from the Shi'ite Safavid power following the battle of Caldiran in 1514, eastern Anatolia remained largely under its indigenous Sunni Kurdish chiefs, who could be assimilated into the ruling elite and relied upon to maintain Sunni orthodoxy and pursue the Sultan's anti-Shi'ite policies. There are a number of similar examples.

But the process of decentralisation, and the situation of regional semi-autonomy, which later developments represent, has been picked out by many commentators, and rightly so. For whatever the original conditions within which provincial elites came to act more or less independently of the centre, the long-term results of such autonomy were the effective paralysis of central power in respect of the real running of the state for considerable periods; the reliance of the state upon ideological motivation alone rather than upon economic control for the maintenance and reproduction of its authority and sovereignty, as well as a proportion of its revenues; and the gradual and piecemeal contraction of the empire territorially as it was progressively less able to muster adequate resources, trained manpower and effective leadership to counter external military pressures. Most important of all, of course, is the fact that the changes reflected also the context of the Ottoman power internationally: the growth of capitalist market relations in western Europe, and especially the speed of technological change, left the feudal Ottoman empire on the margins of what was soon to become the First World. The agrarian and then the industrial revolutions in England, the strength of the European powers, all served first to peripheralise politically and then to colonise economically the Ottoman world for European markets and exports. The efforts made from within this essentially feudal framework of production and power relations to respond to this external challenge, however, were not qualitatively of the sort to lead to real structural change. Draconian reforms undertaken by Grand Vizirs who managed, for a while, to impose a certain unity on the court, and thereby over the empire's resource base, made reconquest and aggressive warfare possible on occasion – the great attack on Vienna in the 1680s, following a successful war against Venice, is a good example. But the structural impact of such reforms was limited, the successes illusory. By the middle of the eighteenth century, even though the *sipahis* continued to occupy their *timars*, albeit on a very much reduced scale, the local landlord class which had entrenched itself in the provinces, allied with provincial military commanders and governors, could defy the Sultan's government more often than not with impunity.

In all these developments, it is important to realise that the absence of juridically-defined private property, the continued possibility for the Sultan arbitrarily to confiscate fortunes and wealth amassed during a career at court, the lack of sanction for privately-held estates and the absence of a formal, titled nobility, are all phenomena belonging properly to the *political* arena of Ottoman state practice, without of course wishing to deny that they provided also both the context for the institutional forms which the Ottoman landed elite took, as well as the ideological authority for the Sultan to intervene directly in *economic* relations.

Yet at the same time, and along with Ottoman state law, they had served as constitutive elements in the evolution of the relations of distribution which dominated during the period from Mehmed II until the later sixteenth century. They represented, in other words, elements of the conditions of existence of that system. As the relations of distribution shifted, however, their functional economic relevance receded, while their political-ideological and symbolic relevance was modified to the changed circumstances. Ideological systems generally (historically) respond only gradually and on a piecemeal basis to shifts or transformations in the conditions of their genesis and evolution. Modifications and shifts in weight or emphasis in the elements which make up a symbolic system can often shore up and give an explanatory and legitimating value to political ideologies long after they have ceased to represent the interests of the dominant class. By the same token, elements of well-established political-ideological narratives can be endowed with new functional relevance, and provide, for different social/political groups, both continued legitimation and stimulus for change in received patterns of practice. Thus it is with Ottoman imperial ideology: the old system, with its rigid division between *askeri* and *reaya*, a division reinforced and hardened by the defeat of the *celali* rebels in the early seventeenth century, still provided the best representation of the perceived interests of both the state and the economically dominant class. This is especially clear in respect of the role of senior and middling bureaucrats and administrators at the capital who, while willing to embrace institutional reforms which did pose a threat to fundamental elements of the old system of fiscal and, more particularly, military administration, did so in order to preserve the authority and centrality of the ruler and the central government, a power which represented both law and justice. As we have seen, the chief opposition came from the *ulema* and those whose interests could be held with them in common. Yet the Ottoman political ideology successfully enabled the 'modernising' element to maintain both the relative political independence of the central establishment and the relative territorial unity of the empire, at least where potential centrifugal and separatist tendencies were concerned. For the very success of the state in its early history, and its consolidation through the fifteenth and into the sixteenth century, gave this ideological system a certain flexibility which, while it conflated theories of the genesis of the state, on the one hand, with theories of its function, on the other, gave it a continued and crucial functional relevance to both the ruling elite and the dominant social groups outside the government.

Government interventions of the sort referred to were regular enough to cement the system of malversation and corruption which became a hallmark of Ottoman administration for later European commentators. Insecurity of tenure of office promoted the maximisation of exploitation, personal gain and alienation of state revenues. But it is also clear that insecurity brought with it a heightened importance to the extensive household and the complex systems of patronage within Ottoman society. High officials placed clients or protégés in the establishment (and the choice of protégé often depended on common ethnic and linguistic identity), such networks serving both to protect individuals from the ruler's whim as well as from his rational policy decisions, and to cement a degree of administrative continuity independent of the Sultan. By the same token, slave members of households entered such networks and reinforced them after they had been promoted or manumitted, continuing to rely upon the system of patronage and support through which they had been brought up or initiated into Ottoman social forms. Such households, eventually forming semi-independent bases of power and authority, came to function as complementary to the central household of the Sultan. The effects of all this, even in the sixteenth century, were in practical terms to disperse authority within the state much more widely than has sometimes been assumed, and to give to the more important members of the ruling class (in the Ottoman sense) a distinct identity outside that of service under the Sultan – even if this identity was only occasionally realised and given expression directly.[70]

I have of necessity had to reduce the complex history and evolution of the internal structure of the Ottoman state in the period after Mehmed II to its barest essentials, and have thereby simplified a series of very complex developments. But for the present discussion the crucial point has been to suggest that in spite of its continuities, both real and apparent, the first decisive factor in the internal political evolution of the Ottoman state was the struggle over the distribution of surpluses appropriated from the rural population of the empire, which took place within the ruling class. The struggle of the state – the Sultans and their advisers – to maintain their control over both the means of production and of distribution provides the context. A second crucial factor hinges on the degree of autonomy which the state was able to enjoy. Up to Mehmed II, the Sultans maintained a rigorous control over the administrative and military institutions which were tools of their policies, reflected through the ideology of Holy War and Islamic expansionism. The *devşirme* elite in theory represented the state and functioned, against any opposition from provincial interests, to promote the ideology of the Ottoman establishment. But even in respect of the source of its personnel and the effectiveness of the *devşirme*, the state in the period from the reign of Mehmed II to the end of the reign of Süleyman I, enjoyed no absolute independence of the interests of the older Turkish aristocracy, the founding elite of the Ottoman state. At the same time, and as became clear in the last years of Mehmed II, and in the war between Cem and Bayezid II, the consolidation of a *devşirme* elite tended to replace rather than merely balance the power of the Turkish tribal nobles.

The factionalism and political fragmentation of the dominant elite at court, the networks of patronage which increasingly from the later sixteenth century tied court and provinces together, were all factors which diminished the Sultan's systemic absolutism, weakened the fragile unity of the state elite, and turned the state itself into an arena for factional interests. The dominance of men appointed directly from the centre, after service in the Sultan's own household and the court, to higher provincial military and administrative positions reduced the value of provincial career structures and denied to many provincials the opportunities which they had previously had to advance themselves in the state's service. This was a feature which became increasingly apparent from the late sixteenth century on, stimulated by the increasing obsolescence of the provincial cavalry forces in the context of the times. At the same time, the increased power of provincial governors, partly a result of the fiscalisation of *tımars*, meant that local networks of patronage and influence became increasingly important (as centrally-appointed officers depended more and more upon regional elites and social networks), stimulated in turn from the middle of the seventeenth century the growth of the provincial *ayan* class.

The contradictions within the state elite, on the one hand, and between state and local interests (which might also be represented by members of the state apparatuses themselves, of course), on the other hand, were expressed most clearly in struggles over the degree of the rate of exploitation, and the relations of surplus distribution.

But the relations of production in respect of the mode of surplus appropriation did not change, although the forms of surplus distribution and the rate of exploitation may have done. The ideological commitment of the Islamic ruling elite to the absolutist rule of the Sultans and the concept of an Ottoman state, on the one hand; together with the corporative substructures of the Ottoman social formation, which held a disparate group of local cultures and social formations together through the medium of local religious and cultural identities (the *Millet* system)[71] under the umbrella of a universalist political ideology, on the other, these are what lent to the Ottoman state its deceptively static appearance, emphasised in addition by the rapid transformation of the western European states in the period from the sixteenth to the nineteenth century, with which – given the invasive effects of capitalist market relations upon the Ottoman economy and society – it was inevitably compared.

But it is significant that when, in the first half of the nineteenth century, the Sultan Mahmud II (1808–39) undertook a series of westernising reforms, designed primarily to adjust the internal balance of power, reinforce the position of the Sultan and re-centralise the government's political and economic control, it was only with the support of an 'enlightened' and 'progressive' westernising faction at court, the inherent structural divisions between the different institutional elements of the ruling class (religious, military, scribal and palatine services), and by dint of a lack of any solidarity among the *derebeys* of Anatolia, that he could impose his will. And the lack of solidarity among the Anatolian nobility was in any case a result of the divisions within the ruling elite which resulted from the failed attempts at reform of Selim III (1789–1807). Mahmud was thus able to isolate key opponents and crush them quickly. The Janissaries were destroyed and the *ulema* faction divided and weakened, again a result of internal splits, for there were reformist elements even here. Nevertheless, Egypt gained its independence; while the tax-farmers and *çiftlik* estates of the Balkans, and the quasi-hereditary *vakıfs* subsisted. The trappings and formal institutional appearance of the older system were done away with, but under the new laws – heavily influenced by western legal principles of property law – many tax-farms on state lands were converted into the secure holdings of secular landlords, thus cementing the position of the provincial landholding elite and preserving the underlying contradiction between central authority and provincial interests.[72] The changes which affected the Ottoman state during the eighteenth and early nineteenth centuries, especially its confrontation with the imperialist and industrialising states of the West, were much more ramified and complex than I have been able to depict here, of course, and I have presented only the briefest of summaries. But I will return to the implications of this survey for a theory of the state in the last section of this article.

VII: THE NATURE OF STATE AUTONOMY

I have looked at the Ottoman case in some detail to make a point. The Ottoman example is the case par excellence where a state elite which is nominally neither hereditary nor class-based dominates, or appears to dominate, a political and socio-economic formation headed by an absolute ruler. The state must thus appear autonomous from the society over which it stands. But the appearance of this structure, perhaps because of its very strangeness to the predominantly European historical/sociological observer, belies the nature of the relationships it embodies. Wherever we look, whether at the centralised empires of central and south America, or the ancient states of China and Asia, the relationships holding between state elites, ruling classes and rulers are complex, dialectical and – crucial for my point – determined by the question of the control over resources. The fact that these relationships appear as political and ideological elements should not conceal this. For whether it is a question of relations of production or of distribution of surpluses, it is such relationships which underlie and are given expression through the dominant forms of political organisation.[73]

These relationships are rarely expressed in non-capitalist contexts through economic categories, of course. On the contrary, they are voiced through symbolic systems and ideologies in which authority and power are the terms of reference, whether earthly or divine.

Most importantly, power is not an abstract, nor is it a disembodied quality of political personalities and relationships. It is rooted in the differential access of individuals, groups and classes to resources (which must include also the possibility or actuality of their being excluded from such resources), and hence is inscribed also within economic relations. This applies equally, of course, to forms of charismatic power exercised at an individual level, as Weber also saw. For this is itself the expression of the mobilisation of emotional narratives and contexts in which the question of access to or exclusion from social resources (however this might be expressed in specific cultural formations) – in other words, control or lack of control over the process and means of reproduction of life – is at stake. The search for power, as Mann has noted,[74] is a search for a means to an end – the (more) effective control or mobilisation of certain resources in order to make possible the achievement of certain goals: the maintenance of political authority, for example, and thus the reproduction of a particular set of social and therefore economic relationships. The ways in which these relationships are expressed, of course, is determined by the general field of cultural tradition and context, and by the specific modes of the distribution of power.[75] This, it seems to me, is the great value of the work of Mann and Runciman: not to demonstrate the absolute autonomy of structures of power, whether *collectively* or *distributively* located, and whether of a broadly economic, coercive or ideological character; but rather to illustrate how these expressions of the fundamental relations of production in a social formation are to be apprehended. Of course, the detailed analysis of a historical social formation, its day-to-day functioning and its developmental trajectory, will not necessarily entail the reiteration of the embedded economic nature of relationships of power and authority, hierarchy and status, either in the vocabulary of the modern analyst or in that of the culture under examination. But this does not mean that it is not the economic structure which provides the framework of action which these specific and culturally-determined practices express and realise.

This is not to say either that the argument from economic relationships takes place at such a level of abstraction or generality that it is of no analytic or heuristic value. I do not wish to collapse all of society into a vacuous category of 'the economic', and then argue on an a prioristic basis that it is therefore 'ultimate'. I do want to argue that analysis must proceed from the premise that social praxis is limited and constrained by economic relationships – relations or production – in the first place, and thus provide a direction for the search to locate the key points at which other expressions of social relations – power, for example – are located and coalesce. It is not to argue that the economic nature of social power as a product of relations of production need ever be made explicit by a culture; it is to argue that it is such relationships, and the contradictions or limitations which they embody, that provide the dynamic and underlying social and cultural potentialities of a social formation, and the individuals who constitute it through praxis.[76]

So are we back to a simple base-superstructure metaphor? *I think not*. First, we know that societies and the way they evolve are looked at in different ways according to what we want to understand about them

– analysis is always functional and directed.[77] Second, we have seen that many social practices and institutions can function as relations of production. It depends what we want to know about a given institution, role or set of practices as to whether we wish or need to relate them to the ultimately economic context within which they are effective. What we need, therefore, is an organic rather than a spatial model of society: all the elements, superficial or not, are vital to the particular appearance and evolution of a society in a specific form. None of the elements stands on its own; but there is, nevertheless, a sense in which certain practices establish a pattern for the ways in which all the other forms actually operate. The economic relationships thus constitute a skeleton which determines both the limits and the basic configuration of a social formation. Just as the different primates have different skeletons, differently articulated but with bodies constructed from the same basic set of corresponding organs and tissues, so different social and economic formations represent different modes of production or combinations of modes of production, their differently articulated relations of production determining the general possibilities and limits of the social practices from which they are constituted. Like the skeleton, therefore, relations of production do not *cause* a social formation; but they do have a determining influence on its physical forms, its capacities to deal with external influences, and its limitations in respect of production, consumption and expenditure of energy. Unlike a skeleton, of course, social relations are dynamic and liable to changes – contradictions and incompatibilities develop as they are overdetermined by both ideological factors and 'interests'. So I do not want to take the analogy too far (skeletons are also subject to change and process!). It is intended merely to illustrate the difference in the way we are able to conceptualise the totality of social relationships and relate their different elements dialectically, without using the spatial base-superstructure metaphor so liable to misconstrual. Such an analogy makes it possible at least to see the determining nature of economic relationships, without at the same time suggesting that they are either causally prior or that they are not themselves determined in their mode of expression by other factors.

These considerations are important when we come to consider the question of relative or absolute autonomy of states and state elites. For it must first of all be clear that absolute autonomy is structurally an impossibility – the personnel and leaders of a state apparatus are always keyed in at some level or another to the social relations of production of their society, no matter how distanced they may be from the actual work of production itself. The Ottoman example discussed above provides ample demonstration of this. Tied as it was, at least initially, to the absolute will of the Sultan, the *devşirme* elite was as bound to the conditions of reproduction of surplus extraction as the economically disabled and politically marginalised Turkish nobility, precisely because they were both the product of that system as it had evolved (by conquest) and because the interests of the *devşirme* elite in respect of the distribution of surplus wealth were, at first, antagonistic to those of the older elite.

But that state institutions and their 'organic' personnel can act autonomously from a non- or only partially-incorporated ruling class in the provinces (however the land and possessions of the latter are held from the legalistic standpoint) should not surprise, and certainly does not run counter to a historical materialist position. Such autonomy is generally relatively short-lived, however, and does not represent an autonomy which seriously challenges the relations of production which makes it possible, although it can certainly – as we have seen – introduce changes into the forms and structures through which those relations of production are expressed. For both groups are dependent upon a particular system of surplus appropriation and distribution. Indeed, it is difficult to see how any state leadership or elite can act for long in a way which fundamentally opposes or conflicts with the long-term interests of the majority of the dominant economic class in society. This question does, inevitably, raise the problem of the qualitative difference between the power of the modern state and that of pre-industrial states. Telecommunications, surveillance and data-processing systems, rapid transportation, massively increased coercive potential, together with the saturation of all social groups by advertising and 'information' systems, all these in the context of political and legal norms which actually permit (as in the UK today) a more or less complete autonomy of action to governments for limited periods, must necessarily qualify the interpretation offered here. But (although a separate discussion is really required) I would argue strongly that even here we can still only speak of a relative (even if extensive and long-lasting) autonomy of states or certain discreet state institutions (for example, security services, defence and so on). The relationships between governments and ruling elites, state fiscal and banking interests and those of investment capital, for example, substantially modify and limit state autonomy. And I would also argue that, to suggest that the modern technocratic state system is fully autonomous is to massively misunderstand the role and constitution of ideology and the nature of contemporary capitalist subsumption.

Even in cases where new state elites have attempted to introduce or impose radically new techniques of production and distribution of wealth, the role of the army and of coercion, and of factional and class or tribal alliances, remain crucial to their success. The reforms and industrialisation programmes inaugurated under Bismarck present a classic instance in which a 'small' and 'progressive' state elite was able to introduce fundamental changes through a process of authoritarian command politics legitimated in traditional nationalist ideology, class alliances and political bargaining. The net winner was, of course, the bourgeoisie; but the unification and the imperialist policies, which necessarily directly involved the army under its officers, drawn from the declining feudal elite, provided a role for elements which clearly had no economic interest in the transformations promoted by the Iron Chancellor.

In the development and extension of world-capitalist market relations, and the development of national elites in non-capitalist countries, similar examples can be found. In emergent industrial and developing states, for example, it has regularly been the state, in the context of the international expansion of capitalist exchange and production relations, and in alliance with key elements of a formative bourgeoisie, the army, and 'commercial profit' propaganda,[78] which has acted to re-structure patterns of industrial and agricultural production, and which has thus led to substantial shifts in relations of production – chiefly from what can be seen as semi-feudal relations (in spite of the presence of modern, bureaucratic government institutions in most cases, staffed, we should note more often than not by elites educated in the industrial first world) to capitalist relations of production, both in respect of the creation of an urbanised industrial working class and in respect of the imposition of a series of discreet monocultural agrarian cash-crop regimes designed to meet the demands for debt servicing, industrialisation and mechanisation. The creation of a large landless sub-peasantry is one concomitant, the consequent urban overcrowding and deprivation another. And inflexibility in agrarian production combined with over-use of fertilisers designed to maximise short-term returns has in many cases resulted in a catastrophic collapse in subsistence levels and the ability of the land to maintain the levels of output required. But in such cases, we need to look carefully at the constitution and structure of the state, especially in respect of the vested interests embodied in its policies, and its situation in an internationalised market context. Once again, it will be seen that fundamentally economic relationships and pressures operate, even if represented through specifically local ideological institutions and practices, interests and responses. And to argue therefore that this is to admit the centrality of purely external causal stimuli is to ignore the fundamental point that capitalist relations, in so far as they are, or have become, entirely international in their effects, are as much an internal as an external element.

As Miliband has pointed out,[79] conflicts between the state leadership and the dominant class, or a fraction thereof, generally means that the state acts in ways which favour other classes (or other fractions of the dominant class). In the Ottoman example, it was in the first instance the *devşirme* who profited from the struggle between the Ottoman ruler and the old Turkish nobility which had given him his empire; and indirectly, the 'subjects', the *reaya*, of the empire benefited, albeit for less than a century, from the anti-aristocratic policies of the Sultans and their slave administration and army; but this was essentially a structure developed to safeguard the state's control of resources, and in no way suggests that the state was somehow independent of society or the economic relations on which its power rested.

It is the conflict over the distribution of resources which tends to promote disintegration or decentralisation should the state elite lose, but which in contrast promotes a strengthening of central authority and a corresponding weakening of oppositional groups if it wins. But it must be stressed that the political autonomy which follows in the latter case is itself clearly to be set in the context of those particular relations of production and distribution.

VIII: BYZANTIUM: AN ALTERNATIVE CASE

Both the Ottoman empire and its territorial predecessor, the East Roman or Byzantine state demonstrate these points. In the Byzantine case, radical changes occurred during the seventh century in respect of the possibilities of maintaining the traditional system of surplus appropriation, whether through state taxes or private landholding, and weakened the broad 'ruling class', the senatorial aristocracy. The changes which occurred made it both necessary and possible for the state, on the one hand, to jump in and centralise the administration of both fiscal and military affairs, and to control appointments to key positions; on the other hand, the Church mobilised its resources to redirect popular attitudes and to legitimate the shift in the relations of distribution which had occurred. The demise of the classical and late ancient municipalities, the failure of the established pattern of organisation to defend the interests of the state against Islam in the 630s and after, all led to a strengthening of the autocratic power of the emperors and their political freedom of action. But the new service elite which the state brought into being in this changed context (initially as a more efficient means of controlling the machinery of surplus extraction) rapidly developed into a service aristocracy and then a hereditary provincial and metropolitan aristocracy, able to alienate and divert resources from the state to its own interests. In the seventh and much of the eighth centuries – like the Ottoman state in the later fifteenth and first half of the sixteenth centuries – the Byzantine state elite could and did act relatively autonomously of the direct, short-term interests of a large section of the dominant social and economic class, who were – again like the Ottoman *kul* elite – more or less dependent on the emperors for titles, positions, status and honours. But it did not act in a direction which actually impaired its power in respect of the prevailing relations of production. And in administering its resources through an intermediate group of officials who eventually developed into an independent and essentially antagonistic 'aristocracy' of provincial and metropolitan landowning and office-holding families, it demonstrated the fundamental problem facing pre-industrial states already referred to: the unavoidable need to invest an intermediate administrative group with the potential to alienate the state's resources to its own advantage.

In the Byzantine case in particular the problem facing the state is clear from the later tenth century on. In spite of their great wealth, the military magnates of Anatolia who were responsible for the reconquests in northern Syria and Iraq still very much represented localised clan and family traditions and loyalties, as did the bureaucratic administrative elite of the Constantinopolitan establishment and provincial civil administration, an elite whose position and wealth was assured through titles, posts and government offices, imperial patronage, and investment in a clientele of supporters and acolytes. All these competed amongst themselves for honour and prestige within the institutional framework of the state's military and bureaucratic apparatus. It was, therefore, not too difficult for a firm, authoritarian soldier-emperor such as Basil II (976–1025), with the help of a loyal guard of foreign mercenaries (the Russian Varangians) – who constituted an independent power-base – to impose drastic sanctions on individual members of this class-in-itself and to introduce draconian anti-aristocratic legislation to protect the economic status of the peasantry, upon whom the state was absolutely dependent for surplus and soldiers. At the same time, Basil promoted a strategy which transferred imperial expansion away from the eastern front to the Bulgarian theatre, where by 1018 his forces had destroyed the powerful Bulgarian empire and re-occupied the Balkans up to the Danube. This rich new province, which the emperor kept firmly under state control by appointing governors and commanders more dependent upon imperial patronage than members of those Anatolian aristocratic clans who had opposed his rule, and by absorbing considerable tracts directly into the imperial estates, provided him with the economic resources through which he could balance the vested interests and the power of the Anatolian factions referred to. It also meant that even after his death a series of much less able emperors was able to lessen the reliance of the state on the military aristocracy by using this new source of wealth, gained through conquest, to pay for more foreign mercenaries and to promote further aggressive military undertakings in South Italy and Sicily.

But the deliberate running-down of the traditional frontier armies or militias (military service was commuted in some areas for a cash payment, which by the 1050s had become a generalised regular exaction), and the dramatic increase in the use of both indigenous and foreign mercenaries as the provincial peasant forces were progressively marginalised, not only directly affected the power of the magnates, but in addition the empire's ability to maintain a coherent defence against sudden attacks. This polarised the factions into which the state elite was divided, and led ultimately to the seizure of the state by a representative of one of the aristocratic clans, the Comneni (initially unsuccessfully between 1057 and 1059, later from 1081 until the end of the twelfth century). And it was from the middle of the eleventh century at first, increasing rapidly through the twelfth century, that the rulers turned to grants of state revenue, in effect lands, in *pronoia*, literally 'in care', in order to raise and maintain soldiers. For although many of these grants were small, the clear alienation of resources from direct state authority had begun, and the process of decentralisation – structurally an unavoidable aspect of all pre-industrial state administration – reasserted itself.[80]

The relative autonomy of state politics – the 'organisational imperatives' of any given state apparatus as determined by both functional and ideological demands – meant that, on the one hand, the political ideology, individual psychologies and personal identities which had developed in each specific cultural tradition dominated the motives and institutions of the staff and leaders of the state apparatuses. But on the other hand, it meant also that the state elite had itself as a class, or a fraction of a class, a vested interest in maintaining that set of institutional practices which were necessarily and systemically in its own best interests. And there is no doubt that, in the Ottoman case, representatives of the state elite understood this field of common interests very well.[81] Of course, this does not mean that the elites to which I have referred were internally undifferentiated blocs with no contradictions and conflicting fields of political and economic practice.

But in both the Ottoman and the Byzantine cases the power elite – the dominant faction of the ruling class – can be distinguished in respect of its economic position in the relations of production, on the one hand, and its political position in respect of the relations of distribution of surpluses.[82]

The problem for the state centre begins when the balance of power – specifically economic power – tips against it, so that the alienation of resources and challenges to the politics of the centre reduce its ability to direct and control the whole. In Byzantium, the strength of the centralised state, the degree of residual autonomy it retained, and its commitment to its resource-base can be seen in the power it was able to exercise until very late in its history in over-riding the legal rights of individual landowners and members of the powerful nobility in order to deprive them of wealth (lands) which represented a threat and a challenge to the authority and power of the emperor.[83]

But it must be emphasised that this residual power does not necessarily represent solid political power based on firm control of resources. Just as with the Ottoman state under its absolutist rulers, we must distinguish between the latent and active exercise of power, between the possibility of using power in a way which reinforces an ideology without threatening a vested interest; and the employment of power, and hence control over sufficient resources, to actually oppose and defeat such a vested interest. To a large extent, this depends on the strength of the dominant ideology, and on the international economic context. In the first case, Byzantine magnates (until the middle of the eleventh century) and Ottoman state officials, members of the elite, concurred with the exercise of the ruler's absolute authority because it reinforced an existing political system in which they could still perceive their own interests (however independent of the state they may in practice have been), and because it clearly did not threaten their class interests. The possibilities for Ottoman officials to advance their careers in the provinces as well as in Istanbul, for example, combined with the entrenched household-patronage networks referred to already, go much of the way to explaining the relative independence from, but continued support for, and obedience to, the central government in the Ottoman period after the seventeenth century.[84] In the second case, a Sultan like Mahmud II had to manoeuvre with extreme caution in the context of the increasing marginalisation of the Ottoman state on the one hand, and its colonisation by western commercial interests on the other (with the fundamental threat that this posed to the old elite), in order to promote a real shift in the internal political-economic balance of power. In contrast, the Byzantine rulers after 1081 (when Alexius I seized the throne) found that only a system of aristocratic clan alliances could maintain the political and ideological apparatus of their state. The centralised state continued to exist, on a decreasing scale, until its extinction in 1453, as did a dependent bureaucracy of non-magnates and a less dependent landed elite. Indeed, it was the great residual power of the imperial ideology, which itself demanded such a state and was inextricably interwoven with the political theology of the Orthodox Church, which made any other trajectory inconceivable. Crucially, the ideological axis was the God-appointed emperor. And long after it ceased to represent the interests of the landed elite, it continued to represent their *perceptions* of how the world functioned. The contradictory nature of this ideological edifice was not understood, in the context of shifting relations of distribution within the elite, as long as ideological attention was fixed on the emperor, rather than on the polity as a whole.

But this no more means that there existed an absolute autonomy of ideologies and ideas than that there is an absolute autonomy of the political. For although the Byzantine imperial ideology retained this hegemonic appeal, it was nevertheless consistently and constantly modified in a piecemeal fashion (attitudes to the Turks, to western Christianity, to the relative position of the concepts 'empire' and 'orthodoxy' in the Byzantine symbolic universe, and so on) in order to render it at the very least commensurate with its social conditions of existence: which is to say, in order that people would continue to make sense of their world within the framework of their symbolic universe and the practices it represented, evoked and, contingently, reproduced. And it is perhaps worth remembering that both elements of the Byzantine ruling elite and the Church, as well as Mehmed II himself, came to regard the conquering Sultan as the legitimate successor of the Byzantine emperors.[85]

Much the same general development in respect of ideological narratives and the shifts which took place within them is evident in the Ottoman experience: only when brutally confronted by the technologies and aggressive economies of the industrialising western powers did this change, as we have seen, and only then was a forlorn attempt made by the central authority to imitate the institutions of the now dominant, and threatening, European powers.

IX: CONCLUSION

I have tried to outline in the foregoing some of the key elements in a historical materialist approach to the analysis of pre-capitalist states and their functioning. Centrally, I have suggested that it remains both legitimate and heuristically necessary to view the relations of production – the 'economic base' in Marx's words – as the primary determining, but not necessarily causal, element in social formations. On this assumption, and employing a coherent set of concepts of modes of production, and the range of historically-attested political and economic relationships they represent, a sound heuristic framework is available through which states can be analysed not simply with a view to describing their structural relationships, but with the possibility of understanding the dialectical nature of these relationships and the elements – practices, roles, institutions – through which they are constituted. By the same token, such a framework makes it possible to understand the contingent value of different practices which lends to them their particular appearance and form. For without the determining economic relationships, there seems to me a real danger that other practices become divorced from the very contexts within which they are initially generated and inscribed, to be apotheosised and attributed with a causal power independent of the culture which determines the extent of their effectivity in the first place. Power is not an abstract, but an embedded set of practices contingent upon specific sets of relationships, moments and constellations of ideas, and rooted ultimately in the relations of production which generate those moments.

This is not to deny, either, the role of the individual. On the contrary, it is to provide precisely the framework through which beliefs and ideologies can be understood to take their strength and dynamism, and to suggest a way of understanding how narratives – discourses of belief and legitimation – can be at the same time both the product of a given set of relations at a particular moment, and yet float free of the relationships for a time once they have become available and articulated.[86]

The fact that, for example, some political leaderships are able for a while to pursue policies and promote strategies which are in fact fundamentally in contradiction to the interests of major sections of society does not, of course, mean that 'absolute' political autonomy is a real possibility. Such policies inevitably end in political or social-economic shifts which rapidly bring the world of the political back within the limits set by the social relations of production.

In this context, it is perhaps important to note also that there are certain universals of state structures which can be observed in both pre-modern and modern states. These include, on the one hand, the fundamental means through which states are able to retain control over their means of political and economic reproduction (which include in particular legal systems, by means of which economic and power relationships are both institutionalised and legitimated), especially the mediating group or class through which the state physically appropriates surpluses and maintains its authority. On the other hand, they include the conflicts which arise between factions of the state elite, or between the state service elite and a less dependent dominant class, or subordinate aristocracies or ruling elites of particular regions within the state's territory. These conflicts are generally concerned with the distribution of surpluses. Again, political ideologies and legal structures constitute an important set of enabling conditions, which affect the outcome of such struggles. In this sense, therefore, while it is clear that there is a multiplicity of forms and appearances of states which can exist under given general sets of political-economic conditions (modes of production), there are actually only a limited number of structurally-possible systems within which pre-industrial social formations could create states – that is, states which moved beyond the stage of tribal confederation and attained a degree of permanence and continuity dependent upon sets of self-reproducing structural relationships. It is instructive to compare societies where states actually fail to reproduce themselves – where, in other words, the absence of some of the key features is apparent – in order to demonstrate the point. But it is also clear that these broad sets of economic relationships – social relations of production – cannot predict exactly either the form of such structures, nor their actual developmental trajectory, at the micro-level: the infinite variety of local factors, as Marx noted, makes this a task for detailed empirical research. That the relationship between the political economy of a society and the mode of expression of its political and power structures is not necessarily 'economic' should not surprise. The relative autonomy of the state and the logic of its organisational structures are perfectly real. But they must themselves be understood as emergent or dialectically generated characteristics of a particular set of relations of production, of a particular set, therefore, of political-economy potentialities.

On reflection, it seems to me that both Marxists and state theorists have misconstrued the force and the direction of the critique of historical materialism which I have discussed in this essay. For, in spite of objections to economic reductionism or determinism, the thrust of the more intelligent arguments against a Marxist perspective are actually directed – quite justifiably – against the failure of historical materialist analysis to devote more space and consideration to the political and to the dialectic between politics, coercive power and ideology. But, as I have tried to suggest, this can take place within a historical materialist framework, since the modes of distribution of economic, coercive and ideological power – to use Runciman's terms – are already determined in their field of effectivity and their potential by underlying and framing economic relationships. And the fact that they may appear to float free of the social contexts of which they must be a product, even if they also act back upon that context (a condition which Marxist theory must anyway insist upon) and hence lead to emergent structures and relationships, cannot alter the framing effects of the social and therefore economic context.

I suggested above that it is the culturally contextual effects of the dialectic between economic and other structures or sets of social relations which lend to social formations belonging to the same conceptual category (mode of production) their unique character and make possible so many different trajectories and developmental possibilities. Such possibilities are constrained by the contradictions inhering in antagonistic – class – production relations. But it is these developmental possibilites as they are realised in the process of change that historians study. *If* it is true that Marxists have traditionally tended to neglect one fundamental aspect – the development and constitutive agency of the state – it is primarily because their political agenda from the 1920s has kept their attention elsewhere and, crucially, because Stalinism itself was quite inimical to any more refined form of state analysis and coercive power – for reasons which must surely be fairly obvious! This is culpable, perhaps, and is certainly also symptomatic of a tendency to class reductionism at certain periods. But it is not a result of any inevitable economic determinism (which, along with material and technical determinism existed long before Marx and Engels) within the theoretical paradigm of historical materialism; and it certainly does not prevent detailed micro-analysis of political structures in all their many effectivities.[87] It is up to Marxist historians to redress the balance and to reformulate the key propositions of historical materialism in a way which takes the intention of these criticisms into account. But of course, research programmes are not constructed randomly: Marxists must also decide how and if political microanalysis is worthwhile. My own response – and, I suspect, that of most readers – would be affirmative. But we need to remember that priorities are expressed differently under different political circumstances. Marxist theory is itself a historical phenomenon, and the fallacy of basing a serious critique of historical materialism solely on the work of certain reductionist representations whose origins and evolution can be historically traced must be apparent, the more so when alternative, more sophisticated, theoretically more coherent and empirically more fruitful models had already begun to be mapped out.

NOTES

1. Mann [1986a]; Runciman [1989 see especially Vol.2]. A third recent publication deals with such phenomena, although its scope is, in fact, more limited, and it does not present particularly new theoretical insights: Tainter [1988]. The classic work is, of course, Moore [1967/1973]; but the first work in the recent generation, which took up critically both Barrington Moore and the Marxist tradition, and one which undoubtedly provided a major stimulus to the whole debate, was Skocpol [1979], who claimed to have developed a real challenge to traditional Marxist views in propounding a theory of 'states for themselves'. For a survey of the debate in respect of capitalist states, see Miliband [1983]; and for a powerful critique of Skocpol, and especially of state theorist and 'institutionalist' perspectives on modern states, see Cammack [1990].
   I should like to thank Halil Berktay, Chris Wickham and Suraiya Faroqhi for their valuable comments and criticism on earlier drafts of this article; in addition, Michael Ursinus and Johann Strauss provided invaluable bibliographical advice and critical discussion on several key topics.
2. Methodological individualism can be encapsulated very briefly as the view that social explanations can ultimately be reduced to the explanation of the actions of individuals, determined by rational choices guided by cultural context and economic need. It has been opposed by 'rational choice' Marxists such as Elster and Roemer to what they condemn as the 'methodological collectivism' of classical Marxism and macro-sociological theory. For good surveys of the debate, the terminology and the literature, see Levine, Sober and Wright [1989]; Wood [1989]. For Mann's work, see Mann [1986b]; see also the introduction to Hall [1986].
3. See in particular Skocpol [1979]; but also the essays in Hall [1986]; Cohen and Service [1978]; Claessen and Skalník [1981; 1978]; Kautsky [1982].
4. Empirical analyses of, and serious interest in, states and their origins owe a great deal to the pioneering efforts of Engels [1877], which presents an evolutionist approach to states as the necessary political apparatus through which class antagonisms are checked and the dominant position of the ruling class is maintained as the social division of labour develops. Engels also believed that states could be formed through a process of conquest and the development of chiefdoms which gradually evolve the institutional apparatuses of states and hence come to represent once again the interests of a dominant elite. See also Engels [1877/78: 197 ff.].
5. Hall's introduction – which I will discuss below – is programmatic.
6. The standard detailed theoretical exposition of this approach remains Poulantzas [1978a]. It should be noted that the notion of 'the last instance' was invoked by Engels [*Marx and Engels*, 1968: 682–83] in an effort to avoid a deterministic and reductionist account. Engels laments the fact that the notion that 'the *ultimately* determining element in history is the production and reproduction of real life' had been already turned into 'the economic element is the only determining one'. 'Marx and I are ourselves partly to blame for the fact that the younger people sometimes lay more stress on the economic side than is due to it. We had to emphasise the main principle vis-à-vis our adversaries, who denied it . . . . Unfortunately, however, it happens only too often that people think they have fully understood a new theory and can apply it without more ado from the moment they have assimilated its main principles, and even those not always correctly. And I cannot exempt many of the more recent "Marxists" from this reproach, for the most amazing rubbish has been produced in this quarter, too . . .'.
7. For a comment on the treatment of the political in Braudel, see McLennan [1981: 136 ff.]; and see in particular Christopher Hill's critique of the Annales approach

to the political [Hill, 1986a]. For a good analysis of the different moral-philosophical strands in Marx's thought and the ways in which these have, or have not, been appropriated by later Marxist writers, see Elster [1985]. For Gellner's critique, see Gellner [1985]; and for a good overview of Gellner's position, see Gellner [1988] (which includes a slightly revised version of the 1985 article under the title 'The Asiatic Trauma', 39–68). But Gellner's criticisms sometimes rest on a willfully blinkered understanding of the potential of Marxist analysis and its political project, a point made in the excellent exposé of Wood [1984: 99–100]. None of this is to deny, either, the threat to a historical materialist approach posed by the dogmatic and entrenched neo-Stalinist social science of the years preceding the Gorbachev era in the Soviet Union and eastern Europe in particular, but still to be found in western Europe and the United States to a degree.

8. Among others on this subject, see Wood [1984: 102].
9. Cohen [1978; 1983]; Laibman [1984].
10. See the excellent brief survey of McLennan [1986]. For a somewhat more positive interpretation (based on the notion that the social relations do not 'fetter' the forces of production themselves, but rather their use and application), see Bertram [1990: 122 ff.], elaborating on McMurtry [1978: 205 ff].
11. A leading protagonist of a realist materialism has been Roy Bhaskar [1982; 1978; 1987]. See also the arguments of Lovell [1980: 9–28 especially]. The debate on this problem and the 're-thinking' of Marxism in British and North American circles has been summarised in McLennan [1984].
12. See McLennan [1984: 156–62].
13. See especially Hillel-Ruben [1979].
14. See Wood [1984].
15. See Elster [1985]. As Elster himself notes, of course, this approach is already present in Marx's work [Elster, 1985: 305]. The 'torch-relay' metaphor is Ernest Gellner's [Gellner, 1980a]. For a more strictly historical materialist approach to this, as well as the part played by both the forces of production, on the one hand, and the context within which these forces are able to be exploited – the relations of production – on the other, see Bertram [1990].
16. See, for example, Burke [1980]. The works of Skocpol, Mann, Runciman and others represent some of the more substantial versions of this comparativist critical approach. For Plekhanov's much earlier response to some of the criticisms implicit in these works, see Plekhanov [1898]; see now Larrain [1986]. Larrain's view, with which I am broadly in agreement, like that of McLennan [1989], argues that a 'reconstructed' historical materialism (although 'reformulated' or even 'more clearly explicated' might be a more appropriate way of expressing what is involved) can retain a strong concept of the structurally-determined nature of social change and history, embracing also the economic, while at the same time maintaining the centrality of human agency, praxis and class struggle, the outcome of which is not in any way pre-ordained.
17. See Elster [1985]; and Roemer [1982], with the valuable survey by Carling [1986]. For a more hostile critical assessment, see Wood [1989].
18. See Anderson [1983: 24].
19. Hall [1986: 5]. In fact, Hall's critique is often too glib and superficial to merit a serious response. It appears to be founded on the assumption that (1) Marxists found their arguments entirely upon the discussions of Marx, Engels and Lenin, which are, it is presumed, more or less free from internal inconsistency, doubt, possible alternatives, and therefore already clearly falsified by more recent work (a position not dissimilar to that of Gellner); and that (2) Marxism has no history (of development, questioning, criticism). Where Lenin proceeds to differ from Marx on certain issues, then his argument 'is scarcely Marxist at all'! [Hall and Ikenberry, 1989: 8]. He takes it (apparently – the dismissal is made very briefly) also that Marxist theory in the Soviet Union, Eastern Europe, Western Europe and the USA represents a more or less undifferentiated block – ignoring thereby that central theme of his

own work: politics. And he concludes that Marx's work has been 'the single most important source of the loss of interest in the state in modern social science' [1986: 3–4] – thereby neatly leap-frogging from Marx–Engels–Lenin, over the Stalinist period, and up to today. The absurdity (and remarkable ignorance) of such views, sadly, is not limited to Hall alone, as Cammack has recently demonstrated in a forensic attack and critique of such writings. Hall's remarks, in fact, clearly represent not a first-hand intellectual confrontation with historical materialist theory, but rather a second- or third-hand dismissal of Marxism based less on theoretical discussion than on political-ideological hostility. In contrast, the work of both Skocpol and Mann, the latter especially, presents a less dogmatic, more pluralist and more constructive approach, as McLennan [1989: 226ff.] clearly demonstrates. Yet for all that, both can be legitimately accused of a similar interpretative over-simplification of historical materialist principles of analysis. Marxists do *not* posit a reductionist, reflection-theory explanation of either politics or state functions: as I will argue at the end of this article, to assume such is to read into Marx and Engels on the one hand, and contemporary Western European and North American Marxist analyses on the other, the political and interpretational priorities of Stalinist dogmatism – a political-ideological mode which was, of necessity, inimical to any close analysis of state elites, the reproduction of state power and its economic mechanisms and the role of charismatic leaders. Contemporary Marxism has certainly suffered (and continues to suffer) from this legacy. But anyone familiar with the writings of, say, Plekhanov, or the less well-known Bogdanov, quite apart from a more 'open' reading of Marx and Engels, will have no difficulty in concluding that a historical materialist approach as such, as opposed to a practical exemplification of highly selective and de-contextualised extracts from their writings, or a particular version extracted from Stalinist historiography, is quite adequate to the tasks for which state theorists have claimed it unsuited.

20. See, for example, the remarks of Thompson [1977]; Nairn [1979: 55ff.]
21. Mann [1986b]; Claessen and Skalník [1978: 3–29]; Cohen [1978: 31–75]; and especially the papers in the third section of Claessen and Skalník [1978].
22. Mann [1986b: 112].
23. Radcliffe-Brown [1940: ixff.]. For the state as an 'institutional form', see Skocpol [1979: 27]. She also believes that Marxists have failed to give the state the attention it deserves: Skocpol [1980: 200]; but see Cammack [1990: 149–55].
24. Mann [1986b: 110]; see Giddens [1982].
25. As I have tried to show in one case study dealing with the social and political crisis in the East Roman/Byzantine world in the later seventh century: Haldon [1986]. Indeed, recent debates over what has been dubbed 'rational choice Marxism' show only too clearly how necessary it is to relate inter-individual practices, attitudes and the construction and patterning of psychologies (micro-foundational analysis) to longer-term tendencies and the structural effects which the interplay between individuals, groups, roles and institutions has in respect of the trajectory followed by any given aspect of a social formation. And these in their turn must then be related to the theoretical and conceptual categories which are designed to provide a framework within which these effects of social practices can be observed, and a heuristic guide through which they and their effects can be understood. It goes without saying that I do not wish to imply a methodological individualism here: macro-phenomena cannot be reduced on a one-to-one basis to their micro-foundations. But there can be no doubt that the specification of the multiplicity of causal relationships which together constitute trends, tendencies, 'structures' and 'events' is an essential foundation for historical and sociological understanding – a point which Marx and Engels recognised quite clearly, even if it has not always been appreciated by all their (theoretical) successors. See Elster [1985]; Roemer [1982]; the survey by Carling [1986]; and the critical appreciations by Levine, Sober and Wright [1987]; Wood [1989]; and Callinicos [1989]; McLennan [1989].

26. Marx, *The Eighteenth Brumaire of Louis Bonaparte*, in Marx and Engels [1968, 96–179; see especially 169ff.]; and *The Civil War in France*, in Marx and Engels [1968: 271–309; see especially 285ff]. These points have been made forcefully and in detail by Miliband [1983].
27. Engels, *The origins of the Family, Private Property and the State*, in Marx and Engels [1968: 461–583; especially 577ff.].
28. As argued by Miliband [1983: 65–7].
29. For some aspects of the debate in respect of the modern state, see the arguments of Miliband and Poulantzas in *New Left Review* 58 (1969); 59 (1970); 82 (1973); the comments of Laclau [1975]; and those of Poulantzas [1976].
30. The formulation begs the question, of course, whether states do always develop in the context of class antagonisms. The answer is empirically testable and unequivocally in the affirmative. Virtually all the comparative historical and social-anthropological work which has examined the question of the origins of states, whether 'primitive' or 'secondary', and from whatever theoretical standpoint, bears this out. See, from a Marxist perspective, Friedman [1984]; and from a non-Marxist (although not a non-materialist) viewpoint, Mann [1986a: 82ff.]; Runciman [1989, Vol.2: 185ff.]; and Cohen [1978: 32ff.]; along with the other essays in the same volume. Note especially Fried [1967; 1978]. The exception is Service [1975], who argues that the state originated in a process of mutual or contractual relations between different groups and ecological niches in a given social-cultural context, in which the state represents the interests of all to their general best advantage. While this may certainly provide an ideological rationale for many state formations both today and in the past, such a narrow and functionalist view has met with little real support.

    For Miliband's comment, see Miliband [1983: 66–7].
31. Whether such divisions are expressed juridically, of course, for example, through a hierarchy of legally-defined statuses is, to a degree, a secondary issue. More importantly, the way in which economic classes are either united or divided internally – by lineage and kinship structures, status groupings and political organisations, local and regional identities or ideological and religious affiliations – is crucial. Because such structures cut vertically across economic divisions, any attempt to explain the politics of societies in terms of economic class position alone, regardless of the praxis-structuring ideological contexts within which people operate, will be valueless. In almost all pre-industrial social formations the general economic structure – the relations of production of society as a whole – is both partially constituted by and at the same time fragmented by such vertical divisions, sometimes setting one element of an economically-dominant group against another, often dividing peasant and pastoralist society along localised kinship and identity lines, and hence uniting at a regional or even more local level both exploiting and exploited classes ideologically. Dominant economic classes may thus suffer politically at the hands of either the state (perhaps allied with other classes) or an alliance of normally politically and economically subordinate classes. But this does not mean that economic relationships are not determinant of the configurations possible within a given social formation. It does mean that, in pre-capitalist society especially, the economic is always expressed through structures – sets of practices – which bear other functions too, as we have seen. And it also means that the political forms through which state power can be exercised, and the policies which rulers can reasonably pursue, will be determined by the relative economic strength and ideological importance of such structures at any given moment. This can be seen very clearly, for example, in the excellent analysis of the internal politics of Greek city-states and the rise of the Roman republic and empire of de Ste Croix [1981]. The 'asymmetrical' nature of class relations in pre-industrial society is a point particularly emphasised by Mann [1986a: 216ff.], but it is hardly new to Marxist analyses.
32. Runciman [1989, Vol.2: 150ff.].
33. See Runciman [1989, Vol.2: 12ff., 148ff.].
34. Runciman [1989, Vol.2: 153].

35. Marx, *Capital* [1970, Vol.3: 791].
36. Marx, *Capital* [1970, Vol.3: 791–2].
37. Marx, *Capital* [1970,c Vol.1: 85 and note 2]. But interestingly, the notion that pre-capitalist modes cannot be economically rooted in the same way as capitalism has crept back in. See, remarkably, Anderson's argument for a superstructural constitution of feudal relations of production [*Anderson*, 1974/1979: 401ff.].
38. Engels, letter to J. Bloch, [*Marx and Engels*, 1968: 682–3].
39. Engels, letter to F. Mehring, [*Marx and Engels*, 1968: 689–93; see especially 690–91].
40. A whole range of efforts to elaborate a more sophisticated version of this model has been undertaken, beginning perhaps most clearly with Lenin, who in his 1908 attack on Bogdanov, entitled *Materialism and Empirio-Criticism* [*Lenin*, 1962] tried to develop what amounts to a reflection theory of ideology and the state (in contrast, in fact, to his more analytical discussion of political organisation). Plekhanov tried similarly to develop a more thoroughgoing account, but in the process produced what some have seen as a reified spatial and sequential model of 'levels' and 'totalities' [*Plekhanov*, 1969: 70]. But it is worth noting that Bogdanov had already begun to develop what was, in many respects, a much more sophisticated and nuanced model of social and economic structures and the nature of determination by the economic [*Bogdanov*, 1897], which was the subject of Lenin's critique, referred to already. See Williams [1986: 38ff.] (I am grateful to Julian Cooper for this reference).

The most recent attempt to defend and explicate the 'base-superstructure' metaphor is Cohen [1978]. Criticism of this model was voiced more forcefully by Althusser and Balibar [1971]; and Poulantzas [1978a; 1978b]. Althusser established a model in which the levels of economics, politics and ideology, made up of specific practices, form a structural totality, in which the idea of determination is replaced by that of structural causality. The economic level remains determinant 'in the last instance', however, since it is the economic which determines which of the levels is dominant by establishing the limits of the relative autonomy of the other levels and allotting them functions necessary to its own reproduction. But it has been frequently pointed out that, while this alternative model challenges crude economic determinism, it actually leaves little changed in respect of the economic 'level'. Indeed, the relative autonomy of non-economic levels depends on their function as necessary to the reproduction of the economic level, and actually creates a split between their conditions of reproduction and those of production in general. This ignores a fundamental aspect of historical materialist notions of the dialectical and processual nature of human praxis. See Glucksmann [1972]; and the essays in Clarke [1980].
41. See Godelier [1978].
42. See Bhaskar [1982]; for Engels, see the letter to J. Bloch of Sept. 1890 [*Marx and Engels*, 1968: 682–3].
43. Mann [1986a: 31], where he argues that this is not a necessary and teleological, but rather a developmental and contingent process. But I do not wish to return to a productive forces determinism in which the primacy of the productive forces alone is fundamental (as implied in Cohen [1978]). Rather, it is both the productive forces and the social relations of production through which they are exploited, harnessed, developed or neglected, which underlies this developmental trend. See Hobsbawm [1984]; and especially Wright [1983: 24–31], where a non-teleological model of the tendency of the forces of production to develop is ably summarised.
44. For the remarks made by Hall, see Hall [1986: 1ff.]; and see Geras [1988: 40–41]; Mouzelis [1988: 117] on the question of the 'downgrading' of the political by Marxists.
45. See Runciman [1989, Vol.2: 155–60].
46. Runciman [1989, Vol.2: 160ff.].
47. In this respect, Runciman's account of historical causation is not far from that of 'pluralist' Marxists such as Sayer [1987]; Gottlieb [1984].

48. Runciman [1989, Vol.2: 40ff., 295]. For a similar approach to practice, perceptions of reality and the structuring role played by narratives, see Haldon [1986], situated firmly within a historical materialist framework of analysis.
49. See Mann [1986a: 6]; Foucault [1979: 81ff].
50. For the major recent discussion see Hindess, Hirst [1975], and the debate which followed, exemplified in the review of Asad, Wolpe [1976]. In respect of specific historical problems, see Wickham [1985]; Berktay [1987]; Haldon [1989], all of which provide recent bibliography and discussion of the main themes.
51. See Haldon [1989]. There has been, of course, a good deal of hostility to the extended use of the concept of feudalism. This has been argued at length by Anderson [1974/1979: 401ff.]; but this hostility has in turn been challenged, notably by Wickham [1985] and Hirst [1975], from different perspectives. For a defence of the extended use, see Haldon [1992, forthcoming].
52. See Berktay [1987]: 311], for the character of feudal class relations. For Amin's tributary mode and its relevance to the feudal mode as employed here, see Amin [1976: 13–16, 18–20]. It should be clear from the general direction of the present argument that I do not believe that any useful analytical or heuristic distinction can in fact be made between 'feudal' (representing 'private' forms of surplus extraction) and 'tributary' (representing 'public' or 'state' forms of the same), as argued by Wickham [1985: 170–71].

For the nature of the constraints imposed by feudal relations of production and distribution, see my forthcoming analysis of feudal state structures and the question of state autonomy, Haldon [1992].
53. For the Ottoman state as exemplifying the Asiatic mode, see Keyder [1976]; İslamoğlu, Keyder [1981]; and in particular İslamoğlu [1987a]. A critical discussion of the Asiatic mode of production: Anderson [1974/1979]: 462–549]; and for a survey of some aspects of the debate, see the essays in Bailey and Llobera [1981]. For the discussion on an Ottoman feudalism, see Lybyer [1913; 1932; 211–13]; and for a survey of the intra-Turkish debate, Berktay [1987: 293 and notes 3, 4]. See now Berktay [1991] for a detailed analysis of the nature of Ottoman feudal relations of production, and the various nationalist historians of the post-1930s period who have denied this.
54. So formulated, for example, by Anderson [1974/79: 365–6]. See also Mardin [1969a].
55. The *devşirme* developed in the first place from the way in which the ruler's fifth portion of booty taken in war (*pençik*) was collected, in the form of young captives who were converted to Islam and trained for the personal service of the Sultan. Probably under Bayezid I (1360–1403) this developed into an institution for the collection of young Christian boys, who would be brought within an entirely Muslim and Ottoman context, trained to the service of the ruler, and providing ultimately the soldiers of the Janissary corps and much of the personnel of the state apparatuses. See Ménage [1960]; Inalcık [1960]; Palmer [1953]; Papoulia [1963]. The average age of *devşirme* recruits seems to have been 14–18 years. See Lybyer [1913: 48].
56. See Runciman [1989: Vol.2, 228]; also Karpat [1968: 74].
57. From the sixteenth century this older (military) title was accompanied by that of *vali*, or governor; and from the later years of the sixteenth century, the large provinces under *beylerbeyis* were referred to also as *eyalets*, originally denoting a semi-autonomous district, a development which reflected the increasing local powers of these governors. See Kunt [1983: 96].
58. For a descriptive account of the Ottoman administration and state structure in the period from the fourteenth to the sixteenth centuries, see in particular İnalcık [1973: 76–118]; Shaw [1976: 112–32]; *CHI* [Vol.1, 300ff.]; Gibb and Bowen [1950–57: Vol.1, i, 45ff., 314ff.]; Kunt [1983: 9–29]. For a detailed summary of the complex set of interlocking relationships which constituted the *tımar* system (and which I have had of necessity to reduce to its most salient characteristics) see Berktay [1991].

59. İnalcık [1973: 65-9]; Alderson [1956]; see Shaw [1976: 112ff.]; and especially Findley [1980a: 13ff].
60. For a brief resumé of the key elements of the fiscal system, the development of tax-farming, and the role of local *ayan* in the growth of large estates, see İnalcık [1980: 311ff.], especially pp.328-33 on tax-farming and estate growth; and pp.313-17 on the ways in which the state was compelled, from the late sixteenth century, to increase and regularise the *avarız* taxes in order to ensure the resources for its central armies and *sekban* infantry units.

For the heterogeneous composition of the early Ottoman elite and the Sultan's retinue, see especially the account in Lindner [1983: 12, 22-25, 32ff.]; and for doubts as to the value of the later ideological legitimation of the early Ottoman conquests by Ottoman writers through the concept of the *Ghaza*, see especially p.24. As regards the *kapıkulları*, the use of slaves was an Islamic secular tradition reaching back in the form represented by slaves as soldiers and state officials to the earliest Abbasid times. But it is important to note that it was for the most part limited to non-agricultural and service spheres of activity: soldiers, personal servants, clerks, administrators, intellectuals, scholars and so on. Slaves could traditionally be educated to a high standard if desired, and intentionally employed as the loyal and totally dependent servants of a ruler. Considered as a member of the master's household, the slave acquired thereby the social status of the master and the household. The Sultan's slaves were thus an element of the Ruling Class, according to Ottoman notions, because of their particularly enhanced status. Indeed, there is some evidence from the mid-sixteenth century that some slaves in private households had actually volunteered for their positions, willingly surrendering their free status in return for the privileged status of slave in a respected household, and the possibilities for social advancement which this opened up to them. See Kunt [1983: 45].

It needs to be emphasised, however, that men of *devşirme* origin often retained a strong sense of their original ethnic and regional identity. Those employed in the palace were highly political, and regularly appear to have used their linguistic and ethnic origins to gain patrons or help clients; and these local identities also gave them an interest in the affairs of their one-time home district, as recent research has shown. Further, hostile or competing groups within the *devşirme* elite itself developed around such identities. And so, in spite of their technical dependence upon the Sultan, there existed a great deal of room for manoeuvre and independent political and economic activity. Of course, the morphology of these relationships must have varied over time, and it is probable that such freedom of manoeuvre was not always so apparent as in the seventeenth century, for which a good study exists. Nevertheless, the point is that the assumed monolithic control of the ruler over the *devşirme* ought not to be taken for granted at any period. See Kunt [1974]; Forand [1971].

Mehmed II's expansion and refinement of the *devşirme* system represents the most developed form of this tradition, and it was taken up elsewhere thereafter, notably by the Safavid Persian rulers in their efforts to escape the influence of the Kızılbaş Türkmen tribes – a strategy closely resembling that of the Ottoman rulers in respect of their relationship with their own Turkish nobility. See CHI [Vol.1, 401-18]. The status of slaves of the Sultan was, in fact, an honour which brought a number of advantages and privileges, a point noted by İnalcık [1973: 87-8]. The best general survey of the development of the Islamic *mamluk*, or slave soldier, tradition, the growth of the ideologies through which it was both made necessary and legitimated (the conflict between the prescriptions of the *Shari'a* regarding secular power, Islamic notions of the tribe as state, the need for the Abbasid Caliphs to protect their interests from various court and religious factions within the state, among others) is Crone [1980] especially pp.74-81. For a general analysis of slavery as an institution and the various forms it has taken under different historical and cultural conditions, see Patterson [1979; 1982].
61. See CHI [Vol.1, 274ff., 284-6]; Shaw [1976: 22ff.]. Note that the term *tımar* (or *iqta'* in the traditional Arabic terminology) might be applied to two different things:

traditionally, it referred to the granting of very extensive regions or districts to individuals in their capacity as governors. In the early Ottoman context, this meant in effect that the leaders of the Turkish warriors and clans became the provincial *beys* of the newly-conquered lands, holding them as *tımar*, from which they and their soldiers and families were to be supported and rewarded. In this case, the ruler made little or no effort to intervene in the internal running of the areas in question. As long as he received the regional military support and revenues, all was well. See below, and note 70. The second sense of the word is applied to the smaller, more closely supervised grants through which the developed Ottoman state of the later fifteenth century raised its cavalry soldiers and administered its revenues. See *CHI* [Vol.1, 153–4]; Lybyer [1913: 210ff.]; and especially Kunt [1983: 12–14], who notes the interchangeability of these technical terms until the mid-sixteenth century.

62. *CHI* [Vol.1, 300ff., 304–5, 308–9]; Beldiceanu [1965]; Shaw [1976: 57f.]; *EI* [Vol.2, 300ff.: 304–5].
63. *Tımars* were divided into three portions: the *iptida*, or 'beginning', for the maintenance of the timariot himself, the main portion for the smaller *tımar* holders; then a second portion for the maintenance of retainers (one for every 3,000 silver coins, or *akçes*); and the *terakki*, or 'bonuses', awarded on an ad hominem basis to certain *tımar* holders, and not passed on from father to son, regardless of whether or not the son continued as timariot after his father's death or retirement. While relatively uniform across the empire, the sources of revenue varied from region to region, sometimes including all the basic customary and religious taxes, sometimes excluding the *öşür*, sometimes other levies, and so forth. Local tradition and custom played an important role in this respect. The best modern descriptive account is Beldiceanu [1980], which supersedes all earlier analyses, although it presents a traditional position in many ways, defining feudalism purely at the level of juridical relationships on the western European model, and bound therefore categorically to reject the notion that the *tımar* system has any connection with feudalism. On the reaction under Bayezid II, see *CHI* [Vol.1, 308–9].
64. For a good survey, see McGowan [1981] especially pp.52ff. On Ottoman land-codes and the intensity of state/timariot supervision, see Barkan [1943]. I am grateful to Halil Berktay for making these texts available and accessible to me. It is worth stressing that *reaya* peasants were dependent on their local timariots over a wide range of issues, covering legal transactions related to their lands and their freedom of movement, and – while the normal form of tax was rendered in cash – they rendered services also in kind and in labour, varying both geographically and chronologically, of course. See Kunt [1983], Berktay [1991] and for a detailed general survey, Faroqhi [1977, 1979].
65. In essence, we are back once again to the fief in its generic sense, as one pole of the centre-periphery continuum: the movement of state formations through various phases of power/authority devolution, from strict central supervision to total alienation of resource consumption is a common feature of all social formations which can be called feudal with respect to their relations of production. It reflects, as I have noted, the problem of central governments in terms of communications, transport, the mode of distribution and consumption of surpluses, and political control. This is brought out well in the discussion of the 'fief' in medieval Islamic states by Cahen [1953], even though Cahen himself (like Beldiceanu – see note 63 above) is of the opinion that these are in no way feudal.
66. On social mobility see especially the examples quoted in Findley [1980a: 36–8. On the concept of *Ghaza* or 'raid' in the context of the *Jihad*, and the ideology based around it, see *CHI* [Vol.1, 269ff. and 283–91]: the concept has been described as the (theological) foundation of the Ottoman state, and certainly constituted the major legitimating motif in respect of Ottoman expansion both against non-believers and other Muslims. Its importance in the original formative process, however, as depicted by Wittek [1938] as fundamental to the establishment of the 'Ghazi state' has been challenged, most recently by Lindner [1983]: see note 60 above.

On the existence of prominent provincial families and households, the complex system of patronage that linked Istanbul to the provinces, and the consequent infiltrative (and therefore weakening) effects these structures had on the degree of central authority in the provinces, see Kunt [1983].

The visible contradiction between the interests of the Ottoman state and those of the Türkmen and other clans, both nomadic and sedentary, in Anatolia in the sixteenth century, is made clear by the violence of Selim I's campaigns to suppress opposition (and Shi'ism) in this region in the first 20 years of the sixteenth century; and, perhaps most tellingly, in the slow subjugation of the Anatolian nomads to central fiscal supervision and surplus appropriation, a process inevitably accompanied also by sedentarisation, brought about both by physical coercion and economic pressure. See especially Lindner [1983: 51–74].

67. For a good general account, see Shaw [1976: 169–216]; *CHI* [Vol.1: 342–53]; İnalcık [1973: 41–52]. On the ruling class in particular, see Findley [1980: 43–68]; Fleischer [1986], for an analysis of the intellectual currents and ideological narratives through which the divisions and vested interests of competing groups were represented; and the careful analysis of Kunt [1983], which examines the composition and evolution of the *Ümera*, the chief stratum of the *ehl-i seyf*, the 'men of the sword', that is to say, the military-administrative elite. See also Bayly [1989] for discussion of the effects of trading and merchant wealth which further complicated the factional interests and loyalties at both the provincial and central levels.

68. On the silver inflation, see Barkan [1975]; but note İnalcık [1978: 90–95]; [1980: 306 note 52, 312f.]; and especially Sundhausen [1983], both of whom point to the fact that the state effected deliberate revaluations of the silver in relation to its gold currency in order precisely to control unofficial price-fixing and price fluctuations, and to preserve intact the relationship between the state and *tımar* incomes and agricultural produce. For the state's need for cash revenues with which to pay its ever-growing central forces at this time, see Kunt [1983: 79–88]; on *vakıf* organisation, see especially Shaw [1976: 162–3]; İnalcık [1973: 142–50]; Gibb and Kramers [1953: 624–8, especially 627]; Lewis [1961: 91–2]; and Yediyıldız [1985] for a general survey. The significance of these 'external' factors, however, has led even very recent commentators to conclude that the Ottoman system was entirely stable until such elements intervened. In fact, the internal stability was both the effect of a particular balance of economic and power relationships, and relatively short-lived. In addition, it was laced with contradictions, both within the ruling elite, and between the Ottoman 'Ruling Class' and the leading elements of the *reaya*: the efforts of *reaya* military men to obtain *kapıkulları* privileges and status, for example, which can be shown to date from at least the 1550s, and the consequent hostility of the Janissaries; the dominant position of a number of *sekban* officers of *reaya* origin, both in the provinces and, in the first half of the seventeenth century, for the central government; and the civil war-like conditions of many regions in the Balkans and Anatolia at times during the seventeenth century, as Janissaries and centrally-mobilised peasant and urban militias fought against *levend* or mercenary units; as well as the rise of the urban *ayan* in the seventeenth century all illustrate this. See Faroqhi [1986] and especially Faroqhi [n.d.]; İslamoğlu and Keyder [1981] 307f.; and on peasant migration and movement, Faroqhi [1984]. On the importance of changes in military technology and their effects on Ottoman warfare, see McGowan [1981] 57; and especially Parry [1970: 835–50], who stresses that it was not simply the use of new technologies as such, which the Ottomans could, and did, acquire and assimilate piecemeal; but rather the development of new tactical formations as the prerequisite for the deployment of this technology, which the Ottoman armies – depending as they did for their tactical structures on socially-embedded organisational forms – were unable to emulate without major reforms. When such reforms were proposed, along with the fundamental structural changes that were their concomitant, the result was a wave of conservative opposition – see below; and Parry [1970: 849–50]. On all these issues, see the survey of İnalcık [1980: especially 288–303]. For the *levend* groups, Griswold [1983: 157ff.] provides an excellent discussion.

69. On the *celali* rebellions, see in particular Griswold [1983] and Cook [1972], the latter arguing that, while demographic pressures certainly played a role, other factors – such as the absence of the military from large areas of Anatolia at this time (in wars against both Persia and Austria) – played an equally important role, especially if it is borne in mind that the nature of Ottoman control and authority rested as much on military and political coercion and supervision as it did on ideological legitimation and law. That there did occur a growth in population in the middle of the sixteenth century is not in itself in doubt. What does appear dubious is that this, rather than demographic dislocation and movement, was at the root of these developments. See İslamoğlu [1987c: 118ff.] and the summary of the arguments of Faroqhi, Erder and Cook in İnalcık [1978: 84–9] with literature. For a good account of the nature and effect of brigandage on local economy and society, see Goffman [1990: 25–33]; and on rural society in general, Faroqui [1977, 1979]; İslamoğlu [1987c]. For the history and development of *vakıf* organisation, see Yediyıldız [1985: especially 9–19; 23–36].

70. On the period of 'decline' and its different aspects, especially the growth of an entrenched provincial landlord class, see *CHI* [Vol.1: 362–9]; İnalcık [1977]; Hourani [1968]; Karpat [1973]; Findley [1980a: Chs. 1–3 especially]; Lewis [1961: 37–8]. Kunt [1983] presents a particularly clear analysis of (1) the decline of the *timar* system in the face of the state's needs for cash for its central armies, on the one hand, and the consequent increasing irrelevance of the traditional provincial forces on the other; (2) the increased importance of the *avarız* taxes, which now became both regularised and standardised; and (3) the importance of households among the military-administrative elite of the empire. The latter played a key role in the undermining of central state authority: the armed mercenaries and servitors of provincial governors were crucial to the maintenance of their position and authority, and as long as their patron was in power, they carried out their policing and fiscal duties, paid and maintained, of course, by their patron himself, not by the state. If the patron lost his post, the retinues could no longer be paid, and extortion and organised brigandage were their only source of income.

On the *ayan* in particular, see Özkaya [1977]; with the important discussion on the various meanings which this term can have, in Ursinus [1982]; further İnalcık [1980: 307ff., 315–16]; and on *çiftliks*, İnalcık [1984]. On the importance of patronage and households, see especially Findley [1980]; and on the *derebeys*, see, for example, for the eighteenth and nineteenth centuries, Gould [1976]. For the demographic contraction during and following the *celâli* wars, a contraction which appears to have reached its nadir in the middle of the seventeenth century, and is eloquently expressed in the records of a number of major urban centres, see Jennings [1976]; Faroqhi [1987: 43ff.], and the warning against exaggerating the decline into a 'crisis' of Todorova [1988].

For the politically-motivated delegation of provincial authority, see, for example, Van Bruinessen [1989]; and on the crucial importance of these anti-Shi'ite policies in respect of Ottoman–Safavid relations and the securing of Anatolia, see Sohrweide [1965] and Imber [1979].

On the *ulema*, see the detailed description of Shaw [1976: 132–9]; and on the *Şeyh-ul-Islam*, or chief *Mufti*, a position established under Süleyman the Great, Shaw [1976: 137ff.]; Lewis [1961: 13–14]; Findley [1980: 61–3]; and especially Faroqhi [1973] for a prosopographical analysis. It is worth noting that traditional assumptions of a clear demarcation between the *ulema* or 'religious institution' and the *devşirme* 'ruling institution' have been challenged and modified. Certainly until the middle of the sixteenth century it seems to have been possible for men to cross over from one 'career' to another with little or no hindrance. Only as a clearly delineated fiscal-bureaucratic administrative establishment entrenched itself – by the middle of the sixteenth century, roughly speaking – were men of *ulema* origins screened out of the secular running of the state. See in particular the remarks of Itzkowitz [1962]. For the political theory of the Ottoman elite and for a discussion of Ottoman

political treatises critical of the *ulema*, see Majer [1980]; and on the vested interests of the palace factions in respect of the Ruling Institution and its traditions, see Wright [1935: 53–60], a dated but still useful comment.
71. There is now a great deal of discussion over the origins and functioning of the *millet* system: traditionally, it was thought that each 'nation' (defined by religious creed) within the Ottoman lands continued to regulate its own internal affairs, so that the *millets* were seen as promoting a certain solidarity of interests across the empire's numerous subject populations. Each *millet* took responsibility for those of its affairs in which the state and the *Osmanlılar* ruling caste had no direct interest – education, religion, justice, provision for the poor, hospitals and welfare, and so on. See Gibb and Bowen [1950–57: 179ff.] for the traditional view; but see now Ursinus [1989], and Braude [1982], who suggests that the whole notion of a *millet* system is a much later projection onto the past.
72. On the divisions within the ruling elite, see Findley [1980: 43ff.], who notes the evolution and progressive differentiation of the various elements which formed it – see especially pp.67–68. For the effects of the French revolution, the rise of Napoleon and the attempted reforms, chiefly military, of Selim III, see Lewis [1961: 40–72]; together with Findley [1980a: 114–20] on perceptions of the need for reform and on the development of reformist and reactionary factions. For the taming of the provincial nobility and the destruction of the Janissary corps, see Lewis [1974: 76–9]; and for the course of Mahmud's reforms, ibid. [79–104]; *CHI* [Vol.1, 364–5]. For a useful comment on the ways in which Mahmud and his supporters gained the upper hand and restored central absolutism by playing off one faction against another, see Hodgson [1974: Vol.3, 228–9].
73. The point has been made before, of course, notably by Anderson [1974: 15–16]. The problem of equilibrium and the nature of direct state intervention in the political relations of distribution is especially clear in the case of the cyclical transformations which distinguish Chinese imperial states and their evolution from the earliest times, for example. Both in the long period preceding the Sung dynasty (960–1279) and thereafter, political power depended upon a complex balancing act between the interests of the centre and those of the (potentially) independent magnates. With the development and extension of the power of the middling and lower gentry under the interested patronage of the Sung, in the form of the meritocratic bureaucracy for which China is well known, the state was able to maintain its pre-eminent position more easily. The system that developed was designed to fragment any opposition to the state's economic and political/ideological control by integrating the middling and lower gentry into the state apparatus, while at the same time reducing the hold of the wealthier class of magnates on the machinery of state in the provinces. See Eberhard [1977: 205ff.], for example. But, as has been pointed out, even here, and in spite of the ideological pre-eminence of the notion of the imperial state and the single emperor, the middling and lower officials of the mandarinate in the provinces were able to usurp state power and revenues at the local level, with only occasional interference from the central authority. And this did not threaten the federal unity of the empire as such. See Beattie [1979].
74. Mann [1986a: 5–7].
75. The question of the actual forms of modes of distribution of power especially concerns Runciman [1989: Vol.2], particularly in his opening analysis, pp.1–86. Poulantzas's detailed discussion of power [1978a: 99–119] combines both a useful critique of the numerous non-Marxist sociological attempts to define and invoke power in social theory; but it is constrained by a structuralist paradigm (structures – practice – overdetermination) which I do not find particularly useful for generating a dynamic analysis of historical change; and by a class-centred method which tends to ignore the complexities and contradictions within the continuum from constituted and constitutive social subjectivity to group and class ideologies and practices, and thus renders empirical analysis one-sided – structures become detached from human subjects in a way which makes causal explanation difficult.

76. This is precisely the point strongly argued by Plekhanov [1898: especially 311ff.].
77. A point made by Mann (among others) in his opening discussion [1986a: 3–4].
78. For Turkish modernisation and reform, see Todorov [1980] and Keyder [1980]. For the position of the Ottoman state as peripheral to the developed capitalist economies of Europe during the later nineteenth and twentieth centuries, see Wallerstein [1980]; İslamoğlu and Keyder [1977]; and for the significance of state dirigist economic and fiscal policies and the creation of a 'state bourgeoisie' (in the process of the Young Turk movement) in respect of modernising both fiscal and credit structures as well as production, see especially Ahmad [1980]; Keyder [1980]; and Sugar [1970]. On the role of the army, see Rustow [1970] and, from a comparative standpoint, Rustow [1963].
79. For an example of 'developing' states, see Cooper [1983]; on Bismarck, see in particular Engels [1964/1968: 59ff.]; and for more recent assessments, Hamerow [1958]; Pascal [1946]. For Miliband's comments, see Miliband [1983: 66]. See especially McLennan [1989: 233–6], for a fuller treatment of this point and a critique of the state-centred argumentation of, for example, Skocpol.
80. Haldon [1989; 1990: 403ff.]. On the magnate clans of Anatolia, the political polarisation of the two dominant factions of the ruling class in the state, and more particularly, on the formation and fragmentation of clan and family alliances within both the provincial and the Constantinopolitan elites, see especially the account of Cheynet [1990]; as well as Morris [1976]; Angold [1984: 59–75]; and, for a slightly less nuanced view, Vryonis [1959]. For a more detailed discussion, see Haldon [1992], with literature. Angold rightly notes the similarities in respect of the antagonisms between central authority and the elite which it had generated and promoted, in both the later Roman state and the Byzantine state of the tenth and eleventh centuries [1984: 68ff.].
81. See especially İnalcık [1980: 283–4]; Wright [1935]; Fleischer [1986].
82. Clearly the non-servile bureaucratic elite of the Byzantine world was much more a part of society in the organic sense – it had not been natally alienated, in Patterson's terms [Patterson, 1979: 34–5; 1982]; and with the exception of the numerically fairly limited number of eunuchs (in comparison with the devşirme elite of the Ottoman state) who served as soldiers and officials in the Byzantine palace and administration, it retained links of clientage and patronage, as well as of regional cultural and social identity, which could vary in degree both by period and by individual. For an analysis of this elite in the eleventh century, see especially the articulate work of Weiss [1973].
83. Haldon [1989: 28–9]; Ostrogorsky [1968: 306].
84. See the remarks of Faroqhi [1985]. Yet again, this point was nicely elaborated by Plekhanov [1898: 294ff.].
85. Compare, for example, Yerasimos [1990]. I am grateful to Suraiya Faroqhi for this reference.
86. I have tried to illustrate this elsewhere, and within a slightly different analytical context: Haldon [1986].
87. One could reasonably argue that much recent state theory has actually led to a sort of state reductionism, in which both the relations of production and, in particular, the role of individuals, are neglected. As McLennan [1989: 224–57] and Cammack [1990] both demonstrate by different means, even the best state-theorist arguments in effect concede the fact of 'relative' autonomy by admitting that states cannot act in a way which is either unconstrained by 'social forces' (which are never specified!), or arbitrary.

REFERENCES

Ahmad, F., 1980, 'Vanguard of a Nascent Bourgeoisie: The Social and Economic Policy of the Young Turks, 1908-1918', in Okyar and İnalcık [1980], pp.329-50.
Alderson, A.D., 1956, *The Structure of the Ottoman Dynasty*, Oxford: Clarendon.
Althusser, L. (and E. Balibar), 1971, *Reading 'Capital'*, London: Penguin.
Amin, S., 1976 (translated by B. Pearce), *Unequal Development*, Hassocks: Harvester.
Anderson, P.A., 1983, *In the Tracks of Historical Materialism*, London: Verso.
Anderson, P.A., 1974/79, *Lineages of the Absolutist State*, London: Verso.
Anderson, P.A., 1974, *Passages from Antiquity to Feudalism*, London: Verso.
Angold, M., 1984, *The Byzantine Empire 1025-1204: A Political History*, London: Longman.
Asad, T., and H. Wolpe, 1976, review of Hindess and Hirst [1975], in *Economy and Society*, 5, pp.470-506.
Bailey, Anne M., and J. Llobera (eds.), 1981, *The Asiatic Mode of Production: Science and Politics*, London: Routledge & Kegan Paul.
Barkan, Ö.L., 1943, *XVI ve XVI*ıncı Asırlarda Osmanlı İmparatorluğunda Zirāī Ekonominin Hukuki v Mali Esasları (Legal and financial principles of the Ottoman empire in the fifteenth and sixteenth century), Istanbul: Istanbul University.
Barkan, Ö.L., 1975, 'The Price Revolution of the Sixteenth Century: A Turning Point in the Economic History of the Near East', *International Journal of Middle East Studies*, Vol.6, pp.3-28.
Bayly, C.A., 1989, *Imperial Meridian*, London: Longman.
Beattie, H.J., 1979, *Land and Lineage in China: A Study of T'ung-Ch'eng County, Anhwei, in the Ming and Ch'ing Dynasties*, Cambridge: Cambridge University Press.
Beldiceanu, N., 1965, 'Recherches sur la réforme foncière de Mehmet II', *Acta Historica*, Vol.4, pp. 27-39.
Beldiceanu, N., 1980, *Le timar dans l'état ottoman (début XIVe siècle-début XVIe siècle)*, Wiesbaden: Otto Harrassowitz.
Berkes, N., 1964, *The Development of Secularism in Turkey*, Montreal: McGill University Press.
Berktay, H., 1987, 'The Feudalism Debate: The Turkish End – Is "Tax vs. Rent" Necessarily the Product and the Sign of a Modal Difference?', *The Journal of Peasant Studies*, Vol.14, No.3, pp.291-333.
Berktay, H., 1991, *The 'Other' Feudalism: A Critique of Twentieth-Century Turkish Historiography and Its Particularisation of Ottoman Society*, London: Verso (forthcoming).
Bertram, C., 1990, 'International Competition in Historical Materialism', *New Left review*, No.183, pp.116-28.
Bhaskar, R.B., 1978, *A Realist Theory of Science*, Brighton: Harvester.
Bhaskar, R.B., 1982, 'Emergence, Explanation and Emancipation', in Secord [1982], pp.275-310.
Bhaskar, R.B., 1987, *Scientific Realism and Human Emancipation*, London: Verso.
Bloch, M. (ed.), 1984, *Marxist Analyses and Social Anthropology*, London: Tavistock.
Bogdanov A., 1897, *Kratkii: Kurs ekonomicheskoy nauki (Short Course in Economic Science)*, Moscow: repr. Academy of Sciences of USSR.
Braude, B., 1982, 'Foundation Myths of the *Millet* System', in Braude and Lewis [1982], pp.69-88.
Braude, B. and B. Lewis (eds.), 1982, *Christians and Jews in the Ottoman Empire*, Vol.1: *The Central Lands*, New York: Holmes & Meier.
Burke, P., 1980, *Sociology and History*, London: Allen & Unwin.
Cahen, C., 1953, 'L'Évolution de l'iqta' du IXe au XIIIe siècle: contribution à une histoire comparée des sociétés médiévales', *Annales E.S.C.*, vol.8, pp.25-52.
Callinicos, A., 1989, *Making History: Agency, Structure and Change in Social Theory*, London: Polity Press.
The Cambridge History of Islam (CHI), 1970, Vol.1: *The Central Islamic Lands*; Vol.2: *The Further Islamic Lands, Islamic Society and Civilisation* (eds.) P.M. Holt, A.K.S. Lambton

and B. Lewis, Cambridge: Cambridge University Press.
Cammack, P., 1990, 'Statism, New Institutionalism, and Marxism', *Socialist Register*, pp.147–70.
Carling, A., 1986, 'Rational Choice Marxism', *New Left Review*, No.160, pp.24–62.
Chapman, J., and J.R. Pennock (eds.), 1983, *Marx and Legal Theory*, New York (=*Nomos*, Vol.24): New York University Press.
Cheynet, J.-C., 1990, *Pouvoir et contestations à Byzance (963–1210)*, Paris: CNRS.
Claessen, H.J.M., and P. Skalník (eds.), 1978, *The Early State*, The Hague: Mouton.
Claessen, H.J.M., and P. Skalník (eds.), 1981, *The Study of the State*, The Hague: Mouton.
Clarke, S., 1980, *One-Dimensional Marxism*, London: Allison & Busby.
Cohen, G.A., 1978, *Karl Marx's Theory of History: a Defence*, Oxford: Oxford University Press.
Cohen, G.A., 1983, 'Reconsidering Historical Materialism', in Chapman and Pennock (eds.) [1983].
Cohen, R., 1978, 'State origins: A Re-Appraisal', in Claessen and Skalník [1978], pp.31–75.
Cohen, R., and E.R. Service (eds.), 1978, *Origins of the State. The Anthropology of Political Evolution*, Philadelphia, PA: Institute for the Study of Human Issues.
Cook, M.A., 1972, *Population Pressure in Rural Anatolia, 1450–1600*, London: Oxford University Press.
Cooper, M.N., 1983, 'State Capitalism, Class Structure and Social Transformation in the Third World: The case of Egypt', *International Journal of Middle East Studies*, Vol.15, pp.451–69.
Crone, P., 1980, *Slaves on Horses: the Evolution of the Islamic Polity*, Cambridge: Cambridge University Press.
de Ste Croix, G.E.M., 1981, *The Class Struggle in the Ancient Greek World*, London: Duckworth.
Eberhard, W., 1977, *A History of China*, London: Routledge & Kegan Paul.
Elster, J., 1985, *Making Sense of Marx*, Cambridge: Cambridge
Encyclopaedia of Islam (EI), 1960 (eds. H.A.R. Gibb and B. Lewis et al.), Leiden: Brill.
Engels, F., 1877, *The Origin of the Family, Private Property and the State* (translated by A. West, introduction by F. Leacock, 1972), London: Lawrence & Wishart.
Engels, F., 1877/78, *Anti-Dühring* (English translation 1939), New York: International Publishers.
Engels, F., 1964/68, *The Role of Force in History. A Study of Bismarck's Policy of Blood and Iron* (transl. J. Cohen), Berlin/London: Lawrence & Wishart.
Faroqhi, S., 1973, 'Social Mobility and the Ottoman Ulema in the Later Sixteenth Century', *International Journal of Middle East Studies*, Vol.4, pp.204–18.
Faroqhi, S., 1977, 'Rural Society in Anatolia and the Balkans during the Sixteenth Century I', *Turcica*, Vol.9, pp.161–95.
Faroqhi, S., 1979, 'Rural Society in Anatolia and the Balkans during the Sixteenth Century II', *Turcica*, Vol.11, pp.103–53.
Faroqhi, S., 1984, *Towns and Townsmen of Ottoman Anatolia: Trade, Crafts and Food Production in an Urban Setting, 1520–1650*, Cambridge: Cambridge University Press.
Faroqhi, S., 1985, 'Civilian Society and Political Power in the Ottoman Empire: A Report on Research in Collective Biography (1480–1830)', *International Journal of Middle East Studies*, Vol.17, 109–17.
Faroqhi, S., 1986, 'Town Officials, Timār-holders, and Taxation in the Late Sixteenth-Century Crisis as Seen from Çorum', *Turcica*, Vol.18, pp.53–82.
Faroqhi, S., 1987, *Men of Modest Substance. House Owners and House Property in Seventeenth-Century Ankara and Kayseri*, Cambridge: Cambridge University Press.
Faroqhi, S., n.d., 'Political Tensions in the Anatolian Countryside around 1600: An Attempt at Interpretation', in *Türkische Miszellen: Robert Anhegger Festschrift* (eds. J.-L. Bacqué-Gramont, B. Fleming, M. Gökberk, I. Ortaylı), Istanbul: Divit Press, pp.117–30.

Findley, C.V., 1980a, *Bureaucratic Reform in the Ottoman Empire: The Sublime Porte 1789–1922*, Princeton, NJ: Princeton University Press.
Findley, C.V., 1980b, 'Patrimonial Household Organisation and Factional Activity in the Ottoman Ruling Class', in Okyar and İnalcık [1980], pp.227–35.
Fleischer, C., 1986, *Bureaucrat and Intellectual in the Ottoman Empire: The Historian Mustafa Ali, 1541–1600*, Princeton, NJ: Princeton University Press.
Forand, P.G., 1971, 'The Relationship of the Slave and the Client to the Master or Patron', *International Journal of Middle East Studies*, Vol.2, pp.59–66.
Foucault, M., 1979, *The History of Sexuality*, Vol.1, London: Allen Lane.
Fried, M.H., 1967, *The Evolution of Political Society*, New York: Random House.
Fried, M.H., 1978, 'The State, the Chicken and the Egg: or, What Came First?', in Cohen and Service [1978], pp.35–47.
Friedman, J., 1984, 'Tribes, States and Transformations', in Bloch [1984], pp.161–202.
Gellner, E., 1985, 'Soviets against Wittfogel: or, The Anthropoligical Preconditions of Mature Marxism', in Hall [1986: 78–108] (repr. from *Theory and Society*, Vol.14).
Gellner, E., 1988, *State and Society in Soviet Thought*, Oxford: Blackwell.
Gellner, E., 1980a, 'A Russian Marxist Philosophy of History', in Gellner [1980b: 59–84].
Gellner, E., 1980b, *Soviet and Western Anthropology*, London: Duckworth.
Geras, N., 1988, 'Ex-Marxism without Substance: Being a Real Reply to Laclau and Mouffe', *New Left Review*, No.169, pp.34–61.
Gibb, H.A.R., and H. Bowen, 1950–57, *Islamic Society and the West*, Vol.1: *Islamic Society in the Eighteenth Century*, London: Oxford University Press.
Gibb, H.A.R., and J.H. Kramers (eds.), 1953, *Shorter Encyclopaedia of Islam*, Leiden/London: Brill.
Giddens, A., 1982, *A Contemporary Critique of Historical Materialism*, London: Macmillan.
Glucksmann, M., 1972, 'A Ventriloquist Structuralism', *New Left Review*, No.72, 68–92.
Godelier, M., 1978, 'Infrastructures, Societies and History', *Current Anthropology*, Vol.19, No.4, pp.763–71.
Goffman, D., 1990, *Izmir and the Levantine World, 1550–1650*, Seattle/London: University of Washington Press.
Gottlieb, R., 1984, 'Feudalism and Historical Materialism: A Critique and Synthesis', *Science and Society*, Vol.48, No.1.
Gould, A., 1976, 'Lords or Bandits? The Derebeys of Cilicia', *International Journal of Middle East Studies*, Vol.7, pp.485–506.
Griswold, W., 1983, *The Great Anatolian Rebellion, 1000–1020/1591–1611* (Islamkundliche Untersuchungen 83), Berlin: Schwarz.
Haldon, J.F., 1986, 'Ideology and Social Change in the Seventh Century: Military Discontent as a Barometer', *Klio*, Vol.68, pp.139–90.
Haldon, J.F., 1989, 'The Feudalism Debate Once More: The Case of Byzantium', *The Journal of Peasant Studies*, Vol.17, No.1, pp.5–39.
Haldon, J.F., 1990, *Byzantium in the Seventh Century: The Transformation of a Culture*, Cambridge: Cambridge University Press.
Haldon, J.F., 1992 (forthcoming), *State Theory, State Autonomy and the Pre-Modern State*, London: Verso.
Hall, J.A. (ed.), 1986, *States in History*, Oxford: Blackwell.
Hall, J.A., and G.J. Ikenberry, 1989, *The State*, Milton Keynes: Open University Press.
Hamerow, T., 1958, *Restoration, Revolution and Reaction: Economics and Politics in Germany, 1815–1871*, Princeton, NJ: Princeton University Press.
Hill, C., 1986a, 'Braudel and the State', in Hill [1986b: 125–42].
Hill, C., 1986b, *The Collected Essays of Christopher Hill*, Vol.3: *People and Ideas in Seventeenth-Century England*, Brighton: Harvester.
Hillel-Ruben, D., 1979, *Marxism and Materialism*, Brighton: Harvester.
Hindess, B., and P.Q. Hirst, *Pre-Capitalist Modes of Production*, London: Routledge & Kegan Paul.

Hirst, P.Q., 1975, 'The Uniqueness of the West', *Economy and Society*, Vol.4, No.4, 446–75.
Hobsbawm, E., 1984, 'Marx and History', *New Left Review*, No.143, pp.39–50.
Hodgson, M.G.S., 1974, *The Venture of Islam: Conscience and History in a World Civilization*, Vol.3: *The Gunpowder Empires and Modern Times*, Chicago, IL: University of Chicago Press.
Hourani, A., 1968, 'Ottoman Reform and the Politics of Notables', in Polk and Chambers [1968: 41–68].
Imber, C., 1979, 'The Persecution of Ottoman Shi'ites According to the Mühimne Defterleri, 1565–1585', *Der Islam*, Vol.56 No.2, pp.245–73.
İnalcık, H., 1960, article 'Ghulam', in *EI*, Vol.2, pp.1085–91.
İnalcık, H., 1973, *The Ottoman Empire: The Classical Age, 1300–1600*, London: Weidenfeld & Nicholson.
İnalcık, H., 1977, 'Centralisation and Decentralisation in Ottoman Administration', in Naff and Owen [1977: 27–52].
İnalcık, H., 1978, 'Impact of the *Annales* School on Ottoman Studies and New Findings', *Archivum Ottomanicum* 6, pp.283–337 (repr. in İnalcık [1985: IV]).
İnalcık, H., 1980, 'Military and Fiscal Transformation in the otoman Empire 1600–1700', *Archivum Ottomanicum*, Vol.VI, pp.283–337 (repr. in İnalcık [1985: V]).
İnalcık, H., 1984, 'The Emergence of Big Farms, *Çiftliks*: State, Landlords and Tenants', in *Contributions à l'histoire économique et sociale de l'empire ottoman. Collection turcica III*, pp.105–26, Louvain (repr. in İnalcık [1985: VIII]).
İnalcık, H., 1985, *Studies in Ottoman Social and Economic History*, London: Variorum.
İslamoğlu-İnan, H., 1987a, *The Ottoman Empire and the World Economy*, Cambridge: Cambridge University Press; Paris: Éditions de la Maison des Sciences de l'Homme.
İslamoğlu-İnan, 1987b, 'Oriental Despotism in World-System Perspective', in İslamoğlu-İnan [1987a: 1–26].
İslamoğlu-İnan, 1987c, 'State and Peasant in the Ottoman Empire: A Study of Peasant Economy in North and Eastern Anatolia during the Sixeenth Century', in İslamoğlu-İnan [1987a: 118ff.].
İslamoğlu, H. and Ç. Keyder, 1977, 'Agenda for Ottoman History', *Reviews*, Vol.1, No.1, pp.31–55.
İslamoğlu, H. and Ç. Keyder, 1981, 'The Ottoman Social Formation', in Bailey and Llobera [1981: 301–24].
Itzkowitz, N., 1962, 'Eighteenth-Century Ottoman Realities', *Studia Islamica*, Vol.16, pp.73–94.
Jennings, R., 1976, 'Urban Population in Anatolia in the Sixteenth Century: A Study of Kayseri, Karaman, Trabzon, and Erzurum', *International Journal of Middle East Studies*, Vol.7, No.1, pp.21–57.
Karpat, K.H., 1968, 'The Land Régime, Social Structure and Modernisation in the Ottoman Empire', in Polk and Chambers [1968].
Karpat, K.H., 1973a, 'Structural Change, Historical Stages of Modernisation and the Role of the Social Groups in Turkish Politics', in Karpat [1973b: 11–92].
Karpat, K.H. (ed.), 1973b, *Social Change and Politics in Turkey: A Structural–Historical Analysis*, Leiden: Brill.
Kautsky, J.H., 1982, *The Politics of Aristocratic Empires*, Chapel Hill, NC: University of North Carolina Press.
Keyder, Ç., 1976, 'The Dissolution of the Asiatic Mode of Production', *Economy and Society*, Vol.5, pp.178–96.
Keyder, Ç., 1980, 'Ottoman Economy and Finances (1881–1918)', in Okyar and İnalcık [1980: 323–28].
Keyder, Ç., 1987, *State and Class in Turkey: A Study in Capitalist Development*, London: Verso.
Köprülü, Mehmet Fuat, 1941, 'Ortazaman Türk-İslâm Feodalizmi' (Turkish–Islamic Feudalism of the Middle Ages), *Belleten* (Bulletin), Vol. 5, No. 19, pp 319–34.
Kunt, İ. Metin, 1974, 'Ethnic-Regional (*Cins*) Solidarity in the Seventeenth-Century

Ottoman Establishment', *International Journal of Middle East Studies*, Vol.5, pp.233–9.
Kunt, İ. Metin, 1978, *Sancaktan Eyalete, 1550–1650 arasında Osmanlı ümerası ve İl İdaresi*, Istanbul: Boğaziçi University Press (translated, extensively revised and re-published as:
Kunt, İ. Metin, 1983, *The Sultan's Servants: The Transformation of Ottoman Provincial Government 1550–1650*, New York: Columbia University Press.
Laibman, D., 1984, 'Modes of Production and Theories of Transition', *Science and Society*, Vol.48, No.3.
Laclau, E., 1975, 'The Specificity of the Political: The Poulantzas–Miliband Debate', *Economy and Society*, Vol.4, No.1, pp.87–110.
Larrain, J., 1986, *A Reconstruction of Historical Materialism*, London: Allen & Unwin.
Lenin, V.I., 1962, *Materialism and Empirio-Criticism*, in *Collected Works*, Vol.14, Moscow: Progress.
Levine, A., Sober, E. and E. Olin Wright, 1987, 'Rational Choice Marxism', *New Left Review*, No.162, pp.67–84.
Lewis, B., 1961, *The Emergence of Modern Turkey*, Oxford: Oxford University Press.
Lindner, R.P., 1983, *Nomads and Ottomans in Medieval Anatolia*, Bloomington, IN: Research Institute for Inner Asian Studies.
Lovell, T., 1980, *Pictures of Reality*, London: British Film Institute.
Lybyer, A.H., 1913, *The Government of the Ottoman Empire in the Time of Suleiman the Magnificent*, Cambridge, MA: Harvard University Press.
Lybyer, A.H., 1932, article 'Feudalism', in *Encyclopaedia of the Social Sciences*, Vol.6, London: Macmillan, pp. 211–13.
McGowan, B., 1981, *Economic Life in the Ottoman Empire: Taxation, Trade and the Struggle for Land, 1600–1800*, Cambridge: Cambridge University Press.
McLennan, G., 1981, *Marxism and the Methodologies of History*, London: Verso Press.
McLennan, G., 1984, 'History and Theory: Contemporary Debates and Directions', *Literature and History*, Vol.10, No.2, pp.139–64.
McLennan, G., 1986, 'Marxist Theory and Historical research: Between the Hard and Soft Options', *Science and Society*, Vol.50, No.1, pp.85–95.
McLennan, G., 1989, *Marxism, Pluralism and Beyond*, Cambridge: Polity Press.
McMurtry, J., 1978, *The Structure of Marx's World View*, Princeton, NJ: Princeton University Press.
Majer, H.G., 1980, 'Die Kritik an den Ulema in den osmanischen politischen Traktaten des 16.–18. Jahrhunderts', in Okyar and İnalcık [1980: 147–53].
Mann, M., 1986a, *The Sources of Social Power, Vol.1: A History of Power from the Beginnings to A.D. 1760*, Cambridge: Cambridge University Press.
Mann, M., 1986b, 'The Autonomous Power of the State: Its Origins, Mechanisms and Results', in Hall [1986: 109–36].
Mardin, Ş., 1969a, 'Power, Civil Society and Culture in the Ottoman Empire', *Comparative Studies in Society and History*, Vol.11, pp.258–81.
Mardin, Ş., 1969b, 'The Mind of the Ottoman Reformer', in S.A. Hanna and G.H. Gardner (eds.), *Arab Socialism*, Salt Lake City, UT: University of Utah Press, pp.24–48.
Marx, K., 1970, *Capital*, London/Moscow: Lawrence & Wishart.
Marx, K. and F. Engels, 1968, *Selected Works*, London/Moscow: Lawrence & Wishart.
Ménage, V., 1960, article 'Devshirme', in *EI*, Vol.2, pp.210–13.
Miliband, R., 1983, 'State Power and Class Interests', *New Left Review*, No.138, pp.57–68.
Moore, Barrington, Jr., 1967/73, *Social Origins of Dictatorship and Democracy*, Harmondsworth: Penguin.
Morris, R., 1976, 'The Powerful and the Poor in Tenth-Century Byzantium: Law and Reality', *Past and Present*, No.73, pp.3–27.
Mouzelis, N., 1988, 'Marxism – Post-Marxism?', *New Left review*, No.167, pp.107–23.
Naff, T., and R. Owen, 1977, *Studies in Eighteenth Century Islamic History*, Carbondale, IL: Southern Illinois University Press.

Nairn, T., 1979, 'The Future of Britain's Crisis', *New Left Review*, No.113-114, pp.43-69.
Okyar, O. and H. İnalcık (eds.), 1980, *Social and Economic History of Turkey* (Papers presented to the First International Congress on the Social and Economic History of Turkey, 1977), Ankara: Meteksan.
Ostrogorsky, G., 1968, *A History of the Byzantine State*, Oxford: Blackwell.
Özkaya, Y., 1977, *Osmanlı İmparatorluğunda Ayanlık* (The Nobility in the Ottoman Empire), Ankara.
Palmer, J.A.B., 1953, 'The Origins of the Janissaries', *Bulletin of the John Rylands Library*, Vol.25, pp.448-81.
Papoulia, B.D., 1963, *Ursprung und Wesen der 'Knabenlese' im osmanischen Reich*, Munich: Beck.
Parker, G. and L. Smith (eds.), 1978, *The General Crisis of the Seventeenth Century*, London:
Parry, V.J., 1970, chapter on 'Warfare', in *CHI*, Vol.2, pp.835-50.
Pascal, R., 1946, *The Growth of Modern Germany*, London: Cobbett Press
Patterson, O., 1979, 'On Slavery and Slave Formations', *New Left Review*, No.117, pp.31-67.
Patterson, O., 1982, *Slavery and Social Death. A Comparative Study*, Harvard MA: Harvard University Press.
Plekhanov, G.V., 1898, 'On the Question of the Individual's Role in History', in Plekhanov [1976: 283-315].
Plekhanov, G.V., 1908/69, *Fundamental Problems of Marxism*, Moscow/London: Progress.
Plekhanov, G.V., 1976, Georgi Plekhanov, *Selected Philosophical Works*, Vol.2, Moscow: Progress.
Polk, W.R. and R.C. Chambers (eds.), 1968, *The Beginnings of Modernisation in the Middle East*, Chicago, IL: Chicago University Press.
Poulantzas, N., 1976, 'The Capitalist State: A Reply to Miliband and Laclau', *New Left Review*, No. 95, pp. 63-83.
Poulantzas, N., 1978a, *Political Power and Social Classes* (Paris, 1968); London: Verso.
Poulantzas, N., 1978b, 'Towards a Democratic Socialism', *New Left Review*, No. 109, pp. 75-87.
Poulantzas, N., 1980, *State, Power, Socialism*, London/New York: Verso.
Radcliffe-Brown, A.R., 1940, *African Political Systems* (eds. M. Fortes, E.E. Evans-Pritchard), London: Oxford University Press.
Roemer, J., 1982, *A General Theory of Exploitation and Class*, Cambridge, MA: Harvard University Press.
Runciman, W.G., 1989, *A Treatise on Social Theory*, Vol.1: *The Methodology of Social Theory*; Vol.2: *Substantive Social Theory*, Cambridge: Cambridge University Press.
Rustow, D.A., 1970, 'The Military: Turkey', in Ward and Rustow [1970: 352-88.
Rustow, D.A., 1963, 'The Military in Middle Eastern Society and Politics', in S.N. Fisher (ed.), *The Military in the Middle East*, Columbus, OH: Ohio University Press.
Sayer, D., 1987, *The Violence of Abstraction: The Analytic Foundation of Historical Materialism*, Oxford: Blackwell.
Secord, P.F., 1982, *Explaining Human Behavior: Consciousness, Human Action and Social Structure*, Beverley Hills, CA/London: Sage.
Service, E.R., 1975, *Origins of the State and Civilisation*, New York: Random House.
Shaw, S., 1976, *History of the Ottoman Empire and Modern Turkey*, 1: *Empire of the Gazis: The Rise and Decline of the Ottoman Empire, 1280-1808*, Cambridge: Cambridge University Press.
Skocpol, T., 1979, *States and Social Revolutions: A Comparative Analysis of France, Russia and China*, Cambridge: Cambridge University Press.
Sohrweide, H., 1965, 'Der Sieg der Safawiden in Persien und seine Rückwirkungen auf die Schiiten Anatoliens im 16. Jahrhundert', *Der Islam*, Vol.41, pp.95-123.
Steensgard, N., 1978, 'The Seventeenth Century Crisis', in Parker and Smith [1978].
Sugar, P.F., 1970, 'Economic and Political Modernization: Turkey', in Ward and

Rustow [1970: 146-75].
Sundhausen, H., 1983, 'Die "Preisrevolution" im osmanischen Reich', *Süd-Ost Forschungen*, Vol.42, pp.169-181.
Tainter, J.A., 1988, *The Collapse of Complex Societies*, Cambridge: Cambridge University Press.
Thompson, G., 1977, 'The Relationship between the Financial and Industrial Sectors in the UK Economy', *Economy and Society*, Vol.6, No.3, pp.235-83.
Todorov, N., 1980, 'La révolution industrielle et l'Empire ottoman', in Okyar and İnalcık [1980: 253-61].
Todorova, M.N., 1988, 'Was There a Demographic Crisis in the ottoman Empire in the Seventeenth Century?', *Études Balkaniques*, Vol.2, pp.55-63.
Ursinus, M.O.H., 1982, *Regionale Reformen im osmanischen Reich am Vorabend der Tanzimat*, Berlin: Schwarz.
Ursinus, M.O.H., 1989, 'Zur Diskussion um "Millet" im osmanischen Reich', *Südost-Forschungen*, Vol.48, pp.195-207.
Van Bruinessen, M.M., 1989, *Agha, Scheich und Staat. Politik und Gesellschaft Kurdistans*, Berlin: Parabolis.
Vryonis, S., 1959, 'Byzantium: The Social Basis of Decline', *Greek, Roman and Byzantine Studies*, Vol.2, pp.159-75 (repr. in Vryonis [1971: II]).
Vryonis, S., 1971, *Byzantium: Its Internal History and Relations with the Muslim World*, London: Variorum.
Wallerstein, E., 1980, 'The Ottoman Empire and the Capitalist World Economy', in Okyar and İnalcık [1980: 117-22].
Ward, R.E., and D.A. Rustow (eds.), 1970, *Political Modernization in Japan and Turkey*, Princeton, NJ: Princeton University Press.
Weiss, G., 1973, *Oströmische Beamte im Spiegel der Schriften des Michael Psellos*, Munich: Institut für Byzantinistik d. Univ. München.
Wickham, C.J., 1985, 'The Uniqueness of the East', *The Journal of Peasant Studies*, Vol.12, Nos. 2 and 3, pp.166-96.
Williams, R.C., 1986, *The Other Bolsheviks*, Bloomington, IN: University of Indiana Press.
Wittek, P., 1938, *The Rise of the Ottoman Empire*, London: Royal Asiatic Society Monographs.
Wood, E. Meiksins, 1984, 'Marxism and the Course of History', *New Left Review*, No.147, pp.95-107.
Wood, E. Meiksins, 1989, 'Rational Choice Marxism: Is the Game Worth the Candle?', *New left Review*, No.177, pp.41-88.
Wright, E. Olin, 1983, 'Giddens' Critique of Marx', *New Left Review*, No.138, pp.11-35.
Wright, W.L. (ed.), 1935, *Ottoman Statecraft: The Book of Counsel for Vezirs and Governors (Nasā'ih ül-vüzera ve'l ümera) of Sarı Meh med Pasha, the Defterdār*, Princeton, NJ: Princeton University Press.
Yediyıldız, B., 1985, *Institution du Vaqf au XVIIIe siècle en Turquie*, Ankara: Turkish Historical Society.
Yerasimos, S., 1990, *La fondation de Constantinople et de Sainte Sophie dans les traditions turques*, Istanbul/Paris: Gözlem Yayınları.

The Search for the Peasant in Western and Turkish History/Historiography

HALIL BERKTAY

In the fragments that he left behind as the draft of an Author's Preface to *The World of the Huns*, the late Otto Maenchen-Helfen [1973: xxvi–xxvii] retold Anatole France's story of the young Persian prince Zemire,

> who ordered his scholars to write the history of mankind, so that he would make fewer errors as a monarch enlightened by past experience. After twenty years, the wise men appeared before the prince, king by then, followed by a caravan composed of twelve camels, each bearing 500 volumes. The king asked them for a shorter version, and they returned after another twenty years with three camel loads, and, when again rejected by the king, after ten more years with a single elephant load. After yet five further years a scholar appeared with a single big book carried by a donkey. The king was on his death bed and sighed, 'I shall die without knowing the history of mankind. Abridge, abridge!' 'Sire', replied the scholar, 'I will sum it up for you in three words: They were born, they suffered, they died!'

Judging from the recent rate at which iconoclastic approaches on the part of quite a few 'non-establishment' historians appear to be converging,[1] equally brief might be the answer to yet another enormous question of what is wrong with Ottoman historical studies, especially as practised in the Turkish centre of the discipline, at the History Departments under the İstanbul and Ankara Faculties of Letters that serve as the traditional training grounds for most professional Ottomanists. In three words: *nationalism, state-fetishism, document-fetishism*. But as even Maenchen-Helfen [1973: xxvii], while admitting that 'in his way, the

---

Halil Berktay is former lecturer in economic history, Faculty of Political Sciences, Ankara University. Permanent address: Başlık Sok. 20/8, 1. Levent, İstanbul, Turkey. Drawing on material from the author's *The 'Other' Feudalism* (forthcoming), this article follows and tries to improve upon two earlier versions: a paper read at the Second National Congress of the Social Sciences organised by the Turkish Social Sciences Association in Ankara on 1 June 1989 (the transcript of which has since then seen print in Turkish together with other Congress papers in *Toplum ve Bilim*, Nos.48–49, pp.61–78), and another read at the Centre for Byzantine, Ottoman and Modern Greek Studies of Birmingham University on 1 March 1990.

king, who did not want to hear it all, was right', still felt compelled to go on and write more than 500 large pages for those who, 'stupidly perhaps, want to know "how it was"', all the more will what may seem an excessively harsh verdict to many inevitably require clarification.

POSITIVISM, HISTORICISM AND HISTORY FROM ABOVE

Let me begin with the last of my key-phrases and try to elucidate what I mean by document-fetishism, lest this be understood to signify that I am against documents and against concrete empirical research in some Althusserian, theoreticist, fashion.[2]

From the sixteenth to the nineteenth century, the study of History developed largely as *a science of documents*. After the Renaissance, which was inhibited by its radical hostility to the (medieval) past in building upon the brilliant beginnings of Valla, Politian and others, Catholic scholars of the sixteenth and seventeenth centuries, who, precisely because 'the defense of history became really a defense of their religion' [Fryde, 1990: 632], made more determined efforts to arrive at strict and universal norms of the critical evaluation of various kinds of documentary evidence. Thus in his *De Re Diplomatica* of 1681, Jean Mabillon was characteristically motivated by a desire – in a formal sense, diametrically opposed to Valla's concern to prove that the 'Donation of Constantine' was a forgery – to demonstrate that the oldest charters of two French Benedictine monasteries were genuine; in the process, he also set out the general rules that must be used to prove the authenticity of medieval records, treating in systematic fashion the various tests involved, including the writing materials, the scripts, the seals and other devices of authentication, the vocabulary, and the official formulas.

On the basis of such gradual accretions, modern historiography was finally established in the nineteenth century, chiefly by the Germans, who, like the Maurist scholars of the seventeenth century in their relation to the Renaissance, were themselves reacting against 'the ungodly and cosmopolitan Enlightenment' [Fryde, 1990: 634]. The centre of this movement was in Prussia, at the newly founded University of Berlin (1809). The German historical school, again in Edmund Fryde's [1990: 635] succinct phrasing, 'prided itself on the scientific precision of its methods, on its determination to get all the details right, and on the scrupulous quotation of sources. This display of exact scholarship represented a great gain for the historical sciences.' German scholarly techniques and the methods of German historical teaching spread to other countries in the course of the later nineteenth century. First 'analysis', comprising 'external' as well as 'internal criticism' of the sources, and then 'synthesis', were integrated into a coherent whole. With this codification of its indispensable assumptions and methodological foundations, History became a discipline for professionals trained systematically at academic institutions.³

This, however, was not the end of Historiography but only its beginning, its emergence from what may be regarded as a whole phase of childhood. It was an indispensable jump for its time; but it also had its limitations, which were left to the better part of the twentieth century to try and cope with. Like progress in practically every other field of human activity, the study of History, too, developed in zigzag fashion, with trade-offs, giving and taking away at the same time. This was reflected in both form/method and content. In breaking away from myth and hearsay, the 'documentary revolution' also had the effect of reducing the concept of historical evidence purely to written sources, records, documents. Ideally, these should begin from a 'point of origin' in the distant past and then come down if possible in an unbroken chain to cover every link in the unfolding of a certain process, phenomenon or institution. This led to a certain 'fallacy of origins' – of substituting legal-institutional beginnings and definitions for material determination. More generally, in the second half of the nineteenth century and early in the twentieth, the general intellectual atmosphere was very positivistic, and this had a strong bearing on how documents came to be regarded by historians – as the Truth, the Whole Truth and Nothing But the Truth. Hence, the reconstruction of historical reality was directly and simply conceived of as discovering individual documents, putting them side by side, and literally taking their arithmetical sum. The corollary was that the historian was thought to stand in relation to his/her material as nothing but a neutral and objective observer and recorder of 'facts', with the story he/she extracted therefrom regarded as the 'only possible' interpretation.

This, of course, was very far from being the case. A sense of the continuity and unity of the historical process had been recovered only at a price. The substitution of Historicism for the Enlightenment attitude to the Middle Ages was not the triumph of balanced objectivity that it was made out to be, but a swing of the pendulum to the other extreme. In the name of *verstehen* (understanding) from within, what it counterposed to a lack of imaginative insight into civilisations different from one's own (at best – swinging into nihilistic negation at worst), was uncritical acceptance of the self-consciousness of an age as the reality of that age – indeed virtual identification with that self-consciousness. What was entirely missing was a notion of ideology as the 'illusion of an epoch', and hence of the contradictory relationship between ideology and the real conditions giving rise to it.⁴ This was reflected in the new scientific historians' naive lack of self-awareness. Whether in Germany, England or France, all were fundamentally inspired by a prejudiced, arbitrary set of assumptions. It was nationalism's quest to invent a national identity supposedly rooted in the past that stimulated all historical research through most of the nineteenth century.[5] The post-Napoleonic patriotic reaction of the Germans, their excessive 'passion for extolling the unique nature of their fatherland and for tracing the roots of this uniqueness through the whole course of German history' [*Fryde*, 1990: 534–5], and the ideas of 'an organic unity of church, state and individual' that they engendered, were not limited to Romantic ultra-restorationists like Friedrich Gentz and Adam Müller in economics [*Roll*, 1938: 217 ff]. For Wilhelm von Humboldt, the effective founder of the German school of scientific historiography, the concepts that had special validity were ideas of religion and of a national state. Ranke, too, was convinced that the description of all human history displays the workings of God's providence, and his famous claim that all he was after was 'merely to show how things actually were (*wie es eigentlich gewesen*)' was married to a paradigm of each nation-state 'naturally' striving to fulfil its individual destiny, which then served to justify the Prussian state and its competitive achievements [*Marwick*, 1970: 34–40; *Tosh*, 1984: 10–12; *Fryde*, 1990: 635]. Later German historians, having contributed to the ideology of German unification (through the nationalistic invention of the 'historic German nation'), continued to praise the triumphs of the Bismarckian state.

More generally, at a time when mass participation, whether in revolutionary or gradualist forms, had not yet fully and actively made itself felt in the construction of modern democracy, history in the West, too, began as the history of the state and history from above.[6] Hence,

> Up to the middle of the last century the chief interest of the historian and the public alike lay in political and constitutional history, in political events, wars, dynasties, and in political institutions and their development. Substantially, therefore, history concerned itself with the ruling classes. 'Let us now praise famous men', was the historian's motto. He forgot to add 'and our fathers that begat us'. He did not care to probe the obscure lives and activities of the great mass of humanity, upon whose slow toil was built up the prosperity of the world and who were the hidden foundation of the political and constitutional edifice reared by the famous men he praised. To speak of ordinary people would have been beneath the dignity of history,

wrote Eileen Power [1963: 18] in 1924. She could have added that women, too, lay entirely below the profession's horizon (witness her own use of only the masculine pronoun), as did peoples outside Europe. In an inaugural lecture delivered to an all-male audience in Strasbourg in 1862, Numa Denis Fustel de Coulanges, one of the most famous of the new 'scientific historians', managed to concentrate many Eurocentrist, racist, statist and patriarchal prejudices into a few lines:

> . . . I shall focus particularly on the Greeks and Romans . . . . Still, the very nature of my subject will often compel me to cast a glance at other nations . . . . I shall even have to call your attention to the Orient, and above all to India, where we shall find men who belonged to the same race as the Greeks and Romans . . . . Among the lofty subjects which Rome and Greece suggest for our study and for your contemplation, I have chosen the family and the state in particular [*Stern* (ed.), 1956: 181–2].

In the West, the thought-methodology of nineteenth century historiography came to be superseded in the twentieth century along various axes of development. On the basis of observing what the spontaneous ideology of these and other narrowly empiricist, positivistic historians was like, more critical minds like R.G. Collingwood [1946] and E.H. Carr [1961] developed some lucid expositions of the ways in which both documents and the historians which work on them are themselves products of socially and historically conditioned selection processes. The idea cuts across all social science and art. Statistics are indispensable for economic analysis, and yet books have been written on *How to Lie with Statistics* [*Huff*, 1954]. In journalism, some classic works have dealt with how cropping a photographic negative in this or that manner can produce utterly different impressions of reality, as in Harold Evans's [1978: 226–7] example of a shot of convicts ordered to help out with flood defences whose leg-irons may or may not be included in the final print. Furthermore, everyone is aware that novelists do not directly reflect reality but select and accentuate only elements thereof (with doctrines like Socialist Realism going so far as to presume to tell writers what they should be concentrating upon) – and yet the very effort to separate History from Literature, Mythology and Parable had led to a situation where historians were somehow thought to be immune to such ideological selectivity in their choice of materials and interpretation. Very soon after Carr, Thomas Kuhn [1962], too, has provided the basis for a more profound philosophical critique of empiricism by demonstrating that human knowledge in virtually every field does not develop along an unbroken evolutionary curve of the gradual quantitative accumulation of more and more individual 'facts'. And while the internal requirements of the discipline cannot be overlooked in favour of a purely externalist approach, it is often shifts in the socially, politically and ideologically determined pressures surrounding historians' intellectual production that dictate a Kuhnian change of paradigm, a relatively sudden transformation in the way evidence is handled and worked into a new discourse.

It is possible, however, to go overboard. Carr [1961: Chs.3, 6] is at his weakest in tackling the question of what makes a particular interpretation or approach better than others; he has great difficulty in establishing an objective derivation for his criteria of preference. Similarly, I do not think that we can go so far as to claim, with Kuhn, that the success of any new theory has no necessary relation to its better grasp of at least some aspect of truth; nor is it easy to agree with Foucault in entirely removing the subject/object dichotomy of the Enlightenment.[7] If we are not to end up in a Structuralist 'randomisation of history' on the Left[8] or in an apology for its degeneration into wilful irrationalism on the Right[9], it is important to persist in regarding past reality, not as something purely 'constructed' [*Berger and Luckmann*, 1967], but as lending itself to improved and richer mental appropriation through successive approximations, though the manner in which these might follow upon one another is likely to be contradictory, non-linear and discontinuous. What a running critique of empiricism has really permitted is not disposing of the concept of empirical evidence altogether but seeing it in a new light, broadening its scope to cover a whole new series of non-documentary sources of information, and initiating the practice of 'reading' the documents themselves (as well as past historians who have worked on them) in a complex, multi-layered way in order make up for their inevitable silences and distortions. To that end, we cannot do without deconstructive criticism; but the purpose of exercises (like the present one) in trying to liberate one bit of history from some partial myths that have plagued it in the past and have come demonstrably to obstruct the progress of knowledge, should be to clear the way for negotiating a new settlement, including what is useful in the findings of the deconstructed historians.

A delicate balance therefore has to be struck between being aware of the ideological fabric and implications of various historical views, and nonetheless exercising restraint in handling each on its own merits. For example, the nature of the effort involved in deciphering an already perpetrated 'overloading', *pace* Maier [1988], of history (in the name of empiricism) by a conservative type of historiography, is likely to require directly confronting and engaging the ideological level. But if going in circles of mutual accusation ('you have your politics, others have theirs'), or perpetuating the split between 'theorists' who despise facts and 'historians' who despise theory, are all to be avoided, there has to be agreement on the principle of scientific inquiry into a knowable object, which is the cornerstone of the autonomy of any separate discipline and within that, of the 'commitment to a shared project of knowledge' [*Maier*, 1988: 62].

What, then, distinguishes this from empiricism? After twists and turns, swings in one direction and backlashes in the other, what we have arrived at, it seems, is no longer a single layer of 'facts' but some more advanced notion, however inadequately defined it might still be, of *three interconnected tiers of evidence, theory and ideology*, with the second being constantly formed by, and mediating between, the others. History narrowly defined deals with the first two (evidence plus theory); Historiography narrowly defined deals with the last two (theory plus ideology). Actually, each is meaningless by itself: Historiography cannot be reviewed and assessed without having some grasp of what it was that people were trying to write about; new History in a certain field cannot be produced (or produced well) without appreciating what was previously done with the same, similar or adjacent bodies of evidence by passing them through the prism of alternative theoretical/ideological viewpoints. A process of mental *tâtonnement* is therefore needed: what is knowable becomes knowable not in itself, but by going back and forth in successive iterations between evidence, theory and ideology, by scrupulously checking History and Historiography against one another.

FEUDALISM – THE LEGALIST, ROMANIST VIEW

What bearing does all this have on Medieval History, particularly as it deals with the peasantry under feudalism? This, first: it is still the case that (Turkish Ottomanists of the orthodox variety aside), even most Westernists, though aware of the existence of, for example, various meanings of feudalism, and of the direction in which they have changed over time, do not devote much effort to exploring this question systematically: always immersed in their first-hand empirical research, they tend to reach into a flowing river of conceptual objects to seize whatever readily comes to hand, without wondering whence the river comes and where it is heading; despite Yeats's warning in 'Sailing to Byzantium' that there is no

> singing school without studying
> Monuments of its own magnificence,

they do not consistently engage in that continuous movement between evidence, theory and ideology, between history and historiography, that I have just spoken of. Consequently, for many, the choice between various definitions of feudalism appears to be completely arbitrary, and consistency all that is important once you have chosen. For others, that consistency, too, is not constantly achievable: even the best Marxist historians, operating with a notion of feudalism as a mode of production, will occasionally incorporate private jurisdiction into their modal definition[10], or will slip into speaking of decentralisation and the privatisation of fiefs as the development of feudalism.[11] And a French Marxist has written a whole book on *Le Féodalisme: un horizon théorique* which deals only with the middle and lower sections of the river bed, not going back to its sources; hence, after sweeping theoretical claims and attacks, its author, too, ends up with a Eurospecific (or even Francospecific) view.[12]

The point is that whilst modern historical science emerged (1) as a science of documents and (2) as the history of the state and the ruling classes, or history from above, it also, simultaneously and on the basis of capitalist development, (3) emerged in Europe, was professionally defined as an intrinsically Eurocentrist discipline – and all three aspects came together in the way the basic concepts in its tool-chest were derived from phenomena that had most impressed themselves on the Western mind. Here, of course, what loomed particularly large was the Roman Empire and its fall, and this was so for real or imagined continuities as well as for discontinuities, breaks or 'jumps' in development.

Thus long before the nineteenth century, the chronology and periodisation of this new body of knowledge were already constructed, without reference to socio-economic processes (or as yet unknown concepts like modes of production), around major political events of European importance: it curved its mental space of Antiquity around Fustel's Greece and Rome; what came after was defined as the Middle Ages by the Renaissance-and-Enlightenment vision of a trough of barbarism between the two summits of Classical and Early Modern civilisation. In phenomenal terms, the distinct emergence of feudalism in the West had followed the collapse of the Roman Empire; hence, not only was the whole notion of feudalism directly reduced to its European manifestation, but all its distinguishing features were also further accentuated through comparison with Rome. This immediately conceptualised feudalism, always at the political level, as the opposite and negation of Rome: a decentralisation ('*the* feudalism') brought about by decline ('*the* transition').

Moreover, the determinants of this feudalisation-as-retrogression, this descent into rural barbarism, were located in a wholly external sphere of 'non-Rome'. Edward James [1982: 3–4] has remarked that even today, medieval historians have a secret distaste for periods of political disintegration and disloyalty to central government; this comes of constantly identifying with the fortunes of the state, as well as with all ancient and medieval authors – Chinese, Indian, Greek, Roman, Arabic, Persian, Western monastic and Byzantine – that have always written from the vantage point of settled civilisations concerning the surrounding 'barbarians'. Accordingly, the Germans, too, had to have been only a destructive force that had caused the collapse of the beloved ancient world.[13] On the other side of the scales, all that the early Middle Ages retained in the way of coherent organisation and 'civilised institutions' had to have been descended from Rome.

This was the first blueprint for feudalism, which established its boundaries; it was by lawyers that, with respect to both continuities and discontinuities, regarding the peasant's lot as well as the internal articulation of the ruling class, it was filled in over time. First, there were the medieval lawyers themselves, who drew upon Roman law to establish the distinction between the 'free' and the 'unfree', and to pretend that the serf was still a slave because a *servus*.[14] Then, around the middle of the sixteenth century, French scholars, searching for the origins of the legal customs of their country, hit upon the study of 'the feudal law', and it was by way of an introduction to this *jus feodale* (not even *féodalité*) that the first systematic work on what would only much later come to be known as feudalism was published by Charles Dumoulin in 1539–58 [*Pocock*, 1957: Ch.1; *Fryde*, 1990: 631]. Let me repeat that statement: it was as part of the history of law and institutions, and in the form of legal treatises, that comprehensive histories of European feudalism initially came to be written.

The importance of this fact cannot be overestimated; it has shaped four hundred years of Medieval History. Art critics and historians like Heinrich Wölfflin [1915] and, more recently, John Berger [1972], have dealt with 'ways of seeing'. What and how does the legal mind 'see'? It is trained to concentrate on form, not content; it always looks for 'precedent' and tries to derive form from previous form – hence the 'developmental fallacy' or the 'fallacy of origins', the obsession with narrow institutional genealogies, the substitution of 'ancestry' for 'explanation' [*McLennan*, 1981: 105] that have plagued several generations of historians. But consequently, the legal mind also emphasises formal continuity over historical and socio-economic change: concerning the conventional legal-juridical definition of feudalism, apart from its other failings: 'even within the narrow range of legal and contractual problems it cannot allow for the time lag between the evolution of legal forms and the changing needs of society', Postan [1961: xiii] once noted. Finally, to an inherent conservatism, a dislike for innovation, the legal mind marries (not a synthetic, but) a catalytic logic: it pursues finer and finer breakdowns, a plethora of 'perfect definitions' each of which will fit exactly, wholly, one case only; its conception of ideal type is never a general category based on some common features, but something that shares no characteristic, that stands aloof from all others. Lawyers make a living by looking for rules not of broad but of the narrowest coverage possible; they are sticklers for detail, they plead technicalities, 'special cases'; successful defence turns on splitting hairs and generating distinctions. Historians have traditionally defined their business as one of searching for the specific, the individual, the particular. But when we come to think of it, there is no real reason why the historian should be concerned only with specifics (and neither is it possible[15]); this is the birthmark of the historian-as-lawyer, not of a hopefully more advanced historian-as-historian that was Marc Bloch's [1931: xxv] ideal (you cannot practice history as the 'science of change' with a legal mind). 'Nineteenth century historiography . . . conceived of its facts in a positivistic manner, i.e. as separate or atomic', Collingwood [1946: 131–2] wrote:

> (i) Each fact was to be regarded as a thing capable of being ascertained by a separate act of cognition or process of research, and thus the total field of the historically knowable was cut up into an infinity of minute facts each to be separately considered. (ii) Each fact was to be thought of not only as independent of all the rest but as independent of the knower . . . .

He added that 'the legacy of positivism . . . is a combination of unprecedented mastery over small-scale problems with unprecedented weakness in dealing with large-scale problems'. This is a good critique of positivistic empiricism; it also happens to be a portrayal of the legal mind at work.

Form over content, legal ancestry over material determination, distinguishing features over common characteristics, as well as a concentration on the state, on relations within the ruling class only, all combined to lead medieval historians, from the sixteenth century onwards, into ever-narrower definitions of feudalism as a very precise set of mutual, contractual obligations between lord and vassal incorporating legal, political, military and ritual elements. Simultaneously, it led them into a search for its 'classical type', its pure stock by gradual variation from which all the other branches or strains could be logically and neatly derived (it was, again, a time when historians believed that peoples borrowed from one another instead of independently inventing similar institutions). Paradoxically, therefore, as empirical knowledge legal, political, military and ritual elements. Simultaneously, it led them into a search for its 'classical type', its pure stock by gradual variation from which all the other branches or strains could be logically and neatly derived (it was, again, a time when historians believed that peoples borrowed from one another instead of independently inventing similar institutions). Paradoxically, therefore, as empirical knowledge expanded and more and more examples of feudalism were discovered, the theoretical effort at definition moved in the opposite direction: the Roman, the Germanic and the Celtic 'roots' of feudalism were pitted against one another; because all additional material was utilised only to exclude and demarcate, the locus of this 'classical type' kept contracting in space and time, boiling down to a contest between its Lombard and Frankish versions [*Pocock*, 1957: 70ff; *Fryde*, 1990: 631]. The latter was eventually decided upon; it became the core of the concept itself, compared with which all other forms would be, by degrees, 'non-classical', 'less feudal' and 'non-feudal'. 'In the pages that follow, I intend to deal with feudalism only in its narrow, technical, legal sense of the word', wrote Ganshof [1944: xvii] in the Introduction to his *Qu'est-ce que la féodalité?*, and thence proposed

> to concentrate on the regions lying between the Loire and the Rhine, which were the heart of the Carolingian state and the original home of feudalism. Further afield, in the south of France and in Germany beyond the Rhine, the institutions that grew up are often far from typical of feudalism as a whole. I shall deal less fully with England, and scarcely at all with Italy.

Only the Paris basin existed, in other words – sometimes delineated as such, but sometimes made into all 'Europe'. For a later edition, the learned professor curtly added, in a cold war footnote, that 'the way in which the word is commonly used by historians in Soviet Russia and other countries behind the Iron Curtain seems to me to be absolutely irrelevant' [*Ganshof*, 1944: xv]. In his Foreword to the third English edition of Ganshof's book, Sir Frank Stenton [1952: ix] approved of this restriction of the treatment to 'the development of what may justly be called "classical feudalism" from its Carolingian origins'. Stenton was on safe ground: through the Norman connection, England lay very close to the pure stock. In the second half of the seventeenth century, Spelman had led the discovery of feudal law in England; he had also postulated the Norman conquest as the beginning of English feudalism [*Pocock*, 1957: *passim.*; *Fryde*, 1990: 632]. For Stenton, too, with his rigidly formalistic definition of a 'classical' type, there was no such thing as an indigenous socio-economic development towards/of feudalism, and hence also no proto-feudalism or feudalism in the

Anglo–Saxon period; 12 years before Ganshof, in his own English Feudalism 1066–66, he wrote that

> It is turning a useful term into a mere abstraction to apply the adjective 'feudal' to a society which had never adopted the private fortress nor developed the art of fighting on horseback, which had no real conception of the specialisation of service and allowed innumerable landowners of position to go with their land to whatever lords they would [*Stenton*, 1932: 215].

Notice key elements: private fortresses, knights, contractual service. And the allegation that 'mere abstractions' are useless (or that in order to be 'useful', terms must somehow always be concrete) flies in the face of everything that is known about the development of science and human thought.

Nearly 30 years after Stenton, in a Foreword to the English edition of Bloch's *Feudal Society*, this formalistic conception was what Postan [1961: xiii], who was no Marxist, was so dismissive about:

> In so far as it concentrates on military service it cannot provide a key to the fundamentals of medieval society or indeed any society; in so far as it concerns itself with contractual principles it conceals from the view the underlying social realities.

And indeed, *féodalité* as decentralised feodo-vassalitic relations of Germanic origin, revolving around an absolute discontinuity and inflexible contrast between Imperial centralism and the Western medieval 'parcellisation of sovereignty', to borrow Perry Anderson's [1974a: 148] term for it, did not include or cover relations of production as existed between different social classes; it only provided the general political framework into which were fitted (not 'feudalism', but) 'manorialism' and 'serfdom'. These two latter terms, themselves also mutually exclusive of one another, were respectively appended to the 'economic' and 'social' spheres that History gradually came to discover, initially as mere additives alongside the 'political', so that there arose a notion of the medieval economy and society from which 'feudalism' somehow stayed aloof.[16] Finally, this separation effect was further magnified by bringing the same legalistic approach to bear on the economy, so that this area came to be defined in terms of (1) a demesne-centred *seigneurie*, (2) 'lords as estate managers', (3) serfs as 'slaves of the soil' – every single one of them postulated this time as continuities emanating from Rome.

Economic continuity, political break: this is quite an inversion, and the gulf distancing it from our present understanding of 'the other transition'

[*Wickham*, 1984] may not always be easy to appreciate in full. How did it happen? I would argue that here, the ideology of the documents and the ideology of the historian mutually reinforced one another. When peasants first began to enter Western Medieval History in the late nineteenth or early twentieth century, it was the fashion to set out the formal structure of the manor or *seigneurie* in terms of legal principles and categories originally derived by medieval lawyers from Roman law. The same was true of serfdom: *servus, servi*, meant nothing but slave(s) or servant(s) as a legal term borrowed from Rome. The inability to delve beyond the level of 'reality' represented by the most readily available documentation seems to have been crucial. In France, which for a long time was the centre of the medieval world [*Bois*, 1984: xi] and then of Medieval History, initial knowledge of the Carolingian era was based on the *polyptyques* of the ninth century. Originating with lordship and with ecclesiastical lordship of the highest rank in particular, these great estate inventories were inevitably axed on the lord's economy, thus providing an exaggerated picture of the extent, role and function of the home farm within the manor. The central estates belonging to abbeys, Bolton [1980: 13–14] remarks, were the most tightly knit, with relatively prominent demesnes and a higher burden of labour services: the monks needed a secure supply of food, and they had the permanent presence and organisation necessary to supervise demesne production. This led medievalists for a long time to believe that what the *polyptyques* said about the eighth and ninth centuries must also be true of the tenth and eleventh centuries, that the demesne or *réserve seigneuriale* had constituted the main component of the manor everywhere and at all times, and that the Middle Ages were universally dominated by large-scale cultivation based on compulsory labour.

In short, what we today speak of as feudalism (in place of a dichotomy between manorialism and *féodalité*) was characterised above all by demesne production and *corvées* (labour-rent) at the economic level. Accordingly, what came to the front in the person of the serf was (once more, with the additional support of the etymology of *servus*), a kind of slavish social type, somewhat more developed than classical slavery but still belonging personally and mostly owing labour services to his/her lord; at the other pole of the fundamental class relationship, that lord or *seigneur* was for his part depicted as the owner-manager of a large, integrated farm, not as a rent-collector. To this accentuation of the Ancient component in the make-up of Medieval social classes and institutions, a totally Imperial embryology was also fitted, so that the lord appeared to have evolved directly from a wealthy member of the Gallo-Roman senatorial class, and the serf from a slave that had been settled on and attached to the land as a *servus casatus*, a 'hutted slave', during what was seen as the continuous transformation of the *latifundium* into the bipartite manor. A simple example will suffice: as the most prestigious compendium of accepted learning, the *Encyclopaedia Britannica* in the late nineteenth century still had no separate Serfdom entry; it simply referred the reader to the Slavery article.[17]

Finally, it remains to note that the model generated by this 100-per cent Eurocentrist process of knowledge was so descriptively specific to certain details, limited in space and time, of the concrete visage of the Western Middle Ages; that is to say, so far removed was it as yet from the level of abstraction and generalisation required by Althusser and Balibar [1972] for a fully scientific concept over a 'semi-scientific' one[18] – that its application to non-European socio-economic formations was excluded from the outset virtually by definition. Indeed, it was that same Eurocentrism which, in order to handle the real or imagined 'otherness' of Oriental societies in Hegelian, essentialist fashion, simultaneously turned out, as the mirror image of an Eurospecific 'feudalism', the explicitly geographical hypothesis of the 'Asiatic mode of production'.[19]

BLOCH: A WATERSHED

A major sea-change came in the late 1920s and the early 1930s with Marc Bloch and the *Annales* school. This is not to say that one man, by himself, rapidly and universally transformed everything. There were individual forerunners; there was also Marxism, which was *the* great alternative at a time when academic history was essentially about the ruling classes, about the deeds of great men, or about law and institutions as if they were hanging in a vacuum and themselves 'making' society. In effect, it was Marxism that *introduced/initiated* material-realistic explanation, demystified ideology, cleared a path for socio-economic history and history from below. Particularly for political reasons, of course, it was formally ostracised by academic historians for a long time. Nevertheless, its impact was considerable, even in the first half of the twentieth century, and the extent to which Bloch quietly allowed himself to be influenced by Marxism is often underestimated.[20]

Classical Marxism, though not in possession of a fully evolved and complete, coherent theory of Feudalism, had nevertheless been quite wary of various misconceptions. Already in *The German Ideology*, under feudalism 'the directly producing class . . . is not . . . the slaves, but the enserfed small peasantry', wrote Marx and Engels [1845–46: 150]. Then in certain passages of *Capital*, Marx himself presented slavery, serfdom and wage labour as the three basic relations of the class organisation of production, recognising serfdom's intermediate status (irreducible to slavery or quasi-slavery) in a broad sense. The third volume of *Capital* also provided an outline of the *modus operandi* of feudal agriculture that, Hobsbawm [1964: 43] has noted, had been missing from the *Formen*; this mature approach included a famous treatment of labour-rent, produce-rent and money-rent as the three possible forms of feudal rent that makes it impossible to identify feudalism with labour-rent only [Marx, 1894: 790–96]. Here, Marx also suggested that if it had not been for the ability of this peasant economy to undertake expanded re-production, there would have been no take-off into trade, urban growth, eventually capital accumulation – a key idea for many participants in both the 'Transition Debate' of the 1950s and the 'Brenner Debate' of more recent vintage. And it was in *Capital*, too, that Marx appears to have been most reluctant to theorise about the 'oriental forms' of serfdom (embodying a fusion of tax and rent) as a separate (Asiatic) mode of production.[21]

Nevertheless, it was Engels who, not approaching pre-capitalist history purely through an inverted teleology[22], was more interested in the different combinations of lordship with the substratum of the village community [Hobsbawm, 1964: 28, 32]; and he further pursued the topic of feudalism, during Marx's last years and after his death, in both *Anti-Dühring* (1877–78) and *The Origin of the Family, Private Property and the State* (1884). In these more mature works, Engels focussed on the replacement of large-scale exploitation (based on slave labour) by small-scale dependent farming as the economic essence of the transition from Rome to medieval feudalism. He thereby emphasised, explicitly, not demesne production but peasant cultivation, and treated the *seigneurie* as a social, political and fiscal unit, but not as a unit of production. This analysis was 'exceedingly acute', says Hobsbawm [1964: 53–4]. One section of *Anti-Dühring*, which also impinges directly on some Turkish debates, is worth greater elaboration. Dühring had claimed that on the basis of technical necessity, feudal overlordship of the land had existed from time immemorial.[23] Engels, in contrast, stressed that village communes and individual peasant holdings had existed freely for millenia before being brought under aristocratic overlordship.[24] He also pointed out that, as in the case of Greece or Rome, the village community and the independent peasantry could be destroyed by another long and complicated process in which slavery rose to the fore. In refuting Dühring's thesis that it was some primordial aristocracy that had called either slaves and/or serfs into being in order to be able to exploit 'tracts of considerable size', Engels [1877–78: 195] asserted that 'during the Middle Ages, peasant cultivation was dominant throughout the whole of Europe'. The implication was that peasants did not need lords to organise production. Furthermore, in *The Origin of the Family, etc.*, Engels [1884: 575], foreshadowing both Bloch and Duby (see below), emphasised serfdom as a new and more progressive relation of production: he drew attention not to the servility but to the semi-freedom of the medieval peasant; he dwelt at great length on the transition from the Germanic free peasantry to serfdom; again prefiguring Bloch (below), he underlined the villein and the 'free manse' as the norm.

On all these points, Engels was ahead of his time; but not many years later, within the academic establishment, too, other scholars were also getting impatient in parallel and related ways with the old approach. Towards the end of their lives, both Marx and Engels were taking a great interest in Russia, which was like an immense laboratory for (what would become) peasant studies: it was there that the survivals of the ancient village commune side by side with various forms of dependence and serfdom made it possible to reconstruct the past of West European feudal institutions in comparative perspective. The acuteness of the agrarian question lent political and ideological motivation to such research, which developed in the hands of democratic reformers and revolutionaries of various kinds. For people like Paul Vinogradoff (who left Russia for Britain largely because of academic and political repression), the brutal reality of serfdom experienced at first hand in daily life transcended the conventional formulae of legalistic ruling class history about the complementarity and organic harmony of social strata; simultaneously it became imperative, in Russia and Eastern Europe, to delve into the path of direct transition from the village commune and the free peasantry into serfdom – to reduce that passage to one out of classical slavery and the Roman villa made even less sense than in the Welsh case (on which Bloch would base his own, similar, argument). It was, in fact, Vinogradoff who, with his classic *Villeinage in England* [1892; the Russian original in 1887], first noted the oppressive, antagonistic character of serfdom as a social relation whilst hypothesising that the Anglo-Norman manor had developed not from a society that somehow had always had serfdom, but from (and by taking over) a society based on the free village community.[25] Asked to write the very first *Encyclopaedia Britannica* entry specifically devoted to Serfdom, Vinogradoff [1911: 664] also emphasised that the notion was 'distinct from those of freedom and of slavery'; alongside the 'classical' path from slavery to serfdom, he went on discuss an alternative path for those parts of Europe that had not fallen under the sway of the slave plantations:

The direction of events towards the formation of serfdom is already clearly noticeable in Celtic communities. In Wales and Ireland the greater part of the rural working classes was reduced not to a state of slavery, but to serfdom .... The Germanic tribes moved on similar lines. Slavery was not a natural institution with them, although it did occur ... it was in the interest of the master to levy tribute and not to organise slave labour. After the conquest of the provinces by the Germanic invaders the Roman stock of coloni naturally combined with German tributary peasants to form medieval serfdom [*Vinogradoff*, 1911: 664–5].

'On the whole serfdom appears as a characteristic corollary of feudalism' and 'it is sure to appear in very different ages and countries', Vinogradoff [1911: 666, 664] added with characteristic breadth of vision.[26] Yet another work strongly modern in its interest in peasant existence was Bennett's *Life on the English Manor*. In his Preface, Bennett [1937: v–vi] criticised 'a rigid adherence to strictly legal considerations': 'The comparatively safe waters of legal status and the like, so well charted for us by Maitland, Vinogradoff, and others, must be left for the open seas.' Moreover, at least in Britain, and as Bennett, writing more than half a decade after *French Rural History*, also gives one to think, Bloch does not seem to have been widely read before the end of the war. Nevertheless, if Medieval History, whether Marxist or non-Marxist, has markedly moved away from a legal-juridical definition of feudalism and of serfdom ever since the 1950s, and can now be shown to have reached, empirically, a working understanding of the Middle Ages as having been based essentially on peasant economy, it is in Marc Bloch's work that the original statement of not one or two but of many or perhaps all of the themes and axes of investigation of that eventual movement may be found.

The development beyond the documentary revolution of nineteenth-century scientific historians towards a more advanced methodology is very much in evidence in Bloch [1931: xxvii–viii], who took to task 'the revered memory' of Fustel de Coulanges as 'not a man on whom the external world made much impact'; for basing his answers solely on 'documents, very ancient documents'; and hence for being 'fascinated by the question of origins' and remaining 'faithful to a strictly chronological approach, by which he moved forward step by step from the most remote to the most recent past'. But with regard to the origins of the feudal system, for example, 'is it unfair to suggest that he would have done better to decide what were the essential features of the finished model before plunging into the mysteries of its inception?' [*Bloch*, 1931:

xxviii]. And in the first paragraph of his own later synthesis of manorial development, Bloch [1941: 235] repeated that warning: 'You cannot study embryology if you do not understand the grown animal.'

Armed with this kind of critical perspective, Marc Bloch put his finger, from inside the profession, on a salient fact that today strikes us, erroneously, as virtually self-evident: since not even small or medium-sized *seigneuries* (which were likely to have smaller demesnes) had estate inventories drawn up, and, more importantly, illiterate medieval serfs, like peasants everywhere, left absolutely no comparable documents, it was most probably the case that a whole vast sea out there of a silent mass of small peasant tenures should be far more extensive and significant within the manor and within the early medieval economy than the demesnes which the *polyptyques* one-sidedly focused on.[27] Restoring the peasantry to this broader, newly defined stage of the Middle Ages, however, depended to a large extent on breaking away from the restricted habit of trying to trace the 'same'(?) institution along as complete a chain of documents as possible (which, incidentally, were all in Latin, hence bearing the mental stamp of and subtly exaggerating the continuity with Rome). At the very least, suggested Bloch – who of course 'read all the pertinent primary and secondary sources' [*Lyon*, 1966: xiii] – this had to be balanced and complemented by another, retrospective, march; himself going out and looking at the French countryside for the ancient traces of the great open fields, for information about soils, ploughs and agricultural geography, and for living peasant tradition, he set out to uncover a bedrock of small peasant possession within a village matrix extending through the ages. Consequently, Bloch's work was a turning point for Medieval History precisely because (a) he refused to be taken in by the technicalities of legal status, discarding the definition of servitude in Roman law to breathe life into the serf not as slave but as small-producing peasant; (b) simultaneously, he also discounted demesne production and labour services, concentrating instead on the peasant holding, and on the fundamental character of the lord as a collector of tax-rent in the long run.

At the simplest level, it is well known by now that in his *Feudal Society*, Bloch [1940: 446] explicitly raised 'a subject peasantry' to first rank in his definition of feudalism; elsewhere, he repeatedly pointed out with respect to this peasantry that its small holdings (and not the demesne) were probably the major part of most manors even in the ninth century, that of its two possible sources, the earlier, unsubjected peasantry of Frankish tribal society (and not Roman slavery) was the more important, and that this was generally reflected in the preponderance of the free manse over the servile manse. Hence 'the jumbled complexity of legal status so characteristic of the tenant populations of seigneurial estates during the early Middle Ages' was 'more or less antiquated' and decidedly secondary, warned Bloch [1931: 83], advising the reader 'not to be led astray by the fair name of "liberty" appearing in this connection' [Bloch, 1931: 84], and unmasking 'the old names which were still on everyone's lips . . . the complex vocabulary which . . . drew heavily on the language of slavery' as not reflecting the reality of 'a now transformed social system' [Bloch, 1931: 90–91]. Whatever the numerical proportions of the technically 'free' and the technically 'servile' in early medieval Europe, Bloch [1931: 84] took 'the free villein' (in the French, not the English, sense) as his ideal type: 'In a way he represents the norm among tenants, the tenant pure and simple.'[28] He then defined the serf by reference to the villein:

> The serf also normally lived on a tenure. In this respect he was subject to the same customs as the body of free villeins, of whatever condition. But he also had to obey certain rules arising from his personal status. Already a villein, he was a villein plus [Bloch, 1931: 85].

Forty-odd years later, for Georges Duby [1974: 40], too, the transition to serfdom involved bringing the circumstances of ex-slaves 'closer to those of free tenants' (instead of vice versa), and was 'one of the great landmarks in labour history and . . . undoubtedly a decisive factor in economic development'. In both Bloch and Duby, therefore, what is emphasised (in contrast to the previously discussed reversion of political break and socio-economic continuity) is the revolution (in the sense of qualitative transformation) that took place in the relations of production in going from a society based on slave labour to a society based on serfdom. Such implied conceptions of feudalism as a set of economic and social relations (and not a set of political forms) share the same intellectual space with a Marxist notion of the feudal mode of production.

But the extent to which Bloch wove these fundamental conclusions into an emphatically non-Romanist and even non-Eurocentric explanation of the evolution (not devolution) of feudal class relations is not often appreciated. The striking thing about section III/1 (on 'The early medieval *seigneurie* and its origins') of *French Rural History* is the near-total absence of any mention of the late-Roman transformation of the slave estate into a bipartite manor. Instead, building on what Vinogradoff had also noticed, Bloch [1931: 74–5] dealt with the *seigneurie* as an 'ancient form of association, deeply rooted in rural tradition', as 'a direct continuation of a much earlier custom, going back certainly as far as the Celtic period if not earlier':

> The picture of Gaul we get from Caesar is of a tribal society largely dominated by chieftains, who were also the wealthiest men of their communities. There can be no doubt that the greater part of this wealth came from the land. But how was it produced? It is hard to visualise these chieftains as directors of large estates cultivated by gangs of slave labour. We are given to understand that their power rested primarily on their 'clients', men who although free by birth were nevertheless their subjects . . . . Everything points to the conclusion that the Gallo-Roman aristocracy was a caste of village chieftains, drawing the greater part of their income from dues owed by their peasant subjects . . . . It thus seems possible, though this is only conjecture, that the regime had its origin in an ancient tribal system: the experience of non-Romanised Celtic societies, for example Wales in the later Middle Ages, seems to suggest that the transition from tribal or clan leadership to seigneurial lordship was a relatively simple matter.
>
> Analogous systems for organising the exploitation of the land were to be found up and down the Empire, *so the essential characteristics of tribal institutions were probably kept alive beneath the Roman façade* [italics added – HB]. Naturally there had to be some adaptation to changed economic and legal conditions. Initially the abundance of slave labour no doubt stimulated the creation of some huge demesnes, but it is by no means certain that many such existed during the Celtic period. The example of Wales is again pertinent, since it proves that a territorial clientele need not be based on the existence of a demesne, still less a demesne of vast dimensions; a chief could derive the whole or larger part of his revenue from dues owed by his peasants . . . .

On the next page, after reviewing the evidence concerning villages named after lords or chieftains, and the adoption of the Latin term *villa* to designate a rural settlement, Bloch [1931: 76] added that

> There could scarcely be a more convincing demonstration that most villages must originally have had a lord. I think we must admit that despite all manner of vicissitudes and inevitable transfer of ownership, the lords of the medieval *seigneuries* were in direct line of descent, by way of the masters of Gallo-Roman villae, from the village chieftains of ancient Gaul.

And what was the medieval subject peasantry descended from? In a 1928 conference, Bloch [1928a: 69] first criticised Meitzen (apart from the latter's racist misconceptions) for having confined his attention to the historic peoples, the Celts, Romans, Germans and Slavs; in 1931, he repeated this criticism, and said that 'one would have to go much further back in time than this, to the anonymous prehistoric groups of men who first created our fields' [Bloch, 1931: 62]. He linked their mode of occupation and appropriation of the soil to the Marxian hypothesis of a primitive communal society:

> This 'rudimentary communism' – to borrow an expression used by Jaurès in the brilliant and prophetic early pages of his *Histoire de la Révolution* – was at once the hallmark of the type of agrarian civilisation which found its expression in open fields with long furlongs, and the very reason for its existence [Bloch, 1931: 48].

Ten years later, in his *Cambridge Economic History* essay on 'The Rise of Dependent Cultivation and Seignorial Institutions', Bloch recapitulated the entire argument. He traced the evolution of the offering of 'presents or dues' by villagers to their chief, initially in return for real services performed by the chief on behalf of the community, into increasingly regularised 'obligations' as the chiefs' power grew [Bloch, 1941: 265]; he explained how a 'gift' might become the basis for a future 'request' and then a 'demand' from the incipient lord [Bloch, 1941: 273–4]. He underlined the ancient free peasant's right of effective possession, from which he could not be excluded [Bloch, 1941: 279–80]. He summed up in the following words:

> In the beginning, we catch glimpses of peasant communities under their chiefs, to whom the various families (in the wide sense) that made up the group owed ritual gifts, and no doubt also assistance in a general way, which would be sure to take the form of certain services . . . . We may assume something of the sort in ancient Europe more or less everywhere. Evidently we are here in touch with one of the oldest lines of cleavage in our civilisation . . . [Bloch, 1941: 283].

> It is particularly tempting to link primitive village organisation with that of the clan or the tribe, and to imagine behind the figure of the lord-to-be, the old man of a group of kindred . . . . This may sometimes have been the actual course of events . . . [Bloch, 1941: 284].

Thus behind the classic *seigneurie* our inquiry reveals long and obscure beginnings. A very ancient structure of rural chiefdoms was the essential nucleus, and about it the centuries deposited their successive layers one by one. Then, the economic conditions of the early Roman era created the great demesnes facing the family holdings of the dependents [*Bloch*, 1941: 290].

Vast perspectives were implied:

> No doubt Eyptian and African evidence can throw a precious light on the origins of the Western *seigneurie*. But only if we ask of them what they can legitimately supply. That is information, not about the actual thing that we are studying, but about analogous things. In short, we must treat them as documents of comparative history.

> And it is on comparative methods that we must rely. On comparisons of the European development with parallel developments that may be studied outside Europe? No doubt. But also, and perhaps mainly, on systematically conducted comparisons of the various regional developments within European civilisation itself . . . [*Bloch*, 1941: 237–8].

There is, clearly, a very strong family resemblance between Bloch's approach and the different combinations of lordship with the substratum of the village community that Engels wanted to explore [*Hobsbawm*, 1964: 28, 32], or the idea, prevalent in late-nineteenth century Marxism, of a universal stage of proto-feudalism emerging directly from primitive communalism and then being capable of heading in different directions [*Hobsbawm*, 1964: 34], or a hypothetical chain of forms of rent-extractive relations that I have suggested elsewhere [*Berktay*, 1987a: 314; *Berktay*, 1990: Chs. IV, V]. If there had not been a Roman past along such a line of development, Bloch is saying, if there had not been large masses of slaves around, then demesnes might not have arisen. We would then have had just tenancies and dues, produce-rent: 'dependent cultivation', the key phrase in the title of Bloch's 1941 essay, stands revealed as the core relation. Whichever way we look at it, demesnes and labour services are secondary, a non-necessary component; they are the medieval heritage, further blown up through the language of the documentation, of a 'Roman façade', a previous slave mode of production. These special features – demesnes and *corvées* – were, moreover, a part of the concrete visage of only the early medieval *seigneurie*; and Bloch's careful account of the line of development from 'great proprietor' to 'rentier landlord', already referred to, leaves no possibility in that direction, too, of building any ideal types on the basis of a demesne-centred manor.[29]

Bloch's basic approach, which despite some ambiguities[30] renders the demesnes-and-labour-services version of feudalism untenable, has had research consequences mainly in two directions. In the West, generations of medieval historians and economic historians since Bloch have been moving in a general way from legal to socio-economic history; major gains have included the mental consolidation of the autonomy of small production,[31] the elaboration of the tribal origins of feudalism,[32] an enhanced understanding of late-medieval urban development and centralisation as not external or antithetical but as internal to feudal society,[33] the proposition that feudalism can arise in 'evolutionary' as well as 'devolutionary' ways,[34] and at least one explicit break with any Ganshovian or Stentonian 'classical type'.[35] In particular, Western historians have been penetrating beyond the successive institutional layers deposited on the relationship of serfdom by a Roman past and a form of private lordship specific to Europe in order to reveal its peasant core. Simultaneously, and inspired by the mass movements of the radical 1960s and 1970s, historians as well as sociologists and anthropologists everywhere have been participating in the progressive discovery of peasant societies in the Third World, thus unifying materials from East and West in an entire literature dealing with every conceivable aspect of peasant life, customs, tenure, communal existence, family and inheritance patterns, and active as well as passive forms of resistance to (and articulation with) the non-peasant world. This stream has nourished publications like *Peasant Studies* and *The Journal of Peasant Studies*; studies like Eric Wolf's [1966] *Peasants* have sought to provide a concise Social Anthropology version, as it were, of categories of Political Economy pertaining to petty commodity production; a more universal outlook on pre-capitalist history, feeding on both Marx and Weber, has thereby arisen. Thus it is no longer surprising to encounter, for example, a study of the *Weapons of the Weak: Everyday Forms of Peasant Resistance* in Malaysia that is directly inspired by

> Marc Bloch, the historian of feudalism, (who) noted that the great millenial movements were 'flashes in the pan' compared to the 'patient, silent struggles stubbornly carried out by rural communities' to avoid claims on their surplus and to assert their rights to the means of production – for example, arable, woodland, pastures [*Scott*, 1985: xvi, with reference to *French Rural History*].

And Rodney Hilton [1973b: 236] concludes his *Bond Men Made Free* with a question-and-answer sequence that, with regard to temporal and spatial continuities, is perhaps more affirmation than denial:

> What could the fate of peasant societies in the present world of almost world-wide commercial and industrial monopoly capitalism have in common with that of the peasant societies of the late medieval world? Clearly, the tasks of leadership in contemporary peasant society have nothing in common with the tasks of the past, except in the recognition that conflict is part of existence and that nothing is gained without struggle.

Like 'La Belle Dame Sans Merci', where 'no birds sing' actually serves to conjure up the absent birds, the effect after 'except' is Keatsian.

THE STATE-SUBSUMPTION OF CLASS FORMATION IN TRIBAL SOCIETY

So, in Europe, the documentation was of a nature which magnified the Roman-slave façade put on the later course of tribal stratification and its crystallisation into the new social classes of the Middle Ages; combined with the intellectual influence of the Renaissance and the Enlightenment, this led, for a time, to the domination of the Romanist view. What would it have been like in the Ottoman Empire? With what formal modulations might we expect its fundamental class relations to have been surrounded and shrouded by virtue of the specific legal-political constitution of Ottoman society and the particular genesis-process corresponding to it?[36] And how would those incrustations be reflected in the documentation of the Empire?

What comparative knowledge and research are good for, is primarily to enable us to expand the range of questions to address to the respective materials that each of us specialise in.[37] And once we ask the correct question, the answer is not so hard to come by. The Ottoman polity was, as its name tells us, an empire. Leaving aside the question of whether it was therefore 'non-feudal' (by the outworn criterion of feudalism-as-decentralisation), it was, in fact, a relatively centralised state by early medieval European standards which, during the fifteenth and sixteenth centuries, had regular land and population surveys at 30- or 40-year intervals, kept careful records of virtually all sources of land revenue, and regulated its system of non-hereditary fief (*timar*) distribution accordingly. Thus everything that had to do with land tenure and the extraction of agricultural surplus from the peasantry, was the subject of documents that were drawn up by the central state. This is no great mystery: it was precisely because the Ottoman Empire took shape as a comparatively late feudalism in the fourteenth century; because it had the benefit of a higher level of liquidity in the Eastern Mediterranean with which to pay a salaried bureaucracy and to equip a 'new model' (janissary: *yeni* = new + *çeri* = troop, soldier) royal infantry army with firearms from an early stage onwards, that it had the necessary organisational ability to do so.[38]

This, I think, is the crux of the problem: what is available to us in the way of documentation on the Ottoman peasant economy are mostly records that have emanated from the central state – for which the peasant was nothing but a subject, a tax-payer; and it is as such and always from the point of view of the state that official documents describe and define him/her, mostly limiting themselves to enumerating the peasant's obligations, which of course lay at the centre of the relationship between the state and the peasant. In other words, it was with the state's view and perception of the peasantry that peasant reality was overlaid. The historical setting for the 'Roman-German synthesis' in the West was that of a relative vacuum left by the collapse of the Roman state; into this loose historical space advanced semi-tribal peoples under their autonomous chieftaincies to set up their numerous barbarian kingdoms. The historical setting for the 'Byzantine-Islamic-Turkish synthesis' in the Near East, however, was a firmer, more structured space dominated by a much more continuous dovetailing of state traditions. To put it in another way, universal processes of class formation in late-tribal (Germanic or Turkic) society, crystallising first behind a 'Roman façade' and then within the fragmented matrix of various petty principalities into the 'private feudalism' of the West, reach us in the Balkans and Eastern Mediterranean in the form of a 'state feudalism' filtered through the prism of a centralised empire. All phenomena actually rooted in the semi-tribal past are taken over, internalised and legalised by the state, so that we are faced, here, with nothing less than a state-subsumption of the transitional forms thrown up in the course of the progressive dissolution and stratification of kinship society.

Thus, for example, through its land and population surveys (*tahrirs*), the Imperial chancery compiled local customary law (*örfi hukuk*), cited it as precedent, codified it, and re-issued it as customary-sultanic law (*örfi-sultani hukuk*, an intermediate term that captures the transformation at mid-point), and even as simply royal or sultanic law (*hukuk-u padişahi* or *yasağ-ı padişahi*, where reference to its customary origins is omitted altogether). Hence, what simply existed as customary law in other tribal and semi-tribal societies, assumed the status of a body of public law consciously and voluntarily legislated by the sultan directly from the top down and apparently without any traditional ancestry whatsoever. And in this context, the same local traditions and usages that, having to do with land occupation and use, mutual rights and obligations, and rates of exploitation, eventually surfaced in England as custumals or manorial bylaws covering small units dominated by an individual lord, emerged when collated by the Ottoman state as a provincial land-code (*sancak kanunnamesi* or *liva kanunnamesi*). Placed at the head of a province- or county-level register (*tahrir defteri*), this would hold sway over a much larger area[39] – making it appear as if it was the state that brought into being all the categories and modalities of peasant existence.

In actual fact, of course, the social relations between the timariot *sipahi* and the *raiyyet* that were incorporated into these *kanunnames* were, as the contents themselves often explicitly state, far more ancient than the state which formalised them.[40] But meanwhile, the semi-tribal Turkish warrior nobility, the original founding aristocracy of the Ottoman Empire, was also undergoing internal transformation, changing composition, being balanced by other elements (in order of appearance: the Christian aristocracies of the Balkans, the *devşirmes*, the local elites of the lands of Classical Islam) co-opted into the military-political elite in the course of a territorial expansion led by the sultan, so that alongside processes of class reproduction through the economy, processes of reproduction of the ruling class through the state were rising to the fore. And this, too, was reflected in such exaggerated fashion by the legal as well as political texts emanating from the central palace elite, that the state as represented by the sultan, around whom this elite gathered, appeared to be independent of and suspended above the ruling class – indeed, to have called it into being and ordained it as nothing more than a group of loyal, salaried civil servants or bureaucrats. In other words, whilst the Ottoman state centre was only partially and temporarily able to sever the umbilical cord connecting it to the economy (in the broad sense), to the ruling class, and to the struggle within it for control over the surplus, it was the state's own ideology, reflected in its legislative activity and documentation, which represented the ruling class as only *kapıkulları*, 'slaves of the Porte', standing the real relationship upon its head and pretending that the autonomy of the state was absolute.[41] At the other end of the social scale, the peasantry, too, stood redefined by the same state ideology and documentation as the *reaya*, 'the protected and shepherded flock'. Hence the fundamental social classes that could be found in virtually any pre-capitalist peasant society were here recast by the state as legally differentiated estates or orders, bolstering the illusion that classes were 'made' by the state instead of the state being derived from a certain class structure, whilst also making it more difficult to detect the universal behind the specific, the suppressed sociological spontaneity underneath the legal garb.

Finally, the concentration of control over land distribution in the hands of some royal line as the vanguard or command-centre of the military aristocracy – yet another common feature of late-tribal societies – also assumed an official, absolute, 'public' character in the Ottoman Empire in the form of so-called *miri* land under the *rakabe* (overlordship or *obereigentum*) of the state, the corollary to which was that all extra-market exactions from the peasant economy, which were the outcome of the contradiction between small production and large ownership and therefore land-rent in the Political Economy sense, were also simultaneously redefined as 'taxes' owed to the state.[42] That is, in fact, what the *çift*, the ancient peasant holding, became: a tax-paying unit; accordingly, all sub-categories of the mass of the *reaya* (the subject peasants attached to the soil), such as the possessors of *tam çift* (full holding) and *nim çift* (half holding), and then the *caba* and *bennak* (all respectively corresponding to the medieval English virgaters, half-virgaters, and cottars and bordars), as well as those truly free cultivators and nomads (*haric-ez defter*, *haymana*) that were as yet not tied to the land, were all placed on the various rungs of a hierarchy of forms which legislation pretended to have 'created'.[43] Apart from the main forms of land revenue, secondary payments like those rendered to each other by the different kinship units (tribes, clans or 'large family groups') of tribal society on the occasion of exchanges of gifts or women or as compensation, blood-money, etc., were also diverted from their traditional channels into the form of fees and fines flowing to the state; examples were bride money or nuptial money (*resm-i gelin*, *resm-i arus*), or the crime and murder fines (*cürüm ve cinayet akçesi*).

In short, within the twists and turns of the legal structure gradually elaborated by this relatively strong central state over time and as it underwent a certain process of acquiring 'depth' and 'weight',[44] we see lurking social classes and class relations that were actually quite universal in character, being rooted in the universal past of tribal society. The money-form of value, Marx [1867] noted, gave rise to a full-blown *commodity fetishism* that served as a veil for real human relationships in capitalist society. In like manner, the state-form assumed by social phenomena, relations and institutions in the Ottoman Empire may be said to have given rise to a certain *fetishism of the state*. And as with commodity fetishism, this other veil of the formally public placed over social reality by a state-fetishist documentation can also be penetrated and removed (not by a preoccupation with outward appearances, but) only through a certain analytical effort that sets out from a broad, comparative empirical base.

To see this, let us go back for a moment to the crime and murder fines (*cürüm ve cinayet akçesi*, or *cerime* for short) mentioned above. As already indicated, in legal theory and at the time of observation, these are fines collected by the state.[45] Any non-comparative descriptivism would be likely to stop at this point and therefore to end up in particularist conclusions. A different kind of clue, however, is provided by the fact that another name used by the Ottoman *kanunnames* to denote the same payment is *kanlık*, which is literally blood-money and immediately suggests, like the Germanic *wergeld* or *wergild*, a payment that was initially the compensation rendered by any murderer's family or clan (not to the state, but) to the kin group to which the dead man belonged. In England, however, in all available Anglo-Saxon laws from the seventh century onward, *wergild* was at least partially a payment to the king by the kin group of the 'guilty' party [Whitelock (ed.), 1979: 391ff; Pollock and Maitland, 1968: 450–52]. And in Wessex in the ninth to tenth centuries, as royal power rose through reorganising society for defence against the Vikings, the kingship that was being progressively redefined in this way also succeeded in imposing itself more and more powerfully on the aristocracy of the kin groups below it.[46] Through such earlier processes, observable also in the Seljukid and then the Ottoman case, might the *wergild* have become something that increasingly went up from the clan leaderships to the king instead of only circulating horizontally within that chieftaincy stratum. Hence it would also seem that the Ottoman crime and murder fines can be situated along the same line of evolution. Now to put it the other way around, it is only juxtaposing Germanic and Anglo-Saxon with Ottoman phenomena, juxtaposing two 'stages' of *wergild* with the somewhat different meanings hinted at by *kanlık* and by *cürüm ve cinayet akçesi*, that enhances our understanding of all of them, and, simultaneously, provides the insights necessary for breaking into the state-fetishism of the Ottoman case in particular. Once one starts looking, similar examples are easy to multiply. In Turkey, Ömer Lütfi Barkan [1939–40] has posited settlements of 'slave sharecroppers' around Bursa and İstanbul as the equivalent of European serfdom in general, thereby arguing that what corresponded to the status of the vast majority of the Western medieval peasantry was only a 'tiny minority' in the Ottoman Empire. If, instead of being regarded as an isolated phenomenon, such prisoners of war settled on the land are studied in conjunction with Henri Stahl's [1980] Romanian '*corvée* villages' or with Slavic 'subject tribes placed under *imperata*, regularly performing services' for the Saxons in Ottonian Germany,[47] this bit of provincialism, too, immediately comes apart.

But for this, of course, agreement on the comparability of Anglo-Saxon with Oghuz-Turcoman processes is a fundamental requirement. It is precisely the validity of such comparative analyses, however, that Turkish nationalist-statist historiography, adding its own ideological glorification and fetishisation of the state to the inherent state-fetishism of the documentation, sets out to deny.

FROM A 'FRENCH' TO A 'PRUSSIAN' PHASE

For virtually all phenomena related to the development of historical studies in the West, as well as for the whole post-positivistic proposition that the fashion in which our various ways of looking at the past follow upon, coexist with, contradict, and eventually displace one another, is inextricably bound up with historians' (and non-historians') changing perceptions of the present, the course of Turkish historiography in the twentieth century provides perfect illustration.

The salient point concerning modern Turkish historiography (as distinct from the school of Ottoman palace chroniclers) is that although it was not always document-fetishist and state-fetishist, in a part of the world where nationalism is obviously a very potent force even today, it, too, was born as a nationalist historiography from the very beginning. Furthermore, although it belonged to a people who had not been conquered but were themselves ancient conquerors and builders of a great feudal empire, it was in a sense a defensive historiography for at least the first half of its existence, from roughly 1900 to around 1935, as it developed not in a vacuum but in a historical space structured by European imperialism (which it was trying to resist), by the Ottoman *ancien régime* (which it had to disentangle itself from and then to overthrow), and by other nationalisms which had preceded it into that space (whose rival claims therefore threatened to crowd it out of history, out of the Near East, even out of Anatolia).

For even by South-east European standards, the Turks were relative latecomers to nation-state building: trade and commodity production, capitalism and the middle classes, Western ideas and an initially mercantile bourgeoisie all took peripheral root among the Christian subject peoples of the Empire, in whose national awakenings their respective churches – benefiting from the autonomies granted to ethnic-religious communities under the Ottoman *millet* system – then came to play an important, overdetermining role.[48] Practically every such national liberation movement and/or the young state that it ultimately gave rise to, moreover, gradually emerged as the favourite of one of the Great Powers who, nourishing ambitions of expanding its sphere of influence through its protégé, provided it with political and material support while also independently bullying, extracting concessions from, and, whenever it found it opportune to do so without antagonising its principal competitors, annexing part of the territories of the Sick Man of Europe.[49] Such were the complex relationships of clientelage (a) between Great Britain and Greek nationalism, from Lord Byron to Venizelos; (b) between Austria-Hungary and Serbia; (c) between Tsarist Russia, with its Panslavist policies, and Bulgaria as well as the Danubian principalities of Moldavia and Wallachia (modern Romania).

There can be no reasonable doubt that through most of the nineteenth and early twentieth centuries, the oppressively corrupt, decadent nature of Ottoman rule, by stifling the potential for socio-economic, political and cultural change, constituted a major obstacle to historical progress. But on the other side of the coin, it seems equally true that in the framework of the stable alliances mentioned above, the aspirations of the Balkan nations went beyond throwing off the Ottoman yoke to obtain state sovereignty and independence: each of them also contemplated carving out, from the rest of the Porte's domains and at the cost of the Turks, little subordinate empires of their own. And the Turks, for their part, even as they were tortuously groping, through the long post-Tanzimat decades, for a new self-definition by permutating elements of 'Ottomanness', 'Islam' and 'Turkicity', were placed in the position of trying to hold the Ottoman Empire together against imperialist encroachment and Balkan revolt, which they often perceived as one.[50]

All this was fully reflected in historiography: variants of the famous '*Byzance après Byzance*' idea first propounded by N. Iorga[51] and repeated by others, for example, suggested that as late as the tenth century, the Turcomans in Anatolia had been so primitive, so purely tribal, so lacking in any legal or administrative traditions of their own, that there was no way they could have created an empire except by enlisting Christian personnel and wholly copying Byzantine institutions as they went along. The political corollary was obvious: the Ottoman Empire was an aberration, a historical accident; as mere slavish imitators, the Turks had no right to continue to rule the lands they had usurped from Byzantium, from the medieval Bulgarian state, or from that of the Serbian prince Stefan Dushan. So much, in fact, was spelled out in an Allied memorandum of 23 June 1919 addressed to the Turkish delegation at the Sèvres Peace Talks: 'Among European Christians as well as the Moslem peoples of Syria, the Arab lands and

Africa, the Turk has done nothing but to ravage and destroy what he has conquered; it is not in the Turkish nature to develop in peace what he has won through war.'52 About a month earlier, the Greek Expeditionary Army, motivated by the *megali idea* and promised a share of the spoils by Lloyd George, had landed in İzmir. So the working partnership in the field and the working partnership in historiography complemented each other: the West prepared to finalise the colonisation of yet another stubborn pre-capitalist polity; Orientalism, fed in this case by the theses of various Balkan nationalisms and by the relative preponderance – compared with Turcology – of both Byzantine and Classical Islamic studies, for all of which it served as the unifying integument, had already accomplished the corresponding mental conquest by consigning the Turks to the ranks of Eric Wolf's [1982] 'people without history'.

To this double hegemony, it was an initially democratic and populist nationalism which in time formulated an effective response. Suffering repression particularly under the Hamidian despotism (1878–1908) as an anti-absolutist oppositional, even clandestine force, this nationalism loosely inspired a new historiography that either became militantly anti-feudal (as when it was directly integrated into a political discourse by Kemalist cadres), or managed to remain coolly detached and objective in its attitude to the Ottoman state. In the hands of its best exponents, this new nationalist historiography adopted a secular, sociological evolutionism in tackling the basic preoccupations of this period, which were: (a) how to extricate a notion of a separate 'history of the Turks' from Islamic history, and (b) how to set out a broad legitimisation of their right to have a sovereign state of their own in Asia Minor. And since both these grand themes, representing moderate ideological commitments, involved bringing Turkish history into the mainstream of world history and elucidating it as a single (but major) strand of a global whole, and since it was on this argument that Turkey's claim of becoming a full and equal member of the community of advanced nations ('catching up with contemporary civilisation,' as Atatürk put it) was based, the cream of the young Republic's historians acquired, in addition to the above virtues, not a xenophobic but a certain humanistic and universalist outlook.

Thus very early in the twentieth century, it was Yusuf Akçura (1876–1935) who outlined a pioneer vision of a nation-state (though he still called it Ottoman) resting on an ethnic, Turkish, foundation, and, more or less simultaneously, suggested a double heritage for Ottoman institutions involving both Islamic and Turkish origins;[53] and after Akçura, who was in many ways a broadly cultured man and a philosopher of history rather than a professional historian, it was in the hands of a real master like Fuat Köprülü (1890–1966) that all the pregnant implications of his predecessor's hypothesis were played out. This is not to say that Köprülü's was the official historiography of the early Republic – a more complex interaction prevailed between the two. After the First and Second Constitutional Periods, the main contribution of the Republican Revolution itself was to remove an already decomposing carcass from the scene, finalising the political solution advanced by Akçura under another name in 1904, and clearing the air of most (but not all) of the poisonous vapours associated with the effort to maintain the empire. This was done in two ways: promulgating a strictly secular state helped to further emancipate the mind from theological scholasticism; the worst excesses of pre-war Panturkism were also eliminated by redefining the soil of Turkish nationalism as only the territory covered by the 'National Oath', that is, Eastern Thrace and Anatolia. Furthermore, Kemalism worshipped at the shrine of Education, and what it did in the way of setting up modern universities and faculties as well as special, autonomously endowed research institutions was far beyond the means of the late Empire.[54]

Beyond this, there were distortions and rough edges. As the philosophers of the French Enlightenment had regarded feudalism as an irrational 'middle age' lacking any historical function or inner logic of its own, so the Kemalists came to paint the relationship between the Ottoman state and themselves in black and white: 'Predicated on the enslavement of the nation', they declared, that state had been 'cruel', 'arbitrary' and 'despotic'; 'the traitors who thronged the palace' had condemned the people to ignorance in order to better 'pillage the country'; as they based 'their wealth and ostentation' on robbing 'the nation with a big stick', they had 'left all Anatolia in ruins', causing 'untold disasters, catastrophes, sorrows'. It was perhaps even more significant that political texts and schoolbooks alike included the Ottoman policy of conquest and expansion in this catalogue of evils: 'the nation' had never had any interest in all the costly expeditions to Vienna, Egypt, Iran; these had been harmful adventures ('Peace in our country, Peace all over the world' was firmly established Turkish foreign policy at the time).[55] And Atatürk himself undertook the potentially dangerous task of providing an entirely irreligious, materialist analysis of the rise of Islam in the desert, as well as a radical critique of the ideological function of religion as pillar of a system that strangled 'individual liberty' and supported an oriental version of the doctrine of the divine right of kings.[56]

This assault on sultan and caliph, on faith and on militarism, helped create a free-thinking atmosphere for more mature assessments. Nevertheless, as history a lot of it was bad history: It was the very opposite of *Historismus*; it had no empathy at all for its object of study. It foisted liberal ideas on to the past: through its insinuations of subjective will and intent, it conflated a statement of the (objective) existence of oppression and exploitation with the suggestion that it should not have been so or that it could have been otherwise. It was also quite wrong not to distinguish between the various phases of the Ottoman Empire and to represent it, for its entire lifespan of six centuries, as uniformly 'reactionary'. Furthermore, liberal ahistoricality extended to the point where the Ottoman sultans were said to have 'usurped national sovereignty' – as if there had been a very ancient Turkish 'nation' steeped in 'freedom' and 'democracy' from time immemorial.[57] This idealisation of Central Asian life (to which the only germ of truth was that nomadic tribalism had in fact been a pre-state mode of existence) was then woven into the even more problematic Turkish Thesis of History, so-called, personally launched by Atatürk in 1928–30. Worried, in the face of colonialist, Orientalising ideology, that the Turks 'would never really, fully be able to appropriate this country for their own if it were admitted that they had only migrated there at a relatively late date' (that is to say from the eleventh century onwards),[58] Atatürk set some of his closest associates to work on the doctrine that the original diaspora of 'Turkish civilisation' from Central Asia had taken place in the seventh millenium BC. 'Turkicising' virtually every single Ancient civilisation under the sky meant, of course, that 'the Turks' had been there in the Near East and Anatolia all along. The idea also served to postulate a Central Asian golden age, bypassing the later Ottoman alternative, which was still politically inadmissible; it suggested that a prehistoric, untainted Turkicity had been subsequently corrupted by Islam – the target of the secularisation reform; it thus sustained as its corollary the Sun Theory of Language, which became the basis for 'pure Turkish' extremism in the linguistic field.[59] Yet, preposterous as it was, the Turkish Thesis of History differed in this important respect from Nazi racism, for example: instead of setting up the Turks as a master race distinct from everybody else, it tended to recover a unity with all world history as 'Turkish' – we are all one, it both asserted and pleaded, we cannot be kept out; in fact we are, ineradicably, mankind. And here we see again that Atatürk was interested in establishing Turkey's European credentials by whatever means possible.[60]

But whatever its political utility, to such amateurishness, Fuat Köprülü, for one, never subscribed; and he it was who gave to the Republic an incomparably better explanation of the evolutionary unity of Turkish history. There are two crucial ways in which his historiography was actually better adapted to the real needs of modern Turkey than the official version. On the way to the Turkish Thesis of History, Atatürk had tacitly agreed with Byzantium-centred Balkan nationalism in estimating that 'the Turks could not, as a tribe, have created an empire in Anatolia. This has to have another explanation' [Afet İnan, 1939: 244; Üçyiğit, 1975: 261, 271]. Köprülü, however, in effect demonstrated how and why it was that they had done precisely that; in other words, instead of positing Tribe and State as two mutually exclusive opposites, in the case of the Oghuz Turks he carefully traced the development, the qualitative transformation, from the one to the other. And secondly, his methodology became the embodiment of everything that could be best in a Republican ideal: an enlightened rationalism, realism, breadth of vision and sober moderation, a democratic humanism, a positivistic but non-reductionist notion of material causality, an emphasis not on heroes or miracles but the *longue durée*; all expressed through a typically French-like stylistic elegance.

Köprülü was strikingly close to his contemporary Marc Bloch on both counts.[61] For this earliest and best follower of the *Annales* school in Turkey, 'the historian's objective' (echoing Bloch's [1931: xxv] own definition of history as 'above all the science of change') was 'to set out the causes of the trajectory in space and time of any given society' [*Köprülü*, 1935: 66]. Again, it was 'understanding the historical development of society' which distinguished the true historian from the traditional chronicler and constituted the dividing line between *l'histoire évenementielle* and modern 'synthetic history' [*Köprülü*, 1935: 65]. As with all 'laws' or or explanations for any kind of motion, the effort to comprehend the movement of society, too, immediately confronted the historian with the problem of distinguishing (in terms of events and institutions) between form and content, outside appearance and inner logic, (in terms of causal factors) between primary and secondary, internal and external [*Köprülü*, 1935: 65; 1946: xx]. Through numerous applications Köprülü revealed that he accepted these primary, internal, determinants of the historical process to be essentially economic and even structured by conflicting class interests – as in his treatment of the social origins of various religious sects, or of the primordial freedom of nomadic tribes and their resistance to incorporation, as a subject peasantry, in any political order.[62] Neither was class analysis ornamentally confined to minor matters; up to a point, it was the main thread Köprülü grasped to unravel the knot of Ottoman origins. Steering clear, in his attitude to the past, of both Enlightenment-type nihilism and historicist identification with the self-consciousness of a bygone age, he clearly held material determination to flow from a given society to its legal-formal constitution: the Anatolian Seljukid state was 'a political manifestation . . . of 13th century Anatolian Turkish society'; its 'centralised' character, its 'solid and orderly institutional framework' was based on the fact that 'in terms of its economic development and degree of division of labour, it was one of . . . the most advanced societies of the Late Middle Ages' [*Köprülü*, 1935: 120] All Turkish-Islamic states were ultimately 'based on a military aristocracy' [*Köprülü*, 1938: 72; 1941: 33; 1946: xvii]; so was the Ottoman Empire [*Köprülü*, 1935: 48, 180, 182]. In fact, to understand the latter, one had to investigate 'the principal elements constituting the *substructure* [italicised in French in the original] of that political organism' [*Köprülü*, 1935: 68], which resided in

> the *stratification* [again the French italics are the author's own] of the various components . . . making up Anatolian Turkish society, their respective and relative positions, the causes underlying their mutual antagonism or adherence [*Köprülü, 1935*: 64–5; also 51–2].

Hence the problem became universally recognisable as what medieval historians today would call one of state formation, no different in principle from, for example, the problem of the formation of the Germanic kingdoms in the Dark Ages; and it was also in a universally recognisable way that Köprülü went about unfolding his solution. The social stratification in question, he said, had slowly taken shape in the course of the Turkic peoples' successive displacements westwards from the tenth to the thirteenth century AD; favoured by the denser presence in the urban hinterland of administrative personnel, jurists, counselors and merchants, all released by the post-Kösedağ (1243) dissolution of the Anatolian Seljukids, it had matured in the frontier marches of Western Anatolia in the early fourteenth century. When the Ottoman war leadership, privileged only by its geographical position, then embarked upon a course of successful expansion against Byzantium, thereby attracting to itself bands of footloose fighters (*gazis* or *alps*, similar to the Germanic companionships, as well as *sipahis*) from all over Asia Minor, *ulema* steeped in the state traditions of High Islam (who also occupied important positions in urban guild structures, and therefore had a double vested interest in seeing peace and order together with the security of the trade routes restored on an Anatolian scale) also closed ranks around the Ottoman dynasty, as did some other noble Turkish houses; whilst the military aristocracy consolidated itself as 'a landed aristocracy . . . resting on very firm foundations' [*Köprülü*, 1935: 180], all got their share of 'the rich *timars* of Rumelia' [*Köprülü*, 1935:

178-9]. This was one of the major secrets of Ottoman state formation – that it was able to sink such firm roots in Europe, building there a power base which it held on to and which allowed it to recover rapidly even after the catastrophic rout of 1402 at the hands of Tamerlane at the Battle of Ankara.

Earlier in this article, I have tried to show that Bloch had to a large extent worked out the elements of a village-level theory of direct transition from Germanic tribalism to feudalism, in which the historical specificities of the resulting West European variety were imparted by the conditioning effect of the previous existence of a developed slave economy. In a Turkish context in the past, I have also argued that similarly, Fuat Köprülü's work in the 1920s and 1930s could be relied on for the building blocks of a comprehensive theoretical appropriation of the Oghuz-Seljukid-Ottoman transition from nomadic and semi-nomadic tribalism to feudal statehood, advancing in three waves and cresting in three successively more developed environments [Berktay, 1983a; Berktay, 1990: Ch. II]. It is that kind of fused anthropological-historical vision that was common to both.[63] And inevitably, it all went hand in hand with a certain universalist outlook: it was precisely at this time, in the early 1930s, that secondary school textbooks dealt with the tenth to sixteenth centuries in terms of 'Turkish-Islamic feudalism', 'Seljukid feudalism' and 'Ottoman feudalism', and only then went on, in comparison with the West European species, to speak of their secondary differences.[64]

Nevertheless, some defects remained. Despite the formidable erudition and intellectual equipment that he brought to bear on the central debate over the rise of the Ottoman Empire, particularly in his first long essay of 1931 on the subject, entitled 'Some Considerations on the Influence of Byzantine Institutions on Ottoman Institutions', Köprülü over-reacted against Iorga-type views by repetitively arguing for a Seljukid against a Byzantine derivation in every instance – and thereby also falling, despite his own injunctions, into the legal-ancestry-over-material-determination trap of pitting one narrow institutional genealogy against another. Even in his much more sociological *Les origines de l'Empire ottoman* (1935), Köprülü persisted in discounting Byzantium; he allowed it some influence for the early days of the Arabo-Islamic state in Egypt and Mesopotamia, less for the Anatolian Seljukids, and least over the Ottomans in the Balkans, thus postulating a falling curve of the invaders' need to borrow.[65] Among other things, this cast the Ottoman principality as already a full-fledged state in the fourteenth century which could do without any further adaptation to new environments. This idea was further reinforced by the role Köprülü accorded to the *ulema* in bridging the gap between the Anatolian Seljukids and the Ottomans: it is not always clear whether this was a facilitating, accelerating factor, or whether it was absolutely determining for state formation. Rereading *Les origines* today, one occasionally has the impression of a vacillation on Köprülü's part between saying that the Ottoman state was born out of tribalism, and saying that it was able to become a state because it followed in the footsteps of previous states (although on balance, his answer to Atatürk's query was closer to the former). Yet again, Köprülü did not proceed very far on the question of the origins of the *tımar* beyond opposing a Seljukid ancestry (from the *iqta*) to a Byzantine one (*pronoia*); he did not, in other words, advance to a theory of the common material determinants of all three, more generally to a theory of the widespread use of the service tenement, the military fief, in all medieval societies. It is impossible not to see in this a rather precise parallel to the futile debate about the Roman, German or Celtic 'roots' of European feudalism. But hence, in the end Köprülü was also hesitant to accept the Seljukids and the Ottomans as feudal.

On all these points, Fuat Köprülü's universalism was still constrained and hampered by the negative aspects of Turkish nationalism – as indeed even the best kind of nationalism is inevitably narrow and exclusionist by definition.[66] The political and military cadres who eventually led the Young Turks Revolution of 1908 and the Kemalist Revolution of the 1920s had for a long time been obliged, as civil servants and army officers, to fight to defend the Empire. Thus the hothouse where they gained the skills and experience which would prove invaluable in the fight to reorganise in 1919–20 (and which explain so much about the precocious victory of Turkey's war *to prevent colonisation*, compared with the lateness of other Third World national *liberation* struggles),[67] also imbued them with an ideology of working for 'the salvation of the state'; this theme was then manipulated by Mustafa Kemal in order to be able to draw all that remained of the Anatolian administrative infrastructure of the Ottoman Empire into the resistance without declaring his radical republican intentions. In the 1920s, too, in comparing the Turkish Grand National Assembly with both Western parliamentarianism and the Soviet system, Atatürk remarked that 'we resemble only ourselves;[68] admissible in the context, this famous early statement of 'third way' thought was nevertheless charged with particularist potential on a wide range of historical issues. It was such beginnings of statism and conceit that were reflected in Köprülü's silences and ambivalences.

But apart from the Turkish Thesis of History and the Sun Theory of Language, within the mainstream of serious historiography in the early 1930s strengths overshadowed weaknesses. Already, however, change was in the air. The new state had consolidated itself to the point where it did not want to pursue social radicalism any further;[69] it therefore began to ally itself mentally more and more with the past, the *ancien régime*, that it had arisen in opposition to. The way the Turkish Revolution entered upon its Thermidor was, moreover, complicated and exacerbated by a series of special circumstances. The Great Depression burst upon the world in 1929. Not being a colony but a sovereign country, Turkey was able to put up a defensive reaction, but one which inevitably involved withdrawing into autarky and trying to industrialise through a much stricter form of dirigism compared with the 'mixed economy' policy, intended to stimulate capital accumulation and private investment, of the 1920s [*Boratav*, 1974: 30ff.; *Boratav*, 1988: 7; *Hale*, 1981: 33ff., 53ff.]. In a way, what was being done in the Soviet Union under Stalinism in terms of concentrating all available talent and resources at the centre, and exercising enormous pressure and discipline from the top down through the party-state apparatus in an effort to pull the backward economy up literally by its own bootstraps, was implemented in Turkey under the reification of Kemalism into Atatürkism. In fact, Turkish five-year industrial plans not only emulated but also partially drew upon Soviet central planning for funds and technical advice [*Hale*, 1981: 56; *Boratav*, 1988: 54; *Tekeli and İlkin*, 1977, 1982]. And as with Stalinism, there were undeniable achievements – through what Korkut Boratav [1988] has called 'initial industrialisation', import substitution created a series of sectors producing key intermediate goods for a large internal market, bolstering a relatively balanced Third World economy with strongly integrated agriculture-light industry circuits. In future years, this would serve as the foundation for further growth and diversification, so that eventually the real plurality of bourgeois interests at the socio-economic level, requiring multi-party political pluralism for its conflicts and contradictions to be expressed and reconciled within the parliamentary arena, would become incompatible with the continuation of a single-party system.[70] Therefore the Kemalist Revolution and then the statist forcing of the pace in the 1930s may be said to have ultimately prepared the way for the 1946–50 transition to parliamentarianism – but this is not often recognised, and part of the reason is that at the ideological level, the Turkish establishment of the 1930s was so hostile to diversity, liberalism, pluralism and individual interest. What it admired in the Soviet Union was not Marxism as a theory and ideology of the oppressed, but the strength of the state, its ability to impose its will on society, to exercise iron discipline in the cause of modernisation.

In this regard, Nazi influence was even stronger. In the end, the systemic and ideological divide with socialism, even state socialism, was too great. By contrast, German state capitalism was, after all, the outgrowth of a historically shaped bedrock of capitalism whose basic class relations and property relations had not been radically altered. Moreover, the promise of fascism was not class struggle but the negation of class struggle. Thus, while whatever influence the Soviet Union had, was bound to remain within the limits of that of an external model, there were greater possibilities for Nazi German influence to become internalised, to forge more organic connections with the Turkish ruling classes at the economic and ideological levels. From the 1920s onwards, Italy was regarded as an enemy because of her threatening claims in the Aegean; on the other hand, in the mid-1930s Dr Schacht's system of bilateral economic relations in the Balkans enmeshed Turkey, too, and an active and voluble pro-German faction emerged in the press, the army and the government.[71]

In this very totalitarian international environment, Turkey's own 'One Party' regime grew more and more rigid. Atatürk, who had retained an Anglo-French orientation in terms of his international sympathies, and who was one of a few European statesmen in the second half of the 1930s with a clear vision of the world being taken down the road to war because of Axis aggression and Western appeasement, died in 1938.[72] His successor, İsmet İnönü, came to be officially called *Milli Şef* in an exact translation of National Leader or *Fuehrer*. In terms of economic policy, too, as prime minister for most of the 1930s, İnönü had been more statist than Atatürk [*Koçak*, 1986: 19ff]. His presidency marked the escalation of the experiment in making the control mechanisms of the Republican People's Party identical with the state apparatus; the balance shifted a bit more towards a pro-German kind of neutrality (until the turning point came in 1942–43 with Stalingrad and North Africa); corporatist ideology ran rampant.[73] At the same time, however, the dominant circles of the Turkish establishment were cautious; they themselves did not want to overcommit themselves in any one direction. İnönü was personally wary of German treachery, breathing a sigh of relief when Hitler launched Operation Barbarossa.[74] Faced with the tug of all these different forces, conservative statism and corporatism were put in the service of consolidating the distinct character and separate posture of the Turkish nation-state, with a self-image of closing ranks in monolithic solidarity to face adversity on its own [*Karpat*, 1959: 73–4]. In these circumstances, the old saying about 'the Turk having no friend but himself', a disconsolate lament for the loneliness of the late Empire, was transformed into a manifestation of overweening pride; to it was grafted Atatürk's 'we resemble only ourselves' dictum, which also assumed a new significance. Together, these slogans came to stand for more than just standing aloof from the global conflict. The political and intellectual drive of the 1910s and 1920s had been aimed at integrating Turkey into the mainstream of world history. The combination of 'we resemble only ourselves' and 'the Turk has no friend but himself' symbolised a contrary trend: a mental reaction directed now at extricating Turkey from that mainstream and that (dissolving) family of nations, and sequestering her in a particular illusory universe of her own where everything could be believed to be different.

This transition of the Turkish Revolution from its 'French' to its 'Prussian' phase was reflected in scholarship in a lagged manner. In the second half of the 1930s, not just the dilettantism of Kemalist political cadres, but academic historiography itself, became tied on much shorter reins to the chariot of a now heavily statist nationalism: abandoning notions of material causality, limitless change (evolution), and universality, it embarked upon a quest (hitherto implicitly rejected) for a static 'golden age' which would not only restore pro-Ottoman thought and sentiment, but also provide justification for the narrowly political conjuncture, for the paternalistic, sometimes quasi-fascist policies and outlook of a dictatorial one-party state. What the Turkish Thesis of History had worshipped in a mythological past, had been, at least, a distorted picture of tribal democracy; but now an infatuation with state power in all its manifestations set in, for which the pre-state paganism of Central Asia could never be the ideal pedestal. Attention was therefore shifted from the seventh millenium BC, and even from the thirteenth century AD, to the times of Mehmed *the Conqueror*, Selim *the Grim* and Suleiman *the Magnificent*; shifted also from the problem of the genesis of the Ottoman state to that of its nature in its prime – but considered in isolation from state formation.[75] On the one hand, the dichotomy between academic historiography and an official history constructed by or for Kemalism's political cadres gradually disappeared as the Turkish Thesis of History fell into disuse particularly after Atatürk's death. On the other hand, academic historiography moved towards an officially sanctioned orthodoxy. It came to reglorify the Ottoman order in a fashion strikingly reminiscent of Metternichian romantic restorationists like Gentz and Müller; hence, not only did it situate itself in a more hostile manner *vis-à-vis* Turkish nationalism's earlier, external, opponents, but also assumed internal functions of the sort of banishing concepts like 'inequality', 'injustice' and 'exploitation' – once readily admitted by prestigious Kemalists as well as by the more marginal and disreputable Marxists[76] – from that Classical Age of the fifteenth to sixteenth centuries. This was done through a theory of the 'non-feudal' nature of Ottoman society, which was not a simple statement about specificities, but ideological code for saying that it represented a perfect class harmony, an organic unity of the interests of the peasant and the state. In pursuing such ends, the founders of the new paradigm once more brought history closer to parable. They adopted an irrational, openly triumphalist, at times race-supremacist, extremely pro-state discourse with regard to the Ottoman Empire; they completely particularised it, cut it off from the rest of humanity, rendered it supra-historical.

THE STATE AS GOD
IN TURKISH NATIONALIST HISTORIOGRAPHY

Köprülü had been a liberal-nationalist; as a typical statist nationalist of the One Party and National Leader periods, it was Ömer Lütfi Barkan (1903–1979) who became the architect of this transformation. It is fascinating to study how individuals are 'selected' for certain historical agencies. Akçura had been a peripatetic, cosmopolitan revolutionary, Köprülü an almost entirely self-made intellectual of the Second Constitutional Period (1908–14), a time of fertile openness. Barkan, nearly 13 years younger, was much more a product of the Kemalist state, which literally ordered him to become a historian.[77] When Barkan died, he was eulogised as the man who had allegedly shed more light than any other on Ottoman history.[78] This should refer more to his pioneering role in opening up the Ottoman archives, I must say, where, in the absence of any ready-to-hand equivalent of the *Monumenta Germaniae Historica* nor even any comprehensive system of classification, Barkan, combining the functions of librarian, copyist, transcriber and translator, had to do everything first by himself and then with a very small team of helpers as he went along. And if he could not take time off to prepare separate editions of the sources, he had to introduce his documentation into the body of his articles. But then, his role as source editor began to intrude upon his historiography, to the point where he gives the impression in his articles of still struggling to master the material, of having begun to write in great haste without proper distillation and assimilation. He is, in many ways, too caught up with his documentation: it is as if he cannot refrain from opening up one treasure chest after another, instead of taking time to reflect, to analyse and synthesise; the documents impose their own order or lack of order upon him, so that he writes gropingly from quotation to quotation; thus, when one of his sources takes a turn from emphasising aspect A to aspect B of a given social institution or phenomenon, Barkan also takes the same turn, although he might have already covered that second aspect several times in the previous pages. Reinforced by empiricism and historicism, his inability to distance himself from his documentation evolves into an unquestioning identification with the judgments and ideological vantage point of his sources, which is that of the Ottoman state; consequently, Barkan's own perspective becomes a fusion of 'the Empire imagined' by itself[79] and by Turkish nationalism in its statist, corporatist phase, from which, also, he cannot take his distances. And a final point in this regard: it is not often noticed that with all his reputation, Barkan never wrote a proper book, a work of synthetic history; instead, he *initiated* a whole tradition of publishing books composed of an introduction followed by transcribed, edited texts of documents, such as one or more *kanunnames*, a complete *defter*, or the daily records of a major construction site – that documents can somehow speak for themselves would seem to have been the underlying assumption.

In the West Barkan is better known for his exploration of Braudelian frameworks for the study of Mediterranean-wide price and population movements, for which reason he is sometimes taken as the *Annales* school's Turkish representative par excellence. But in Turkey, he is considered the pioneering authority on matters of land tenure and peasant status, where the methodology he employed was a far cry from that of Köprülü or of the *Annales*. Not that he did not have a good empirical grasp of the underlying realities of Ottoman rural society: he knew very well that it was composed of two principal classes called the *askeris* (the military) and the *reaya* (the tax-paying subjects, more specifically the peasantry); that of the permanent privileges of the *askeris*, the most important, the right to receive and hold *tımars* (in other words the existence of a fief system), was the consequence of a material necessity common to all medieval societies; and that the *reaya* for their part were 'permanent and hereditary tenants' attached to the soil.[80]

But despite all this, for Barkan, the universalist notion of an 'Ottoman feudalism' was anathema: he castigated this idea as the concentrated expression of the anti-Ottomanism of the Kemalist Enlightenment. In typical Rankean fashion, he himself first called for *verstehen* by cautioning against 'passing value judgments' to argue that 'if one were to apply our modern notions of justice' to the Ottoman state and class system,

> it would be impossible to accept that they represented a just and fair class harmony in any way.
>
> We, however, taking into account the economic and political necessities of the times, and refraining from looking for forms

of class conflict and class exploitation everywhere in accordance with certain socialist conceptions, must here make an effort to understand that regime in an objective way.[81]

'Socialist conceptions', in other words, meant applying 'modern notions of justice' to the Ottoman Empire; it was this that led to 'looking for . . . class conflict and class exploitation', and ended up in 'value judgments'. If only such errors were eliminated, it would be possible to accept that the Ottoman regime represented 'a just and fair class harmony'; this would constitute an 'objective' understanding of Ottoman society. This, presumably, was value-free history. But feudalism existed in Europe and did seem to incorporate lack of freedom; and since Turkish historians could not by themselves rewrite all world and medieval history, the key lay in making Ottoman history into a special terrain where the evils of first feudalism, then capitalism and finally socialism did not penetrate –

> O, how wonderful would it have been, if all this business about capitalism and socialism had not arisen to bedevil the world, and if that Ottoman phenomenon, which was after all the ideal golden age, had been prolonged down to the present. . . .

Barkan was quoted as having said outright even in his later years.[82] Such particularising procedures have always been a major feature of romantic 'third way' thought, and fitted the special requirements of the late 1930s perfectly.

But after all, did the Ottoman military caste, comprising both large and small fief-holders, not possess a monopoly of the right to bear arms and of eminent rights over the land? And were not both European serfs and Ottoman *reaya* thereby attached to the soil and compelled to surrender all or part of their surplus in the form of taxes and/or rents? Were they not, therefore, basically the same type of producers: 'a subject peasantry', in Marc Bloch's characterisation for the West, enmeshed in the same type of exploitative subordination and dependence? Despite the supposition, widespread in Turkey and abroad but not based on close readings, that Barkan practised economic and social history, it is in his way of handling such potential objections that at least in his first period, up to around 1950, Barkan's thinking stands revealed as formalism of a very narrowly *legalistic* sort.[83] Of course, said Barkan [1939–40: 674], socio-economically serfs and *reaya* were not dissimilar; 'the differences between the two must not be exaggerated.' But, he continued,

> the point that is particularly necessary for the historian, is not the broad similarities of the sociologist that are obtainable through successive abstractions, but the specific forms assumed by general

laws and directions of evolution under the influence of factors specific to time and place and of particular historical circumstances [Barkan, 1939–40: 675].

This amounted to an outright rejection of the sociological approach that Köprülü had espoused; by driving a wedge between history and sociology,[84] it allocated to the Barkanian 'historian' a role close to what Köprülü had dismissed as that of the traditional *vakanüvis*, the chronicler.

Emphasis on legal form enabled Barkan to move East and West as far apart as possible. On the European side of the comparison, he followed the trend then prevailing in Western Medieval History to dismiss any German influence as of no consequence whatsoever [Barkan, 1957: 12, 33, 35], and to characterise feudalism – in comparison with Roman central administration – as decentralisation, the parcellisation of sovereignty, the disappearance of public law and order, even statelessness. In the same context, he spoke of the transition to feudalism as a process of economic strangulation:

> Hence, we may conceive of the system we call feudalism as having emerged in economic terms through the dispersal of state authority in the hands of former functionaries and tax-farmers who ... came to appropriate the functions and prerogatives that had originally been conditional upon their public office.... The feudal regime which imparted its distinctive features to Western Europe from the ninth century onwards, was the consequence on the political stage of the economic weakening suffered by this society, which thereby declined into an entirely rural economic system [Barkan, 1957: 43].

This was not intended merely as an account of what actually happened in European history; it was a definition of feudalism and of the transition to feudalism in general. Within that framework of a postulated continuity of demesne-centred 'large estates', managed by lords as 'landed capitalists', from late Roman times to the early Middle Ages, he also, predictably, maintained that serfdom (which he persistently rendered in Turkish as 'slavery of the soil') was but one of the two main ways of 'utilising slave labour in agriculture': in origin, the serf was a slave that had been given a tiny plot of his own by his owner and master, to whom he and his offspring continued to belong unless formally manumitted;[85] similar stigmata borne by medieval serfs attested to the fact that they were the direct and 'true descendants' of slave ancestors – and with his strict adherence to the search for the specific, difference of legal form over similarity of socio-economic content was what mattered.[86] Hence for Barkan, too, the transition from slavery to serfdom was more of a continuity than a discontinuity; it introduced no new quality to mark feudalism as a social system. What did provide a threshold of discontinuity to peg a definition of feudalism on, was the political decentralisation of the Dark Ages, the breakup into closed, self-contained units. This was feudalism conceived, consistently with Barkan's methodological preferences, as a set of legal-political forms, at the superstructural level.[87]

This was ordinary enough; but Barkan went further: On the Ottoman side, he focused on the state as 'maker' of the legal form of social relations. Fascinated by an Ottoman documentation that viewed all phenomena through the eyes of the central bureaucracy and gave an exaggerated picture of the state's power and degree of actual control, Barkan, in the name of 'approaching the Ottoman Empire on its own terms', took all this at face value. The contrast between Köprülü and Barkan extends to even matters of style: Whilst the former's lucidity was the perfect vehicle for his rationalism, the latter's convoluted, tortuous, circular sentences would also appear to have served a purpose; when one stops to dissect them, it is not logical clarity but impossibly rhetorical assertion that comes out. Thus Barkan engaged in some great bombast about the Ottoman Empire in its heyday as manifesting 'a gigantic state will and power that subsumed everything' [Barkan, 1937: 288], that 'bent human and physical laws to its omnipotent state will' [Barkan, 1937–38: 738]. And when he announced from the rostrum of the Second Turkish Historical Congress in 1937 that it had constituted 'an extremely well-organised and fully statist order ... a tremendous example of a regime in which everyone worked for the state and the state worked for everyone' [Barkan, 1937: 288], he was in effect bouncing back from the Classical Age to the Turkish establishment of his day that elite's own self-image as an idealised historical reconstruction – indeed, some among the high-ranking political cadres of the Republican People's Party present on such ceremonial occasions might have wondered whether they were hearing something out of their own propaganda documents. Neither was this the end of the parallel with nineteenth-century statist nationalism in Prussia. Instead of going from society to state, as Köprülü did, Barkan posited the state as a datum in itself, as the prime mover of history and society, as the creator of 'particular historical circumstances'. The Empire, he wrote, represents a strange creature of a *sui generis* type, and appears to pursue objectives all its own. In this system, everything and everybody have been mobilised in the service of a single goal; and that goal is the State, which is both the means and the end of the regime, and which is represented in the person of the emperor. As far as this objective, that is above and beyond all social classes and ethnic groups, is concerned, these other strata are nothing but functionaries . . . [Barkan, 1937–38: 787–8].

Thus in place of Fuat Köprülü's 'military aristocracy [which] consolidated itself as a landed aristocracy', we get 'civil servants', and the whole relationship between them and the state is inverted. At the same stroke, the founding of that state becomes a 'miracle' of 'the compelling power of the Turkish sword that represented a new cause' [*Barkan*, 1937–38: 758, 769]; it is held to reflect 'in blinding brilliance, the richness of the sources of vitality of the Turkish race that set it up' [*Barkan*, 1937–38: 728]. Again, the rise of the Empire demonstrated, says Barkan [1937–38: 725], 'how a gigantic and omnipotent state will power, further tempered in the fire of the political strife and upheavals that it let loose upon the world, could manipulate all sorts of economic, social and demographic forces to create an order and harmony all its own'. *All of the above* were written in 1937–38 and need to be read against that background. It was a time when Nazi directors like Leni Riefenstahl were advertising Hitler's great review of the Wehrmacht in Nurenberg as 'The Triumph of the Will', when fascist poets from D'Annunzio to Ezra Pound were celebrating the *sturm und drang* of war as the supreme excitement and the ultimate test of a nation's soul, when the Axis was preparing to visit its brand of virility upon the democratic effeminacy of the rest of the world.

What bearing did all this have on the status of the Ottoman peasant? Liberal ahistoricality was an easy target for Barkan. As if to speak of the fact of peasant subjection meant to imply that in that age it could have been otherwise, he mocked the imaginary suggestion that 'those who made the [Ottoman] laws . . . [should have] given any great thought to whether they should be inspired by a concept of absolute *liberty* that just was not in the nature of things'.[88] To this he counterposed the idea that the *reaya*'s subjection and attachment to the soil was somehow 'natural' on the grounds that if he were allowed to move about, the state would lose revenue: the *sipahi* would be unable to collect part of the 'taxes' that were allocated to him as his *timar*, his fief;

consequently, he might fail to carry out his military duties [*Barkan*, 1975: 881]. And why did the timariot as 'the representative of the state' have a right to peasant surplus? Because 'the Empire and its sword-bearers were engaged in fighting against the infidel host, against their much more primitive regimes which represented a terrible and destructive force of oppression for the peasant classes'; it was, again, 'natural' – 'entirely natural, that in return for such military duties as were not at all easy, they should partake of the peasant's produce in the form of tax in kind . . .' [*Barkan*, 1937–38: 728].

Here, Barkan clearly employed double standards: *all* medieval ruling classes claim to be protecting the peasantry in return for what they get from it, and such 'protection' is nothing but preventing other aristocracies from getting in on 'their' peasantry's harvest – 'the infidel host' which Barkan spoke of in unscholarly fashion, adopting the Islamic ideology of the Ottoman state as his own, would have pretended as much if it had been they who conquered Anatolia. Furthermore, any Western feudal lord could have asserted that he needed to have his serfs tied down to the land in order not to lose revenue; *given* unequal class relations, this was just as 'natural'. But this does not seem to have deterred Barkan from concluding, with typical casuistry, that only the subject status of European serfs was really 'unfreedom' because it was the result of 'arbitrary' constraints imposed by individual lords within the context of private law; by contrast, the limitations on the freedom of the reaya did not amount to 'unfreedom' because they were imposed by the Ottoman state as 'reasonable' measures of public law for the purpose of ensuring that its 'fiscal needs' were covered. Compared with the absolutised unfreedom of the Western serf, which was alleged to be derived from and not too different from that of the slave, the *reaya* was 'a free peasant'; hence, Ottoman society was not feudal but simply subordinated to a just and fair system of imperial taxation stipulated by public law. The assertion that this did not incorporate any (feudal) exploitation clearly rested on a mystification of the Ottoman state as a supra-historical Being that acted out of its own *raisons d'état*.[89]

There were further consequences. On the basis of that supposed superiority of the Ottoman system to the 'much more primitive regimes' of 'the infidel', Barkan interpreted the Turkish expansion in Europe as a 'liberation' *en masse* of the Balkan peasantries from 'serfdom', therefore from 'feudalism'. For descendants of the conquered peoples, he was insultingly lyrical on this subject:

From being the slaves of innumerable petty lords who were bodily eliminated on the battlefields, they moved to the status of being only the protected *reaya* ... of a great Empire ... the arrival of the Imperial order must have meant for them the solution of a social problem, the achievement of a great Land Reform on an international scale ... [Barkan, 1937–38: 758].

And *reaya* 'freedom' meant that those who made 'land reforms' for others did not need them in their own country: in a very long article he published in 1939–40, precisely at a time when such questions were being debated in Turkey, Barkan [1939–40: 674] stated his *double* intention to 'emphasise the particularities of the Ottoman system *and of our present-day social structure*' (italics mine), and deduced that while western and eastern Europe had from the end of the nineteenth century onwards been shaken by social turmoil, because 'we' had had 'no serfdom', Turkey had 'always been able to maintain a social structure healthy enough to obviate the need for such peasant movements and land reforms in the course of her economic and social history' [Barkan, 1939–40: 677]. Thus Barkan was very conscious in his own way of the link between past and present (though his inference was self-contradictory: elsewhere in his work, he admitted a certain 'feudalisation' in the sense of the rise of private landlordism in the eighteenth centuries; there was therefore no direct line of descent from the sixteenth century *reaya* to the late Ottoman and then the Republican peasantry). And of course, in a manner he did not intend or perceive, he epitomised a very tight – too tight – relationship between the political front and the front of historiography: Just looking at the last two examples, we can see that in his person, the Thermidor broke with the Enlightenment of the Revolution across the board – it broke with Akçura's parliamentary defence of land reform, it broke with the Kemalists' renunciation of Ottoman imperialism, as it broke with Köprülü in methodology.

LOOKING TO THE FUTURE

Turkish academic historiography has never recovered. The Barkanian paradigm, propagated through decades of increasing nationalist conservatism, has, firstly, sentenced that orthodox, semi-official historiography to document-fetishism of the most naive kind possible – to taking the contents of Ottoman state documents literally, without any prior ideological deconstruction. At worst, this allies itself to the increasing subservience of Establishment historians to the practical, short-term policy objectives of the modern state at any given moment. Thus throughout the 1980s, the Turkish Historical Society devoted a large part of its energies to disproving Bulgarian and Armenian claims – arguing, for example, that because repairs to Balkan churches were eventually allowed when local Christian communities petitioned the Porte for permission, the Ottoman state was actually as 'fair' and 'just' as it self-righteously claimed to be in its self-appraisal.[90] Here the abolition of the institutional autonomy of the Turkish Historical Society by the military after the coup of 12 September 1980 is only part of the story; it cannot obscure the facility with which official Turkish historiography, given its ideological tenor of statist nationalism, descends to such propaganda activity. And at best, the illusion that historical truth can be seized simply by putting documents together has reduced generations of students to document transcribers – a few such documents for a graduation thesis, a few more for a doctoral dissertation, a few more for the rank of a full professor. This has been noted by others.[91] What has been missed is its connection with Barkan's empiricist and historicist precepts and with Barkan's personal example as a role model.

This effect is, secondly, reinforced through the chauvinistic insularity engendered by particularism: told that the Ottoman Empire was 'not feudal', meaning that it was all different, Turkish Ottomanists by and large do not undertake any secondary reading outside their own field; most of them remain rather ignorant of the sophisticated developments of the last 60 years in History, and in European Medieval History in particular. As their ambitions and energies are constantly channelled into appropriating more and more of the inexhaustible supply of documents in the Ottoman archives, they become further removed from those intellectual sources which could inform them about the proper questions to ask of their documents – sources which in time could endow them with a sweep and breadth of vision more like Köprülü's (and Köprülü [1935: 67], too, insisted that Seljukid-Ottoman history be studied by the same advanced methods as were being brought to bear by Bloch, Febvre and others in the 1930s on the Western Middle Ages). Again, this has been İnalcık's hidden resource.[92] By contrast, not reading secondary literature having to do with societies outside the Near East has become a permanent trait of the Barkanian historian. It does give rise to some strange claims. Soberly regarded, Ottoman land and population surveys (*tahrirs*) were the means for the ruling class of taking a full inventory of its sources of revenue and ensuring an airtight surplus-extraction process. Barkan [1937–38: 776], however, went through a veritable Wagnerian crescendo about 'an immense accomplishment, . . . a manifestation of power capable of defying a thousand and one vested interests in order to bend the entire universe to the absolute imperative of the state . . .' Perhaps, if he had had at least an inkling that English kings, through the Domesday Book and the Hundred Rolls, were doing similar things from the late eleventh century onwards, he could have preserved a sense of proportion that was much needed.

Finally, and most importantly for our present purposes, as a result of all this exaltation of the Ottoman state, the supposedly 'free' peasant neither breathes nor stirs in most of Turkish historiography. As I have already explained, since the 1930s, one major feature of the second historiographical revolution in the West has been history from below; particularly important for medievalists has been peasant history. This is not a matter of neglecting the political arena, the ruling classes or the state, of one-sidedly insisting that history from below is the only good and correct history,[93] but of redressing the balance. But because of the overwhelmingly statist, elitist character of the Barkanian discourse, there has been no such development in Turkish historiography: constantly extolling the virtues of the state and the 'freedom' of the *reaya* ends up by burying that *reaya* and not investigating at all the supposedly 'greater scope' of their activity.[94] As in W. H. Auden's poem on 'The Unknown Citizen', ironically subtitled 'To JS/07/M/378 This Marble Monument Is Erected by the State' (and significantly dated March 1939, when Barkan was writing his two most important articles), corporatism in real life and corporatism in historiography keep setting up monuments to the state, not to the common man:

> Was he free? Was he happy? The question is absurd:
> Had anything been wrong, we should certainly have heard.

Likewise, once İnalcık [1973: 112] knows that 'the *reaya* were undoubtedly in a happier position', how can he keep to his promise 'to write the history of the people' [İnalcık, 1983]?

Barkan [1937: 281], too, once made the same promise; and yet, for him and for most Ottomanists, the peasant has continued to exist purely in terms of his obligations towards the state, that is, as tax-payer only. Here we have, then, another confluence of the historian's ideology with the built-in ideology of the documentation, for this is precisely how the state saw and dealt with the peasant – as the tiniest cog in its administrative machinery. Hence, one looks in vain in the *İslam Ansiklopedisi*, the Turkish edition, for any separate entry on the *raiyyet* or the *reaya*: this basic productive class of Ottoman society, probably comprising more than 90 per cent of the population, has not been deemed worthy of an article in itself. There are independent entries for all the taxes it paid, however, and its general obligations are described all over again as part of the lengthy, Barkan-written 'Timar' entry [Barkan, 1974]. In other words, there is no notion of the autonomy, reproduction, life-activity of the peasant economy. In fact, Turkish historians of the traditional school may easily be demonstrated to understand 'the economy' to comprise only trade, guilds, money, urban production. İnalcık's [1973] *The Ottoman Empire: The Classical Age 1300–1600*, for example, which has been the standard synthetic textbook in the field for nearly 20 years, after devoting the first six chapters of Part One to political-military history, moves to Part Two: The State, where we get Chapter 7 on the Ottoman dynasty, Chapter 8 on the method of accession to the throne, Chapter 9 on the 'class' (that is, estate) system, Chapter 10 on law, Chapter 11 on the palace, Chapter 12 on the central administration, and Chapter 13 on provincial administration and the *tımar* system. Then, Part Three: Economic and Social Life deals with international trade, the road network, urban population, guilds and merchants in two chapters (14, 15). Where in all this is the peasantry, that vast, primordial bedrock of Ottoman society? To be sure, it is in Chapter 12 – under 'provincial administration'. There could hardly be any clearer demonstration of what is meant by statist history.

All these epi-phenomena indicate that official, nationalist Turkish historiography is at a dead end. The past history of that historiography constitutes part of the history of ideas of Republican Turkey, and can best be understood against the background of the ebb and flow of the Kemalist Revolution. For the two decades preceding the founding of the Republic in 1923 and for the better part of the following decade, the relatively liberal nationalism that marked the upsurge of that forerunner of delayed, Third World-type democratic revolutions, liberated historians from the shell of late Ottoman thought and society, and instilled in them the seeds of some of their most brilliant reconstructions. From the second half of the 1930s, however, that same nationalism, not oppositional but in power, and statist, retrogressively shackled historiography, saddled it with some very conservative and xenophobic paradigms, so that it became ossified, parochial and hidebound, not just in terms of its world outlook but also in its teaching habits, topics and methods of research, its texts, its lack of debates, its entire discourse.

Years ago, Bryce Lyon [1966: xiii] wrote of Marc Bloch's conviction that agrarian history could no longer be discussed principally in legal and institutional terms. It made no sense to speak of peasants, animals, crops, fields and ploughs as though they were only items of revenue and terms at law. He felt that the armchair historian of Paris writing about seignorialism could never come to grips with the subject. What did such a historian know about rural mentality, the daily routine of farming, the smells of hay, manure and pigs?

In the course of his mental preparations for writing *French Rural History*, Bloch read Maitland's *Domesday Book and Beyond*, and pondered whether 'such an approach would not be even more fruitful with less attention to legal problems. Had not previous historians been too engrossed in the origin of institutions . . . ?' [*Lyon*, 1966: xiv]. Lucien Febvre, for many years Bloch's closest friend and collaborator, also spoke disparagingly of Henri Sée's 'legalism and aridity of approach', and after mentioning Fustel and Jacques Flach, too, by name, added that 'these historians – all of them, without exception – knew nothing at all about agriculture as it is practised. In 1932 I was forced to say of them "their peasants always plough with cartularies, using charters for ploughshares"' [*Febvre*, 1966: xix]. In the Prologue to his *Life on the English Manor*, already referred to above,

> The sun rose early, for it was late June, but not much earlier than the peasants of the little village of Belcombe, in the year 1320. As the light strengthened, bit by bit the village became visible, and the confused medley, in which here a roof and there a bit of a wall stood out, began to arrange itself as a narrow street with flimsy houses dotted about in little groups,

began H.S. Bennett [1937: 4]; he went on to describe how villein serfs might have risen, breakfasted 'with a lump of bread and a draught of ale' before proceeding to the fields to cut hay for a few hours on a Sunday morning in order to be back in time for Mass. In the rest of his book, Bennett explored the daily structure of peasant existence, its smells and dusty roads, the food they ate and the songs they sang, how the stained glass windows of the village church served them as their most tangible scriptures.

More than half a century later, we in Turkey still do not have a single comparable work capable of being entitled Life in the Ottoman Village – nor is there likely to be one as long as the *raiyyet* remains 'an item of revenue and a term at law', continuing to plough with *kanunnames*, using *fermans* for ploughshares. This is not to say that no Turkish historians have been producing interesting and valuable work – as I write I have before me Huricihan İslamoğlu-İnan's [1991] very recent *Osmanlı İmparatorluğu'nda Devlet ve Köylü* (State and Peasant in the Ottoman Empire), which notes that in guaranteeing an average degree of exploitation capable of permitting the peasant economy to reproduce itself, the Empire actually ruled by consent not despotism; Ottoman 'justice' was the ideological codification and consecration of this settlement. But such excitement has always come, and will be coming, from those that in one way or another are outside, or distanced from, the official framework.[95]

Of that institutionalised mainstream, what the Arab scholar William Haddad has generally observed is surely true: 'The nation-state is the Prison of the Mind.'[96]

NOTES

1. See, in particular, contributions in the last few years by Akarlı and Fleischer [1990], Suraiya Faroqhi [1988, 1991] and others – all cited in the present author's second article [*Berktay*, 1991] below.
2. In the late 1960s and early 1970s, when theoreticism as a form of idealism was in its heyday, Lucio Colletti [1973: 377], for example, accorded such primacy to subjectivity and consciousness as to claim that 'the working class cannot constitute itself as a *class* without taking possession of the scientific analysis of Capital'. Althusserian structuralist attempts, such as those by Hindess and Hirst [1975, 1977], to write history by reasoning from first principles, proved 'particularly unacceptable to historians' because of 'their theory of knowledge' [*Wickham*, 1985: 189, note 5], and provoked E.P. Thompson's [1978] angry over-reaction in *The Poverty of Theory*, the anti-theoretical extremism of which was criticised, among others, by Raphael Samuel [1981b, 1981c] and by Stuart Hall [1981]. In Turkey, A.S. Akat, an AMP theorist of the same years, conflated a way of proceeding to a theory of history on the basis of historical subjects' own consciousness (which is historicism), with a way of proceeding to theory from empirical evidence in general (with which, as a materialist principle, there is nothing wrong), when he wrote that it was impossible 'to construct a theory of history by using concrete history to make generalisations', for 'attempting to use historical (social) phenomena that take place in concrete time and space in order to create a theory of history (and society) is bound to land us in empiricism (and historicism)' [*Akat*, 1977: 36]. He asserted, furthermore, that 'the method of science is *always* to move from the most abstract to the most concrete inorder to mentally reproduce the concrete as a synthesis of multiple and complex determinations' [*Akat*, 1977: 36]. It was misleading of Akat [1977: 36, note 2; 37, note 5] to cite Marx and Engels in support of his contentions: in the *Grundrisse*, Marx [1857–58: 101] affirmed the concrete as 'the point of departure in reality and hence also the point of departure for observation and conception'. In his 'Afterword to the Second German Edition' of *Capital* in 1873, Marx [1867: 19] again spoke of 'analysis' and 'synthesis', 'method of inquiry' and 'method of presentation', as two stages of the same process of knowledge: *inquiry* proceeded from the concrete to the abstract; then, *presentation* went once more from the abstract to the concrete. Furthermore, 'the method of rising from the abstract to the concrete is only the way in which thought appropriates the concrete' [*Marx*, 1857–58: 101]. Guy Bois [1984: 13] has also warned that

The abyss of speculation is no less fearsome [than that of empiricism]. The dead ends of a historiography heavily impregnated with nineteenth century positivism are arousing violent reactions today, often stimulating, but sometimes victims of speculative idealism. This shift becomes a threat if theoretical effort dominates the historian's work to the detriment of 'direct penetration into the historical material', to adopt a formula Pierre Vilar used in a recent and important article.... It is not true that models of the functioning of pre-capitalist economic systems can be drawn up simply by picking up here and there materials that historians have collected.

As for concrete applications, Robin Law [1981] has written a sharp critique of the procedures adopted and results obtained by Althusserian historians in an African context.

3. The summary in this section has been deliberately based on some recent introductions to History for undergraduates, such as those by Arthur Marwick [1970] and John Tosh [1984], as well as another 'standard' article by Edmund Fryde [1990], which captures the swings of Historiography from one extreme to another, resulting in a non-linear but zigzag development, in very sophisticated fashion.
4. See, in particular, the discussion by Tosh [1984: 141–2] of where Marx stood in relation to the historicising historians.

> Just as one does not judge an individual by what he thinks about himself, so one cannot judge such an epoch of transformation by its consciousness; but, on the contrary, this consciousness must be explained from the contradictions of material life, from existing conflict between the social forces of production and the relations of production.

wrote Marx [1859: 4] in one famous 'Preface'.
5. After those by Benedict Anderson [1983] and Gellner [1983], another recent study by Hobsbawm [1990] has also dwelt upon the ways in which nationalism and its invented 'national history' actually preceded the nation and the nation-state on the stage of history. The relationship between nationalism and historical and archaeological studies has also been variously commented upon by François Georgeon [1980: 50] and İlber Ortaylı [1982: 73]. On 'the decline of nationalistic history in the West', see P.M. Kennedy [1972].
6. It must be added that throughout the pre-industrial era, this prejudice, too, rested on a certain material basis: As long as labour productivity was so low that only a surplus extracted in tiny bits from a very large mass of direct producers could feed the state as well as a ruling class that was a very small minority, the contrast between the misery and ignorance of the former and the splendour of the latter, between hovel and palace and between a maximum of subordination and another maximum of dominance, was so extreme as to make it very difficult to perceive of the one as actually resting on the other. There seemed to be no inner connection between the two – so totally were the direct producers excluded, except at very exceptional times, from active historical agency. I have dealt with this problem elsewhere [Berktay, 1986c].
7. Kuhn [1962], while portraying the development of science as a series of peaceful interludes punctuated by intellectually violent revolutions in which one conceptual world view is replaced by another, makes no distinction between the linear evolutionism of a steady, cumulative acquisition of knowledge, and the more sophisticated idea that what results from these discrete jumps must move, in the long run, in the direction of closer approximations to truth. If one dispenses with this latter minimum in extreme post-modernist, relativistic fashion, how can there be any scholarly agreement on warranted against unwarranted conclusions? For the same reason, it would seem necessary and desirable to preserve a certain non-identification of the subject with the object. Hence, while I see Foucault's [1977: 31] point when he speaks of not 'writing a history of the past in terms of the present' but of 'writing the

history of the present', I have difficulties with his notion of a 'non-duality between ideas and practice' [Poster, 1984: 15].
8. See Perry Anderson's [1983] critique of Structuralism on the grounds of its 'exorbitation of language' [40–45], its 'attenuation of truth' [45–48], and its 'randomisation of history' [48–51].
9. Charles Maier [1988: 44] relates how he and many others 'felt uncomfortable' when William H. McNeill [1986] 'devoted his [American Historical Society] presidential address to a plea for restoring the role of myth in history'.
10. Thus Rodney Hilton [1976b, 1984] insists that lordly jurisdiction was not superstructural but part of the 'feudal relations of production'. If this were so, contradicting the universalism of a modal definition, focussing on the exploitation of a dependent peasantry by a landowning class, that Hilton himself has done so much to develop, feudalism would still be specific to Europe. John Haldon [1991], in contrast, has introduced a conceptual distinction between the relations (or the mode) of production at the economic level, and the non-economic conditions for the continuous operation of that mode of production. Guy Bois [1984: ix–x] has pointed out, against Brenner, that even in the capitalist mode, non-economic conditions and frameworks are needed to sustain the transfer of surplus – the 'autonomy of the economic', in other words, is not the privilege of capitalism. I might add that as a non-economic condition for surplus extraction, lordly jurisdiction could very well be replaced by imperial legislation and state jurisdiction – as was the case with the Ottomans. Did this change the mode of production? In both cases, a small-producing peasantry was the fundamental substratum.
11. See, for example, the identification of privatisation as a 'tendency towards the development of feudalism' by Guy Bois [1980: 62–3], as well as my earlier theoretical response directed at both Wickham [1985] and Bois [Berktay, 1987a: 299].
12. Alain Guerreau [1980: 41ff] *begins* his exploration of the theoretical horizons of feudalism directly with the nineteenth century, and with Guizot, Fustel and Flach. There is no broader epistemological questioning of the sixteenth to seventeenth centuries – of the formative period of Eurocentrist history, ruling class history, legal history of institutions from above. And both in his book and in his interventions at the now-defunct Société d'Étude du Féodalisme of the late-1970s, his comments on the role of the Catholic Church as the point of origin for much of early medieval documentation verge on positing a separate Church as the crucial element in the systemic reproduction of feudalism [Guerreau, 1979–80: 22–3]. Also see Le Goff's Preface [Guerreau, 1980: 12–3].
13. For some statements on the ways the vantage point of the Romans has been built into our observations and knowledge of the Germans, see Todd [1972: 2–3]; Todd [1975: 9ff]; Wallace-Hadrill [1971: 1] ('For facts we must wait till the Romans speak.'). An earlier work by Wallace-Hadrill [1952: Ch.1] is tinged with regret over the passing of classical civilisation. When E.A. Thompson [1948: 54–5; 1952], in his work on late Roman revolts in Gaul and Spain, spoke of the alliance of interests between the barbarians and the oppressed masses of the Empire, Wallace-Hadrill [1962: 27, note 2] again objected: 'While accepting a good deal of Thompson's case against the landlords . . . I believe he overlooks the grim truth that extortion and corruption are often the price of protection, and that many are willing to pay that price . . .'. Recent literature has been of a different mind [Musset, 1975: 167; Pounds, 1974: 10, 18].
14. Both Bloch [1928a: 59–62] and Homans [1942: 233] point out that the distinction between 'free' and 'bond', particularly in England, was one that revolved around access to royal courts as against manorial courts only. Homans [1942: 235] then explains that 'In their great work of simplification which made the common law . . . what the lawyers did was take from the Roman law the doctrine that men were either serfs (*servi* = slaves) or freemen, and try to apply it to the distinction between men who held land in villeinage and those who held land by other tenures.' Adds Titow [1969: 57ff.]: 'Students must be warned at this point not to take the writings of the contemporary lawyers on the subject of

freedom too literally . . .'.
15. Philosophically speaking, there is no specific without the general; or, the specific is only the specific within the general – they are simultaneously constituted by reference to one another. John Tosh [1984: 133-4] has provided a good discussion of the inevitability of 'recognising patterns' and therefore of blurring the conventional distinction between the subject matter of History ('what happened in the past') and Sociology ('how societies work'), also incorporating Philip Abrams' explanation of the indissoluble link between the two disciplines: The two-sidedness of society is such that every social action is both a choice and at the same time determined. Actions become institutions and institutions are changed by actions in turn.
16. This was pretty much standard procedure in American undergraduate teaching in the 1950s and 1960s. In his popular *History Handbook of Western Civilization*, for example, McNeill [1949: 301ff.] went by this formal distinction between 'feudalism' and 'manorialism'. And it is how I, too, received my introduction to medieval history: my course syllabus for the academic year 1965-66 at Yale University begins with an introduction on how medieval Europe was never entirely 'feudal (politically)'. nor entirely 'manorial (economically)', nor entirely 'divided into freemen and serfs (socially)'. I have previously cited this in print [Berktay, 1983b: 309, note 35].
17. In the Ninth Edition (1875-89), Vol.XII (1887), Serfdom is treated only in the 'Slavery' entry by J.K. Ingram [1887: 129-44] and then very briefly [136-7]. The 'Feudalism' entry in the same edition (Vol.IX, 1879) has *nothing* to say on the peasantry throughout its four pages; it is entirely about kings and retinues, magnates and royal authority, and efforts to restore the latter.
18. Note that this now reverses Stenton's preference for 'a useful term' over a mere abstraction. The point is that we must have *all*: empirical observations as well as half generalisation and full generalisation; each has its place in the process of knowledge.
19. Wickham [1985: 170] has pinpointed a significant symmetry: 'The real problem about the Asiatic mode is that it is too politically and legally specific. Like the private-justice-and-serfdom-and-labour-service version of the feudal mode, it has too many institutions arbitrarily attached to it for it to be of much help as an economic category.'
20. Among the participants at an international symposium in 1986 commemorating the 100th anniversary of Marc Bloch's birth, it was Guy Bois in particular who addressed himself to this question [Berktay, 1986a].
21. Against Varga [1967: 101], I do not think that 'Oriental forms of serfdom' and 'the AMP' come to the same thing. What is at issue is not whether the East had any kind of specificity at all; rather, it is whether that specificity really amounted to a qualitatively distinct, different kind of relation or mode of production. O'Leary [1989: 110-18] also seems to have missed this point in his 'Capital: Volumes I and III' discussion.
22. Hobsbawm [1964: 43] has noted that Marx in particular was 'not concerned with the internal dynamics of pre-capitalist systems except insofar as they explain the preconditions of capitalism'. This, in retrospect, was probably the methodological point of origin of classical Marxism's mistakes regarding pre-capitalist history. For the problem of the extent to which any ancient or medieval society had realised or was capable of realising those preconditions is not, in any logical and necessary way, the beginning point of a meaningful and comprehensive inquiry into pre-capitalist history. A good case, indeed, can be made for the alternative position: full analysis and then theoretical reconstruction of the basic elements of all pre-capitalist social formations should precede, and should be undertaken initially without any reference to, the question of the eventual transition or non-transition to capitalism.

With Marx, it was more of a habit to annex pre-capitalist history to his analysis of capitalism, which his life's work was organised around; Engels, with more encyclopaedic interests, was less prone to this error. And hence, 'Engels's *historical* judgements are nearly always superior to those of Marx. He possessed a deeper knowledge of European history, and had a surer grasp of its successive and salient structures', Perry Anderson [1974b: 23, note 12] has observed.

23. To be fair, this inversion is still quite widespread. Allowed to survive through the lack of integration between Anthropology and (Ancient and Medieval) History, it is perhaps the decisive weakness that has to be overcome in visualising, in broad outlines, a general but multi-variant transition from tribal to feudal society.

24. It was at this point, and by way of demonstrating how late it could be before lordship overtook the hitherto free peasantry, that Engels [1877-78: 195] let drop a remark which has been popular with non-Turkish AMP theorists of older generations whilst earning him the dislike of AMP theorists in Turkey: 'The Turks first introduced a form of feudal ownership of land in the countries conquered by them in the East.' Still, Engels was mistaken in thinking that this was the first appearance of feudalism in the area.

25. This Russian connection has been studied by Gatrell [1982]. It is interesting to note that some years ago, when Alan Macfarlane [1978] attacked the notion of a peasant history for England, he also attacked what he saw as the harmful influence of historians and sociologists of Russian origin on English medieval studies. This was then criticised by Hilton [1980].

26. By correlating serfdom with feudalism, these expressions both echo the idea, which Hobsbawm [1964: 34] says was prevalent in late- nineteenth century Marxism, of a universal stage of proto-feudalism as the first form of class society, and simultaneously prefigure a much later statement by Takahashi [1952] to the effect that serfdom constituted the social form of existence of human labour under feudalism, as well as another by Rodney Hilton [1984: 85]: 'The exploitation of servile peasants by a landowning class in widespread in world history, from Asia to the Americas, from ancient to modern times. If this is the feudal mode of production, then feudalism has been almost everywhere, at some time or another.' Incidentally, once it moved beyond treating Serfdom under Slavery, there seem to have been only two signed 'Serfdom' or 'Serfdom and Villeinage' articles in the *Encyclopaedia Britannica* before it split up into separate *Micropaedia* and *Macropaedia* editions : that by Vinogradoff [1911], which came down into the 1960s, (it is still in the 1965 edition) and then another one by Hilton [1970b], coupled with his 'Manor' entry [Hilton, 1970a] from the late 1960s on.

27. A few examples just to show how much this is now part and parcel of the modern approach: 'The peasants have left no records behind' [*Titow*, 1969: 1]. 'These writings are exclusively concerned with the most extensive and efficiently managed estates . . .' [*Duby*, 1974: 13-5] Again, they were 'all written in the context of great estates' and 'great estates were far from extending over the whole Western countryside. They happen to be all that the sources disclose for us, or nearly so. Almost total darkness prevails beyond their boundaries . . .' [*Duby*, 1974: 78-9, 89]. Bolton [1980: 9] is very similar: 'There are records enough . . . but all were made for or by lords. For the most part we have to see the peasantry, the mass of the population, through the lord's eyes, and this inevitably gives us a one-sided view.' And perhaps in riskier fashion, Duby [1974: 95] has also argued that this '*système domanial*' was already obsolete at the time of Irminon's *polyptyque*:

Because it lacked strength, the shell of the great estates crumbled away, undermined by the resistance, conscious or otherwise, of those 'poor', 'humble' and 'weak' men who toiled in the fields. . . . Every polyptyque describes a partially decomposed organism, whose disintegration it was unsuccessfully trying to slow down.

28. This repeats an earlier statement by Bloch [1928a: 60]: 'The one-time villein, the tenant pure and simple, if I may so call him . . .'
29. Typically, *French Rural History* brackets the treatment, in section III/1, of 'The early medieval *seigneurie* and its origins', with: 'I. The Main Stages in the Occupation of the Soil', 'II. Agrarian Life' (both of which deal with peasant existence and activity as independent of, and anterior to, lordship), and 'III/2. From great proprietor to rentier landlord' (which points up the brevity of the period of relatively intense demesne cultivation).
30. I have criticised the Blochian idea of an *'ambiance sociale totale'* elsewhere [*Berktay*, 1987a: 320–21, note 1]. Evelyne Patlagean [1988] has made a crucial point by observing that there is no place in Bloch's conception of feudalism for the feudal state; this sets very strong Eastern limits to his comparative horizons.
31. I would include under this heading: emphasis on the non-slave, free German antecedents of medieval serfdom [*Hodgett*, 1972: 24–6; *Duby*, 1974: 40; *Musset*, 1975: 132]; further evidence that manors with large demesnes were relatively limited in number, transitional, and restricted to Northern France and the Paris basin [*Pounds*, 1974: 51, 53–4, 65; *Bolton*, 1980: 13–4; *Duby*, 1974: 90, 92, 95]; the elucidation of the process whereby labour services began to be commuted, not in the thirteenth century, as Ö.L. Barkan [1939–40, 1957] followed his Western contemporaries in believing, but much earlier [*Postan*, 1937; *Titow*, 1969: 43–63; *Bolton*, 1980: Ch.1; *Hilton*, 1973a; *Duby*, 1978a]; analyses of the relationship between the lord's economy and the peasant's economy that begin and proceed not at the legal but at the economic level, and concentrate on change instead of static definitions [*Kosminsky*, 1935, 1955, 1956; *Kula*, 1962; *Dyer*, 1980]; rising understanding of the ability of serfs, imbedded in the matrix of the village community and protected by custom and tradition, to undertake individual and/or collective resistance, so that lords did not exactly have a free hand in their supposedly 'arbitrary' encroachments [*Knight*, 1934; *McNall Burns*, 1941: 329; *Homans*, 1942: 109, 235–6; *Hodgett*, 1972: 33; *Faith*, 1984: 49; *Dyer*, 1984; *Mann*, 1986: 395, 397, 399; *Hilton*, 1990a, 1990b]; dawning awareness that effective possession or effective privacy extended so far down in the village community that 'villein charters' (which should have been legally inadmissible) and village land markets were probably 'as old as the village itself' [*Postan*, 1960: 132] – opening up to an entire new literature on peasant family structures, life-cycles and inheritance customs [*Faith*, 1966; *Goody, Thirsk and Thompson* (eds.), 1978; *Goody*, 1983; *Smith* (ed.), 1984]; explicit discounting of labour-rent as a non-essential element under feudalism [*Hilton*, 1976a: 14–5]; finally, explicit theoretical generalisations about the manor as a collection of petty farms [*Bloch*, 1940: 246; *McNall Burns*, 1941: 328; *Wolf*, 1966: 49] and about the feudal mode of production as a 'petty mode of production' subordinated to 'feudal bonds and feudal exploitation' [*Dobb*, 1962: 9, 11].
32. On the one hand, more and more comparative historians and sociologists have come to stress just how exceptional the slave mode of production is in history [*Hopkins*, 1978: 99 and note 2; *Dunn*, 1982: 63, 65–6; *Wickham*, 1988: 188]. Secondly, and independently of research on slavery, yet still within the framework of the European transition from late Roman to medieval society, the Romanist view has been weakened by research on aspects of class formation among the Germans [*E.A. Thompson*, 1948, 1952, 1965, 1966; *Wallace–Hadrill*, 1952, 1962, 1971; *Todd*, 1972, 1975; *Musset*, 1975], and Duby [1974] has provided a whole account of this transition in terms of a polarisation into 'warriors and peasants' where the Roman

heritage is mostly dealt with in a small section entitled 'Fascination with Classical Models'. Thirdly, authors as diverse as George Thomson [1949] and Henri Stahl [1980] have left accounts of primitive land systems in Africa, among the ancient Greeks and in Romania, which allow us to form a more coherent picture of the process Bloch hypothesised as the gradual settlement of clans as villages, their placing under lordship, and the consequent transformation of gifts into land rent.

33. Starting with the position taken by Dobb [1950, 1953] in the 'Transition' debate, this literature includes contributions by Hibbert [1953], Hilton [1953, 1976a, 1976b, 1979, 1984], and Merrington [1975]. Gervase Rosser [1988: 45] has provided a concise summary of what it all means, including additional references.

34. In post-war literature, this idea was first advanced by Owen Lattimore [1957], and then picked up by Hobsbawm [1964: 62–3].

35. Immediately after the mid-October 1978 conference on 'Mediterranean Feudalisms' in Rome, 'My first and immediate impression is', wrote Duby [1978b], that 'it is certain that one can no longer talk of a "classical" feudalism: that model's day is over. Neither is there any "perfect" feudalism; or rather, they are all more or less perfect, in their own fashion.'

36. For a discussion of the conceptual relationship between the common material basis of all feudal societies and their specific genesis-processes, see an earlier article [Berktay, 1987a: 311–12].

37. The best defence of the comparative method in this regard has again been provided by Bloch [1928a: 44, 51; 1928b], particularly in the former article where he relates how he had been able to break through the dogmatic assumption that no enclosures had taken place in France simply because he happened to be familiar with the English literature.

38. This argument about the underpinnings of Ottoman centralism, too, has already been set out in Berktay [1987a: 317–18].

39. Careless talk about the Ottomans having had 'a comprehensive system of public law' notwithstanding, the land *kanunnames* were in many ways unlike modern law. They were not deduced in logical fashion from certain abstract principles; they represented compilations of local custom and tradition. The relative strength of the Ottoman state enabled them to be codified not on the scale of a single manor or village, but on the larger scale of a *sancak* or *liva*. Nevertheless, in the face of the physical, cultural and historical diversity of a pre-modern agrarian society, even by an 'omnipotent' state that was the maximum achievable.

40. Whenever it is a matter of settling what 'ancient custom' was, Ottoman *kanunnames* will, depending on the region, refer to how things were, for example, under the Karamanids or the Akkoyunlus (the White Sheep tribal confederation), so that a picture emerges of other, previous *sipahis* 'eating' the revenue of this or that village in traditional proportions. And sometimes an entire sub-system of land tenure, such as the half-state, half-estate system, will thereby be revealed to date from pre-Ottoman times [İslamoğlu-İnan, 1987: 107–11]. The first Ottoman ruling class was a product of the fusion of the military classes of Anatolia and the Balkans; the peasantry, which remained where it had always been, was 'fused' by coming under the overlordship of the new state.

41. Here I am grateful to John Haldon for having allowed me to see, from 1989 onwards, drafts of his major contribution to this collection [Haldon, 1991].

42. I would like to put an earlier argument about the error involved in positing too sharp an opposition between 'tax' and 'rent' [Berktay, 1987a] in even stronger form. What we mean when we speak of tax-rent is not a combination of two distinct phenomena but rent-in-tax-form. If legal origins and derivation are so important, why not pay attention to Islamic jurists on this point: In the Ottoman case, they provided a theoretical justification for collecting *öşür* by saying that since the *raiyyet* was a tenant on state land, the *öşür* was the rent (*icare*) of the land. To see why they were basically right, let us turn to the *malikane-divani* (half-state, half-estate) system. Suppose, first, that there is only a pre-conquest private landowner that confronts the

tenant cultivator: this is a case of pure rent. Then, after the conquest, suppose that a *sipahi* is appointed over them, to whom part of the revenue of the land has to be diverted. What happens here is that *part of the rent* becomes codified as the state's (*divani*) share, as 'tax'. When we look beyond this intermediate stage to one in which the pre-conquest landowner has disappeared completely, we arrive at a situation in which *the whole rent* has passed into 'tax'. As state *rakabe* swallows up pre-conquest ownership rights, the Ottoman timariot takes the rent that used to go to the landowner; this is the secret of 'tax'. And the *sipahi* does not pay any 'taxes' precisely because these are actually rents-in-tax-form, whereas the timariot, as a member of the military class, partakes of the class monopoly of the land. This is his birthright from which he cannot be excluded.

Now another demonstration by way of negative example: in his seminal paper on this subject, in an early footnote, Barkan [1939: 54, note 1] defined the *malikane* (estate) share as being 'in the nature of the rent of the land, and belonging to its owner . . .' But of course, he had (elsewhere and always) defined *öşür* in general as the rent of land belonging to the state. He then faced a dilemma: in the *malikane-divani* system, if the 'estate' share was rent, what was the 'state' share? If it was not rent, how could *öşür* in general be rent? In a marginal note in his own copy, he questioned himself in so many words [*Barkan*, 1939: 160, note (*) added by the editors]. The only possible solution is the one I have indicated here: we are faced with subdivisions of what is all rent in the Political Economy sense.

43. For such gradations within Western medieval village society, see descriptions by Bennett [1937: 61–73], Hilton [1978], Miller and Hatcher [1978: 22–5], Dyer [1980: Ch.4], Bolton [1980: Ch.1]. The same gradations existed within Byzantine village society, too, running from a *zeugaratos* (full yoke-holder) through a *boidatos* (half yoke-holder) down to an *aktemon* (a peasant with none). I am grateful to Alan Harvey [1989: 16–19, 37–8, as well as personal communication] for this information.

44. For an explanation of these concepts, see the section on 'Centralisation and Decentralisation in the Ideology of Empire' in my second article below [*Berktay*, 1991].

45. *Timars* were administratively classified into those termed to be *serbest* (literally 'free') and those that were not. This revolved around the right to collect certain dues variously called the *rüsum-i serbestiye, niyabet*, or *bad-ı heva*. Their most significant component were the crime and murder fines, which symbolised the entire 'privilege to pursue and arrest criminals, and, after having obtained the *kadı* court's verdict, to implement the sentences passed, including collection of all monetary fines' [*Barkan*, 1975: 884]. This privilege was hotly contested among the *askeris*: while many dues in this group came in time to be collected by all large or small fief-holders within their own fiefs, the right to collect the lucrative crime and murder fines in particular remained the jealously guarded prerogative of those higher up that held the *serbest timars*. As for petty timariots, at best, they had to split half and half with their superiors; in some localities, they had to turn all such income over to their *serbest timar* superiors.

46. Michael Wood [1987: 94, 100, 103ff.] gives an account of the effects of war and military organisation on class formation under Alfred and his successors, and notes the parallel with what was happening in tenth-century Germany under Henry I. I would like to thank Chris Wickham for the references on the *wergild* in Anglo-Saxon times.

47. I have relied for this information on a paper on 'Early Medieval Warfare' read by Karl Leyser on 4 December 1989 at a Birmingham Medieval Society Seminar.

48. What Hobsbawm [1962: 171; 1990: Ch.2, especially 67ff.] has shown in general about the role of religion in the early definition of 'national' identity and aspirations, or of 'popular proto-nationalism', is particularly valid in this regard.

49. For a similar analysis, see Kitromilides [1989]. Tsarist Russia played an especially prominent role in this regard. 'Like the British liberal, the Russian Panslav saw

Ottoman rule over Balkan Christian peoples in the darkest colors', notes Barbara Jelavich [1973: 9]. 'Freedom, in almost every instance, was attained with the aid of the Russian armies' [Jelavich and Jelavich, 1965: 45].

50. Thus the Young Turks pursued a policy of the 'alliance of various elements' (*ittihad-ı anasır*) of the Empire, which turned the Committee of Union and Progress into the guardian of the existing state in confrontation with its subject peoples. Revolutionaries were transformed into conservatives in the process.

51. On Iorga's life and double career, see the essay by Maurice Pearton [1988] in a whole volume on 'historians as nation-builders' in Central and South-east Europe edited by Deletant and Hanak [1988] – which however contains nothing on Turkey, the locus for 'a nationalism too far', it seems, where Köprülü of course would be Iorga's counterpart.

52. Re-translated into English from the Turkish text provided by Osman Olcay [1981: lxxii].

53. Akçura's life and thought have been exhaustively and passionately studied by François Georgeon [1980], on whom I have relied heavily in forming my mental picture of Köprülü's intellectual antecedents [*Berktay*, 1983a]. Representative of a group of talented middle class Turkish intellectuals from the vicinity of Kazan in Southern Russia who kept circulating between that country, Turkey and France; learned, cosmopolitan product of far more than just an Ottoman education; participant in four revolutions in two defunct empires in 1905, 1908, 1917, and 1919–23; member of the Grand National Assembly throughout the 1920s (where he took a stance in favour of land reform and progressive labour legislation on the left wing of the Republican People's Party); and the first president of the Turkish Historical Society in 1932, Yusuf Akçura's real claim to historiographical fame rests on the *Essai sur l'histoire des institutions du Sultanat ottoman* which he submitted as a graduation dissertation to the Ecole des Sciences Politiques in Paris in 1903. These institutions, said Akçura, were not of purely Islamic but also Turkish descent. Of the Turks, Akçura wrote that among the traditions these warlike nomads of Central Asia had tenaciously held on to even after passing into the sphere of Islamic civilisation were: (1) patriarchy; (2) collective property over the land embodied in the person of the *khan*, who as leader of the people concentrated great authority in his hands – but one which was nevertheless defined and circumscribed by (3) the existence of *yasag* and *töre* as bodies of customary law; and (4) the appearance of an aristocracy around the *khan* and over the tribal rank and file. Why was this so important? As Georgeon has explained, by putting Islamic law on the same plane as Turkish customs, Akçura attributed not an divine and hence absolute, but only a relative, historical, value to the former, thus secularising the history of the Turkic peoples, which he also moved towards integrating with world history. Furthermore, by pinpointing the emergence of 'public institutions' in embryonic form (kingship, royal eminent rights, an aristocracy, customary law) *within* the tribal social stratification of the Turkic peoples as the real beginnings of full-fledged state organisation, he improved on the mechanistic external determinism represented by both the Byzantine-based and the Classical Islam-based versions of the Orientalist paradigm.

54. These special research institutions were the Turkish Historical Society and the Turkish Language Society, both of which Atatürk endowed out of his own private estate. On the significance of the formal independence thereby granted to research in history and linguistics, a variety of commentators are united, including İğdemir [1973: 3–5], Üçyiğit [1975: 261], Karal [1975: 258–9, 265], Ortaylı [1982: 79], and Tunçay [1981: 300]. This institutional autonomy, however, was terminated after the 12 September 1980 military coup in Turkey.

55. A full review of this revolutionary attack is included in a useful essay on 'Kemalism and the State' by Perinçek [1986: 129–90, especially 142–3]. Gündüz Ökçün [1968: 258] also quotes extensively from a speech by Mahmut Esat Bozkurt at the İzmir Economics Congress of 1923, where this leading Kemalist ideologue repudiated Ottoman expansionism in very similar language. Alternatively, see

Berktay [1983b: 286, note 12].
56. See Atatürk [1986] for the full text of a very interesting manuscript that came to light only in the 1980s. Also see Perinçek [1986: 158].
57. An earlier discussion is in Berktay [1983b: 285–6], with reference to both Mahmut Esat Bozkurt and Atatürk.
58. Related by Atatürk's adopted daughter Afet İnan [1939: 245–6], whom he had sent to Europe to read history and physical anthropology. Made vice-president of the Turkish Historical Society in 1932, it was she and some other politically loyal associates who were set to work on the new theory that the very first states in Anatolia and elsewhere had all been founded by the 'brachycephalic Turkish race'.
59. But the reader must beware of seeing this as a uniquely Turkish craze. Romantics glorified the primitive everywhere, and the linguistic 'invention of tradition' in nineteenth-century Wales by Iolo Morganwg and others [*Morgan*, 1983] was no less outrageous than some of the etymologies proposed by the advocates of 'pure Turkish'.
60. This did not exclude resorting to a quasi-racist, pro-Turkish strain in European physical anthropology, represented by E. Pittard and others, whose influence over this first phase of 'ethnological' Turkish nationalism has been sensitively traced by Taner Timur [1984].
61. Born four years after Bloch, Fuat Köprülü (or Köprülüzade Mehmet Fuat, as he was called in those days) developed precociously in the midst of the 'hitherto unseen vitality imparted to intellectual and literary activity' by the Young Turks Revolution of 1908 [*Inalcık*, 1968: 289], and joined the editorial boards of major nationalist-populist publications like *Türk Yurdu* (The Turkish Fatherland) and *Halka Doğru* (To The People) – both founded or co-founded by Yusuf Akçura – in 1911–12. Inspired by nationalism to investigate Turkish literature and history, he gradually dissociated himself from the romantic Turkist fervour of his twenties to adopt a moderate liberal position in politics; while this occasionally estranged him from some of the more radical Kemalist reforms, it was perhaps better for his historiography not just because it created a certain defensive distance (which was lacking in Akçura), but also because it provided him with the right temperament for studying the past and continuity with the past – one is reminded here of the paradox of the Roman Catholic and Maurist scholars of the sixteenth and seventeenth centuries. In his Preface to the first Turkish edition of *Les origines de l'Empire ottoman*, Köprülü [1959: 7–10], who read everything, and imbibed French positivism and Durkheimian sociology in his youth, dwelt at great length on his further debt to the *Annales* school. As for the other side of this relationship, the *Annalistes* were certainly aware of Köprülü: Lucien Febvre [1937] personally reviewed *Les origines* in a very favourable way.
62. Köprülü used terms like 'bourgeois', 'petty bourgeois' and 'working class' freely to denote the merchant burghers, guild masters, journeymen and ordinary labourers of medieval Islamic and Anatolian towns. Thus, the *Halvetiyye*, for example, were 'a bourgeois sect that had preserved its Sunni constitution'; it was normal for the *Kazeruniyye* or the *İshakiyye* or the *Mürşidiyye*, too, 'to appear, more or less like other urban denominations, in Sunni form' since they were also 'rooted in the petty bourgeoisie and the working class'; but it was really the *Mevlevis* who were the preferred representatives of 'the higher aristocracy and the upper and middle bourgeoisie' [*Köprülü*, 1935: 161–3] – and who, as such, 'directed violent accusations and even slanders at nomadic Turcomans' which reflect 'the social antagonism between nomads and sedentary populations' [*Köprülü*, 1943a: 435–6, 444; 1935: 99].
63. For the Western reader, Bloch's interest in social anthropology hardly needs to be demonstrated – *Les rois thaumaturges* (1924) is proof enough. Köprülü's is, if anything, more pervasive for being less explicit: his repeated accounts of the breakdown of the Turcomans' kinship-based internal cohesion in the course of being settled territorially and on the basis of individual subordination to the Seljukid sultan

[*Köprülü*, 1938, 1941, 1943a, 1943b, 1944] would be inconceivable otherwise. He specialised, a Yugoslav historian has said, 'in the dark ages stretching from the first clans to the rise of to the rise of the Ottoman Empire' [*Filipovic*, 1955: 30].

64. These were no ordinary schoolbooks: intended to set secondary education on a new footing, they were collectively written and edited by the first nucleus of the Turkish Historical Society in the summer of 1931 [*İğdemir*, 1973: 7, 10].

65. This was not empirical proof but three hypotheses put together, as he admitted [*Köprülü*, 1931: 27, 206–7, 213, 216, 223–4; *Köprülü*, 1935: 181; *Köprülü*, 1938: 52, 56, 57]. But as such, it was not even very logical because it overlooked the fact that the geographical movement involved was one of getting closer and closer to the centre of Byzantine civilisation, where all the institutions of the latter were living on in concentrated and integral form.

66. An entire new literature on processes of nation-state formation in comparative perspective, once more exemplified by B. Anderson [1983], Gellner [1983] and Hobsbawm [1990], amply demonstrates how nationalism is *always* defined by reference to an 'enemy' or an 'other'.

67. I have previously argued this point through contrasts between Mustafa Kemal on the one hand, and Jomo Kenyatta and Vo Nguyen Giap on the other; between the three years it took for the Turkish Nationalists to advance from defeat and occupation to victory in 1919–22, and Mao Zedong's concept of 'protracted war' [*Berktay*, 1987c].

68. This was during a long address to the Grand National Assembly on 1 December 1921. Some members of the opposition had criticised the supremacy of the revolutionary Assembly on the grounds that it 'was neither democratic nor socialist; it did not resemble anything in the textbooks of political theory'. In response, Mustafa Kemal admitted that what they were doing was neither (Western-style) 'democracy' nor (Soviet) 'socialism'. Instead, he said, it was a type of government, based on the new principle of 'national sovereignty', that life itself had given birth to:

> ... We are a poor and labouring people striving to preserve our existence and independence. Let us know where we stand ... Gentlemen! In order to preserve these rights of ours and to secure our independence, we have to pursue a social doctrine which considers it right and just to resist, with our entire national being, imperialism that is trying to destroy us and capitalism which is trying to swallow us wholesale ... So what if it doesn't resemble democracy, it doesn't resemble socialism, it doesn't resemble anything! Gentlemen, we should be proud of not resembling and not forcing ourselves to resemble anybody. For, gentlemen, we resemble only ourselves!

69. It was at this time, for example, that proposals such as Akçura's for radical labour legislation and land reform were rejected and shelved. For a brief history of perennial debates on land reform without any tangible outcome, see Keyder and Pamuk [1984–85].

70. In this regard, Republican Turkey may be said to have had a parliamentary headstart of two or three decades on many other Third World countries precisely because she had an equivalent headstart in achieving national independence and then undertaking her own statist experiment in accelerated, internal market-based development. This also explains why, although Turkish pluralism is not so solid that the country has been entirely able to evade military coups in the past, nevertheless these interventions have been much weaker and shorter-lasting than those that have plagued much of Africa, Latin America or Southeast Asia for many decades [*Berktay*, 1987c].

71. Throughout this period, the Communist Party was always banned and underground. Right-wing extremists, however, including some ultra-nationalist historians of Tsarist Russian origin, were free to propagate 'liberating' the Turkic peoples of the Soviet Union with German support [*Koçak*, 1986: 173ff., 189, 191, 293ff.]. This amounted to a revival of the Panturkist dream that had been rejected by the Kemalist Revolution [*Georgeon*, 1980: 79–81, 83].

72. Mete Tunçay's [1981] on the consolidation of the One Party regime and Cemil Koçak's [1986] on the National Leader period proper are two long and exhaustive studies that dovetail neatly into one another. For Atatürk's foreign policy orientations, see Koçak [1984–85: 13–14]. For the parting of ways between Atatürk and İnönü in the former's last years, also see Koçak [1986: 17–37].
73. For the gradual identification of the RPP with the state, see Karpat [1959: 73ff.]. For the shift towards a pro-German kind of neutrality in 1941–42, see Koçak [1984–85: 21–3; 1986: 176, 183–4]. For the change after Stalingrad and North Africa: also Koçak [1984–85: 23ff.; 1986: 259ff.]. For the eventual crackdown on the pro-German 'Turanist' movement: Koçak [1986: 294ff.].
74. Koçak [1984–85: 21–2] for the maintenance of a precarious balance; again Koçak [1986: 173–4] for how 'the war had moved away from us'; also a personal testimony by İnönü's son-in-law, Metin Toker [1974] – I am grateful to Cemil Koçak for bringing this last source to my attention.
75. The point about isolating the study of any mature state from the study of its formation, its genesis-process, is important. It is this operation which, by cutting off certain characteristics of some 'classical' period from their earlier forms, renders them pure, timeless and absolute. All relative scales are obliterated; it is then that the state appears as the source, the beginning of things. The corollary is that the 'secret' of any state and/or state society can best be deciphered by going back to its formation, its specific genesis. Any ruling class, any founding stratum that seems to 'disappear' from the scene at a later stage is sure to be found there, in the primordial slime of state formation.
76. For the official aversion that had set in at this time, in the late 1930s, to any kind of talk about social classes, see Karpat [1959: 71].
77. Nearly 15 years younger than Köprülü, Barkan (1903–1979) appears to have owed all the major turning points in his life to the Kemalist state. Having grown up in Edirne and attended Edirne Teachers' School, he started his working life as a primary school teacher. After three years, he enrolled at the Faculty of Letters of İstanbul University (still called the *Darülfünun*) in 1924; graduating with a certificate in Philosophy, he was given a state scholarship to receive further training at the Faculty of Letters in Strasbourg for an eventual secondary school teaching career. There, he read not history but general philosophy, sociology and psychology; returning to Turkey in 1931, he was appointed to the Lycée of Eskişehir as a philosophy teacher. Then came the higher education reform of 1933, during which the universities were reorganised, ranks and job definitions established, and talented individuals from secondary education promoted to various academic posts. Barkan, too, was made an associate professor of history at the newly founded Institute of the History of the Turkish Revolution at İstanbul University. The significance of this move has, till now, gone uncommented upon precisely because there have been no proper biographical-ideological studies of modern Turkish historians. At the time the IHTR was the equivalent of an Institute of the History of the CPSU(B) under Stalin – a stronghold of statist ideology where no deviation from the party line would be brooked. Barkan remained within this framework from 1933 to 1937, during the high tide of totalitarianism in Europe and the heyday of the Turkish statist experiment. It was there that he drafted his first articles on Ottoman history, including the famous paper he delivered to the Second Turkish Historical congress in 1937, to be referred to below. It was only in late 1937 that he was transferred to the Chair of Economic History and Economic Geography of the new Faculty of Economics. Thus Barkan was a functionary, a civil servant himself before he came to posit the *sipahis* as nothing but civil servants. And at the time that he spoke of the Ottoman system as 'an order in which everyone worked for the state and the state worked for everyone' [*Barkan*, 1937: 288], the author himself was working for the state and living in an ideological climate where this was standard state propaganda.

78. See, for example, the series of obituaries in the daily *Milliyet* by Lütfü Güçer [1979], Süreyya Barkan [1979], Uluğ İğdemir [1979] and Ali Gevgilili [1979], as well as an appreciation by Robert Mantran [1980].
79. In the same sense that the theory of complementarity and harmony between 'the Three Orders', pace Duby [1980], is nothing but *'l'imaginaire du féodalisme'*.
80. For such observations and statements tending in a relatively universalist direction, see: Barkan [1937-38: 726, 738-9, 743, 745, 748, 775, 782-3, 786]; Barkan [1939-40: 669, 674, 683]; Barkan [1964: 17-19, 26]; Barkan [1970: 166-7]; Barkan [1974: 806, 815, 817]; Barkan [1975: 885-7, 881].
81. By itself, Marxism did not have that much political influence in Turkey when this was written. Radical Kemalists, on the other hand, were politically untouchable but theoretically vulnerable. What Barkan was, consciously or unconsciously, doing in this paragraph, amounts to attacking the anti-Ottomanism of Enlightenment-type Kemalist nihilism by attributing it to socialists, thus killing two birds with one stone.
82. Quoted by Y.S. Tezel [1975: 373], these words are not to be found in the official text of the minutes of the discussion that took place after Barkan [1975] presented his 'Feudal System and Ottoman Timar' paper at a conference in 1973. Nevertheless, they are *echoed* there as well as throughout Barkan's published work (see note 88 below); furthermore, they have never been denied or contradicted after appearing in print 16 years ago, when Barkan was still alive.
83. In terms of subject matter, Barkan's output falls into two main parts. It was only with his 1950 review of Braudel's *La Méditerranée* that he moved on, in the post-war era of Turkey's opening up to the world economy, to historical demography, Ottoman budgets and fiscal surveys, the daily accounts of monumental urban construction projects in İstanbul, and the differential effects of the sixteenth-century price revolution on the Eastern Mediterranean. Before that, land tenure and peasant status formed his original interest and sole topic of concentration for at least 15 years beginning with 1937. Suraiya Faroqhi [n.d.] has perceptively observed that 'in this early period Barkan appears mainly as a legal historian.'
84. What if the Historian, as narrowly defined by Barkan, should, by focusing purely on the individual and the particular, arrive at one conclusion (say, about the 'non-feudal' nature of Ottoman society), whilst the Sociologist, allowed his/her 'successive abstractions', should conclude the opposite, namely, that it was 'feudal'? Let us note that Barkan is very much aware of this possibility, that he even accepts it as probable. But could these two distinct findings then be allowed to exist side by side without infringing upon each other, so that in effect we have separate 'truths' for History and Sociology, and not even an overarching framework for integration, for ordering the hierarchy, between the two?
85. And since Barkan thought of the bulk of European serfdom as arising from the settlement of Roman slaves on the land, like Dühring, he, too, in effect recast medieval peasant cultivaltion as having been invented by lordly action.
86. As indicated above, Barkan went to Strasbourg when Bloch was there, but studied philosophy instead of history. It is to his credit that he still read Bloch's *French Rural History*, which appeared in 1931 – the year Barkan returned to Turkey – probably in the mid-or late 1930s, for there are references to it in his major articles of 1937-38 and 1939-40, where he set out his basic argument for serfs as no better than 'slaves of the soil'. Yet such use as he makes of that work is the very opposite of what Bloch intended. *French Rural History* embodies a very anti-legalistic spirit, as I have tried to demonstrate; Barkan, however, resorts to it time and again in support of all his legal points – it is as if Bloch's injunctions to the contrary were not there at all.
87. And such has been the authority of Barkan, and, following him, of Halil İnalcık, that pegged to their ruling orthodoxy of Ottoman 'differentness', this outmoded notion of feudalism still dominates the Turkish scene in the social sciences. Baykan Sezer [1978: 47, 62], for example, a sociologist working within the framework of traditional empiricism, speaks of 'unanimous agreement' on this point: 'Even the

simplest knowledge of history might tell us that centralism and feudalism are mutually incompatible.' On the same page, the author heaps further abuse on 'such absurdities as centralised feudalism'. In another article of the late 1970s, initially published in English as well as Turkish and hence widely read and reproduced, two AMP theorists also assumed that disdain for 'terms as far-fetched as "centralised feudalism"' was only natural [İslamoğlu-İnan and Keyder, 1977: note 16]. Apart from Barkan, the influence of Perry Anderson [1974a: 148], with his emphasis on 'the parcellisation of sovereignty' as 'constitutive of the whole feudal mode of production', was probably decisive for Turkish AMP theory. And at the economic level, too, for AMP theorists as for Barkan, West European feudalism has been a kind of semi-slave process, organised by lords as big entrepreneurial farm managers, revolving around demesne production based on compulsory labour.

88. Barkan [1937–38: 741]; italics in the original. At this point in his career Barkan actually went so far as to deride liberalism and liberty, the individual and the Code Napoleon, Adam Smith and the French Revolution. He scoffed at 'the individualistic and liberal notions of the Code Napoleon that were once very much the fashion'; he regretted 'a time when the liberal system ... had been accepted as if it were inevitable' [Barkan, 1937–38: 742]. But he congratulated himself that, particularly in matters of land tenure, 'an absolute and uncurtailed right of usufruct, of the sort envisaged by the Code Napoleon, has today been rejected and discarded everywhere' [Barkan, 1937–38: 743]. He said all this to *defend*, in the name of *verstehen*, the propriety of the *raiyyet's* attachment to the soil.

89. A matter of style determined by content, which harkens back to the early conditioning of the historical profession: on each possible point of comparison between Ottoman and medieval Western institutions, in sum and in part, with respect to his overall argument and *vis-à-vis* secondary phenomena like the Ottoman marriage dues (not really like *formariage*, he says, but more in the nature of a modern municipal charge) or the Ottoman warchest tax (the *avarız*, which he says was not really like the *taille* in that it was not 'arbitrary' because it was 'legislated' and therefore part of 'public law'), Barkan reads very much like a lawyer haranguing the court by trotting out every single sophistry available, without regard to whether they are self-contradictory or not, and without regard to the ultimate meaning and worth of the end being sought.

90. This makes about as much sense as any hypothetical assertion by some future historian that Turkish undergraduates enjoyed 'freedom' of organisation in the 1980s because the law says that they were allowed to seek the 'permission' of their university chancellors to set up student unions. Nevertheless, the 10th Turkish Historical Congress in 1986 was largely given over to the sort of propaganda campaign mentioned in the text [Berktay, 1986b], and the 11th Congress in 1990 was not much better.

91. Including Professor Bekir Sıtkı Baykal [1975: 317], who once complained that 'instead of elucidating a problem by screening the sources and imbibing their contents, the sources in question are often presented in their entirety'.

92. In contrast to Barkan, who was shaped by a rigidly claustrophobic statism, Halil İnalcık was still going through his basic training when a new wave of opening up and Westernisation hit post-Second World War Turkey. For a start, he was a student of the very coherent, organised and articulate Köprülü, who was always in touch with international currents. Then from 1945 onwards, İnalcık's career took him repeatedly to Europe and the United States. He worked with Paul Wittek in London in 1949; at various times, he taught, wrote or did research at Columbia, Princeton and Pennsylvania, and he has been permanently at Chicago since 1972. Since 1954, a major part of his output has been published in English. Thus, the continuity of his basic paradigm apart, he has taken full advantage of an age of ampler opportunities to enter the global mainstream in a way that was not possible for his predecessors. The positive effects of interdisciplinary contact, and of the rigour

imposed by producing for the world market, are not to be underestimated. If Barkan was a rude barbarian chieftain pitching his tents outside the city walls, İnalcık would be an urban aristocrat.

93. 'Yet for all the fascination held by popular movements, Marxist history is not just "history from below" (and neither Thompson nor Hill has ever suggested that it is). Struggles between classes are ultimately resolved at the political level, and it is through control of the state that new dispositions of class power are sustained. In fact it can be argued, though it is not very fashionable to do so, that "history from above" is just as important a perspective for Marxist historians' [Tosh, 1984: 145]. Also see an editorial note by Raphael Samuel [1981a].

94. Machiel Kiel [1985: 66] has been perhaps a bit too trusting in his reliance on the major Turkish historians: '. . . Our brief outline of the Ottoman system has perhaps shown to the reader that in the Ottoman system the peasant groups had more room for action and greater opportunities for lending material support to art than peasants in a real feudal society as known in Western European history . . .'. Those actions and opportunities would have to be shown independently, not deduced from (claims on behalf of) the system.

95. Mostly educated at least partially abroad, and with many presently or in the past employed in England, Germany or the USA, a growing group of scholars are distinguished by *not* being nationalist and/or statist in their world view and by *not* being document-fetishists in their methodology. This is not a matter of 'Marxists versus non-Marxists'; these minimal common features, I have argued, are enough to define them as 'non-establishment' [Berktay, 1987b, 1990–91].

96. Quoted by Kiel [1985: 18].

REFERENCES

Akarlı, Engin and Cornell Fleischer, 1990, 'Taking Stock of Ottoman History', unpublished discussion paper read at the Rockefeller Foundation Seminar on Ottoman History held at St. Louis, USA, on 12–15 April 1990.

Akat, A.S., 1977, 'Tarihi Maddecilik ve Kapitalizm-Öncesi Toplumlar: Asya Toplumu-Feodalite Tartışmasına Yeni Bir Yaklaşım' (Historical Materialism and Pre-Capitalist Societies: A New Approach to the Asiatic Society-Feudalism Debate); *Toplum ve Bilim* (Society and Science), No.1, 34–48.

Althusser, Louis and Etienne Balibar, 1972, *Reading Capital*, London: New Left Books.

Anderson, Benedict, 1983, *Imagined Communities: Reflections on the Origin and Spread of Nationalism*, London: Verso (fourth impression 1987).

Anderson, Perry, 1974a, *Passages from Antiquity to Feudalism*, London: New Left Books.

Anderson, Perry, 1974b, *Lineages of the Absolutist State*, London: New Left Books.

Anderson, Perry, 1983, *In the Tracks of Historical Materialism*, London: Verso.

Atatürk, Mustafa Kemal, 1986, 'Hz. Muhammet ve İslamiyet Üzerine Elyazıları' (Manuscripts on Mohammed and Islam), *Saçak* (İstanbul), No.26.

Barkan, Ö.L., 1937, 'Osmanlı İmparatorluğunda Kuruluş Devrinin Toprak Meseleleri' (Land Problems in the Period of the Rise of the Ottoman Empire), in Barkan [1980: 281–90].

Barkan, Ö.L., 1937–38, 'Osmanlı İmparatorluğunda Çiftçi Sınıfların Hukuki Statüsü' (The Legal Status of the Agrarian Classes in the Ottoman Empire), in Barkan [1980: 725–88].

Barkan, Ö.L., 1939, 'Malikane-Divani Sistemi' (The Half-Estate, Half-State System), in Barkan [1980: 151–208].

Barkan, Ö.L., 1939–40, 'XV ve XVI'ncı Asırlarda Osmanlı İmparatorluğunda Toprak İşçiliğinin Organizasyonu Şekilleri' (Forms of Organisation of Agricultural

Labour in the Ottoman Empire in the Fifteenth and Sixteenth Centuries), in Barkan [1980: 575–716].

Barkan, Ö.L., 1957, İktisat Tarihi (Ders Notları). Kitap II: Orta Çağda Batı Avrupa Memleketlerinin Sosyal ve Ekonomik Teşkilatı (Economic History Lecture Notes. Book II: The Social and Economic Organisation of West European Countries in the Middle Ages), İstanbul Üniversitesi İktisat Fakültesi Yayınları (Publications of the Faculty of Economics of İstanbul University), No.97.

Barkan, Ö.L., 1964, '16 Asrın İkinci Yarısında Türkiye'nin Geçirdiği İktisadi Buhranların Sosyal Yapı Üzerindeki Tesirleri' (The Social Consequences of the Economic Crises of the Second Half of the Sixteenth Century in Turkey), in İktisadi Kalkınmanın Sosyal Meseleleri (Social Aspects of Economic Development), İstanbul.

Barkan, Ö.L., 1970, 'Research on the Ottoman Fiscal Surveys'; in *Studies in the Economic History of the Middle East* (ed. M.A. Cook), Oxford: Oxford University Press, pp.163–71.

Barkan, Ö.L., 1974, 'Timar', in Barkan [1980: 805–72].

Barkan, Ö.L., 1975, 'Feodal Düzen ve Osmanlı Timarı' (The Feudal System and the Ottoman Timar); in Barkan [1980: 875–95].

Barkan, Ö.L., 1980, *Türkiye'de Toprak Meselesi. Toplu Eserler 1* (The Agrarian Question in Turkey, Collected Works, Vol.1), İstanbul: Gözlem Yayınları.

Barkan, Süreyya, 1979, 'Osmanlı Tarihi Gün Işığına Çıkarken' (As Ottoman History Emerges Into Daylight); *Milliyet*, 17 Ekim/October.

Baykal, Bekir Sıtkı, 1975, [Interventions during the Seminar on 'The Teaching of History in Turkey' held in Ankara on 13, 14, 15 November 1975], in *Felsefe Kurumu Seminerleri* (Seminars of the Philosophical Society), Ankara, 1977.

Bennett, H.S., 1937, *Life on the English Manor: A Study of Peasant Conditions 1150–1400*, Cambridge: Cambridge University Press; reprinted 1962.

Berger, John, 1972, *Ways of Seeing*, Harmondsworth: Penguin.

Berger, P. and T. Luckmann, 1967, *The Social Construction in Reality: A Treatise in the Sociology of Knowledge*, Harmondsworth: Penguin.

Berktay, Halil, 1983a, *Cumhuriyet İdeolojisi ve Fuat Köprülü* (Republican Ideology and Fuat Köprülü). İstanbul: Kaynak Yayınları.

Berktay, Halil, 1983b, *Kabileden Feodalizme* (From Tribe to Feudalism). İstanbul: Kaynak Yayınları.

Berktay, Halil, 1985, 'Tarih Çalışmaları' (Historiography), in *Cumhuriyet Dönemi Türkiye Ansiklopedisi* (Encyclopaedia of Republican Turkey), Vol.9, Fasc. 78. İstanbul: İletişim Yayınları.

Berktay, Halil, 1986a, 'Uluslararası Marc Bloch Kollokyumundan İzlenimler' (Impressions of an International Symposium on Marc Bloch), I, II, *Tarih ve Toplum* (History and Society), Nos.32, 34.

Berktay, Halil, 1986b, 'İdeolojik Milliyetçilikten Propaganda Güdümlülüğüne' (From Ideological Nationalism to Guided Propaganda); *Tarih ve Toplum* (History and Society), No.35.

Berktay, Halil, 1986c, 'Osmanlı Devletinin Yükselişine Kadar Türklerin İktisadi ve Toplumsal Tarihi' (Economic and Social History of the Turks up to the Rise of the Ottoman Empire); in *Türkiye Tarihi* (History of Turkey), Cilt/Vol.1 (ed. Sina Akşin), İstanbul: Cem Yayınları pp.23–136.

Berktay, Halil, 1987a, 'The Feudalism Debate: The Turkish End: Is "Tax-vs.-Rent" Necessarily the Product and Sign of a Modal Difference?'; *The Journal of Peasant Studies*, Vol.14, No.3, pp.291–333.

Berktay, Halil, 1987b, 'Nokta Dergisinin Tarih Sorularına Cevaplar' (Answers to the newsweekly *Nokta's* questions on history); *Saçak*, No.47, İstanbul.

Berktay, Halil, 1987c, 'Türkiye'nin Özgüllükleri Üzerine Düşünceler' (Thoughts On Turkey's Specificities), I, II; *Saçak*, Nos.41, 42, İstanbul.

Berktay, Halil, 1990, 'The "Other" Feudalism: A Critique of 20th Century Turkish Historiography and Its Particularisation of Ottoman Society,' unpublished Ph.D. thesis, University of Birmingham.

Berktay, Halil, 1990–91, 'The Rise and Current Impasse of Turkish Nationalist Historiography', forthcoming in German translation in *Periplus* (Yearbook of Non-European History), Heidelberg, No.1.
Berktay, Halil, 1991, 'Three Empires and the Societies They Governed: Iran, India and the Ottoman Empire'; *The Journal of Peasant Studies*, this volume.
Bloch, Marc, 1928a, 'A Contribution Towards a Comparative History of European Societies', originally published in *Revue de Synthèse Historique*; also in Bloch [1967: 44–81].
Bloch, Marc, 1928b, 'A Problem in Comparative History: The Administrative Classes in France and in Germany', originally published in *Revue historique du droit français et étranger*; also in Bloch [1967: 82–123].
Bloch, Marc, 1931, *French Rural History: An Essay on Its Basic Characteristics* (translated from the French by Janet Sondheimer), Berkeley and Los Angeles, CA: University of California Press.
Bloch, Marc, 1940, *Feudal Society*, Vol.1: The Growth of Ties of Dependence; Vol.2: Social Classes and Political Organisation (translated by L. A. Manyon), Chicago, IL: University of Chicago Press.
Bloch, Marc, 1941, 'The Rise of Dependent Cultivation and Seignorial Institutions', in *The Cambridge Economic History of Europe, Vol.1: The Agrarian Life of the Middle Ages* (ed. M.M. Postan), Cambridge: Cambridge University Press; second edition, pp.235–90.
Bloch, Marc, 1967, *Land and Work in Medieval Europe: Selected Papers* (translated by J. E. Anderson). London: Routledge & Kegan Paul.
Bois, Guy, 1980 [Remarks during the discussion following Harbans Mukhia's paper], *Compte rendu des séances de la Société d'étude du féodalisme*, 1979–80, III–IV, pp.54–63.
Bois, Guy, 1984, *The Crisis of Feudalism: Economy and Society in Eastern Normandy, c. 1300–1550*, Cambridge: Cambridge University Press; Paris: Editions de la Maison des Sciences de l'Homme.
Bolton, J.L., 1980, *The Medieval English Economy 1150–1500*, London/Melbourne: Dent.
Boratav, Korkut, 1974, *Türkiye'de Devletçilik* (Statism in Turkey), Ankara: Savaş Yayınevi (second edition, 1982).
Boratav, Korkut, 1988, *Türkiye İktisat Tarihi 1908–1985* (Economic History of Turkey 1908–1985), İstanbul: Gerçek Yayınevi.
Carr, E. H., 1961, *What is History?* Harmondsworth: Penguin.
Colletti, Lucio, 1973, 'Marxism: Science or Revolution?', in *Ideology in Social Science* (ed. Robin Blackburn), London: Collins/Fontana, pp.369–77.
Collingwood, R. G., 1946, *The Idea of History*, Oxford: Oxford University Press (reprinted 1986).
Deletant, Dennis and Harry Hanak (eds.), 1988, *Historians as Nation-Builders: Central and South-East Europe*, London: Macmillan.
Dobb, M., 1950, 'A Reply', in Hilton (ed.) [1976: 57–67].
Dobb, M., 1953, 'A Further Comment', in Hilton (ed.) [1976: 98–101].
Dobb, M., 1962, 'Transition from Feudalism to Capitalism', lecture delivered at the University of Bologna, 24 March 1962, and first published in Italian in *Statistica*, April–June 1962; also in Maurice Dobb, *Papers on Capitalism, Development and Planning*, New York: International Publishers, pp.2–16.
Duby, Georges, 1974, *The Early Growth of the European Economy: Warriors and Peasants from the Seventh to the Twelfth Century* (translated by Howard B. Clarke), Ithaca, NY: Cornell University Press.
Duby, Georges, 1978a, 'Medieval Agriculture 900–1500', in *The Fontana Economic History of Europe, Vol. One: The Middle Ages* (ed. C.M. Cipolla), London: Collins/Fontana, pp.175–220.
Duby, Georges, 1978b, 'Féodalités méditerranéennes', *Le Monde*, 27 Oct., p.32.
Duby, Georges, 1980, *The Three Orders: Feudal Society Imagined* (translated by Arthur

Goldhammer; with a Foreword by Thomas N. Bisson), Chicago, IL: Chicago University Press.

Dunn, Stephen P., 1982, *The Fall and Rise of the Asiatic Mode of Production*, London: Routledge & Kegan Paul.

Dyer, Christopher, 1980, *Lords and Peasants in a Changing Society: The Estates of the Bishopric of Worcester, 680–1540*, Cambridge: Cambridge University Press.

Dyer, Christopher, 1984, 'The Social and Economic Background to the Rural Revolt of 1381', in *The English Rising of 1381* (eds. R.H. Hilton and T.H. Aston), Cambridge: Cambridge University Press pp.9–42.

Engels, Friedrich [1877–78], 1976, *Anti-Dühring: Herr Eugen Dühring's Revolution in Science* (translated by Emile Burns), New York: International Publishers.

Engels, Friedrich [1884], 'The Origin of the Family, Private Property and the State', in: Karl Marx and Friedrich Engels, *Selected Works in One Volume*, London: Lawrence & Wishart, 1968, pp.455–593.

Evans, Harold, 1978, *Pictures on a Page*, London: Heinemann.

Faith, Rosamond, 1966, 'Peasant Families and Inheritance Customs in Medieval England', *Agricultural History Review*, No.14.

Faith, Rosamond, 1984, 'The "Great Rumour" of 1377 and Peasant Ideology', in *The English Rising of 1381* (eds. R.H. Hilton and T.H. Aston), Cambridge: Cambridge University Press, pp.43–73.

Faroqhi, Suraiya, 1988, 'New Approaches to Ottoman History', second draft of a paper read at the International Symposium on 'Legalism and Political Legitimation in the Ottoman Empire and in the Early Turkish Republic, ca. 1500 to 1940' held at Bochum on 1–3 December 1988.

Faroqhi, Suraiya, 1991, 'In Search of Ottoman History', paper read at the International Symposium on 'The State, Decentralisation and Tax-Farming, 1500–1850: The Ottoman Empire, Iran and India' held at Munich on 2–5 May 1990, in *The Journal of Peasant Studies*, this volume.

Faroqhi, Suraiya, n.d., 'Ömer Lütfi Barkan', entry submitted to the *Encyclopaedia of Great Historians* (ed. Lucien Boia), Westport, CT: Greenwood Press.

Febvre, Lucien, 1937 [review article on *Köprülü*, 1935], *Annales d'histoire économique et sociale*, Vol.IX, No.43, pp.100–101.

Febvre, Lucien, 1966, 'Preface', in Bloch [1931: xvii–xxi].

Filipovic, N., 1955, 'Müellif Hakkinda Not' (Note on the Author) (translated into Turkish from the original in *Porjekio Osmanske Carevine*, pp.5–12, by M. Tayyip Okic), and included in Köprülü [1981b: 21–31].

Foucault, Michel, 1977, *Discipline and Punish* (translated by Alan Sheridan), New York: Pantheon.

Fryde, Edmund B., 1990, 'The Study of History', *Encyclopaedia Britannica*, fifteenth edition, Vol.20, pp.559–73.

Ganshof, F.L., 1944, *Feudalism* (translated by Philip Grierson), first English edition, with a Foreword by Sir F.M. Stenton, 1952; third English edition, fourth impression, London: Longman, 1971.

Gatrell, Peter, 1982, 'Historians and Peasants: Studies of Medieval English Society in a Russian Context', *Past and Present*, No.96.

Gellner, Ernest, 1983, *Nations and Nationalism*, Oxford: Oxford University Press.

Gevgilili, Ali, 1979, 'Osmanlının Sırları ve Prof. Barkan' (The Secrets of the Ottomans and Professor Barkan); *Milliyet*, 28 Aug.

Georgeon, François, 1980, *Aux origines du nationalisme turc: Yusuf Akçura (1876–1935)*, Paris: Editions ADPF.

Goody, Jack, 1983, *The Development of the Family and Marriage in Europe*, Cambridge: Cambridge University Press.

Goody, Jack, Thirsk, Joan and E.P. Thompson (eds.), 1978, *Family and Inheritance: Rural Society in Western Europe 1200–1800*, Cambridge: Cambridge University Press.

Guerreau, Alain, 1979–80 [Remarks during the discussion following Helene Antoniadis's paper], *Compte rendu des séances de la Société d'étude du féodalisme*, III–IV, pp.5–24.

Guerreau, Alain, 1980, *Le Féodalisme: un horizon théorique* (Preface de Jacques Le Goff), Paris: Editions Le Sycomore.
Güçer, Lütfü, 1979, 'Barkan ile Aydınlanan Tarih' (A History That Barkan Shed Light Upon); *Milliyet*, (?) Sept.
Haldon, John, 1991, 'State Theory and the Medieval State: Some Comparative Perspectives', *The Journal of Peasant Studies*, this volume.
Hale, William, 1981, *The Political and Economic Development of Modern Turkey*, London: Croom Helm.
Hall, Stuart, 1981, 'In Defence of Theory', in Samuel (ed.) [1981: 378–85].
Harvey, Alan, 1989, *Economic Expansion in the Byzantine Empire 900–1200*, Cambridge: Cambridge University Press.
Hibbert, A.B., 1953, 'The Origins of the Medieval Town Patriciate'; *Past and Present*, No.3.
Hilton, R.H., 1953, 'A Comment', *Science and Society*, Fall; also in Hilton (ed.) [1976: 109–17].
Hilton, R.H., 1970a, 'Manor', *Encyclopaedia Britannica*, fifteenth edition, Vol.14, pp.801–3.
Hilton, R.H., 1970b, 'Serfdom and Villeinage', *Encyclopaedia Britannica*, fifteenth edition, Vol.20, pp.244–8.
Hilton, R.H., 1973a, 'The Manor', *The Journal of Peasant Studies*, Vol.1, No.1, pp.107–9.
Hilton, R.H., 1973b, *Bond Men Made Free: Medieval Peasant Movements and the English Rising of 1381*, New York: The Viking Press.
Hilton, R.H., 1976a, 'Introduction', in Hilton (ed.) [1976: 9–30].
Hilton, R.H., 1976b, review article on Anderson [1974a and 1974b], *The Journal of Peasant Studies*, Vol.5, No.3, pp.271–83.
Hilton, R.H., 1979, 'Towns in English Feudal Society', *Review* (Binghamton), Vol.III, No.1, pp.3–20.
Hilton, R.H., 1980, review article on Macfarlane [1978], *New Left Review*, No.120.
Hilton, R.H., 1984, 'Feudalism in Europe: Problems for Historical Materialists', *New Left Review*, No.147, pp.84–94.
Hilton, R.H., 1990a, 'Seigneurie française et manoir anglais fifty years later'; in *Marc Bloch aujord'hui. Histoire comparée et sciences sociales*, Paris: Editions de l'Ecole des Hautes Etudes en Sciences Sociales.
Hilton, R.H., 1990b, *The Change Beyond the Change: A Dream of John Ball*, London: The William Morris Society.
Hilton, R.H. (ed.), 1976, *The Transition from Feudalism to Capitalism*, London: Verso.
Hindess, Barry and Paul Q. Hirst, 1975, *Pre-Capitalist Modes of Production*, London: Routledge & Kegan Paul.
Hindess, Barry and Paul Q. Hirst, 1977, *Mode of Production and Social Formation*, London: Routledge & Kegan Paul.
Hobsbawm, E.J., 1962, *The Age of Revolution 1789–1848*, New York: Mentor.
Hobsbawm, E.J., 1964, 'Introduction', in Karl Marx, *Pre-Capitalist Economic Formations* (translated by Jack Cohen; edited and with an Introduction by E.J. Hobsbawm), London: Lawrence & Wishart.
Hobsbawm, E.J., 1990, *Nations and Nationalism Since 1780: Programme, Myth, Reality*, Cambridge: Cambridge University Press.
Hodgett, Gerald A.J., 1972, *A Social and Economic History of Medieval Europe*, New York: Harper Torchbooks, reprinted 1974.
Homans, George Caspar, 1942, *English Villagers of the Thirteenth Century*, Cambridge, MA: Harvard University Press.
Hopkins, Keith, 1978, *Conquerors and Slaves*, Cambridge: Cambridge University Press reprinted 1980.
Huff, Darrell, 1954, *How to Lie with Statistics*, New York: Norton.
Ingram, J.K., 1887, 'Slavery', *Encyclopaedia Britannica*, fifteenth edition, Vol.2, pp.129–44.
İğdemir, Uluğ, 1973, *Cumhuriyetin 50. Yılında Türk Tarih Kurumu* (The Turkish Historical Society in the Fiftieth Year of the Republic), Ankara: The Turkish Historical Society.

İğdemir, Uluğ, 1979, 'Osmanlı Dünyası ve Yitirdiğimiz Bilgin Barkan' (The Ottoman World and Barkan the Scholar We Have Lost), *Milliyet*, 12 Sept.
İnalcık, Halil, 1968, 'Türk İlmi ve M. Fuad Köprülü' (Turkish Scholarship and Köprülü); *Türk Kültürü* (Turkish Culture), Year VI, No.65 (March).
İnalcık, Halil, 1973, *The Ottoman Empire: The Classical Age 1300-1600*, London: Weidenfeld & Nicolson.
İnalcık, Halil, 1983, [Interview done by the newsweekly *Nokta*], *Nokta*, No.27, p.45.
İnan, Afet, 1939, 'Atatürk ve Tarih Tezi' (Atatürk and His Thesis of History), *Belleten*, Vol.III, No.10, pp.243-6.
İslamoğlu-İnan, Huricihan and Çağlar Keyder, 1977, 'Agenda for Ottoman History', *Review* (Binghamton), Vol.1, No.1, pp.31-55.
İslamoğlu-İnan, Huricihan, 1987, 'State and Peasants in the Ottoman Empire: A study of the Peasant Economy in North-central Anatolia during the Sixteenth Century', in *The Ottoman Empire and the World Economy* (ed. H. İslamoğlu-İnan), Cambridge: Cambridge University Press; Paris: Editions de la Maison des Sciences de l'Homme, pp.101-59.
İslamoğlu-İnan, Huricihan, 1991, *Osmanlı İmparatorluğu'nda Devlet ve Köylü* (State and Peasant in the Ottoman Empire), İstanbul: İletişim Yayınları.
James, Edward, 1982, *The Origins of France: From Clovis to the Capetians, 500-1000*, London: Macmillan.
Jelavich, Barbara, 1973, *The Ottoman Empire, the Great Powers and the Straits Question, 1870-1887*, Bloomington, IN: Indiana University Press.
Jelavich, Charles and Barbara Jelavich, 1965, *The Balkans*, Englewood Cliffs, NJ: Prentice-Hall.
Karal, E.Z., 1975, Interventions during the Seminar on 'The Teaching of History in Turkey' held in Ankara on 13-14-15 November 1975, in *Felsefe Kurumu Seminerleri* (Seminars of the Philosophical Society), Ankara, 1977.
Karpat, Kemal, 1959, *Turkey's Politics: The Transition to a Multi-Party System*. Princeton, NJ: Princeton University Press.
Kennedy, P.M., 1972, 'The Decline of Nationalistic History in the West, 1900-1970', *The Journal of Contemporary History*, No.7, pp.77-100.
Keyder, Çağlar and Şevket Pamuk, 1984-85, '1945 Çiftçiyi Topraklandırma Kanunu Üzerine Tezler' (Theses on the 1945 Law on Land Reform); *Yapıt* (Ankara), No.8.
Kiel, Machiel, 1985, *Art and Society of Bulgaria in the Turkish Period*, Assen/Maastricht: Van Gorcum.
Kitromilides, Paschalis, 1989, '"Imagined Communities" and the Origins of the National Question in the Balkans', *European History Quarterly*, Vol.19, pp.149-94.
Knight, Melvin, 1934, 'Serfdom', *Encyclopaedia of the Social Sciences*, Vol.13, New York: Macmillan, pp.667-71.
Koçak, Cemil, 1984-85, 'İkinci Dünya Savaşı Yıllarında Cumhuriyetin Barış Politikası' (The Peace Policy of the Republic During World War II), *Yapıt*, No.8, Ankara, pp.12-28.
Koçak, Cemil, 1986, *Türkiye'de Milli Şef Dönemi 1938-1945* (The National Leader Period in Turkey, 1938-1945), Ankara: Yurt Yayınları.
Köprülü, Fuat, 1931, 'Bizans Müesseselerinin Osmanlı Müesseselerine Tesiri Hakkında Bazı Mülahazalar' (Some Considerations Concerning the Influence of Byzantine Institutions on Ottoman Institutions), reprinted in Köprülü [1981a].
Köprülü, Fuat, 1935, *Les origines de l'Empire ottoman*, Paris: E. de Boccard; Turkish text reprinted in Köprülü [1981b].
Köprülü, Fuat, 1938, 'Ortazaman Türk Hukuki Müesseseleri: Türk-İslam Amme Hukukundan Ayrı Bir Türk Amme Hukuku Yok mudur?' (Medieval Turkish Legal Institutions: Is There No Turkish Public Law Distinct From Islamic Public Law?); *Belleten* (Ankara), Vol.II, Nos.5-6, pp.39-72.
Köprülü, Fuat, 1941, 'Ortazaman Türk-İslam Feodalizmi' (Medieval Turkish-Islamic Feudalism); *Belleten* (Ankara), Vol.V, No.19, pp.319-34.

Köprülü, Fuat, 1943a, 'Anadolu Selçuklu Tarihinin Yerli Kaynakları' (Local Sources for Anatolian Seljukid History), *Belleten* (Ankara), Vol.VII, No.27, pp.379–522.
Köprülü, Fuat, 1943b, 'Osmanlı İmparatorluğunun Etnik Menşei Meseleleri' (Problems of the Ethnic Origins of the Ottoman Empire), in Köprülü [1981b: 183–307].
Köprülü, Fuat, 1944, 'Kayı Kabilesi Hakkında Yeni Notlar' (New Notes on the Kayı Tribe); in Köprülü [1981b: 309–56].
Köprülü, Fuat, 1959, 'Önsöz' (Foreword), in Köprülü, [1981b, 3–16].
Köprülü, Fuat, 1981a, *Bizans Müesseselerinin Osmanlı Müesseselerine Tesiri* (The Influence of Byzantine Institutions on Ottoman Institutions), İstanbul: Ötüken, 1981.
Köprülü, Fuat, 1981b, *Osmanlı İmparatorluğunun Kuruluşu* (The Origins of the Ottoman Empire), İstanbul: Ötüken, 1981.
Kosminsky, E.A., 1935, 'Services and Money Rents in the Thirteenth Century', *Economic History Review*, Vol.V, No.2.
Kosminsky, E.A., 1955, 'Feudal Rent in England', *Past and Present*, No.7.
Kosminsky, E.A., 1956, *Studies in the Agrarian History of England in the Thirteenth Century* (translated from the Russian by Ruth Kisch; edited by R.H. Hilton), London: Basil Blackwell.
Kuhn, Thomas, 1962, *The Structure of Scientific Revolutions*, Chicago, IL: University of Chicago Press; enlarged second edition, 1970.
Kula, Witold, 1962, *An Economic Theory of the Feudal System: Towards a Model of the Polish Economy 1500–1800* (translated from the Italian edition by Lawrence Garner), London: New Left Books.
Lattimore, Owen, 1957, 'Feudalism in History', *Past and Present*, No.12.
Law, Robin, 1981, 'How not to be a Marxist Historian: The Althusserian Threat to African History', in Samuel (ed.) [1981: 313–19].
Lyon, Bryce, 1966, 'Foreword', in Bloch [1931: ix–xv].
Macfarlane, Alan, 1978, *The Origins of English Individualism*, London: Basil Blackwell.
McLennan, Gregor, 1981, *Marxism and the Methodologies of History*, London: New Left Books.
McNall Burns, Edward, 1941, *Western Civilizations: Their History and Their Culture*, Vol.I, New York: Norton; seventh edition, 1968.
McNeill, William H., 1949, *History Handbook of Western Civilization*. Chicago, IL: University of Chicago Press; fourth impression, 1959.
McNeill, William H., 1986, 'Mythistory, or Truth, Myth, History, and Historians', *American Historical Review*, No.91, pp.1–10, also in William H. McNeill, *Mythistory and Other Essays*, Chicago, IL: Chicago University Press.
Maenchen-Helfen, J. Otto, 1973, *The World of the Huns*, Berkeley and Los Angeles, CA: University of California Press.
Maier, Charles S., 1988, *The Unmasterable Past: History, Holocaust, and German National Identity*, Cambridge, MA: Harvard University Press.
Mann, Michael, 1986, *The Sources of Social Power, Vol.1: A History of Power from the Beginning to AD 1760*, Cambridge: Cambridge University Press, reprinted 1988.
Mantran, Robert, 1980, 'In Memoriam', in *Memorial Ömer Lütfi Barkan* (ed. Robert Mantran), Paris: Bibliothèque de l'Institut Français d'Etudes Anatoliennes d'Istanbul, pp.vii–xvii.
Marwick, Arthur, 1970, *The Nature of History*, London: Macmillan; reprinted with corrections, 1976.
Marx, Karl, 1857–58, *Grundrisse: Foundations of the Critique of Political Economy (Rough Draft)*, (translated with a Foreword by Martin Nicolaus), Harmondsworth: Penguin Books in association with *New Left Review*, 1973.
Marx, Karl, 1859, *Preface and Introduction to a Contribution to the Critique of Political Economy*, Peking: Foreign Languages Press, 1976.
Marx, Karl, 1867, *Capital, Vol.1*, New York: International Publishers, 1967.
Marx, Karl, 1894, *Capital, Vol.3*, New York: International Publishers, 1967.
Marx, Karl and Friedrich Engels, 1845–46, *L'Idéologie allemande*. Selected passages in *Sur les sociétés précapitalistes. Textes choisis de Marx, Engels, Lénine* (Preface de

Maurice Godelier, Centre d'Etudes et de Recherches Marxistes), Paris: Editions Sociales.
Merrington, John, 1975, 'Town and Country in the Transition to Capitalism', *New Left Review*, No.93; also in Hilton (ed.) [1976: 170–95].
Miller, Edward and John Hatcher, 1978, *Medieval England: Rural Society and Economic Change 1086–1348*, London: Longman.
Morgan, Prys, 1983, 'From a Death to a View: The Hunt for the Welsh Past in the Romantic Period', in *The Invention of Tradition* (eds. E.J. Hobsbawm and Terence Ranger), Cambridge: Cambridge University Press, pp.43–100.
Musset, Lucien, 1975, *The Germanic Invasions: The Making of Europe AD 400–600* (translated by Edward and Columba James), London: Paul Elek.
Olcay, Osman, 1981, *Sevres Antlaşmasına Doğru (Çeşitli Konferans ve Toplantıların Tutanakları ve Bunlara İlişkin Belgeler)* (Towards the Treaty of Sèvres – The Minutes of Various Conferences and Meetings and Related Documents), Ankara: Faculty of Political Sciences, Ankara University.
O'Leary, Brendan, 1989, *The Asiatic Mode of Production*, London: Basil Blackwell.
Ortaylı, İlber, 1982, *Gelenekten Geleceğe* (From Tradition to the Future), İstanbul: Hil Yayın.
Ökçün, A. Gündüz, 1968, *Türkiye İktisat Kongresi, 1923 – İzmir* (The Turkish Economics Congress, İzmir 1923), Ankara: Faculty of Political Sciences.
Patlagean, Evelyne, 1988, 'Europe, seigneurie, féodalité: Marc Bloch et les limites orientales d'un espace de comparaison', *Studi Medievali*, Centro Italiano di Studi Sull'alto Medioevo, Spoleto, 3e Serie, XXIX, II, pp.515–37.
Pearton, Maurice, 1988, 'Nicolae Iorga as Historian and Politician', in Deletant and Hanak (eds.) [1988: 157–73].
Perincek, D., 1986, *Osmali'dan Bugüne Toplum ve Devlet* (State and Society from the Ottoman Empire to the Present), İstanbul: Kaynak Yayınları.
Pocock, J. G. A., 1957, *The Ancient Constitution and the Feudal Law. A Study of English Historical Thought in the Seventeenth Century*. Cambridge: Cambridge University Press, a reissue with a Retrospect, 1987.
Pollock, S. and F. W. Maitland, 1968, *History of English Law*, Cambridge: Cambridge University Press, second edition.
Postan, M. M., 1937, 'The Chronology of Labour Services', in Postan [1973: 89–106].
Postan, M. M., 1960, 'The Charters of the Villeins', in Postan [1973: 107–49].
Postan, M. M., 1961, 'Foreword', in Bloch [1941: Vol.1, xi–xv].
Postan, M. M., 1973, *Essays on Medieval Agriculture and General Problems of the Medieval Economy*, Cambridge: Cambridge University Press.
Poster, Mark, 1984, *Foucault, Marxism and History*, Cambridge: Polity Press; third edition, 1990.
Pounds, N. J. G., 1974, *An Economic History of Medieval Europe*, New York: Longman; reprinted 1983.
Power, Eileen, 1963, *Medieval People*, London: Methuen; tenth edition with a new chapter.
Roll, Eric, 1938, *A History of Economic Thought*, London: Faber; fourth edition, 1973.
Rosser, Gervase, 1988, 'London and Westminster: The Suburb in the Urban Economy in the Later Middle Ages', in *Towns and Townspeople in the Fifteenth Century* (ed. J. A. F. Thomson), Stroud, Gloucestershire: Alan Sutton, pp.45–61.
Samuel, Raphael, 1981a, 'People's History', in Samuel (ed.), [1981: xv–xxxix].
Samuel, Raphael, 1981b, 'History and Theory', in Samuel (ed.) [1981: xI–lvi].
Samuel, Raphael, 1981c, 'Editorial Note [to Debates Around *The Poverty of Theory*]', in Samuel (ed.) [1981: 376–8].
Samuel, Raphael (ed.), 1981, *People's History and Socialist Theory*, London: Routledge & Kegan Paul.
Scott, James C., 1985, *Weapons of the Weak: Everyday Forms of Peasant Resistance*, New Haven, CT: Yale University Press.
Sezer, Baykan, 1978, 'Türk Toplum Tarihi Üzerine Tartışmalar' (Debates On Turkish

Social History); *Toplum ve Bilim* (Society and Science), No.4, pp.46–62.
Smith, Richard M. (ed.), 1984, *Land, Kinship and Life-Cycle*, Cambridge: Cambridge University Press.
Stahl, Henri, 1980, *Traditional Romanian Village Communities. The Transition from the Communal to the Capitalist Mode of Production in the Danube Region* (translated by Daniel Chirot and Holley Coulter Chirot), Cambridge: Cambridge University Press; Paris: Editions de la Maison des Sciences de l'Homme.
Stenton, Frank, 1932, *The First Century of English Feudalism 1066–1166*, Oxford: Clarendon Press.
Stenton, Frank, 1952, 'Foreword', in Ganshof [1944].
Stern, Fritz (ed.), 1956, *The Varieties of History from Voltaire to the Present*, New York: Vintage Books; revised edition 1973.
Takahashi, Kohachiro, 1952, 'A Contribution to the Discussion', in Hilton (ed.), [1976: 68–97].
Tekeli, İlhan and Selim İlkin, 1977, *1929 Dünya Buhranında Türkiye'nin İktisadi Politika Arayışları* (Turkey's Search for an Economic Policy During the 1929 Depression), Ankara: Middle East Technical University.
Tekeli, İlhan and Selim İlkin, 1982, *Uygulamaya Geçerken Türkiye'de Devletçiliğin Oluşumu* (The Formation of Statism in Turkey on the Threshold of its Implementation), Ankara: Middle East Technical University.
Tezel, Y.S., 1975, Interventions during the Seminar on 'The Teaching of History in Turkey' held in Ankara on 13–14–15 November 1975, in *Felsefe Kurumu Seminerleri* (Seminars of the Philosophical Society), Ankara, 1977.
Thompson, E.A., 1948, *A History of Attila and the Huns*, Oxford: Clarendon Press.
Thompson, E.A., 1952, 'Peasant Revolts in Late Roman Gaul and Spain', *Past and Present*, No.2, pp.11–23.
Thompson, E.A., 1965, *The Early Germans*, Oxford: Clarendon Press.
Thompson, E.A., 1966, *The Visigoths in the Time of Ulfila*, Oxford: Clarendon Press.
Thompson, E.P., 1978, *The Poverty of Theory and Other Essays*. London and New York: Merlin Press.
Thomson, George, 1949, *Studies in Ancient Greek Society: The Prehistoric Aegean*, New York: The Citadel Press; reprinted 1965.
Timur, Taner, 1984, 'Batı İdeolojisi, Irkçılık ve Ulusal Kimlik Sorunumuz' (Western ideology, Racism, and the Problem of Our National Identity), *Yapıt* (Ankara), No.5, pp.7–30.
Titow, J.Z., 1969, *English Rural Society 1200–1350*, London: Allen & Unwin.
Todd, Malcolm, 1972, *The Barbarians: Goths, Franks and Vandals*, London: Batsford; second impression, 1980.
Todd, Malcolm, 1975, *The Northern Barbarians 100 BC–AD 300*, London: Basil Blackwell; revised edition, 1987.
Toker, Metin, 1974, 'İnsan Olarak İnönü' (İnönü as an Individual), *Hürriyet*, 4 Feb.
Tosh, John, 1984, *The Pursuit of History*, London and New York: Longman; eighth impression, 1989.
Tunçay, Mete, 1981, *Türkiye Cumhuriyetinde Tek-Parti Yönetiminin Kurulması, 1923–1931* (The Formation of One-Party Rule in the Turkish Republic, 1923–1931), Ankara: Yurt Yayınları.
Üçyiğit, Ekrem, 1975, Interventions during the Seminar on 'The Teaching of History in Turkey' held in Ankara on 13–14–15 November 1975, in *Felsefe Kurumu Seminerleri* (Seminars of the Philosophical Society), Ankara, 1977.
Varga, Eugene, 1967, 'Sur le "mode de production asiatique"', *Recherches Internationales*, Nos.57–58, pp.98–117.
Vinogradoff, Paul, 1892, *Villeinage in England*, Oxford: Oxford University Press.
Vinogradoff, Paul, 1911, 'Serfdom', *Encyclopaedia Britannica*, eleventh edition, Vol.24, pp.664–7.
Wallace-Hadrill, J.M., 1952, *The Barbarian West 400–1000*, London: Basil Blackwell; revised edition, 1985.

Wallace–Hadrill, J.M., 1962, *The Long-Haired Kings and Other Studies in Frankish History*, London: Methuen.
Wallace–Hadrill, J.M., 1971, *Early Germanic Kingship in England and on the Continent*, Oxford: Clarendon Press.
Whitelock, Dorothy (ed.), 1979, *English Historical Documents*, Vol.1. London: Eyre Methuen, second edition.
Wickham, C.J., 1984, 'The Other Transition: From the Ancient World to Feudalism', *Past and Present*, No.103, pp.3–36.
Wickham, C.J., 1985, 'The Uniqueness of the East', *The Journal of Peasant Studies*, Vol.12, Nos.2–3, pp.166–96.
Wickham, C.J., 1988, 'Marx, Sherlock Holmes, and Late Roman Commerce', *The Journal of Roman Studies*, Vol.LXXVIII.
Wolf, Eric, 1966, *Peasants*, Englewood Cliffs, NJ: Prentice-Hall.
Wolf, Eric, 1982, *Europe and the People Without History*, Berkeley and Los Angeles, CA: University of California Press.
Wood, Michael, 1987, *Domesday: A Search for the Roots of England*, London: Book Club Associates.
Wölfflin, Heinrich, 1915, *Principles of Art History* (translated in 1932 by M.D. Hottinger from the seventh German edition of 1929), New York: Dover Publications.

Ottoman History by Inner Asian Norms

ISENBIKE TOGAN

INTRODUCTION

The Ottomans founded a state and an empire in which diverse traditions played an important role. It was truly an empire based on a multiple heritage: the Inner Asian, the Anatolian, the Byzantine, the Islamic and Near Eastern and finally the European. The inter-relationships of these different structures and influences contribute to the richness of the Ottoman culture and make the history of the Ottoman Empire a fascinating subject of study, especially as we are dealing with an empire that sustained itself for 600 years. However, students of Ottoman history, using different historical methodologies, differ in their analyses of the structure of the empire over time. Given the multiple heritage of the Ottoman Empire, the major schools of historical research that have developed in European and Islamic history are well represented in Ottoman studies.[1] Therefore current historiography presents rich analogies, parallels and contradictions to both European and Islamic history. Yet the Inner Asian heritage of the Ottoman Empire presents a weak front, although we are fortunate to have a few good studies addressing this issue.[2] Work on the Ottoman Empire's Central Asian antecedents has rarely been undertaken by specialists in Inner Asian studies, but usually takes the form of contributions by Ottomanists to Inner Asian history.[3] Inner Asian history therefore has not so far

---

Professor Isenbike Togan is at the Department of History, Washington University in St. Louis, MO, USA. A first version of this article was presented as a paper to the 'Conference on Ottoman History as Part of World History, Causes and Considerations' (St. Louis, 1990). Ottomanist friends and colleagues have supplied her with copies of their work and thereby provided inspiration for this study. While attending a conference on the Age of Süleyman the Magnificient (20–22 June 1987), a paper by Professor Halil İnalcık first induced her to ask the question she has tried to answer in the present article. A year later when she had the good fortune to read Rifa'at Abou-el-Haj's manuscript on *The Nature of the Ottoman State*, she began to formulate her ideas. Within the collegial atmosphere of the Center for the Study of Islamic Societies and Civilisations at Washington University in St. Louis, a Rockefeller Residency Grant enabled her to discuss some of the issues. Here she would like to express her gratitude to Rifa'at Abou-El-Haj, Engin Akarlı, Suraiya Faroqhi, Cornell Fleischer and Barbara Flemming for their comments and their encouragement. Of course, all errors are hers. The author dedicates this article to Francis Woodman Cleaves and the late Joseph F. Fletcher with gratitude and fond memories.

offered as much of a methodological stimulus to Ottoman historiography as Islamic or European history.

One major reason has been the general orientation of Inner Asian studies. It is generally accepted that the steppe formations were ephemeral states. Hence not their 'short' duration, which was considered axiomatic, but their emergence has been of interest for scholars. However, we also encounter the tendency to concentrate on the 'steppe' as a form of alternative system, a tradition that started with O. Lattimore [1940]. Within this perspective the 'short' durations of different dynasties are not as relevant as their inner dynamic, their systemic characteristics. Seen from this vantage point, the durability of the Ottoman Empire attracts the attention of the historian of Inner Asia. Even for the historian of China, Ottoman durability constitutes a valid issue. Ottoman continuity in change attracted the attention of the Chinese philosopher Kang Yuwei, who in passing through İstanbul in 1908 remarked that the Ottomans had attained constitutional monarchy while the Chinese had not [*Spence*, 1981: 75]. This remark points to the fact that the Manchu dynasty lost its legitimacy in the turn-of-the-century political changes, but the Ottoman dynasty did not. Which factors were responsible for holding together the Ottoman ruling elite? Hogdson [1974: III, 104] thinks that the state apparatus played a crucial role.

Suraiya Faroqhi [1990] ascribes this staying power to the flexibility of the Ottoman system. But what was the basis of this flexibility? What kind of an analogy can we draw between the flexibility in Ottoman politics and the flexibility that we observe in Inner Asian tribal and imperial politics? Inner Asian politics, similar to tribal politics in other regions of the world, present a make-shift appearance due to this flexibility, that we sometimes conceptualise as 'segmentary opposition'. Our vision of Inner Asian structures is still rudimentary. Can analysis of the Ottoman case from an Inner Asian perspective enlighten us about the weak and strong points of these structures?

In the light of the questions above, this article compares the structural changes that the Mongolian and the Ottoman systems went through in the course of their respective existences. The reasons for this choice are several. First of all, neither empire is typical; the Mongols did not form an 'ordinary' steppe empire, nor was the Ottoman Empire typical of a sedentary state. Second, the stimulating effect that the Mongolian imperial traditions had on Ottoman statecraft is recently being acknowledged more and more, so that we can assume a common administrative tradition. Third, for both of the empires we are in possession of abundant source materials and a number of brilliant studies which make comparison feasible. For our purposes, the

Mongolian empire under the Great Khans until 1259 and Mongol rule in China after 1260 will be taken into consideration, while, in the Ottoman case, the entire period of the Empire's existence will be dealt with. The state and the empire that the Mongols founded, and then continued to develop in China under the dynastic name Yuan (1260–1368), presents a stimulating example of a steppe formation on sedentary soil which, in a period of approximately 180 years (1190–1368), went through different phases of historical development, and presents significant analogies to the Ottoman experience. For a comparison of developmental phases we will use the basis of certain common traits which are discernible in population and frontier policies, the adherence of both states to the role of trade routes in empire building, and the tendency of both governments to mete out different treatments to different regions in their respective empires.

In the comparative approach developed here, the notions of 'redistribution of resources and power sharing' and 'accumulation of resources and monopoly of power' will be used as analytical tools. The former two features are frequently encountered among tribal structures and, particularly, among Inner Asian steppe formations. The latter are characteristic of sedentary formations. Both the Ottoman and Mongol empires consisted of populations that were sedentary and others that were nomadic, the latter being mostly of tribal origin. In both cases we witness the problems of articulation or non-articulation of nomadic and sedentary traditions. A close examination, however, reveals that both of the empires employed redistributive as well as accumulative policies at different time periods, and that the choice of one or another of these policies is not related to nomadism or the sedentary life alone. By using redistribution and accumulation of resources as well as power-sharing and monopoly of power as analytical tools, I am seeking a pattern that will help us to better understand the dynamics of the two empires.

In my comparison I will use Inner Asian and, particularly, Mongolian or Turco-Mongolian terminology, so as to present an outlook from the Inner Asian vantage point. My aim is twofold. By analysing Ottoman history with concepts formed when studying Inner Asian dynamics, I hope firstly to raise new questions and generate a discussion on the Ottomans and Inner Asia, beyond the well-established problématique of racial, linguistic and cultural affinity, which has dominated previous discussion.

Second, I hope that by such an analogy we Inner Asianists will better understand the durability of the Ottomans in relation to 'ephemeral' Inner Asian formations. I strongly believe that any further discussion in relation to Inner Asian history can only start from an Inner Asia-centred approach. By using different paradigms from those established by a study of European and Islamic history, we may develop a better understanding of the dynamics of Inner Asian or Ottoman history and, thereby, the dynamics of history in general.

I: TRIBAL POLICIES OF THE OTTOMANS AND MONGOLS

In my comparison, I will start with the tribal policies of the Ottomans and the Mongols. In terms of Inner Asian history it is the mobilisation or distribution of human resources – rather than of land – that is crucial in the formation of steppe empires. A further consideration is that in both cases, people of tribal backgrounds played a fundamental role in the formative periods of both empires. As a second step, I will present a structural analysis of the inter-related dynamics of the Mongolian empire, from its beginnings around 1190 to 1368, the date when the last legitimate Qaghans had to acknowledge that times had changed, and left their seat on sedentary soil in China.[4] As the third step I will proceed to analyse the structure of the Ottoman empire within the paradigms of the Mongolian 'World Empire', as it appeared from a Chinese vantage point. I will, not however, carry the comparison much into the nineteenth century as, at this stage, such a comparison needs to be made within a world historical perspective. Finally, I will point out common features and differences, and formulate new questions that can be asked as a result of these proceedings.

Both the Mongols in their homeland and the Ottomans grew out of populations that were nomadic and had a tribal background. I consciously use the phrase 'populations of tribal background' to differentiate them from 'tribes'. Neither the Ottoman nor the Mongol empire allowed 'tribes' in the narrow sense of the word to play a role at the level of the central government. Both formations grew together with their conquests, and one can discern certain resemblances between their infiltration into foreign territory, as well as their frontier and colonisation policies which were essentially anti-tribal.[5] The anti-tribal policies of the Seljukid, Mongolian and also Ottoman governments are clearly visible in their policies toward their respective frontiers, namely, the *uc* and *tamma* [İnalcık, 1954; Hsiao, 1978]. Because the central governments of the Seljuks, Mongols and Ottomans were anti-tribal in character, they had to develop power bases outside of the tribal context. But even though these states developed outside of their respective 'home bases', Mongolia or Anatolia also served as the respective states' defensive base against populations and interests that had been established earlier;

solidarity based on tribal kinship or urban networks was crucial here.

In the sense that new polities established themselves outside the home base as against the earlier solidarities, the consequent policies look exclusive. Because these polities primarily depended on a group of principal participants (*gazi*, or *nökör*), both the Mongolian and the Ottoman empires have been described in ethnic terms, namely, as Mongol and Turkish, a description which is incorrect for either empire. At the core, in the new political organisations, which at the beginning were mobile, an inclusive policy was maintained. Thus we see people of diverse backgrounds participating in the central administrations of both Ottoman and Mongol empires. At this early period, the core and the periphery were not distinctly separated. It was especially through participants who served in turns at the core and the periphery, that a bond between the two ends was created. This channel was to play a crucial role in maintaining a balance and in providing resilience to the formations.

Both the Mongolian and the Ottoman formations expanded by dispersing the original tribal populations, thus leading to the formation of two empires on the 'frontiers' of older polities and astride trade routes. Moreover, by dispersal the original tribal populations could develop new cultural forms within the cosmopolitan environments they entered. This conscious 'frontier' policy made it possible to wean former tribal populations away from their tribal loyalties and induce them to develop loyalties toward the new centre. By dispersal populations were not expelled from the polity, but charged with an official mission on the frontier. Seljuk, Mongol and Ottoman frontier policies passed through three consecutive stages:

(1) infiltration of people of tribal backgrounds into a new 'frontier' zone (Seljuks into Asia Minor, Mongols into North China);
(2) colonisation and settlement on the new 'frontier', undertaken first by military and then by bureaucratic means;
(3) subordination of pastoral nomadic people and tribal groups to the state administration and the establishment of bonds between the centre and the periphery.

While the first two stages were common to most political structures emanating from the steppe, the third was unusual. For although the Mongols attempted subordination policies, they were not able to institutionalise them. Institutional subordination is a uniquely Ottoman practice and can only be compared to the later Qing (Manchu Chinese) practices of the eighteenth and nineteenth centuries.

Both the Mongols and the Ottomans dealt with tribal populations in three different regions, which differed according to proximity of the tribes to the seat of the relevant central government.

(1) Core Economic Area

In both empires the core area was predominantly agricultural and devoid of tribal groups or populations. The Balkans beyond Edirne and South China south of the Huai River were both key economic areas producing the tribute grains essential to the respective central governments. In China, the core economic area was not partioned as 'appanages' (allotted households), but remained under direct imperial control. In the Ottoman Empire's core area, direct central control existed, but a large part of the arable land was distributed to cavalrymen, who owed service in exchange for the peasant taxes alloted to them [*Togan*, I, 1979].

(2) Strategic Areas Surrounding the Capital (Istanbul and Qanbaligh/ Beijing)

As an intermediate zone separating the core agricultural area and tribal areas, the strategic importance of these areas was due to their position, linking the political centre of gravity with the key economic area. In both the Mongolian and Ottoman empires, this area was protected by troops directly under the control of the central government. At the beginning individual nomads were enrolled in these units. However, in both empires these soldiers of nomad background were not tribally organised, but possessed a strictly military organisation, even though they supported themselves by animal husbandry. In the Ottoman context, these troops were known as the *yörük*. In the Mongol Empire a similar role was played by the 'Mongol Troops' *menggu jün*, and under the Qing the troops consisting of former bannermen fell into the same category. At a later date these troops were gradually replaced by military units under more direct government control, who were preferably selected from groups whose ethnic origin differed from that of the populations they were expected to control. The Ottomans had their janissaries, while the Mongols in China employed Qipchaq, Qangli and Alan troops [*Hsiao*, 1978].

(3) Areas Adjacent to Trade Routes

These areas include those colonised by tribal populations or by people of tribal origin. Ottoman colonisation policies in the Balkans can be understood as a conscious policy of this type. At the time of the Mongolian conquests all of Turkestan (east and west), but especially the Semirechie region was the meeting ground of major long-distance trade routes. It is then no wonder that the Chinggisid princes who had acquired shares (patrimony) in quite distinct parts of the empire, lined up their encampments along routes leading towards Qaraqorum, with Jochi along Irtish, Chaghadai along Ili and Ögedei along Emil [*Barthold*, 1935: 180-81]. Also when the central government allotted households in North China to the princes and notables, locations along trade routes were preferred. In both the steppe regions and in North China, the Mongols stationed troops. Yet in order to sustain the reproduction of the riches of the key economic area in South China, the Mongols avoided bringing troops and tribal populations into this area. Moreover, South China was not located at a crossroads of intercontinental trade routes, a fact which strengthened the Mongolian administration's resolve to keep the princes, the commanders and their troops out of South China. The Ottomans, on the other hand, developed a complex system which included both colonisation and protection of the riches of the key economic area. By incorporating the nomadic populations into the army on an individual basis [*Togan* I, 1979], the trade routes were guarded by people of tribal origin. At the same time, these troops protected the agricultural areas from incursions of pastoral tribes acting on their own initiative.

II. THE OTTOMANS AND MONGOLS: INTER-RELATED POLICIES

As a next step, we will discuss how populations of tribal origin were dispersed into frontier regions, either within the army of conquest or in independent 'conquering' units. For this purpose I will present an overview of the major structural changes which occurred in the history of the Mongolian Empire. We have already noted that, on principle, agricultural areas were kept separate from the pasture lands of the nomadic populations incorporated into the army of conquest. A selective approach to the utilisation of land and the administration of populations was part and parcel of Mongol political and economic policy, which aimed at something which we would today call 'world order'. As I have argued elsewhere, the Mongols seem to have referred to this 'world order' as *jasagh* [*Togan*, ms]. For the Mongols this world order developed within the army of conquest, and the word itself is attested as meaning 'army (military) order' [*Haenisch*, 1962: 86]. In the initial stages of the Mongolian polity *jasagh* implied both equality and hierarchy. *Jasagh* in general is rendered as 'law'. However, the backbone of this initial army order was not law as we understand it today, but inclusiveness, a policy of incorporating people of different backgrounds within the army of conquest. This spirit of inclusiveness permeated the empire, but also became the source of many tensions. Tensions arose among other things, because the Mongolian administration also showed exclusive tendencies at the top level. As a result of these policies and developments, the Mongols were able to keep at bay problems arising from tribal circles.

The systematic incorporation of tribal populations into the structure of the state and empire saved the Mongols from 'internal troublemakers'. The incorporation or complete exclusion of troublemakers enabled the Mongols to focus their attention on issues related to the formulation of steppe traditions and the articulation of those steppe traditions with the traditions of the sedentary regions. We see these developments especially in the economic and political sphere [*Allsen*, 1987]. Steppe traditions favoured redistribution of economic resources and sharing of political power. These steppe traditions from time to time clashed with sedentary traditions, which tended to be accumulative in the economic sphere and monopolistic in the political realm [*Togan and Lam*, 1989]. At the same time the two traditions also interacted, particularly during transitional periods of unusual ideological complexity.[6]

Phase I (1190–1206)

During this period, the Mongol ruling groups created a 'core' state based on *horizontal* relationships among communities whose primary occupation were pastoralism and warfare. This core incorporated different soldiers (*nökör*), irrespective of their ethnic background, creed or language; they were considered to form a group of companions. This organisation was based on inclusion and led to the emergence of the Mongolian state on the frontiers of Inner Asia and China astride the major trade routes [*Ratchnevsky, 1983; Cleaves, 1982*]. The dominant ideology favoured reciprocity and power sharing among companions.

Phase II (1206–34)

During this phase a polity was formed in which *personal* relationships dominated. But earlier horizontal relationships within the context of an army of conquest were now transformed into vertical ones. This resulted in hierarchies. No differentiation existed between civil, military and commercial nodes of power. Conquered populations were divided among comanders of the army of conquest. The political ideology of the period sharply differentiated members of the ruling group from the subject populations. Resources were redistributed from taxpayers to tax takers. Only within the imperial family do we find vestiges of the previous ideology of power-sharing. Otherwise power was now delegated to members of the ruling group within the hierarchical structures of the army of conquest.

Phase III (1251–59)

During this short period, we encounter the beginnings of *impersonal and institutional* relationships. Civil and commercial nodes of power perform separate functions, but military and civilian functions are performed by the same people. These years constitute a transition period towards the formation of a centralised authority [*Allsen, 1987*] and witness considerable ideological conflict. In the economic sphere, resources are redistributed, while in the political sphere accumulation of power is the rule. Within the ruling family, power-sharing is limited to fewer and fewer members, while the right to govern is now limited to a specific line.

Phase IV (1260–94)

Further *institutionalisation* and division of labour are characteristic of this period. Civil and military spheres are now separated, taxation centralised, while in certain spheres of commerce monopolies are instituted. A hereditary stratum of 'princes' comes into being, who along with local religious personnel and sedentary bureaucrats constitute the centre of power. During this bureaucratisation process, some of the earlier commanders become high level bureaucrats, so that the word for commander *noyan* acquires the meaning of 'official'. Concomitant with these changes, a central army without local roots is created. Troops are recruited from the Qipchaq and Alans in Western Eurasia. Merchants, who earlier were partners in state-building, become subordinated as state merchants. We also witness a further dispersal of the earlier 'tribal' elements into the periphery. Central authority, in its search for a balance between the accumulative central apparatus and the key economic area producing the tribute grain, builds the Grand Canal for the provisioning of the capital. Concomitantly the central government cedes a certain autonomy to local 'gentry' in this core area.

The political ideology of the period stresses accumulation both in economics and power relations. Conflicts arising from accumulative policies are solved temporarily by separating out limited spheres in which redistributive modes continue to be applied [*Hsiao, 1978; Rossabi, 1988; Endicott-West, 1989*].

Phase V (1295–1328)

The centre becomes ceremonial in a transition from centripetal accumulative policies to consolidation of dynastic power. This process is symbolised by lateral succession within the ruling family, a system that enables the share-holders of power to compete by putting forward their own candidates among the imperial princes. The contraction of the dynasty in the political sphere is paralleled by the enlargement of the ruling circles and the formation of cliques. Bestowal of princesses plays a role in enlarging the ruling group, as the newcomers are incorporated without creating permanent aristocracies. Thus a new centre is formed, incorporating both old and new shareholders of power. These consist of princes, core army, scholar officials and local gentry, the configuration as a whole is known as 'Conquerors and Confucians'.

On the ideological level, redistributive patterns re-emerge and benefit the newcomers. Representatives of the core economic area and the sedentary periphery are included in the ruling group, but the nomadic periphery continues to be excluded. This re-emergence of redistributive patterns and power-sharing is also apparent from the marriage customs of the dynasty [Dardess, 1973; Holmgren, 1986].

Phase VI (1328–68)

In this phase, we observe constant conflict at the centre, described as clashes between 'conservatives' and 'reformists'. The views and aspirations of the reformist sedentary periphery turn into the ideology of the central apparatus. The conflict between redistribution and accumulation is resolved in favour of accumulation. Even power-sharing ultimately favours central autocratic authority, for as the sedentary periphery feels in control it attempts to eliminate other power-sharers.

On the ideological level, emphasis shifts from redistribution to accumulation and from power-sharing to autocracy in the sedentary domains. Redistributive ideology and power-sharing are upheld in the nomadic periphery with attendant fragmentation of political authority, thus leading to the emergence of new tribes and retribalisation.

Phase VII

The people of the sedentary periphery take over the state and found a new dynasty, the Ming 1368–1644. The political ideology of the time emphasises the accumulation of power in the hands of a newly formed ruling group, which legitimises itself by assigning autocratic powers to the recently enthroned Ming Emperor.

In the Mongolian case, the ruling groups demonstrate considerable flexibility, which involves fairly abrupt changes of political style. A redistributive mode is adopted in the early stages of empire formation, which facilitates the incorporation of new elements into the ruling group. The latter can thereby expand the territory under its control. Since the ruling group is both flexible and inclusive, what has been termed the 'ladder of success' is accessible to quite a few people regardless of class or ethnic backgrounds. However, at a later stage, the ruling group switches to an accumulative mode, thereby contracting and consolidating its power at the same time.

III. THE OTTOMAN EMPIRE AND THE MONGOL 'WORLD EMPIRE'

Flexibility and inclusiveness are also familiar themes in the policy of the Ottoman Empire, when one examines it according to Inner Asian norms. Like its Mongolian counterpart, the Ottoman world order as exemplified by sultanic law (*Kanun*) stood for inclusiveness and for an open society. Although the '*kanun*' was a creation of the Ottoman ruling group and upheld the latter's privileges, its stated intention was to make justice available to everyone. However, the Ottomans were far more successful in transforming their ideas of 'world order' into reality than the Mongols had ever been, and in the Ottoman Empire during its period of florescence, the '*kanun*' was applied more consistently than was ever true of the *jasagh*. In the following presentation I will give a partly narrative and partly analytical account of Ottoman empire building. I deliberately use Inner Asian terminology in parenthesis, so as to point to parallel traditions.[7]

Phase I (1290–1360)

In this phase, there develops a political core group, based upon *horizontal* relationships among communities whose primary occupation was pastoralism and predatory warfare. This core was an organisation incorporating, as companions, people irrespective of their ethnic background, creed or language. This organisation that sometimes has been called *bölük* [İnalcık, 1981] was based on inclusion. Thus came into being the principality of Osman, forerunner of the Ottoman state, securing itself a place on the frontiers of Islam between the Seljuks and the Byzantines. This polity was founded by a '*gazi*' leader in frontier politics and warfare, along with his 'companions' (*nököd* < sing. *nöker*) [Lindner, 1983]. *Gazis* as warriors were joined by dervishes who played an important part among these groups from the beginning; their role may be compared to the role of merchants in the Mongolian formation. (The merchants who were really the Mongols' partners in state building were called *ortak* or *ortogh* [*Togan* I, 1984; *Allsen*, 1989, *Endicott-West*, 1989].) Among the Ottomans the partners (*ortak*) of the ruling group were not merchants but dervishes and religious scholars. Thus while the

Mongols based themselves on a secular platform, mediating between competing religious groups while committing themselves to none, the Ottomans were closely associated with Islam right from the beginning. The relationship among participants in the political enterprise was primarily one between companions, and therefore reciprocity and equality were the norms. This trend can also be observed within gender relations. Women were active partners in negotiations and transactions with friend and foe, possessed forms of organisation (for instance, the so-called 'Sisters of Rum') and established relations of interdependence between members of different communities within the political core. The political ideology current in this milieu emphasised reciprocity and power-sharing among companions.

Phase II (1360–1453)

However, slowly horizontal relationships changed into vertical ones. This process began when sizeable numbers of men entered the service of the 'companions (*nököd*)'. These men were later called *sipahi*, meaning 'mounted', and they functioned like the Mongolian *albatu* of the later times, those free people who owed services to their leaders [*Schurmann*, 1956b; *Vladimirtsov*, 1944]. The obligation (*alba*) of the *sipahi* was to serve in the army and supply additional men recruited from local subject populations, called *cebelu*, meaning 'armoured'. The case of the *sipahi* shows us how the Ottomans used concepts and terminology on a more 'individualistic' basis than was current in Inner Asia, where the *nökörs* are referred to only as followers.

The Ottomans used *cebelu* for soldiers who had been recruited by individual participants in the polity, namely, the *sipahi*. Soldiers from subject populations recruited by the Ottoman central administration were called *yeniçeri*. The parallel to the Mongolian usage is evident, as in Mongolian the term *çeri* (*cherig*) also was used for soldiers from subject populations. *Yeniçeri* thus meant *cherig* organised in a new style. Whereas the Mongols did not distinguish between different methods of recruitment, the Ottomans devised fine distinctions which later gave them more elbow-room and greater flexibility. In Ottoman parlance, the *sipahi* who supplied *cebelu* was called *tımarlı sipahi*. While in the Mongolian context, the warrior's obligation (*alba*) was emphasised, the Ottoman term specified that the *sipahi* was a cavalryman equipped with a source of livelihood. This source of livelihood had a parallel in the Mongol context, namely a share in the population allotments (*qubi*) assigned to every warrior. Again there is an important distinction between Mongolian and Ottoman terminology: Mongolian parlance emphasises rights according to earlier tribal customs, which take the form of a *qubi* (share). Ottoman parlance emphasises the institutional patterns, that is, the sources of continuity. Although a *tımarlı sipahi* was given a specific share (*qubi*) of the revenues collected from the local population, the concept of 'share' was not emphasised in Ottoman usage. The term *qariyatu* ('those with a relation'), which the Mongols came to use for subject populations, the Ottomans rendered by the term *reaya*, usually translated into English as 'flock'. At this juncture it can only be said that both *reaya* and *qariyatu* denote a following and are thus not emic but etic terms, reflecting the terminology of the rulers.

During this period, the Ottoman leaders were also first addressed as '*bey*', corresponding to *noyan* in Mongolian. At this juncture one-person leadership was not developed; dual leadership and sharing of power among elder and younger brother (*aqa* and *ini* in the Mongolian terminology) was also current among Ottomans. The Ottomans, like the Mongols, did not distinguish between civil and military authority. However, their judiciary personnel consisted of the *kadi's* (judges trained according to the precepts of Islam), whereas Mongolian judges (*jarghuchi*s) from the earliest times onwards were 'secular' officials.

At about this time, the Ottoman rulers also instituted palace guards (Mongolian counterpart: *keshig*) and a standing army constantly at the beck and call of the central government (Mongolian counterpart: *ghol*). These military men were recruited from the local population, and called *yeniçeri*. The establishment of the *yeniçeri* as a military unit recruited from the subject populations represent an early divergence from the redistributive pattern that dominated the Ottoman centre's relations with the *tımarlı sipahi*. Candidate janissaries joined the army not as a privilege but as an obligation, and with a hierachically structured army at the centre, little remained of the 'companionship-in-arms' which had previously characterised relations between the Sultans and their followers.

With the introduction of the *yeniçeri*, the Ottomans quite early in the history of their state attempted to include military talent from the subject population. In this respect, the Ottomans went much further than the Mongols, who, as we have seen, also had an inclusive army of conquest. But among the Mongols the guards (*keshig*) were recruited from the leading families who had been participants in early stages of the polity; in the Ottoman context, the equivalent policy would have been to recruit the guard from the sons of the *sipahi* leaders most favoured at court. Unlike the Mongols, the Ottomans did not keep the descendants of the early members of the polity at the centre, but sent them to guard the frontiers as quasi-independent *uc beyi*. This method was also employed by the Mongols, as part of their policy of population dispersal. Among the Mongols, leadership both at the centre and at the periphery was open to the descendants of those who had founded the initial polity, but among the Ottomans, only leadership at the periphery was open to members of this group.

With the establishment of the *çeri* (*keshig*) at the centre, the Ottoman rulers assumed greater importance, however they still functioned as lords (*beys*) among other *beys*. But with time, the Ottoman rulers assumed the role of the overlord, *khan* in Turco-Mongol parlance, and called themselves *han*. However, they continued to form marriage alliances with other *bey* families. But I am not sure whether the Ottoman ruling family gained status by these marriages, and whether these were cases of hypogamy for the dynasties marrying their daughters into the Ottoman ruling family. My impression is that there was no ranking involved among the dynasties, perhaps because the Ottomans were latecomers into the community of *beys*. When the Mongols established their *keshig* as a symbol of the centre, they previously had eliminated most of their rivals. By marrying the daughters of defeated rivals, princes of the Mongol ruling family asserted themselves and gained status. Their partners on the other hand acknowledged defeat by accepting hypogamy, and this situation is sometimes described as 'descending from their ranks'.

Close associates of the participants in state-building acquired their *qubi*-shares in titles and households; this presupposes the notion of 'sharing', a phenomenon that historians have called *ülüş* [*Togan, Zeki Velidi*, 1970: 284–301]. But as mentioned earlier, personages who received major shares of the ruler's resources were associated with the periphery as *uc beyi* or *akıncı beyi* and their connection with the centre remained tenuous. In the meanwhile, the House of Osman, as the ruling family, concentrated power as the polity's centre and developed as a dynasty.

In this second phase political ideology fluctuated uneasily. At certain times, Ottoman rulers were willing to share power, particularly with commanders active on the Rumelian frontiers. But accumulation of power was also noticeable, particularly with respect to the remaining Anatolian principalities; and this trend precipitated Timur's intervention in Ottoman affairs. In terms of leadership during the reign of Bayezid we observe a shift from sharing power to rule by a single ruler. Yet after the 1402 defeat by Timur joint rule by brothers reasserted itself within the dynasty. Moreover, the Ottoman Sultans in Anatolia had to reckon with a number of principalities, previously conquered by Ottoman arms, but reestablished by Timur. But during the reign of Murad II, one-man leadership was once again firmly established.

Phase III (1453–1512)

After 1453 the trend is towards an institutionalisation of the central authority. Centralising politics and the tools of centralisation emerged in the Ottoman Empire as in the corresponding phase of Mongol rule. Yet there was a major difference. Whereas the Mongols could only achieve a monopolisation of authority at the centre by allowing members of the ruling group larger slices of revenue, thereby continuing to operate in a redistributive mode, the Ottomans were able to combine a monopoly of power with accumulative trends in the fiscal sphere as well [*Togan and Lam*, 1989]. The nodes of opposition to the policies of accumulation are again very different. In the Mongolian case, opposition came from the members of the ruling family itself and from an earlier core of the 'companions' and their descendants.

The Ottomans, on the other hand, had by this phase resolved the problems related to the ruling family, at least in theory. Due to the institution of fratricide at the beginning of each reign, the Sultan was secure from competitors until his own sons grew up. Ottoman rulers had also eliminated all the other centrifugal forces, namely, earlier companions of the rulers and Anatolian *beys*. The latter were either eliminated or kept busy at the frontiers, and hence had autonomy in the periphery but no status at the centre. Their autonomy at the periphery, however, made them participants in the overall order of the Empire.

Opposition to Ottoman accumulative policies came from the nomadic populations of the realm. But this obstacle was overcome by various means. Nomads were attacked by the central government's troops, decimated and induced to settle or emigrate. In no case did the central government give in to the demands of its nomad subjects [*Togan I*, 1979]. But the opposition of the religious establishment could only be resolved by a new balance of redistribution [*Fleischer*, forthcoming], which involved not the peripheral military (the *tımarlı sipahi*) but landed religious establishments (*evkaf*) both in the central provinces and on the periphery. Disagreements over redistribution were also voiced by the central military organisation, the *yeniçeri*. These struggles over redistribution are of special interest to the historian, as they indicate that the religious establishment and the janissaries claimed a share in political power; these groups were to remain major contenders down to the nineteenth century.

On the ideological level, certain parallels exist between Ottomans and Mongols. Again we encounter a conflict between redistribution in the economic sphere and accumulation in the political sphere. Political writings of the time reflect growing accumulation. Thus the historian

Aşıkpaşazade bitterly criticised increasing taxation and the growing distance between rulers and ruled.

Phase IV (1512–66)

Institutionalisation is the major aspect of this period, especially apparent under Süleyman the Lawgiver. Separation of the military and civil spheres is not as clear as among the Mongols in China. The most outstanding characteristic of this period is the creation of a new centre of power at the Palace. Servitors of the Sultan (*kul*) are recruited from the old elite but also from the conquered population, leading to the formation of a standardised bureaucracy. Among the Mongols the same function was carried out by the *keshig*, the 'guard'. However, the *keshig* consisted of the sons of the earlier 'companions', and thus constituted the elite of society, later connected to the hereditary stratum of 'princes'. They thereby became an exclusive element, while the Ottoman *kul* system allowed the inclusion of selected representatives of the conquered population and of 'outsiders' who had been in the service of foreign, particularly Iranian rulers. Yet channels for exclusive promotion were also allowed to the sons of important officials who were recruited into the Palace as *müteferrika*. Here we encounter another aspect of Ottoman flexibility; however, this privilege applied only to the first generation of officials' descendants.

Mongolian central authority, in its search for a balance between the accumulative central apparatus and the tribute-grain-producing key economic area, had built the Grand Canal for the provisioning of the capital. While the Mongolian government ceded a certain autonomy to local 'gentry' in the core area, the Ottoman government seems to have done this in a more selective way, as Margaret Venzke [1990] shows in her study on Ottoman Aleppo and Damascus. In this context, certain merchants also acquired a political role, even though it remained minor. In earlier phases, Muslim merchants, the so-called *ortak*, had been partners of the Mongols, yet with the creation of princedoms, merchants had been brought under control in a situation reminiscent of Hodgson's military patronage state [*Hodgson*, 1974, Vol.2]. The merchants became instrumental in the provisioning of the capital as 'state merchants' [*Schurmann*, 1956a]. At the same time local religious personnel and sedentary bureaucrats were incorporated by the Mongols into the administrative centre, but as subordinate elements. Among the Ottomans, on the other hand, the trend was more consistent with their earlier policies. Merchants had never been political partners, and now as 'state merchants' they were employed in the provisioning of the capital [*Genç*, 1989; *Greenwood*, 1990]. Religious personnel retained their participatory role, and they became more and more firmly established as one of the pillars of the bureaucratised state.

During this period of institutionalisation, the Ottomans also made a distinction between *reaya* who were sedentary and cultivated the soil, and those who were nomads and called *il*. Among the Mongols such a distinction between nomad and sedentary subject populations did not exist. The Mongolian ruling group made a distinction between those subjects who submitted, whom they called *il*, and those who refused to submit, whom they called *bolgha*, 'rebel'. After submission, most of the *il*s were made part of the conquering armies. By the same token, the nomads did not acquire the status of tribute-paying subjects. Later on in history, when subjugation was no longer at issue, subject populations, whether nomad or sedentary, were all called *qariyatu*. Here, we again see a difference between the Mongolian and Ottoman policies. The Mongols were primarily interested in the subordination of tribal and nomadic people, and in incorporating them into the hierarchical system of the army of conquest. Thus the latter became part of the ruling group. The Ottomans, on the other hand, were more interested in balancing political power and economic strength; as a result merchants were not admitted to the councils of the rulers, while an influential current of opinion, derived from Ibn Khaldun, held that Ottoman administrations should not involve themselves in profit-making activities.

Ottoman tribal policies were also aimed at creating a balance between political and economic power. Tribes (*aşiret*) in eastern Anatolia were allowed to maintain their political and ethnic identity with little gain on the economic front, while nomadic populations in the west were not tribally organised (*yörük*) but could enrich themselves by involvement in the market; these non-tribal *yörük* also had economic ties with the central government apparatus. As mentioned earlier, still other nomads were incorporated into the army, serving on the periphery [*Togan*, 1979]. In other cases tribes which the central government regarded as dangerous were despoiled and killed off. However, among those who continued to be part of the Ottoman Empire, tribal leaders did exist. But in the course of time the latter were transformed into administrators of their own tribes on behalf of the Ottoman government, and stopped being autonomous leaders of their tribes in peace and war. By accepting to be part of the Ottoman Empire, tribal leaders limited intertribal warfare and adopted a non-predatory policy, concentrating upon civilian matters. They certainly did not live in a particularly peaceful world; but now their problems were not so much with one another but with the Ottoman centre. Other earlier military leaders in the Ottoman Empire also acquired a place in the civil administration. Ottoman commanders and chiefs of police were called *subaşı* (leader of the soldiers), comparable to the Mongolian terms *jaghun-u noyan, mingghan-u noyan, tümen-ü noyan* which denote a *noyan*, namely, a leader of a hundred, thousand, ten thousand soldiers; these military leaders also in time acquired civilian functions. Another commander who performed administrative duties was the Ottoman *sancak beyi* meaning the bearer of a banner, a position resembling the *touxia* commanders among the Mongols in China [Ratchnevsky, 1966]. Both of these positions emerged at a time when there were no clear-cut boundaries between military and civil administration; officials retained their military character, but functionally they became more and more involved with civilian matters. Thus administrators retained a flexible position and could be employed in both the military and civilian realms. Among the Mongols in China, however, the changeover from a military to a civilian function was definitive.

The Mongolian *noyan* became a purely civilian rank and came to correspond to the Chinese *guan* 'a high official'. The *touxia*, namely, the commanders with banners of their own did not acquire civilian functions and their offices simply disappeared. Some of the commanders were made *guan* and thus lost their military role. Their troops were made to join the peasent households in Northern China. As the position of the *sancak beyi* could be incorporated into the Ottoman civil administration, whereas the Mongolian equivalent, the *touxia*, could not, the Ottoman government remained especially flexible. The Ottomans seem to have achieved flexibility by retaining a dual system of ranking, in which military and civilian functions were carefully balanced.[9]

As a result, the Ottomans were able to function on a dual level, with centralisation and subordination at the centre and autonomy at the periphery. The Mongols in China, however, adopted the Chinese system of ranking which was purely civilian in principle; moreover, their peripheral 'nomads' were incorporated into the central system as followings of princes. But this solution encountered fierce opposition from those who did not wish to closely be integrated within the system. This opposition could not be resolved by a centre that put sedentary interests first. As the nomadic periphery was not integrated into the central state, centre and periphery went their separate ways, a Mongolian version of the division between the steppe and the sown. The subsequent collapse of Mongolian administration in China is to be understood in this context.

Phase V (Seventeenth and Eighteenth Centuries)[10]

In terms of general characteristics, the Ottoman polity shows features that parallels those of the Mongolians in Phase V, even if the genesis is different. Instead of going into long detail, I will repeat what I have already said for the Mongols, mentioning the appropriate Mongolian institutions or groups in parenthesis.

> The centre becomes ceremonial in a transition from centripetal accumulative policies to a consolidation of dynastic power. This process is symbolised by lateral succession within the ruling family, a system that enables the share-holders of power to compete by putting forward their own candidates among the imperial princes. The contraction of the dynasty in the political sphere is paralleled by the enlargement of the ruling circles and the formation of cliques. Bestowal of princesses plays a role in enlarging the ruling group, as the newcomers are incorporated without creating permanent aristocracies. Thus a new centre is formed, incorporating both old and new shareholders of power. These consist of the Ottoman Palace (princes), core army, the *ulema* (scholar officials) and urban and rural notables (local gentry), the configuration as a whole is known as the Sultanate of Women (Conquerors and Confucians).

The peculiarity of this era is not so much the change in actors, as the shift of emphasis from a monopoly of power in the hands of the Sultan to a renewed sharing of power. Power is not any more monopolised by the Sultan alone, it is a group of power-holders who count. At the same time, there is a distinct change in terms of goals and values. Martial values are replaced by a civilian value system. This change is most apparent in the household of the Sultan, the Palace. Earlier a ruler's charisma and his success on the battlefield were the factors deciding his success. Later in the early seventeenth century self-willed rulers like Genç Osman were confronted with serious opposition; their will to dominate was not tolerated; however, there were also great exceptions like Murad IV (1623–40). To mention another example: down to the late sixteenth century, princes had been sent out to the provinces to develop their character and administrative skills. But from the late sixteenth century onwards, neither an outstanding character nor administrative skills were needed for the members of the dynasty. They only needed to play their role patiently while awaiting their turn according to the rules of seniority.

A shift of emphasis towards civilian values can also be observed in the administration of justice. Both the Mongol and the Ottoman rulers claimed that their chief duty was to bring justice. The Mongols used *jarghuchi* (judges) whose functions were not defined as civilian, as those functionaries also commanded armies. From the outset the Ottomans appointed civilian judges, trained in the Islamic sciences.

These civilian judges also functioned as 'military judges' (*kadıasker*), a term which denoted one of the highest ranks in the judicial hierarchy. No army commanders were ever appointed as judges. This does not mean, however, that military commanders did not dispense justice. At certain times, commanders of armies acting as governors held 'court' in the tribal fashion. But these were extraordinary times, times of 'martial' law as we would call it today. The Ottoman system differed from the Mongolian due to the religious training of the *kadı* and the extension of his civilian functions into the military-administrative realm. From the beginning the *kadı* was instrumental in implementing a balance between the taxpayers and the tax collectors, interfering in case of abuse. He possessed jurisdiction over disputes between the subject population (*reaya*) and the *tımarlı sipahi* and thus was responsible for keeping fundamental class conflict within manageable limits. As a result of this position the Ottoman *ulema* were able to carve for themselves a secure place in the Ottoman polity.

At this crucial juncture the Mongols failed. They employed merchants as tax collectors, and encouraged merchants to become tax farmers, thus giving rise to much resentment as these merchants also lent money at high interest so that the taxpayers were caught up in a vicious cycle. Among the Ottomans, on the other hand, when tax farming became prevalent in the seventeenth and eighteenth centuries, even where the tax farmers were merchants, they tended to identify with local interests. Some of these tax farmer merchants developed into *ayan* (notables). Sometimes the opposite development occurred, in that the local *ayan* won control over tax farming, keeping local funds in the locality instead of remitting them to the centre. One of the very effective local forces were again the *ulema*, including *muftis*, the *kadıs* and other religious dignitaries and scholars. They came from various social backgrounds, upholding the Muslim ideal of equality, so that in each locality they also acted against any kind of aristocratisation. As they controlled pious foundations (*vakıf*, pl. *evkaf*) they asserted themselves quite effectively.

For a long time the *ulema* shared the inclusive spirit of the Ottoman state and empire; recruitment was not limited to one particular social group, but open to anyone who possessed the means and the will to undergo an arduous period of training. In the late fifteenth century, they successfully resisted accumulative trends in state policy that would have harmed their own independent existence, keeping their hold on the *vakıf* down into the nineteenth century.

Independent control of *vakıfs* by the *ulema* implied retaining some redistributive trends in the economy while accumulative tendencies ruled at the centre of power. Nor was this an isolated case, as the allotments of the *tımarlı sipahi* were also aspects of a redistributive policy in the provinces, that went hand in hand with accumulative taxation policies at the centre. Thus accumulative tendencies found expression in the dynasty and the central government apparatus, whereas redistributive tendencies dominated in the provinces both among the *ulema* and the *tımarlı sipahis*. By the seventeenth and eighteenth centuries such redistributive tendencies were no longer confined to the *ulema*, but also evident in tax-farming, in the emergence of the *sekban* as alternative provincial forces sustained not by allotments from the central administration but out of funds provided by provincial administrators.

Because the state apparatus was able to accommodate both accumulative and redistributive tendencies, it was flexible. Or maybe it was able to accommodate the two modes because of its flexibility. In either case it is evident that the *ulema* planted the seeds for future developments simply by holding on to their *evkaf*. Because the Ottomans had by this time acquired 'flexibility' as an administrative tool, they could adjust to the pressures of the seventeenth and eighteenth centuries. Islam with its emphasis on equality among Muslims and on a society open to all, was another factor which strengthened the position of the *ulema* in their effort to enforce redistributive policies. In the eighteenth century the *ulema* nolens volens underwrote the expenditures of the central government by allowing the siphoning off of *evkaf* revenues to pay the salaries of 'civil' offials [*Faroqhi*, 1985]. Concominant with these developments in the periphery, the *ulema* at the centre were co-opted into the bureaucracy and developed tendencies toward hereditary office holding; this phenomenon again demonstrates the tension between redistributive and accumulative tendencies which characterised Ottoman history throughout the centuries.

CONCLUSION

From the above comparison of the development of the Mongolian and Ottoman empires along a line of analysis inspired by Inner Asian formations, the Ottomans stand out by two traits: first, by developing dualistic structures and, secondly, by their tendency to orient themselves towards the needs of civilian populations. In the course of time, their administration acquired further skills maintaining these dualistic structures even though modes of recruiting completely changed. In spite of a strict differentiation between the taxpayers and the political class, the ladder of success was kept open. Yet this system had its limitations. In the pre-nineteenth century period, political mobility was available to those who confessed Islam, although they did not need to be born Muslims. But in the nineteenth century the empire evolved into a loose structure with many nodes of power deriving their strength from religious, linguistic and cultural affinities. This ultimately resulted in the dissolution of the empire into a large number of nation states, which claimed to be based upon 'open societies' in the modern sense of the word [*Tietze*, 1990].

The general histories of the Ottoman and Mongolian polities from the thirteenth to the nineteenth century can be summarised as the articulation of redistributive (tribal) traditions with accumulative (imperial) institutions. This articulation manifests itself in the way redistributive traditions were maintained at the periphery while the centre switched to accumulative policies.[11] 'Inner Asian' redistributive traditions go hand in hand with power-sharing, with many autonomous nodes of power. The *bey* phenomen as discussed above constitutes the first step towards such an articulation. Once the *bey* is not bureaucratised in name and function, but incorporated into the system of governance, redistributive as well as power-sharing tendencies are incorporated into the larger system. This might be termed synchronic flexibility, the ability to incorporate accumulative and redistributive tendencies within the same system. In the fifteenth century, the Ottomans allowed redistributive tendencies to prevail in the borderlands. But an important subgroup of the political class, namely the *ulema*, adopted these redistributive and power-sharing tendencies and thereby spread them throughout the system, so that by the seventeenth century, there existed a strong alliance in favour of power-sharing, namely, peripheral *beys*, the new *ayan* and the *ulema*, while the janissaries and irregular soldiers also demanded a share in political power.

During the early seventeenth century 'Sultanate of Women', moreover, the Palace as an institution acquired political power. Alliances in favour of power-sharing were active well into the nineteenth century. By that time, however the actors had completely changed, and a system of recruitment which had little connection with the official ideology was taking over. With the lesser *ayan* in the periphery, the households of the more important pashas and the new scribes arising from within the multilingual commercial circles of the capital demanded a share of power. By comparison, the old 'guard', namely the janissaries, the Palace, the older, established *ayan* families and the *ulema* were all eclipsed by the newcomers. Thus the *ulema* who until the nineteenth century had been indispensable for the functioning of society became dispensable. Avenues of upward mobility, clogged by the eighteenth century with hereditary office holding opened up again. However, the new changes did not favour redistributive and power-sharing patterns. The accumulative trends that became dominant in the nineteenth century are symbolised in the radical changes that we define as 'westernisation' or 'modernisation'. These historical developments might also be described as 'diachronic flexibility', the ability to gravitate between redistributive and accumulative modes over time.

From the larger perspective, however, the major reason for sociopolitical change in the nineteenth-century Ottoman Empire is the accommodation of the newcomers. The previous distribution of power is wiped out; all resources which had been redistributed earlier are brought under control of the centre and the polity thus functions in an accumulative mode. The western ideology was the necessary vehicle for the newcomers, who wanted to create their own world within the changing world system. Because the newly adopted accumulative patterns did not have to be adopted wholesale from abroad, because they were traits already present in the dualistic system of redistribution and accumulation, the Ottoman dynasty was able to give legitimacy to the system in a period of dramatic change. Dynasty and state remained legitimate as long as they accommodated and incorporated the changes demanded by newly arising social groups. The flexibility of the dualistic system permitted this. In another context, there might have been a revolution or a dynasty change, whereas in the nineteenth century, the Ottoman dynasty could still absorb, accommodate and incorporate change after half a millenium of rule.

NOTES

1. Methodological differences among Ottoman historians have developed along two different lines. In the 1960s and 1970s, the main disagreement was between Marxists and non-Marxists. At present, the interpretation of sources is the main issue debated: one group of scholars claims to 'let the texts speak for themselves', while their opponents believe in a contextual and constructural interpretation of the available sources. The situation is complicated by the fact that certain Ottomanists emphasise the uniqueness of the Ottoman Empire, while their opponents seek world historical patterns in Ottoman material. Generally the wish to 'let the texts speak for themselves' and the assertion of Ottoman uniqueness form part of the same world view, which also implies a distinctly anti-Marxist stand. On the other hand, contextual and constructural interpretation and the search for world historical patterns do not necessarily imply a Marxian world view, although such a combination is possible.
2. The Turkish historian Mehmet Fuat Köprülü is one of the best examples of such an approach.
3. The Turkish historian Zeki Velidi Togan is a notable exception. His own Central Asian background played an important role in his approach.
4. This idea was first outlined in Togan [1984] and later developed further in Togan and Lam [1989].
5. The following section is based on a previous paper, 'The Evolution of Ottoman Tribal Administration', presented to the Center for Middle Eastern Studies, University of Chicago, 1987 (unpublished).

6. This overview is based on my own earlier periodization of Mongolian rule in China [Togan, 1984]. Chan Hok-lam [1981] also sees similar patterns. From the historiographical point of view Dardess [1973], Langlois [1981], Morgan [1986], Allsen [1987], Rossabi [1988], Barfield [1989], Endicott-West [1989] are indispensable for an understanding of the problems involved.
7. For Inner Asian, in this case Mongolian and Turkic terminology, consult G. Doerfer [1963–75], Cleaves (various articles). For Ottoman terminology compare the relevant articles in the *Encyclopedia of Islam*.
8. I am indebted to Metin Kunt and Cornell Fleischer who brought the *müteferrika* to my attention.
9. I am indebted to Cornell Fleischer for the 'dual ranking system'.
10. I am indebted to Rifa'at Abou-el-Haj for making his manuscript '*The Nature of the Ottoman State, 1560s to 1700*' available to me.
11. What I call redistributive traditions here, can also be called tribal or steppe traditions. I think, however, that when we say steppe we rarely think of the relationship between the steppe and, on the one hand, the desert or the sown, on the other. These traditions were prevalent among Turco-Mongolian populations of Inner Asia and also among the Arabs of early Islam.

REFERENCES

Abou-El-Haj, forthcoming, 'The Nature of the Ottoman State, 1560s to 1700'.
Allsen, Thomas T., 1987, *Mongol Imperialism*, Berkeley, CA: University of California Press.
Allsen, Thomas, 1989, 'Mongolian Princes and their Merchant Partners, 1200–1260', *Asia Major*, 3rd Series, Vol.II, No.2.
Barthold, Wilhelm, 1935, Zwölf Vorlesungen über die Geschichte der Türken Mittelasiens, Berlin: Deutsche Gesellschaft für Islamkunde.
Barfield, Thomas, 1989, *The Perilous Fontier: Nomadic Empires and China*, Oxford: Blackwell.
Chan Hok-lam, 1981, 'Chinese Official Historiography at the Yuan Court: The Composition of the Liao, Chin, and Sung Histories', in *China under Mongol Rule*, (ed. John D. Langlois), Princeton, NJ: Princeton University Press, pp.56–107.
Cleaves, Francis Woodman, 1982, *The Secret History of the Mongols*, Cambridge, MA: Harvard University Press.
Cleaves, Francis Woodman, 1940–, Series of articles on cultural and institutional aspects of Mongols in China published in the *Harvard Journal of Asiatic Studies*.
Dardess, John W., 1973, *Conquerors and Confucians: Aspects of Political Change in Late Yuan China*, New York: Columbia University Press.
Doerfer, Gerhard, 1963–75, *Türkische und mongolische Elemente im Neupersrischen*, 4 vols., Weisbaden: Franz Steiner Verlag.
Endicott-West, Elizabeth, 1989, *Mongolian Rule in China: Local Administration in Yuan China*, Cambridge, MA: Harvard University Press.
Endicott-West, Elizabeth, 1989, 'Merchant Associations in Yuan China: The Orto', *Asia Major*, 3rd series, Vol.II, No.2.
Faroqhi, Suraiya, 1985, 'Civilian Society and Political Power in the Ottoman Empire: A Report in Colective Biography (1480–1830)', *International Journal of Middle East Studies*, No.17.
Faroqhi, Suraiya, 1990, 'Towns, Agriculture and the State in Sixteenth-Century Ottoman Anatolia', *Journal of the Economic and Social History of the Orient*, Vol.XXXIII, No.2.
Fleischer, Cornell, 1987, 'Power of the Person, Authority of the State', Paper presented at the Symposium on The Age of Suleyman the Magnificent, Chicago, 1987.
Fleischer, Cornell, forthcoming, 'From Şehzade Korkud to Mustafa Âli: Cultural Origins of the Ottoman *Nasihatname*', to be published in *The Social and Economic History of Turkey* (eds. Bernard Lewis and Heath Lowry), İstanbul: Isis Yayınları.

Fletcher, Joseph, 1986, 'The Mongols: Social and Ecological Perspectives', *Harvard Journal of Asiatic Studies*.
Genç, Mehmet, 1989, 'Osmanlı İktisadi Dünya Görüşünün İlkeleri', *Sosyoloji Dergisi*, Vol.3, No.1.
Greenwood, Anthony, 1990, 'İstanbul's Food Provisioning and the Ottoman Economy', Paper presented at the Center for the Study of Islamic Societies and Civilizations, Washington University at St. Louis, Missouri.
Haenisch, E., 1962, *Wörterbuch zu Manghol und Niuca Tobca'an*, Wiesbaden: Franz Steiner Verlag.
Holmgren, J., 1986, 'Observations on Marriage and Inheritance Practices in Early Mongol and Yüan Society, with Particular Reference to the Levirate', *Journal of Asian History*, Vol.20, No.2.
Hsiao Ch'ing-ch'ing, 1978, *The Military Establishment of the Yuan Dynasty*, Cambridge, MA: Harvard University Press.
Hodgson, Marshall G.S., 1974, *The Venture of Islam*, 3 vols., Chicago, IL: Chicago University Press.
İnalcık, Halil, 1954, 'Ottoman Methods of Conquest', *Studia Islamica*, Vol. II.
İnalcık, Halil, 1981, 'The Question of the Emergence of the Ottoman State' *International Journal of Turkish Studies*, Vol.II, No.2.
İnalcık, Halil, 1987, 'State and Rural Economy', Paper presented at the Symposium on The Age of Suleyman the Magnificent, Chicago.
Jackson, P., 1978, 'The Dissolution of the Mongol Empire', *Central Asiatic Journal*, Vol.XXII.
Lattimore, Owen, 1940, *Inner Asian Frontiers of China*, New York: American Geographical Society.
Lindner, Rudi Paul, 1983, *Nomads and Ottomans in Medieval Anatolia* (Uralic and Altaic Series), Bloomington, IN: Research Institute for Inner Asian Studies.
Morgan, David, 1986, *The Mongols*, Oxford: Blackwell.
Ratchnevsky, Paul, 1966, 'Zum Ausdruck "T'ouhsia" in der Mongolenzeit', in *Collectanea Mongolica: Festschrift für Professor Dr. Rintchem zum 60. Geburtstag*, Wiesbaden: Harrassowitz.
Ratchnevsky, Paul, 1983, *Činggis-Khan*, Wiesbaden: Franz Steiner Verlag.
Rossabi, Morris, 1988, *Khubilai Khan: His Life and Times*, Berkeley, CA: University of California Press.
Schurmann, H.F., 1956a, *Economic Structure of the Yüan Dynasty*, Cambridge, MA: Harvard University Press.
Schurmann, H.F., 1956b, 'Mongolian Tributary Practices of the Thirteenth Century', *Harvard Journal of Asiatic Studies*, No.19.
Spence, Jonathan D., 1981, *The Gate of Heavenly Peace: The Chinese and Their Revolution 1895-1980*, New York Viking.
Tietze, Andreas, 1990, 'An Alternative Approach to the Ottoman Period of Decline', paper presented at the Conference on Ottoman History as Part of World History, Causes and Considerations (St. Louis).
Togan, Isenbike, 1973, 'The Chapter on Annual Grants in the Yüan shih in Mongolian and Chinese History', unpublished Ph.D. dissertation, Harvard University.
Togan, Isenbike, 1979, 'Differences among Semi-nomadic Groups in the Ottoman Empire' (in Turkish with and English summary), *Boğaziçi Üniversities: Dergisi*, Vol.7; also Japanese translation in *Toyo Gakuho*, Vol.62 (1981).
Togan, Isenbike, 1984, 'The Mongols' Trade Partners: A Study of Chinese Trade under Mongol Rule' (in Turkish with an English summary), *Toplum ve Bilim*, Vol.25/26.
Togan, Isenbike (ms), 'Flexibility and Limitation in a Steppe Formation: The Legacy of the Mongolian World Empire (in preparation).
Togan, Isenbike and Yuan-chu Lam, 1989, Review of Thomas T. Allsen, *Mongol Imperialism: The Policies of the Grand Qan Möngke in China, Russia and the Islamic Lands, 1251-1259* (Berkeley, CA: University of California Press, 1987) *Journal of American Oriental Studies*, Vol.109, No.2.

Togan, A. Zeki Velidi, 1970, *Umumi Türk Tarihine Giriş*, 2nd printing, İstanbul: İstanbul Üniversitesi Edebiyat Fakültesi.

Venzke, Margaret, 1990, 'The Question of Syria in the Ottoman Land Regime of the Sixteenth Century', Paper presented at the Center for the Study of Islamic Societies and Civilizations, Washington University of St. Louis, Missouri.

Vladimirtsov, B.Y., 1944, *Moğolların içtimai Teşkilatı* (translated by Abdülkadır İnan), Ankara: Türk Tarih Kurumu.

In Search of Ottoman History

SURAIYA FAROQHI

Ottoman history has a somewhat special position within Middle Eastern history.[1] At least since the inception of 'modern style' or 'Republican-mode' Ottomanist historiography in the 1920s, Ottoman history has been studied on the background of European history and the paradigms characteristic of the latter. Fuat Köprülü began his work on the origins of the Ottoman Empire with a refutation of Gibbons' claim that the Ottoman state had originated in 'a tribe of 400 tents', and proceeded to analyse the social, cultural and economic structures of thirteenth and fourteenth-century Anatolia. In his view these structures constituted a *conditio sine qua non* for Ottoman success. Köprülü equally responded to the work of European mediaevalist historians [*Köprülü*, 1959; *Berktay*, 1983: 82]. Thus Ömer Lütfi Barkan's close ties to Fernand Braudel and the *Annales ESC*, and Halil İnalcık's later involvement with Wallerstein and the Ottoman history concerns of the Fernand Braudel Center are not the peculiar personal orientations of these two scholars, but indicate a long-term trend [*Braudel*, 1966; *Barkan*, 1951; *İnalcık*, 1978]. It is worth noting that this involvement with European history was the work of Turkish scholars of strong Republican and nationalist convictions, whose views on domestic policy during the 1960s and later might be described as liberal-conservative. European practitioners of Ottoman studies did not play any significant role in generating this orientation.

Among European historians, Fernand Braudel was probably the first to propose that on the level of socio-economic structure, there existed a common dimension between the Ottoman world and early modern European states. This idea was taken up by Ömer Lütfi Barkan whose

---

Suraiya Faroqhi is at the Nahost-Institut Ludwig-Maximilians-Universität Munich, Germany. For incisive comments, the author thanks Engin Akarlı, Cornell Fleischer, Raoul Motika and Isenbike Togan. In addition, Rifa"at Abou-El-Haj, Tülay Artan, Halil Berktay, Büsra Ersanlı Behar, Selim Deringil, Nükhet Sirman Eralp, Peter Gran, Bozkurt Güvenç, Cemal Kafadar, Resat Kasaba, Roger Owen, Elizabeth Özdalga and Ilhan Tekeli have discussed with her many of the issues touched upon in this article. To all these fellow scholars, she is profoundly grateful, particularly to Tülay Artan for allowing her to read her forthcoming book in manuscript. Of course her colleagues are in no way responsible for the many errors and misunderstandings that this study is bound to contain.

work on the 'price revolution', demographic history and the condition of agricultural labourers can be regarded as a response to Earl Hamilton, the French school of historical demographers and Marc Bloch [Barkan, 1980; Barkan, 1975a]. Turkish historians concerned with the Ottoman Empire and interested in European and American historiography have all acted on the assumption that a broad knowledge of early modern European history can serve as a source of assumptions to be tested and paradigms to be played out in the Ottoman context. Ottoman history down to the present day has remained a net importer of paradigms. Even so, explicit comparisons rarely have been attempted. It is possible that the Feudalism-Asiatic Mode of Production controversy, with its obvious political overtones, has discouraged attempts at comparative history[2]. Ömer Lütfi Barkan and Halil İnalcık both responded to the controversy by insisting that the Ottoman polity was an entity *sui generis*, and this became the dominant view in the Turkish academic establishment [Barkan, 1975b]. As a result young scholars were further discouraged from overt comparisons with European societies.

However, the notion that a knowledge of European social and economic history is a distinct advantage to the Ottoman historian was never seriously challenged. There have been major historians who did not seek to acquire such a familiarity; Mustafa Akdağ and Cengiz Orhonlu are the most obvious examples [Akdağ, 1963; Orhonlu, 1974]. But to my knowledge very few people have ever claimed that concern with European history was a danger to the Ottoman historian, likely to lead him/her to ask the wrong questions of his/her material.

On a different plane, however, a concern of this kind can be read out of Andrew Hess's work on Ottoman-Spanish warfare in the Mediterranean [Hess, 1978]. Hess perceives his work as a challenge to Braudel's vision of Mediterranean unity. He reasserts the cultural and political divisions whose existence Braudel had not denied, but which constitute only a minor theme in the latter's great work on the Mediterranean. According to Hess, however, the wars of the sixteenth century ended with Spain and the Ottoman-Moroccan polities mutually 'turning their backs' upon one another. Hess does not attempt to refute the existence of economic conjunctures common to the Mediterranean as a whole, but in his view these matters pale into insignificance *vis-à-vis* a major conflict in the political and cultural field.

The present article defends a rather different view. I assume that both Ottoman and European history of the modern period were not monolithic entities. Regional differences between the Aegean seaboard and the semi-autonomous principalities of the Ottoman-Safavid border region were profound. In the same way it is mistaken to see early modern

Europe as consisting only of England, Holland and possibly France. Spain, the Italian principalities and the Germanies with their declining populations, economic involution and – in the latter two instances – political dislocation also formed part of seventeenth-century Western Europe [*de Vries*, 1976]. Given this degree of internal diversity both within the Ottoman Empire and early modern Europe, convergence and a mutual 'turning of backs' could and did exist side by side. In this study, I emphasise convergence, not because I would deny the existence of disjuncture, but because I believe the premises underlying many historical studies on the 'rise of the West' to be mistaken. I oppose the essentialist thinking which underlies so many comparisons between 'East and West', and plead for a relatively late divergence between the two, for the role of historical contigencies in causing disjuncture, and for the importance of economic, social and cultural contradictions within the two socio-economic formations in question. As a result, historical process, which according to a Europe-centred essentialist world view constitutes a unique privilege of 'the West', is discovered in the Ottoman Empire as well. On the other hand the stagnation and decline attributed to the post-sixteenth-century Ottoman Empire not infrequently had parallels in early modern Europe.

BORDER CULTURE

Convergent phenomena may be studied in different frameworks. To begin with, certain parallels may be regarded as forming part of a border culture [*Bennassar and Bennassar*, 1989]. For frontier districts were not only the realm of almost perpetual fighting. Whenever there was a lull in the Habsburg-Ottoman wars of the late seventeenth century, certain Ottoman pashas and Habsburg frontier commanders exchanged gifts, polite letters and sometimes even military secrets ['*Alî*, 1981: 30–31, 36–7][3]. Spanish soldiers, abandoned to the hunger and boredom of *presidio* life in North Africa were more than ready to desert to the Muslim side (and to return when homesickness became too hard to bear). Fishermen from Sardinia, Calabrian farmers and inhabitants of the Balearic islands were not adverse to a career as corsairs in the Ottoman navy. From the records of the Inquisition, we know that certain people crossed and recrossed what was after all one of the most serious ideological barriers of the time. Even love for a spouse might cause people to change sides [*Bennassar and Bennassar*, 1989: 300–301].

Nor was this 'border mentality' limited to common soldiers, peasants or fishermen. A seventeenth-century Spanish nobleman and officer, Gutierre Pantoja, readily became a Muslim after he had been captured, sold to the Sultan's Palace and made to enter the pages' school [*Bennassar and Bennassar*, 1989: 126ff.]. If his account is correct, he rose in the Ottoman navy to become *tersane kethüdası*, that is, he obtained a rank immediately below the supreme commander of the Ottoman fleet. Apparently Gutierre Pantoja did not feel many qualms of conscience because of the way in which he changed sides. Nor did Cigalazade Yusuf Sinan Paşa, who obtained an elevated rank in the Ottoman central administration of the sixteenth and seventeenth centuries, ever hide his familiy ties to Italy, where his mother continued to live [*Islam Ansiklopedisi*, 1950: Vol.3, 161–4]. There may have been an 'Iron Curtain' separating Christendom and Islamdom; but more often than we had hitherto considered possible, this curtain was lifted just high enough for individuals and small groups to move back and forth.

Moreover, there exist similarities between Ottoman and early modern European culture which are not readily ascribed to border contact. To a person attuned to European Renaissance buildings, the Süleymaniye is immediately accessible in a fashion that most late medieval Byzantine buildings are not, since symmetry, a clear hierarchy of spaces, monumental façades, vistas and a concern with technical excellence are common to classical Ottoman and European Renaissance architecture. A recent study of the sixteenth-century Ottoman architect Sinan points to the existence of certain features in classical Ottoman building which remind us of the European Renaissance, and parallels have been drawn between Sinan and Palladio [*Kuran*, 1987: 245–6]. We know that Sinan never visited Italy, and was not familiar with the architectural theory of the Italian Renaissance. Nor do we possess any evidence that would allow us to explain these similarities as the result of cultural borrowing on the part of Italian Renaissance architects – even though such a possibility should not be excluded a priori [*Kuran*, 1987: 246]. Given our present knowledge, we should probably regard such affinities as part of a common Mediterranean culture, which included many traditions shared between Muslims and 'people of the Book'. After all, a sixteenth-century Muslim who refused to share a cell with an 'atheist' fellow prisoner found a sympathetic hearing among the Inquisition judges – judges who almost condemned this very same man to death at the stake [*Bennassar and Bennassar*, 1989: 72].

THE EARLY MODERN STATE IN EUROPE AND THE OTTOMAN EMPIRE

Ottomans and early modern Europeans also had certain political experiences in common. However, this aspect of their lives has rarely been studied. Quite to the contrary, since the times of Busbeck, who wrote his travelogue in the middle of the sixteenth century, writers comparing Ottoman and European polities have dwelt almost exclusively on contrasting features [*Von Busbeck*, 1926: 64–6]. To begin with the composition of the ruling class, the Ottoman Empire of the sixteenth century lacked an aristocracy with control over land, while this group continued to hold the reins of power in all European states until well into the nineteenth or even twentieth century. By contrast, members of the Ottoman governing class, legally slaves of the Sultan, were totally beholden to the ruler, at a time when a major noble of the Habsburg Empire, William of Nassau-Orange, led a rebellion in the Low Countries, and the Polish aristocracy established total control of the Polish-Lithuanian state. By contrast the Ottoman Empire of the sixteenth century in Busbeck's eyes appeared as a society with little regard for ancestry. Service to the Sultan and the ruler's pleasure constituted the only basis for high rank and political power.

Busbeck's comparisons involve a certain manipulation of reality. The Ottoman Empire did not possess a land-holding nobility – even the *ayan* of the eighteenth and nineteenth centuries never boasted a local power base comparable to the French or English aristocracy. But this does not mean that the Ottoman ruling group was free of aristocratic pretensions. Particularly after affiliation with the 'great household' of a vizier or pasha had become a standard means of elite recruitment, what might be called a grandee mentality became characteristic of the Ottoman ruling class [*Abou-El-Haj*, 1984: 88–9]. Whether we stress the similarities or the differences between European and Ottoman ruling classes will depend upon our overall view of the two societies involved. As long as we insist that 'Oriental despotism' and European absolutism cannot be analysed within one and the same category, we will stress the differences, while the opposite starting point will lead us to emphasise similarities [*Anderson*, 1974: 361–94]. But the proof of the pudding is in the eating, and only future scholarship will show whether the manipulations undertaken in this article make more sense than those of my predecessors.

When discussing European feudalism and the Ottoman system of state and society, we often select the most decentralised 'medieval' phase of European history and compare it with the Ottoman Empire in its most 'centralised' stage, that is, in the shape it took on during the Süleymanic period, particularly the 1550s and 1560s. In the seventeenth century, things had changed quite appreciably. The heads of major households and high-level *ulema* families now exhibited certain features that we associate with an aristocracy, and Linda S. Schilcher has even discovered 'estates' in nineteenth-century Damascus [*Schilcher*, 1985]. Today we know that to be a *kul* was not the same as to be a slave to a private person, and that *kul* retained family, regional and factional loyalties which they needed to 'fit in' with their loyalty to the Sultan as best they might [*İnalcık*, 1973: 87; *Findley*, 1989: 25; *Kunt*, 1974]. After 1695 long-term tax-farming rights were granted primarily to people who were already members of the Ottoman ruling class, and who thereby were able to establish themselves permanently in the provinces they administered [*Genç*, 1975: 241]. Even though very few among these provincial powerholders ever envisaged independence, the Ottoman Empire of the seventeenth and eighteenth centuries was still much more decentralised than it had been in the time of Süleyman the Lawgiver (1520–66).

On the other hand, European feudalism also evolved in time, and in the sixteenth century, centralised, absolutist states were emerging. We must not forget that Busbeck wrote his remarks about the Ottoman system of government not as a dispassionate observer, but as a political polemicist. A faithful adherent of his Habsburg ruler, he hoped that the latter would gain the same kind of independence from the local aristocracy that Sultan Süleyman had already achieved. All over Europe, there were tendencies in the direction of royal absolutism. Given this political agenda, Busbeck was not interested in the checks and balances which limited the Ottoman ruler's power even in the mid-sixteenth century, such as the self-recruiting governing class of Egyptian Mamluks, Cairo or Damascus militias, the established landed families of Syria, or the semi-independent principalities of the border region [*Raymond*, 1973–74; *Abu Husayn*, 1985; *van Bruinessen*, 1978]. Given the continous struggle of the Habsburgs to limit the prerogatives of 'their' aristocracies, Ottoman 'despotic' government was regarded as a model by 'political pamphleteers' such as Busbeck, and if he had not found such a thing in real life, he might easily have invented it.

THE JOYS AND PITFALLS OF COMPARISON

To be fruitful as a scholarly endeavour, comparative history must take into account both similarities and dissimilarities between the two societies forming the objects of comparison. Phrased in such an abstract fashion, this statement will not be disputed by anyone and therefore is scarcely worth making. But the implications are much more controversial, and the comparative historian, by stressing either similarities or differences, willy-nilly reveals aspects of his/her political and cultural agendas. When addressing the differences between European absolutism and 'Oriental despotism' (or any other political category in which we may place Ottoman government) scholars usually imply that the Ottoman Empire developed along completely different lines from early modern Europe. According to this viewpoint, the intrusion of European commercial and military power, which became more intense in the early nineteenth century although it was familiar from earlier periods as well, created a radical break in Ottoman history. The latter is thereby divided into a 'traditional' and a 'modern' phase, and these two phases can be examined more or less in isolation from one another. The 'modern' period is studied within the paradigms of European history and mainly (though no longer exclusively) by using European sources. As to the 'pre-modern' period, it is usually assumed that the Ottoman Empire was a phenomenon *sui generis*, which because of its unique characteristic cannot be profitably compared with any other state and/or society.

In the last few years, this paradigm has come under increasing attack. Ottomanist historians dealing with the pre-Tanzimat period have known for a long time that the reforms undertaken between 1838 and 1876 had solid roots in Ottoman history. The first indicators which showed that the peasants' rights of possession were evolving in the direction of full property rights were observed as early as the sixteenth century [*Barkan*, 1980: 291–375]. Rules of inheritance increasingly resembled those prescribed by the Islamic religious law (*şeriat*) for private property, and where alienation and inheritance were involved, the tenants of state lands and private owners were in a broadly comparable position even before the land law of 1858. Moreover we know that at least from the middle of the sixteenth century onward, there was a significant group within the Ottoman bureaucracy whose members possessed little *medrese* training, and whose way of handling political issues was highly pragmatic.[4] Thus the progressive adoption of European-style higher education during the second half of the nineteenth century appears as a less alien importation than adherents of the traditional-modern dichotomy had originally assumed.[5] It is of some significance that the empirical data which allow us to question this dichotomy have for the most part been known for a long time, but only now are we beginning to appreciate their implications for our overall view of Ottoman history.

The 'traditional-modern' dichotomy now has come under critical scrutiny, not only in Ottoman history but, to name but one example, in Chinese history as well.[6] Insistence on the cultural and political bifurcation between the Ottoman Empire and Europe and acceptance of the 'traditional-modern' dichotomy generally go together. As the dichotomy between 'traditional' and 'modern' has become problematic, emphasis on the 'peculiar' character of Ottoman history today is less obligatory than had been the case in the recent past.

Scholars who dwell upon parallel developments in Ottoman and European history often wish to express their conviction that 'history' and 'dynamic' were by no means special characteristics of Western Europe. They equally feel impatient with the assumption that a few European traders, ambassadors and politicians were able to inject 'the forces of change' into the Ottoman system, which the latter had been unable to generate on its own. Historians of India are in a similar position, and some of them have proposed interesting solutions. A recent account of the genesis of the 'Second British Empire' during the late eighteenth and early nineteenth centuries combines an Ibn Khaldunian model of tribes breaking out of their habitats beyond the frontiers of settled civilisation with twentieth-century research on the growth of trade throughout early modern Western and Southern Asia [*Bayly*, 1989: 27ff.]. Expanding trade and the resultant enrichment of provincial elites made it more difficult for the central governments of the Ottoman, Safavid and Moghul states to maintain control over outlying provinces. Tribal horizons expanded not only in the sense that more goods became available, but the tribesmen also accepted models of a purified religion – this latter factor was important in the Wahabi rebellion, which shook the Ottoman Empire during the early years of the nineteenth century.

Trade-induced dislocation of the major Asian empires had little to do with European commerce; for research particularly on Ottoman and Indian trade has shown that internal exchange was of major significance, and that trade relations among the three Muslim-ruled empires were also going strong. If this model constitutes an adequate reflection of reality, then the expansion of the British Empire in the latter half of the eighteenth century became possible because a dynamic generated in England coincided with a crisis caused by political and economic processes particular to the major states of the Islamic world. This model may appear less 'neat' than many of its predecessors, which were based on the assumption that all crises occurring in the eighteenth-century Islamic world constituted long-term consequences of European imperialism. But the model introduced by Bayly does possess the merit that the three large-scale societies of the eighteenth-century Islamic world are no longer regarded as so many inert masses, only catapulted into history by the activities of European states and merchants.

For reasons that concern European historiography a rejection of the 'traditional-modern' dichotomy in Ottoman history is now easier to defend that would have been the case 20 or 25 years ago. In recent years European historiography has chosen to emphasise not the 'modernity of the sixteenth century' but rather the persistence of the old order in late nineteenth and early twentieth-century Europe [*Hauser*, 1963; *Mayer*, 1981]. Again, this is not purely a result of historical research, for an ideological dimension is present as well. Historians stressing the continuities between British governmental systems before and after the parliamentary reforms of 1832 have been described as 'proving that nothing happened' [*Bayly*, 1989: 236]. The conservative thrust of such a statement cannot be denied. But emphasis on continuities is equally popular among historians who cannot be described as conservatives. In this instance the disillusionment following the defeat of the reformist (or, in Third World countries, revolutionary) movements of the 1960s and early 1970s is largely responsible. It has become apparent that 'old' structures have a tough life of their own, and 'new' ones are difficult to establish. Recent studies emphasising continuities from the late Middle Ages to the mid-twentieth century are so numerous that a detailed discussion is impossible. As a dramatic instance one might mention Ruggiero Romano's and his associates' assertion that industrial capitalism came to Italy only after 1945, and that Mussolini's law forbidding peasants to leave their villages was a last attempt to revive serfdom [*Romano*, 1980: 24, 33–4]. Concerning France in the late nineteenth century and during the first half of the twentieth, researchers have dwelt on the archaic features of life in the more outlying provinces. In Eugen Weber's view, the peasants of many outlying regions only turned into Frenchmen during the 25 years preceding 1914 [*Weber*, 1976]. Even in 1940, the lifestyles of farmers living in the remoter parts of the country were rather reminiscent of the eighteenth century. For German history, this new current of research has had an unexpected consequence. From the 1950s and particularly the 1960s onward, certain historians had attributed the rise of Nazism in Germany to a special form of historical development (*Sonderweg*). Proponents of the *Sonderweg* theory had assumed that the victory of Nazism occurred because throughout the nineteenth century the German bourgeoisie was weak, modern forms of associational life were underdeveloped and the forces representing the old order remained strong. But if this was true everywhere in Europe, it is not possible to build an explanation of a specifically German development upon this state of affairs [*Wehler*, 1988: 240; *Maier*, 1988].

As recent studies of European history emphasise continuity and persistent archaic features, the comparative historian who wishes to dwell on Ottoman-European parallels can easily locate a variety of possible subjects. Generally these parallels refer to social and political structures forming part of the 'old order'. As a good example, one might mention the *ancien régime* complexity of jurisdiction and taxation in eighteenth-century France, which bears a certain family resemblance to the Ottoman situation of the same period. Regulations dating back one or two centuries had never been formally abolished, but for the most part, their scope of application was merely limited. At the same time new rules and practices were successively superimposed upon one another [*Cezar*, 1986]. 'On the ground' this often led to a complicated imbrication of rights to revenue, so that much local experience was needed in order to operate in any given setting. There were also some remarkable parallels between Ottoman urban life and its counterpart in Sicily or southern France. Towns whose main economic basis consisted not of trade and crafts but of agriculture were widespread throughout the Mediterranean basin [*Romano*, 1980: 27].

Emphasis on persistent archaisms is justified as a corrective against naive assumptions concerning a clearly identifiable 'take-off' into modernity, but the approach involves intellectual difficulties of its own. Admittedly European governments and societies of the period around 1800 are quite different from those encountered today. Once we accept the 'archaic' character of the nineteenth century world we are forced to locate most major changes within a fairly short period of time, from 1914 to 1990 or even from 1945 to 1990. But this amounts to assuming another 'take-off' period, only this time fairly close to our own day. It is difficult to deny that in our own lifetimes and those of our parents, we have indeed witnessed major social, political and economic changes, to say nothing of the concomitant 'explosion of knowledge'. Yet the intellectual objections against a once-and-for-all 'take-off' remain valid whether applied to the late eighteenth century or to our own day, and this question will probably occupy historians during the next few years.

For however brief a span, 'the wind of the times' fills the sails of the comparative historian dealing with the Ottoman Empire and Europe, and we enjoy the benefits of an at least partially auspicious scholarly conjuncture. Yet a rather serious problem remains unresolved. When we compare two items, we assume that they can be placed in a common category, or to put it more colloquially, that we are not comparing chalk with cheese. But what do we call the common category which encompasses Ottoman state and society as well as their early modern European counterparts? The debate concerning the 'feudal' or 'Asiatic' Mode of Production was meant to supply an answer to this question. At least indirectly, this discussion involved a comparison between the Ottoman Empire and Europe, as well as comparisons with India, China and Iran [İslamoğlu and Keyder, 1977; İslamoğlu-İnan, 1987: 1–26; Berktay, 1985: 245–78]. However, most scholars are at home with only one or at most two of the historical disciplines involved, and to proceed merely on the basis of a limited corpus of secondary literature often results in unfortunate misunderstandings.

This difficulty has prompted scholars such as Marshall Hodgson and Maxime Rodinson to forego taxonomic refinements and establish very broad categories, encompassing a wide variety of pre-capitalist social formations [Hodgson, 1974: Vol.1, 45ff., 105ff.; Rodinson, 1978: 58–68]. This solution can be challenged in its turn; for a broad category such as 'agrarianate societies' does not allow us to explain why these societies followed a variety of historical trajectories. Many historians apparently despair of ever finding a solution to the problem, and have moved on to other matters. Today the debate is being continued by only a very few Ottoman historians, and the present study tries to deal with the question on a much more naïve level. Comparing 'surface phenomena' from the social and political realms, the question of internal dynamic is left more or less in abeyance. Of course, the naïveté involved is really a *fausse naïveté*, because by deciding to not look at one's predecessors one does not make the work of these scholars disappear. Certainly the emphasis on Ottoman-European parallels in my case involves the assumption that Ottoman and European societies diverged at a late date, presumably during the second half of the eighteenth century. This assumption makes it incumbent upon the historian to show how and where this divergence came about. But much more research is needed before we can even begin to answer this question.

CHANGES IN COURT CEREMONIAL AS INDICATORS OF POLITICAL CHANGE

Recent studies of Ottoman administration between about 1550 and 1700 have shown that by this time, the Sultans were no longer expected to rule in person, but presided over an administration consisting of 'grandee' heads of households. Failure in war and the inability to maintain a balance between rival houses of viziers and pashas could cost the Sultan his throne. Regencies were frequent and presented difficult but not insoluble problems. This indicates that government by a 'grandee'-directed bureaucracy had become institutionalised. In a sense, the growing influence of Palace School graduates in provincial administration may have made it unnecessary for the Sultan to intervene in day-to-day politics.

During the last few years, researchers have shown that this change in power relations was expressed in a new kind of court ceremonial [Abou-El-Haj, 1984; Kunt, 1983; Necipoğlu-Kafadar, 1986]. In the pre-Süleymanic period, and even during the Lawgiver's early years, the Sultan's legitimacy depended upon his acceptance by the military, which was by no means automatic. Legitimacy was maintained by having the Sultan frequently appear in front of his soldiers, and particularly dine in state in the outer appartments of the Palace, where he could be seen by a large number of military men. During the early stages in Süleyman's career, he also participated in festivities accessible to the İstanbul public. But in the Lawgiver's later years, these appearances were curtailed as no longer consonant with the dignity of the ruler, and when the Sultan did appear in public, he often remained silent and was in turn greeted in hieratic silence. Little research has been done on seventeenth-century court ceremonial, but apparently a major change occurred in the early eighteenth century, when it became common for Sultans to participate in 'private' festivities. Ahmed III and his successors attended parties in the seaside villas (yalı) of his relatives and grandees. Here the ruler was inaccessible to soldiers and townsmen, but could be seen by whomever his host invited. The destruction of the pleasure resort of Sa'adabad during the rebellion of Patrona Halil in 1730 demonstrates that this new form of court amusement was regarded as unacceptable by a large number of soldiers and Istanbul townsmen [And, 1982; Aktepe, 1958]. But while yalı parties were probably less conspicuous after 1730, the yalı continued as a major site of court life. Eighteenth-century princesses were often assigned a seaside residence soon after they were born, or at the very latest when they were affianced to high-level members of the Ottoman ruling establishment.

Ottoman ceremonial was vastly different from its contemporary French counterpart. The Ottoman ambassador Yirmisekiz Mehmed Çelebi commented on the fact that Louis XV as a child-king was expected to show off recently acquired accomplishments to foreign visitors, a gesture which the ambassador regarded as incompatible with the dignity of a Sultan [Göçek, 1987: 41–2]. Yet starting from the middle of the century, the French court in turn de-emphasised public ceremonial in favour of private and ostensibly 'rural' pleasures – Marie Antoinette and her companions playing at shepherdesses in the Petit Trianon come to mind as a prominent example. The ideological context of this changeover was specifically European: There was a distinct trend toward privacy and 'bourgeois' habits both among nobles and wealthy commoners, and the royal family was not necessarily the trendsetter in this respect [Darnton, 1981: 215–56].

We do not really know what prompted the change in eighteenth-century Sultanic behaviour on the ideological level, since eighteenth-century court culture has been as little studied as the history of this period in general. However, we can exclude cultural borrowing from French practice, as the Ottoman Sultans engaged in a round of ostensibly private pleasures in the very early eighteenth century, before a comparable trend had become notable at the French court. Moreover, Rousseauism, an important factor in the studied 'naturalness' of the late eighteenth-century European aristocracy, was of no significance at the Ottoman court. This state of affairs is worth commenting upon, since the Tulip Period presided over by Ahmed III is generally regarded as the first period of Ottoman history in which large sections of the upper class became interested in cultural contact with Europe. Apparently, borrowing became possible upon a background of convergence.

Recent analyses of Ottoman Palace construction have dwelt upon the impact of court ceremony on the shape, decoration and location of buildings [*Necipoğlu-Kafadar*, 1986]. This type of research question has been very fruitful, and it is worth remembering that a similar approach was developed by art historians dealing with medieval churches [*Gombrich*, 1984: 176]: The temporary structures erected for the reception of Renaissance kings and queens have been intensively studied. As these buildings were cheap to put up, it was possible to create whole sets of interrelated symbolic images in a short timespan, which would have been quite impossible if more costly materials had been used [*Yates*, 1985]. Now Ottoman public festivals were also numerous, well documented and ornate, and have attracted attention because of the many opportunities they provided for games and performances. But at the same time, these festivals asserted the legitimacy of the dynasty and transformed the streets of Istanbul into a stage setting, while the decorations put up at such occasions sometimes allow us to decipher the functions of the surviving kiosks and pavilions [*And*, 1982: 73ff.].

URBAN HISTORY

Notions of the 'Oriental city' for a long time have bedevilled the study of Ottoman cities, even though in the last 30 years, there have been several attempts to lay the ghost. Conventional wisdom assumes that Ottoman cities possessed no privileges and no corporate identity, because Islamic religious law (*şeriat*) was supposedly hostile to the notion of intermediate bodies inserting themselves between the individual and the community of believers (*ümmet*). As a result the town was considered unable to develop any specifically urban institutions. Supposedly Middle Eastern towns also lacked clear-cut boundaries, so that it became difficult to determine who was a townsman and who a villager. However, Ottoman urban historians have never gone as far as certain students of Mamluk Syria, who assume an unbroken continuity between towns and their rural hinterlands, and consider a region consisting of several oasis towns plus the surrounding countryside as the most appropriate unit for historical study [*Lapidus*, 1969: 60–69].

One reason for insisting on the importance of the town as a research topic is the fact that the Ottoman upper class was intensely urban. The best example of this consciousness ist the ten-volume travel account of Evliya Çelebi, who views the Ottoman territories as an accumulation of cities, linked to one another by a network of roads [*Evliya*, 1896–1938]. Every city is described according to a fixed format, beginning with the etymology of the name and its (more or less mythical) history and including an account of citadels, mosques, picnic grounds and locally famed foods. Evliya gives no descriptions of villages, and the countryside appears as a no-man's land, populated by its very special 'fauna' of Beduins, robbers and roving rebels. By this account Evliya implies that the Ottoman state is only fully present in its cities, only cities have a history, and no member of the Ottoman elite would live outside of towns and cities. This view is all the more interesting because it is partly inaccurate; at least in seventeenth-century Syria, we do find gentlemen's seats located in villages [*Abu-Husayn*, 1985: 143]. As a result it is legitimate to regard the town as a fundamental unit in Ottoman social history. Members of the Ottoman elite knew quite well where a town began and where it ended. Even though Ottoman cities did not possess urban privileges or a highly developed set of institutions particular to the city, the level of social cohesion was often quite high.

In late sixteenth-century Ankara, local notables negotiated with one another and with members of the Ottoman central administration, and arranged to protect their home town against roving brigands by the construction of a city wall [*Ergenç*, 1981]. These men certainly did not passively wait for the Ottoman central government to take the initiative. If we adhere to Traian Stoianovich's classification scheme of autonomous, dependent and semi-dependent cities, major Anatolian towns such as Ankara should therefore be regarded as 'semi-dependent' and not as 'dependent' [*Stoianovich*, 1970; *Ergenç*, 1981]. This conclusion is important for the historian wishing to compare Ottoman and European cities of the early modern period. For from the sixteenth century onward the autonomy of the mediaeval European city was either destroyed by the onslaught of the absolutist state (one might cite as examples the fate of La Rochelle or the Spanish cities after the Comuneros revolt) or else made meaningless because the cities in question lost most of their economic significance (Nuremberg and Augsburg) [*Braudel*, 1979: Vol.1, 453ff.].

The leading cities of the seventeenth century were state capitals, which depended for their survival on aristocracies and royal courts. Neither Paris nor London nor Madrid were ever centres of industry, and even the economic roles which many capitals eventually acquired were due to the presence of a centralised administrative apparatus. Thus Paris became the leading capital market of France because tax farming was central to the financial business of the kingdom. Given this state of affairs, it is legitimate to say that in the Ottoman Empire as in early modern Europe, major cities were closely dependent on the central administrations of the states on whose territories they were located. This situation however did not preclude an appreciable degree of social cohesion on the part of townsmen, and in certain instances Ottoman cities flourished because local inhabitants seized the opportunities arising from political conditions. The *pax ottomanica* opened up trade routes, and city-wide arrangements for defence sometimes permitted the inhabitants to retain a reasonable share of their earnings, which they invested, among other things, in larger and more ornate houses or public buildings [*Raymond*, 1979].

THE PROBLEMS OF TRADE

Studies of capital formation in the Ottoman Empire have emphasised the tension between merchants and the state. An older school of thought had held that Ottoman Muslims were culturally averse to trade, and concentrated upon administration, war and agriculture, leaving commerce (apart from the politically determined Istanbul trade) to non-Muslims. Supposedly the money market was also off-limits to Muslim Ottomans, due to the *şeriat*'s prohibition of usury. However, from the 1960s and 1970s onward, historians have demonstrated that these assumptions were quite mistaken. Well into the seventeenth century, Ottoman Muslims traded in Venice in appreciable numbers, the lending of money at interest was widely practised by pious foundations and the Muslim population at large, and legal devices were used to 'get around' the prohibition of interest-taking [*Kafadar*, 1986; *Jennings*, 1973; *Mandaville*, 1979]. In this context, it is worth remembering that Ottoman lenders of the sixteenth or seventeenth centuries generally had fewer inhibitions about admitting that they took interest than the major Italian bankers of the fifteenth century. When the Medici bank was at the height of its power, the managers of branch banks were explicitly instructed to avoid all business deals that involved the overt taking of interest, while the managers of small Ottoman mosque foundations had no qualms of this kind [*de Roover*, 1963: 12].

Muslim Ottomans also dominated the late-fifteenth-century commerce of the Black Sea and were active in the caravan trade linking the various Anatolian regions to one another and to the capital [*İnalcık*, 1979]. Contrary to a still widespread prejudice, the activities of merchants were not illegitimate in the eyes of the power-holding bureaucrats. Merchants trading over long distances were exempt from many of the limitations imposed upon craftsmen and shopkeepers [*İnalcık*, 1969]. 'Mainstream' Ottoman bureaucrats subscribed to the view that tax-paying subjects, including merchants, should be permitted to earn money without competition from members of the political class, so that they would be placed in a position to pay taxes. Not that this rule was universally observed. Occasionally viziers and other high-level administrators used their privileges as members of the elite in order to make a profit from trade [*Kunt*, 1977]. But most Ottoman officials of the late sixteenth and early seventeenth centuries apparently subscribed to the Ibn Khaldunian view that such an infringement of the division of labour current in the Ottoman polity could only lead to serious difficulties, and viewed it as a sure sign of decline.

This debate regarding Ottoman trade has some remarkable parallels where seventeenth-century Russia is concerned, if I correctly understand a recent monograph on Russia's internal trade [*Bushkovitch*, 1980]. The author is critical of an older 'received opinion' that merchants were pressed into state service (particularly tax collection) and as a result were unable to form significant capital reserves. But closer study has demonstrated that Moscow traders had considerable staying power, and European merchants did not succeed in ousting their local competitors from the internal market. Russian traders on the whole fared better than their Polish–Lithuanian counterparts, and the state provided them with limited but by no means negligible protection. By Bushkovitch's interpretation, state service was a source of profits to at least some of the luckier and more astute merchants.

This discussion of Russian trade does not include the 'ideological' aspects of the matter, that is the views that Czars, boyars and Russian officials took of merchant activities. Both Bushkovitch's study and the work of recent Ottoman economic historians revolve around the notion that the state provided opportunities for merchant profit, even though Russian boyars and Ottoman officials ruled their respective polities without admitting merchants to their councils. Moreover, recent historians of Ottoman trade and commerce-oriented ideology agree with Bushkovitch that the state's aloofness from trade did not immediately expose local merchants to ruinous competition by European traders. In the Russian case, state service provided merchants with opportunities for enrichment while Ottoman long-distance traders also enjoyed privileges vis-à-vis their poorer fellow townsmen. Both in the Russian and in the Ottoman case, recent historians no longer assume that the state's towering stature in comparison to 'the economy' was necessarily a drawback to the formation of merchant capital.

Quite possibly this more flexible stance can be explained by the experience of the post-Second World War period, when a number of Third World countries achieved a degree of industrialisation by fostering the development of a local bourgeoisie. Modern Turkish describes this process by a special expression, namely 'devletin eliyle adam zengin etmek', that is, 'to enrich a man by the hand of the state'. This colloquialism refers to the enrichment of a small commercially oriented elite through preferential tax regimes and other privileges, in the hope that these people will then invest their profits in industry. Slightly more remote in time, Keynesian financing to overcome the depression of the 1930s and the reconstruction experience in post-war Europe have also habituated scholars to a situation in which the state creates opportunities for private investment and capital formation. Historiography took up this theme, with a certain time-lag.

ATTITUDES TOWARD 'PRIMITIVE STAGES' IN OTTOMAN
AND EUROPEAN HISTORY

In the nineteenth and twentieth centuries the writing of history usually took place within the nationalist paradigm; and this also applies to scholarly work on both Ottoman and Russian history. However, the elaboration and more remote consequences of this paradigm have been rather different in the two instances involved. It appears that for long periods of time little research was done on seventeenth-century Russian commerce because it was regarded as backward, and other topics were preferred in consequence [Bushkovitch, 1980: x]. A similar claim of 'primitiveness' could certainly be advanced for the history of Anatolia in the fourteenth and fifteenth centuries, after the fall of the Seljuk sultanate and before the extension of the Ottoman Empire into areas beyond the northeastern tip of the Anatolian peninsula. Yet studies of this time-span, known as the 'beylik period' for a long time have been popular among both Turkish and non-Turkish Ottomanists (most recently Zachariadou, [1983]). The paucity of sources has acted as a challenge; scholars have squeezed the last drop of information out of a few inscriptions, chronicles and occasional references in early

Ottoman or Venetian documents. In addition, the limited extension of these principalities and the fact that sources and secondary literature are equally limited in volume, have ensured the continuing popularity of *beylik* period monographs as thesis topics, since this field allows a young scholar to show his/her ingenuity. None of the researchers who have produced monographs on the *beylik* period have ever complained about the 'primitiveness' of their chosen subject, and usually the lack of documentation is ascribed to wars, fires and other vicissitudes, rather than to the fact that few written documents were produced in the first place.

However, it is possible to put another and less pragmatic interpretation upon this approach.[7] In Republican-mode Turkish historiography the *beylik* period is annexed to the early history of the Ottoman Empire in a number of interesting ways. When the Ottoman *beylik* was founded in the area of Söğüt, Iznik and Bursa during the closing years of the thirteenth century, it was for a long time a small poorly documented entity which acquired a potential for expansion only because it was located close to the Byzantine frontier. When reconstructing early Ottoman history, it is therefore necessary to constantly look beyond the Ottoman frontiers, and this proceeding has become standard practice since it was inaugurated by Fuat Köprülü [*Köprülü*, 1959: 105–6]. Particularly the number of Ottoman buildings surviving from before the destruction of the first Ottoman Empire in the battle of Ankara (1402) is very limited, and a history of Anatolian art and architecture during this period is only possible if the structures put up by different ruling dynasties are studied together. This situation has encouraged twentieth-century scholars to regard the Anatolian *beyliks* as predecessors and quasi-extensions of the Ottoman Empire. While it is of course well-known that the Ottoman principality defeated its competitors in war and eliminated their ruling dynasties, this aspect of fourteenth to early sixteenth-century Anatolian history generally recedes into the background.

Turkish historians of the Republican period generally assume the existence of a clear break between the Turkish Republic and the Ottoman Empire. But at the same time they regard the Turkish Republic as a 'successor state' to the Empire in a sense that is quite different from the manner in which Yugoslavia, Hungary or Greece are also 'successor states'. Therefore Ottoman and *beylik* period history are defined as part of the national history of the Turkish Republic. However, this does not apply to classical Greek, Roman or Byzantine history, even though major sites of these three civilizations are located in Anatolia and Thrace, and historians or archeologists have occasionally suggested that the boundaries of national history be redrawn in order to include these disciplines as well. However, very few Turkish writers on history, often from outside the academic community, have emphasised continuities between the history of antiquity, Byzantium and the Ottoman period.[8] For the most part, such continuities, mostly on the level of popular culture, have attracted the interest of journalists and literary figures opposed, in one way or another, to the notion of a Turkish–Islamic synthesis without the slightest leavening of cosmopolitan traits.[9] Given the formidable barriers between academic and non-academic intellectuals in present-day Turkey, such currents have had almost no impact upon established Ottoman historiography. Thus the *beylik* period is regarded as part of a long and glorious imperial tradition, and the 'primitiveness' or otherwise of state and society during this period becomes more or less irrelevant.

Ottomanist historians' attitudes *vis-à-vis* the *beylik* period stand out even more clearly when we compare them to the views that prevailed about 30 years ago among quite a few German historians with respect to the Dark Ages. In those days, scholars felt that they had freed themselves of the normative aesthetic canons of classical antiquity, and the non-classical abstract art of the Dark Ages was highly prestigious.[10] Moreover, at least in West Germany, those were the days when the cold war and the beginning integration of the Federal Republic into the European Community gave quite a boost to the study of the Christian, pre-French, pre-German empire of the Merovingians. This perspective was, of course, quite anachronistic, and today would (hopefully) convince no one at all. Suffice it to say that in this context the 'Dark Ages' had a considerable and sometimes quite romantic appeal, and scholars either minimised the primitiveness or else viewed it as a positive attraction.

Nor is a romantic view absent from historiography on the early Ottoman Empire and the *beylik* period as a whole. Particularly in publications intended for a broader public, the fact that we know very little about Sultan Osman, Sultan Orhan or their immediate successors seems a positive advantage, and authors are free to project their private social utopias on to this little documented period.[11] Romantic imagination is centred upon 'origins' in a manner familiar from nineteenth- and early twentieth-century historical writing; not by chance are frontier heroes and religious men popular topics with historians working within the paradigm of Republican-mode Turkish historiography. But the utopia most frequently projected upon *beylik* period history is the exaltation of social and political harmony. Conflict between the different states of post-Seljuk Anatolia is played down, and relations between the different social groups present in mediaeval

Anatolian states are presented as largely non-antagonistic. With only slight exaggeration, we might say that this difficult and conflict-ridden period is viewed exclusively from an Ottoman point of view. From the victor's perspective, the outcome of the struggle is decided in advance and the struggle itself becomes irrelevant. The rise of the Ottoman Empire is regarded as almost a necessary consequence to its frontier location and social organisation.

THE 'SEVENTEENTH CENTURY CRISIS'

For almost 30 years, there has been a debate among European historians concerning the interpretation to be given the political, economic and demographic difficulties which could be observed in almost all European countries at varying times after the year 1600. Holland was the only country whose 'Golden Age' coincided with the seventeenth century. England certainly experienced a period of growth and laid the foundations of future prosperity. Yet the Civil War period was characterised by considerable commercial reverses, while earlier in the century the Dutch took over the place of the English in Russian trade and challenged their competitors in the eastern Mediterranean. On the other hand, these difficulties pale into insignificance when compared to the massive crisis affecting those regions which were crossed by the armies fighting the Thirty Years War [*Parker and Smith* (eds.), 1978; *Parker*, 1987]. Not only in the Germanies, but also in Bohemia, Poland and Burgundy widespread destruction and depopulation occurred. Moreover, in the second half of the seventeenth century, France was affected by a long-lasting economic depression, and the efforts of Colbert to further French trade were only moderately effective in a period when most Marseilles merchants judged that they could not afford to take any risks [*Léon and Carrère*, 1970: Vol.2, 188–9]. Long-term depression also had very negative effects upon the French peasantry. With agricultural prices low while taxes increased steadily, peasants were indebted and many of them lost their land to local *coqs de village*, who had enriched themselves by tax collection and usury. In Northern France the ownership of a team of horses, which in this area was indispensible to an economically viable enterprise, was rare enough that the fortunate owner was considered to form part of the village elite [*Goubert*, 1968: 198].

In spite of the catastrophic situation in the countryside, French merchants ultimately overcame the trade depression, and between about 1730 and 1780, French trade in the Mediterranean entered upon a period of renewed prosperity. The situation was rather different in

Northern Italy, which had been one of the chief centres of European trade, industry and finance between the twelfth and sixteenth centuries. Venetian textile industries declined, and present-day scholars are still debating whether Venetian cloth was priced out of the market by high wages or by the numerous taxes to which it was subjected [*Rapp*, 1976: 140]. Venetian and other North Italian entrepreneurs found profits from trade so insecure that they invested in the countryside, and Italy became an exporter of wine, olive oil and silk thread.[12] Profits from these trades were high enough to support the luxurious lifestyle affected by the upper classes, but Italy was ousted from its place in the centre of the European world economy.

In spite of these well-documented individual crises, there is considerable debate among seventeenth-century historians, who are very far from agreeing that the European economy as a whole was going through a period of crisis. In part this is due to the fact that Holland, and England to a lesser extent, do not fit into the overall crisis-ridden pattern. Moreover, recent work on seventeenth-century Spain has cast considerable doubt on our notions of the 'decline of Spain', once considered the classical example of the seventeenth century crisis [*Kamen*, 1980]. Another difficulty stems from the fact that economic reverses did not all occur at the same time, even though many contemporaries, and Voltaire in their wake, considered 1640 a time of troubles for the entire Eurasian continent.

Certain scholars have attempted to link the economic difficulties of the period with the vagaries of the weather. The seventeenth century was a time of cool, rainy summers and cold winters, which caused harvest failures in many parts of Europe [*Le Roy Ladurie*, 1983]. But climatic events, like other natural catastrophes, never affect human societies in an unmediated fashion. The historian Emmanuel Le Roy Ladurie, when dealing with climatic changes in historical times, specifically warns the reader that the effects of climate upon agriculture are so complex that he prefers to not discuss them [*Le Roy Ladurie*, 1983: Vol.1, 23–4]. On the other hand, we now have evidence of demographic stagnation and decline for many seventeenth-century societies living under a wide variety of political regimes. We therefore need to find causes for these difficulties that are not too parochial and may have led to population decline in many different parts of the Old World.

One such overall explanation starts out from the frequency, long duration and general savagery of seventeenth-century wars. In the European context, these wars have been linked to state formation; in many places, centralised absolutist regimes were springing up, and many of the rulers concerned saw war as the means of consolidating their power both on an international and on a domestic level. Earlier historiography had usually adopted the viewpoint of the rulers involved in the contest. Only in the last decades, under the impression of two World Wars and the dangers arising from the arms race, have a few iconoclastic historians challenged this perspective and insisted on the proximity of state formation and organised crime [*Tilly*, 1985]. In the same vein, it has been pointed out that war-related mobilization of people and resources may well have constituted a burden which was too heavy for the fragile economies of that time [*Steensgaard*, 1978]. The overall technical level of production did not increase significantly in the seventeenth century, and taxes became progressively more burdensome. In the long run, economic crises were bound to occur. This explanation has the merit that the major cause for economic crisis is non-parochial and yet allows us to explain why different economies experienced the crisis at different times, and at varying degrees of severity. For not all rulers 'overloaded' the fragile economies of the territories which they controlled to quite the same degree, and not all economies were equally vulnerable. At the same time, Steensgaard's model, similar to most other explanations invented by historians, reflects a concern of the time in which it was devised, in this instance, the rising costs of the arms race.

Many Ottoman historians will respond quite readily to the suggestion that the seventeenth century was a period of demographic and economic difficulties. Before the first quarter of the century had elapsed, population decline was visible in certain parts of the country, and by the 1640s some of the more important Anatolian towns had shrunk to about the half the size they had possessed in the 1580s [*Jennings*, 1976: 39]. Most seventeenth-century tax records are a much less reliable source for population data than their sixteenth-century predecessors; but the overall impression for those parts of the Ottoman Empire which have been studied to date is one of demographic decline [*McGowan*, 1981: 114]. Foundation accounts show that by the middle of the seventeenth century, even wealthy pious foundations were confronted with major budget deficits, while the decline of industries such as the Bursa silk and the Salonica woollen cloth manufactures must have had negative repercussions on these two important cities [*Faroqhi*, 1988; *Braude*, 1979; *Çızakça*, 1980].

Certain scholars consider these phenomena as symptoms of the 'decline of the Ottoman Empire', but particularly a historian working in a comparative perspective will be disinclined to accept this view. After all certain parts of Anatolia recovered during the middle years of the seventeenth century, while between 1700 and 1770, many regions of the Ottoman Empire experienced a marked economic revival [*Goffman*,

1990: 142ff.; *Fukasawa*, 1987]. In my view, many Ottomanist historians, when writing about 'decline', have joined the depression of the early 1600s and that of the early 1800s. This was made easy due to the fact that both these periods coincided with intensive involvement of English, French and Dutch merchants in the eastern Mediterranean, and it is possible that there existed a connection between outside involvement and the downturn of the Ottoman economy. Moreover, a concern on the part of Turkish scholars with the process by which the Ottoman state was turned into a semi-colony from the closing years of the eighteenth century onward coincided with an Orientalist concern with the 'decline of the Islamic world'. Orientalists writing about the mediaeval caliphal period had long dominated the profession, and had never been quite comfortable with the notion that the decline which followed the Mongol or even the Seljuk invasions had not been as irreversible as they had assumed.[13]

While Ottoman historians and those dealing with Moghul India were able to convince their colleagues that a 'silver age' of Islamic civilisation occurred in the sixteenth and seventeenth centuries, this modification of the previous paradigm was accepted but grudgingly, and Ottomanist scholars of the mid-twentieth century rarely challenged the paradigm of 'early and long-lasting decline' in an explicit fashion. Quite to the contrary. A major historian such as Ömer Lütfi Barkan adopted this paradigm, and linked it to the idea that the Ottoman state and society, which he regarded as unique repositories of social and cultural values, were destroyed by economic and political trends originating in Europe [*Barkan*, 1975a: 26]. Only in the most recent historiography do we find attempts to analyse the notion of decline, to study this concept as a phenomenon in intellectual history, and thereby to limit its wholesale and tendentious application.

A MAJOR LACUNA

The present study does not discuss the role of class in Ottoman society *vis-à-vis* its early modern European counterparts, although this is one of the crucial issues facing the social historian. But while there is an extensive literature on the applicability or otherwise of the concept of class to late mediaeval and early modern European realities, Ottoman historians to the present day shy away from the issue. As a result we do not possess any serious discussion concerning the different types of class concept which may – or may not – be appropriate to Ottoman realities. At the bottom of this reticence lies the assumption previously alluded to, that class tensions did not exist in classical Ottoman society, and that classes only formed after the intrusion of European capital in the nineteenth century. However, there is ample evidence for class tension in the rich Ottoman documentation of the sixteenth and seventeenth centuries.[14] While it is obvious that the class concept must be redefined for the Ottoman context, it is a mistake to assume that the inhabitants of the Ottoman Empire lived in classless harmony.

In addition, European mediaeval and early modern historiography contains a rich and intensive discussion of other social groups whose solidarities and conflicts affected society as a whole, such as the faction, the clan, the extended family or even the literary coterie. Where the pre-nineteenth-century Ottoman Empire is concerned, we know that such groups existed, but they have not been investigated in any detail [Fleischer, 1986: 23ff.]. Therefore it is still too early to say to what extent these and other groups furthered the social integration and self-consciousness of the Ottoman political class. Now that Ottoman and early modern European historiography are less remote from one another than they used to be, the time has come to discuss social conflict in a more sophisticated manner than was possible in the past.

CONCLUSION

This rapid *tour d'horizon* demonstrates that Ottoman and early modern European historians share quite a few concerns. Most prominent is the rejection of a hard-and-fast boundary between 'traditional' and 'modern'. Most European historians no longer believe that there was a point of 'take-off' in social as well as in economic history, and that once this point of no return had been passed, a society was firmly launched on the road to 'modernisation'. Many Ottoman historians no longer believe that 'modern' armies, educational systems and forms of property-holding came in as completely alien importations. Historians in both disciplines today conceive of social change as a multi-layered process, and inequalities between regions of a country or empire form part of the model rather than mere 'special conditions' characterising this or that individual case. Tensions are acknowledged between people advocating different kinds of change, and those changes ultimately adopted are the results of class alignments and class conflicts within a given society. This emphasis on complexity is almost a 'period characteristic' of present-day historiography, which is on the whole hostile toward the attempts at sweeping synthesis so characteristic of the 1960s and early 1970s [Bayly, 1989: 14].

While parallels between European and Ottoman historiography of the early modern periods strike the eye, it is more difficult to explain them. Explanatory factors can be grouped in three categories. To begin with, a certain stage in the discovery of primary sources may determine why a given set of scholarly attitudes prevails at a given time. An emphasis on the publication and interpretation of individual documents is common when the number of documents known is still limited. This stage can be observed in European mediaeval history during the nineteenth century and in European Ottomanist historiography during the 1920s and 1930s.

On the other hand the 'document fetishism' rightly criticised in recent publications on Ottoman history is at least partly a response to the overwhelming amount of primary sources whose existence first became known during the 1940s and 1950s, and accessible to a broader group of scholars from about 1960 onward. This explanation may seem pedestrian. Many authors dealing with the history of scholarship de-emphasise dynamics internal to a given field, and point out that the broader political, social or philosophical concerns of a given time period are more important in determining the direction of research even in a specialised discipline such as Ottoman history [Cohen, 1984: 7, 153]. It is certainly true that the availability of sources is less of a constraint than it appears at first sight. When the scholarly concern is there, historians are often quite inventive in locating the requisite sources, while mountains of primary material will remain neglected when interest is lacking[15].

'Document fetishism' can also be explained by the positivist stand which has been a characteristic of Ottoman historiography throughout the twentieth century, and we may explain this phenomenon by the manner in which Ottoman chroniclers used the official documents available to them, and not simply by the example of late nineteenth and early twentieth-century European scholarship. On one level the 'document fetishism' of Ottomanists thus can be explained by the unreflected imitation of an attitude characteristic of the relevant primary sources. But when all is said and done, the historian also constructs his/her views of history in a constant dialogue with primary and secondary sources. The intellectual framework within which Ottoman history is practised is as yet poorly developed, and this state of affairs has made us susceptible to the 'occupational disease' of being overwhelmed by our documents.

On another level, recent historiography on the Ottoman Empire is marked by a certain disenchantment with the central state. The *ayan* of the eighteenth and early nineteenth centuries are today regarded as a product of Ottoman state and society, and sponsors of interesting cultural activity[16]. The moral opprobrium with which they were viewed by early 'Republican mode' historians has largely disappeared. We no longer see the Ottoman state as the main or even exclusive source of economic dynamism, an assumption which dominated the historiography of the sixteenth and seventeenth centuries until quite recently[17]. Rather it is now admitted that state policies can also be the source of economic crisis, and decentralisation may have positive side effects where economic growth is concerned. This refusal to see the centralised national state as the *non plus ultra* of political history is also visible in branches of European historical scholarship. The cautiously positive evaluation of the 1648 treaties of Munster and Osnabruck, which put an end to the Thirty Years War and established a congeries of independent states in the Germanies, might be cited as a case in point [*Parker*, 1987: 317–8]. On quite a different plane the vogue of 'community studies' in which borrowings from anthropology are very obvious, also indicate a widespread conviction that centralised states and their bureaucracies are not the only subjects that a historian may legitimately study.

This tendency certainly has its roots in the life experiences of the historians concerned. Some of those who have lived through the difficult 1970s and 1980s in Turkey have come to regard the central state and its institutions as a potential source of disruption in their personal and scholarly lives. The tensions of the Vietnam War have affected American historians and social scientists dealing with East Asia more profoundly than the average Ottomanist historian working in the United States. Even so, the Vietnam War occurred when many American and European historians presently active in the field were at their most impressionable age, and has contributed toward disillusionment with powerful centralised states. Moreover, the repercussions of Near Eastern conflicts of the present day have made quite a few researchers sceptical of the nation state paradigm as a whole. In the context of Western Europe, concern about protecting individuals from the interventions of an omnipotent bureaucratic apparatus has been growing in recent years, while Eastern European scholars have yet other reasons for regarding all manner of centralised bureaucratic machineries with profound distrust. It is difficult to imagine Ottoman historiography developing in a vacuum, completely isolated from all these different and yet converging experiences.[18]

But apart from common features whose main source is in the mind and approaches of historians, we also encounter parallels involving 'real' phenomena. At times the research worker may experience some difficulty distinguishing between the two, since what in one context appears to be part of the researcher's approach, under different circumstances may turn into a feature of reality as constructed by the historian. The obverse is of course true as well. A scholar may choose to write a book on internal trade in the Ottoman Empire and discover that urban development was tied more closely to internal than to foreign trade. On one level, this is an empirical observation. But at the same time, this observation may find its place in an overall 'internalist' approach, which emphasises the historical significance of internal developments vis-à-vis dynamics 'imported' from Western Europe [İslamoğlu-İnan, 1987: 12ff.]. By the integration into this particular context, an individual empirical observation changes character and becomes part of the 'overall approach'. Parallels between Ottoman and European historical experiences are easy to challenge; the obvious objection is that the researcher pointing them out is motivated by a set of basic social or philosophical assumptions, which are not necessarily shared by the scholarly community as a whole. But then the same is true of those who, in the traditional manner, emphasise the diverging experiences of early modern Europe and the Ottoman world.

NOTES

1. In choosing the title for this article I was inspired by Cohen [1984].
2. This controversy, in which Sencer Divitçioğlu defended the idea that the Ottoman Empire should be regarded as an example of the Asiatic Mode of Production and (among others) Mübeccel Kiray the notion of a 'feudal' Ottoman society, raged in the late 1960s and early 1970s. Compare Divitçioğlu [1971].
3. I owe this reference to Mr Dieter Thalmayr.
4. Among the authors of 'advice' literature of this period, Koçu bey might be placed in this category. Kātib Çelebi, known for his religious learning, towards the end of his life was highly critical of many contemporary representatives of organised religion. Compare İnalcık [1973: 185].
5. Findley [1989: 131–211] discusses the education and intellectual attainments of nineteenth-century Ottoman officials within the 'traditional-modern' paradigm.
6. Compare Cohen [1984] for the attitudes of American historians working on nineteenth and twentieth-century China.
7. I owe these ideas to Isenbike Togan.
8. For two exceptions compare İnalcık [1958] and Keyder [1987]. Keyder regards the history of Byzantium and the Ottoman Empire as essentially cyclical.
9. Views of this kind were expressed in the literary circle surrounding Cevat Şakir (Halikarnas Balıkçısı) and later by Azra Erhat.
10. The 'rehabilitation' of non-classical ancient art was not an innovation of the 1950s, but began in the early years of this century. Concerning the political overtones of Dark Ages historiography in the Federal Republic of Germany compare the exhibition 'Werdendes Abendland an Rhein und Ruhr', Essen, Villa Hügel, 1956.
11. The vogue of the *ahis* in popular historiography can be explained in part by this inclination.
12 Sella [1974: 4 418–20] discusses Italy's industrial decline and successful competition on the part of newer industrial locations.
13 For this reason Marshall Hodgson insists on the expansion of the Islamic world in fifteenth and sixteenth centuries, and upon cultural florescence in the 'Gunpowder Empires' [*Hodgson*, 1974: Vol.3, 14–15].

14. See Faroqhi [forthcoming]. For a discussion of the different ways in which the term 'class' can be used compare Wehler [1988: 171-2].
15. As proof for theses claims, we may cite the development of *histoire des mentalités* in France. Fifty years ago, most historians would have thought that lack of sources made it impossible to study the progress of secularisation among eighteenth-century French provincials, changes in courtship patterns among peasants or the evolution of intra-family relations. With growing interest in such topics, scholars have located sources which hitherto had remained unexploited, or else used well-known sources in new ways. Compare Vovelle [1982].
16. Compare Arel [1986: 43-76]. The author is currently working on a broadly-based study of fortified houses in the Aegean coastlands of Anatolia.
17. However, İnalcık [1969] emphasises the role of individual craftsmen and merchants; this article may be regarded as one of the first moves away from a purely state-centred approach in Ottoman economic history.
18. Of course, it is always difficult to 'handle' these experiences. Research directions always mirror the life experiences of the scholar involved, but at the same time, the need to guard against anachronisms, sloppy use of sources and subjective distortions or over-interpretations remains paramount.

REFERENCES

Abou El-Haj, Rifa'at, 1984, *The 1703 Rebellion and the Structure of Ottoman Politics*, İstanbul; Leiden: Nederlands Instituut voor het Nabije Oosten.
Abu-Husayn, Abdul Rahim, 1985, *Provincial Leaderships in Syria, 1575-1650*, Beirut: American University of Beirut.
Akdağ, Mustafa, 1963, *Celâlî Isyanları*, Ankara: Dil ve Tarih Coğrafya Fakültesi Yayınları.
Aktepe, Münir, 1958, *Patrona Halil Isyanı (1730)*, İstanbul: Edebiyat Fakültesi Yayınları.
"Ali, 1984, *Der Löwe von Temeschwar. Erinnerungen an Ca"fer Pascha den Älteren, aufgezeichnet von seinem Siegelbewahrer "Ali* (eds. and trs. Richard Kreutel and Karl Teply), Graz: Styria.
And, Metin, 1982, *Osmanli Şenliklerinde Türk Sanatları*, Ankara: Kültür ve Turizm Bakanlığı Yayınları.
Anderson, Perry, 1974, *Lineages of the Absolutist State*, London: Verso/New Left Books.
Arel, Ayda, 1986, 'Cincin köyünde Cihanoğullarına ait Yapılar', V, *Araştırma Sonuçları Toplantısı*, Vol.I, Ankara: TC Kültür Bakanlığı.
Barkan, Ömer Lütfi, 1951 review of Braudel, 1966, *Iktisat Fakültesi Mecmuası*, Vol.XII, pp.173-91 (This review refers to the 1949 edition of Braudel's work).
Barkan, Ömer Lütfi, 1975a, 'The Price Revolution of the Sixteenth Century: A Turning Point in the Economic History of the Near East', *International Journal of Middle East Studies*, Vol.6, pp.3-28.
Barkan, Ömer Lütfi, 1975b, 'Feodal Düzen ve Osmanlı Timarı', *Türkiye Iktisat Tarihi Semineri, Metinler/Tartışmalar* (eds. Osman Okyar and Ünal Nalbantoglu), Ankara: Hacettepe Üniversitesi Yayınları.
Barkan, Ömer Lütfi, 1980, *Türkiy'ede Toprak Meselesi*, İstanbul: Gözlem Yayınları.
Bayly, C.A., 1989, *Imperial Meridian: The British Empire and the World 1780-1830*. London; New York: Longman.
Bennassar, Bartholomé and Lucille Bennassar, 1989, *Les Chrétiens d'Allah. L'Histoire extraordinaire des renégats, XVIe-XVIIe siècles*, Paris: Perrin.
Berktay, Halil, 1983, *Cumhuriyet Ideolojisi ve Fuat Köprülü*, İstanbul: Kaynak Yayınları.

Berktay, Halil, 1985, 'Tarih Çalışmaları', in *Cumhuriyet Dönemi Türkiye Ansiklopedisi*, İstanbul: İletişim Yayınları.
Braudel, Benjamin, 1979, 'International Competition and Domestic Cloth in the Ottoman Empire, 1500–1650: A Study in Undevelopment', *Review*, Vol.II, pp.437–54.
Braudel, Fernand, 1966, *La Méditerranée et le monde méditerranéen au temps de Philippe II*, 2 vols., 2nd edition, Paris: Librairie Armand Colin.
Braudel, Fernand, 1979, *Civilisation matérielle, économie et capitalisme, XVe–XVIIIe siècle*, 3 vols., Paris: Armand Colin.
van Bruinessen, Martinus, 1978, 'Agha, Shaikh and State: On the Social and Political Organisation of Kurdistan', Ph.D. Dissertation, Utrecht: author's publication.
von Busbeck, Oghier Ghiselin, 1926, *Vier Briefe aus der Türkei* (ed. and tr. Wolfram von den Steinen), Erlangen: Verlag der Philosophischen Akademie.
Bushkovitch, Paul, 1980, *The Merchants of Moscow 1580–1650*, Cambridge: Cambridge University Press.
Cezar, Yavuz, 1986, *Osmanlı Maliyesinde Bunalım ve Değişim Dönemi (XVIII. yydan Tanzimat'a Mali Tarih)*, İstanbul: Alan Yayıncılık.
Cohen, Paul, 1984, *Discovering History in China: American Historical Writing on the Recent Chinese Past*, New York: Columbia University Press.
Çızakça, Murat, 1980, 'Price History and the Bursa Silk Industry: A Study in Ottoman Industrial Decline, 1550–1650',: *The Journal of European Economic History*, Vol.XL, pp.533–50.
Darnton, Robert, 1981, *The Great Cat Massacre and other Episodes in French Cultural History*, New York: Vintage Books/Random House.
Divitçioğlu, Sencer, 1971, *Asya Üretim Tarzı ve Osmanlı Toplumu*, İstanbul: Köz Yayınları.
Ergenç, Özer, 1981, 'Osmanlı Şehirlerindeki Yönetim Kurumlarının Niteliği Üzerine Bazi Düsünceler', in *VIII. Türk Tarih Kongresi, Ankara, 11–15 Ekim 1976, Kongreye Sunulan Bildiriler*, 2 vols., Ankara: Türk Tarih Kurumu Basımevi.
Evliya Çelebi, 1896–1938, *Seyahatnamesi*, 10 vols. İstanbul: Ikdam Matbaasi et al.
Faroqhi, Suraiya, 1988, 'A Great Foundation in Difficulties: Or Some Evidence on Economic Contraction in the Ottoman Empire of the Mid-Seventeenth Century', in *Mélanges Professeur Robert Mantran* (ed. Abdeljelil Temimi), Zaghouan: Publications CEROMDI.
Faroqhi, Suraiya, 1992, 'Political Activity among Ottoman Taxpayers and the Problem of Sultanic Legitimation (1570–1650)', *Journal of the Economic and Social History of the Orient*, Vol. 35.
Findley, Carter V., 1989, *Ottoman Civil Officialdom: A Social History*, Princeton, NJ: Princeton University Press.
Fleischer, Cornell, 1986, *Bureaucrat and Intellectual in the Ottoman Empire: The Historian Mustafa Âli (1541–1600)*, Princeton, NJ: Princeton University Press.
Fukasawa, Katsumi, 1987, *Toilerie et commerce du Levant d'Alep à Marseille*, Paris: Éditions du Centre National de la Recherche Scientifique.
Genç, Mehmet, 1975, 'Osmanlı Maliyesinde Malikâne Sistemi', in *Türkiye Iktisat Tarihi Semineri, Metinler Tartışmalar* (eds. Osman Okyar and Ünal Nalbantoğlu), Ankara Hacettepe Üniversitesi Yayınları.
Goffman, Daniel, 1990, *Izmir and the Levantine World, 1550–1650*, Seattle: University of Washington Press.
Gombrich, Ernst H., 1984, *Aby Warburg. Eine intellektuelle Biographie* (tr. Matthias Fienbork), Frankfurt/M.: Suhrkamp.
Göçek Fatma Müge, 1987, *East Encounters West: France and the Ottoman Empire in the Eighteenth Century*, New York; Oxford: Oxford University Press.
Goubert, Pierre, 1968, *Cent mille provinciaux au XVIIe siècle, Beauvais et le Beauvaisis de 1600 à 1730*, Paris: Fayard.
Hauser, Henri, 1963, *La modernité du XVIe siècle*, Paris: Armand Colin.
Hess, Andrew, 1978, *The Forgotten Frontier: A History of the Sixteenth-Century Ibero-African Frontier*, Chicago, IL: Chicago University Press.

Hodgson, Marshall, 1974, *The Venture of Islam: Conscience and History in a World Civilization*, 3 vols., Chicago, IL: University of Chicago Press.
İnalcık, Halil, 1958, 'The Problem of the Relationship between Byzantine and Ottoman Taxation', in *Akten des XI. Internationalen Byzantinisten-Kongresses* (eds. Franz Dölger and Hans–Georg Beck), Munich: Beck.
İnalcık, Halil, 1969, 'Capital Formation in the Ottoman Empire', *Journal of Economic History*, Vol.29, pp.97–140.
İnalcık, Halil, 1973, *The Ottoman Empire: The Classical Age*, London: Weidenfeld & Nicolson.
İnalcık, Halil, 1978, 'Impact of the *Annales* School on Ottoman Studies and New Findings', *Review: Journal of the Fernand Braudel Center*, Vol.1, pp.69–96.
İnalcık, Halil, 1979, 'The Question of the Closing of the Black Sea under the Ottomans', *Archeion Pontou*, Vol.35, pp.74–110.
Islam Ansiklopedisi, Islam Alemi Tarih, Coğrafya, Etnografya ve Biyografya Lugatı, 1950– , İstanbul: Milli Eğitim Basımevi.
İslamoğlu, Huri and Çağlar Keyder, 1977, 'Agenda for Ottoman History', *Review*, Vol.1, pp.31–57.
İslamoğlu–İnan, Huri, 1987, 'Introduction: "Oriental Despotism" in World-System Perspective', in *The Ottoman Empire and the World Economy* (ed. by Huri İslamoğlu–İnan), Cambridge: Cambridge University Press; Paris: Maison des Sciences de l'Homme.
Jennings, Ronald, 1973, 'Loans and Credit in Early 17th Century Ottoman Judicial Records: The Sharia Court of Anatolian Kayseri', *Journal of the Economic and Social History of the Orient*, Vol.XVI, pp.168–214.
Jennings, Ronald, 1976, 'Urban population in Anatolia in the Sixteenth Century: A Study of Kayseri, Karaman, Amasya, Trabzon and Erzurum', *International Journal of Middle East Studies*, Vol.7, pp.21–57.
Kafadar, Cemal, 1986, 'A Death in Venice 1575: Anatolian Muslim Merchants Trading in the Serenissima', *Raiyyet Rüsûmu. Essays presented to Halil İnalcık on his Seventieth Birthday by his Colleagues and Students* (eds. Bernard Lewis et al.), *Journal of Turkish Studies*, Vol.10, pp.191–218.
Kamen, Henry, 1980, *Spain in the later Seventeenth Century, 1665–1700*, London; New York: Longman.
Keyder, Çağlar, 1987, *State and Class in Turkey. A Study in Capitalist Development*, London: Verso/New Left Books.
Köprülü, Fuat, 1959, *Osmanlı Devletinin Kuruluşu*, Ankara: Türk Tarih Kurumu Basımevi.
Kunt, Ibrahim Metin, 1974, 'Ethnic-Regional (*Cins*) Solidarity in the Seventeenth-Century Ottoman Establishment', *International Journal of Middle East Studies*, Vol.5, pp.233–9.
Kunt, Ibrahim Metin, 1977, 'Derviş Mehmed Paşa, Vezir and Entrepreneur: A Study in Ottoman Political-Economic Theory and Practice', in: *Turcica*, Vol.IX, pp.197–214.
Kunt, Ibrahim Metin, 1983, *The Sultan's Servants: The Transformation of Ottoman Provincial Government 1550–1650*, New York: Columbia University Press.
Kuran, Aptullah, 1987, *Sinan: The Grand Old Master of Ottoman Architecture*, Washington: Ada Press Publishers; İstanbul: Institute of Turkish Studies.
Lapidus, Ira M., 1969, 'Muslim Cities and Islamic Studies', *Middle Eastern Cities* (ed. I.M. Lapidus), Berkeley, Los Angeles, CA: University of California Press.
Léon, Pierre and Charles Carrère, 1970, 'L'appel des marchés', in *Histoire économique et sociale de la France* (eds. Fernand Braudel and Ernest Labrousse), 4 vols., Paris: Presses Universitaires de France.
Le Roy Ladurie, Emmanuel, 1983, *Histoire du climat depuis l'an mil*, 2 vols., Paris: Flammarion.
Maier, Charles, 1988, *The Unmasterable Past. History, Holocaust and German National Identity*, Cambridge, MA: Harvard University Press.

Mandaville, Jon, 1979, 'Usurious Piety: The Cash-Vaqf Controversy in the Ottoman Empire', *International Journal of Middle East Studies*, Vol.X, pp.289–308.

Mayer, Arno, 1981, *The Persistence of the Old Régime; Europe to the Great War*, New York: Pantheon Books.

McGowan, Bruce, 1981, *Economic Life in Ottoman Europe: Taxation, Trade and the Struggle for Land, 1600–1800*, Cambridge: Cambridge University Press; Paris: Maison des Sciences de l'Homme.

Necipoğlu–Kafadar, Gülru, 1986, 'The Formation of an Ottoman Imperial Tradition: The Topkapı Palace in the 15th and 16th Centuries', Ph.D. dissertation, Harvard University, Cambridge/MA: University Microfilms.

Orhonlu, Cengiz, 1974, *Osmanlı İmparatorluğunun Güney Siyaseti, Habeş Eyaleti*, İstanbul: İstanbul Universitesi Edebiyat Fakültesi Yayınları.

Parker, Geoffrey and Lesley Smith (eds.), 1978, *The General Crisis of the Seventeenth Century*, London: Routledge & Kegan Paul.

Parker, Geoffrey, 1987, *La guerre de trente ans* (tr. André Charpentier), Paris: Aubier.

Rapp, Richard, 1976, *Industry and Economic Decline in Seventeenth Century Venice*, Cambridge, MA: Harvard University Press.

Raymond, André, 1973–74, *Artisans et commerçants au Caire au XVIIIe siècle*, 2 vols., Damascus: Institut Français de Damas.

Raymond, André, 1979, 'La conquête ottomane et le développement des grandes villes arabes. Le cas du Caire, de Damas, et d'Alep', *Revue de l'Occident musulman et de la Méditerranée*, Vol.1, pp.115–34.

Rodinson, Maxime, 1978, *Islam and Capitalism* (tr. Brian Pearce), Austin TX University of Texas Press.

Romano, Ruggiero, 1980, 'Versuch einer ökonomischen Typologie', in *Die Gleichzeitigkeit des Ungleichzeitigen. Fünf Studien zur Geschichte Italiens* (tr. Eva Maek–Gérard), Frankfurt/M.: Suhrkamp.

de Roover, Raymond, 1963, *The Rise and Decline of the Medici Bank 1397–1494*, Cambridge, MA: Harvard University Press.

Schilcher, Linda S., 1985, *Families in Politics: Damascene Factions and Estates of the 18th and 19th Centuries*, Stuttgart: Franz Steiner Verlag.

Sella, Domenico, 1974, 'European Industries 1500–1700', in *The Fontana History of Europe: The Sixteenth and Seventeenth Centuries* (ed. Carlo M. Cipolla), Glasgow: Fontana Books.

Steensgaard, Niels, 1978, 'The Seventeenth Century Crisis', in *General Crisis of the Seventeenth Century* (eds. Goeffrey Parker and L.M. Smith), London: Routledge & Kegan Paul.

Stoianovich, Troian, 1970, 'Model and Mirror of the Pre-modern Balkan City', in: *La ville balkanique XVe–XIXe ss, Studia Balcanica*, Vol.3, pp.83–110.

Tilly, Charles, 1985, 'War Making and State Making as Organised Crime', in *Bringing the State Back In* (eds. Peter B. Evans, Dietrich Rueschemeyer and Theda Skocpol), Cambridge: Cambridge University Press.

Vovelle, Michel, 1982, *Idéologies et mentalités*, Paris: François Maspero.

de Vries, Jan, 1976, *The Economy of Europe in an Age of Crisis 1600–1750*, Cambridge: Cambridge University Press.

Weber, Eugen, 1976, *Peasants into Frenchmen: The Modernisation of Rural France 1870–1914*, Stanford, CA: Stanford University Press.

Wehler, Hans–Ulrich, 1988, *Aus der Geschichte lernen?* Munich: C.H. Beck.

Wittek, Paul, 1938, *The Rise of the Ottoman Empire*, London: The Royal Asiatic Society of Great Britain and Ireland.

Yates, Frances A., 1985, *Astraea, The Imperial Theme in the Sixteenth Century*, London: Ark.

Zachariadou, Elizabeth A., *Trade and Crusade. Venetian Crete and the Emirates of Menteshe and Aydın (1300–1415)*, Venice, Istituto Ellenico di Studi Bizantini e Postbizantini di Venetia.

Three Empires and the Societies They Governed: Iran, India and the Ottoman Empire

HALIL BERKTAY

An international symposium on 'The State, Decentralisation and Tax-Farming, 1500–1850: The Ottoman Empire, Iran and India' was held at Munich on 2–5 May 1990 under the auspices of the Nahost-Institut of the University. It was preceded by at least two other gatherings of somewhat similar tone and intent as well as, partially, composition: the Bochum Conference of 1–3 December 1988 on 'Legalism and Political Legitimation in the Ottoman Empire and in the Early Turkish Republic', and the Rockefeller Foundation Seminar on Ottoman History held at St. Louis, USA, on 12–15 April 1990. Various people involved in hitherto relatively isolated, individual efforts over the past five years to 'take stock of' [*Akarlı and Fleischer*, 1990] and to formulate 'new approaches' [*Faroqhi*, 1988] to Ottoman history gradually drew together at these three venues in diverse yet collective dialogue. What many among them probably had in terms of strong common ground, despite inevitable differences, was perhaps best expressed by Cornell Fleischer and Engin Akarlı [1990: 1–3] in a discussion paper they read at St. Louis only two weeks before Munich when they singled out for criticism: (1) 'the nationalistic perspective' of Republican Turkish scholarship; (2) an 'elitist and statist tradition' that is 'perhaps as old as the art of historical writing' and which 'pays little attention to . . . nomads, peasants, artisans and shopkeepers' in reducing history to ruling-class history from above; as well as (3) mutual otherisation by Western/Christian and Eastern/Islamic societies and bodies of scholarship. Here most of the researchers involved would seek the underlying causes of the methodological and conceptual backwardness of Ottoman historical studies. 'Assumption 1: Ottoman

---

Halil Berktay is former lecturer in economic history, Faculty of Political Sciences, Ankara University. Permanent address: Başlık Sok. 20/8, 1. Levent, Istanbul, Turkey. The first draft of this article was initially presented as one of the two summing-up reports (following upon that by Steven Blake of St. Olaf's College, Minnesota) at the Munich conference. The author would therefore like to thank all those present during the discussion on 5 May 1990 for their invaluable comments and criticism while emphasising the personal nature of the final interpretation.

history is not history at all', Suraiya Faroqhi [1988: 1] had therefore commented in a satirical vein in an earlier draft of her own, and she as well as Akarlı and Fleischer [1990: 4] recommended 'comparative analyses and bringing Ottoman history into the history of the world' as an antidote.

Comparisons with who or what? Traditionally, comparisons with the West had been high on the agenda for (Turkish) Ottomanists [Faroqhi, 1991]; inspired in turn by the Kemalist Revolution's drive to join the ranks of advanced nations in the 1920s – 'catching up with contemporary civilisation', as Atatürk put it [Berktay, 1990a: 112] – and then by the Republic's retreat into statist autarky in the 1930s, they had opted first for a relatively universalist and later for a particularist position [Berktay, 1987: 321–3, notes 3–4; Berktay, 1990a: 173–9], though their grasp of Western medieval history was not very impressive to begin with and became increasingly obsolete in time [Berktay, 1990a: Chs. III and V]. Meanwhile, another possible axis of comparison with other Asian empires went neglected except for noting the most obvious affinities and ideological continuities – such as the 'Counsel for Princes' literature – and then perhaps impounding them in the notion of a 'Near Eastern state' [İnalcık, 1973: 65–9]. A pity, because apart from the subjectivist derivation of that dubious concept [İslamoğlu-İnan and Keyder, 1977: section 1] and the particularist uses to which it has been put [Berktay, 1990a: 284–5] this is and has always been a very fruitful direction of inquiry – as the Munich symposium amply demonstrated by throwing doubting Ottomanists together with Indianists and Iranists who had all been basically going their separate ways.

WHAT DO MEDIEVAL STATES DO WHEN THEY RULE?

The overall theme proposed for the conference, of course, was one that was particularly conducive to productive exchange, focusing as it did on features that more or less permanently marked all three historical processes: (i) relatively strong central government (both the reality and its ideological offshoots – the latter pervasive enough even today to cause some historians to speak of 'strength' or 'centralism' without qualifications), though it was not altogether able to avoid lapsing into (ii) phases of decentralisation before recovering totally or partially; (iii) other quasi-cyclical alternations, frequently related or parallel, between periods dominated by military fiefs and those in which tax-farming rose to the fore.

But why was this so, and why is it important? At Munich, what might with some luck turn out to be interdisciplinary collaboration of an enduring sort was just beginning, and, understandably, most participants were as yet ready and willing only to volunteer descriptive information concerning their own specialities while asking prudent questions of others. Thus among the 17 papers presented, many dealt with the empirical details of various tax-farming or revenue-sharing systems as practised in Ottoman [*Özbaran*, 1990; *Çızakça*, 1990; *Veselá*, 1990; *Matuz*, 1990; *Salzmann*, 1990], Persian [*Fragner*, 1990; *Zarinebaf-Shahr*, 1990] or Indian [*Alam*, 1990; *Subrahmanyam*, 1990; *Rothermund*, 1990] territories; but a comprehensive, theoretical definition of tax-farming – such as modern sociological investigations of contemporary peasant communities in underdeveloped countries are likely to undertake – as well as an analytical exploration of its crucial importance for these three empires (and indeed for many other pre-capitalist societies of a certain minimum size in other parts of the world) was not easily attempted by historians. Yet to do so is to pose the larger question, to borrow a phrase from Therborn [1978], of what medieval states did when they ruled – a question which is, in fact, best answerable by looking at those laboratories for developing advanced statecraft that were Persia, India and the Ottoman Empire.

To see this, we have to consider ancient and medieval class formation and the formation of land rights in unison. In an incomparably more Eurocentrist age, and often following in the wake of what was then available in terms of academic learning or even conventional wisdom in fields outside their main areas of concentration and independent research, even the founders of classical Marxism were not above believing that only the ancient East had been marked by an absence of private property.[1] Today we know, however, that a complex terminology of land *tenure* – from the Latin *tenere*, 'to hold', since everybody 'held' land of someone else – was universally required to express the hierarchy of interlocking land rights that was such a striking feature of practically all 'traditional' societies.

As I have pointed out elsewhere [*Berktay*, 1987: 306–7], these usually consisted of (a) the king's/emperor's highest overlordship; (b) the rights of aristocratic/bureaucratic fief-holders and/or landowners; (c) the rights of the village community; (d) the rights of the peasant household. Peasant society existed from time immemorial, so to speak; it was much more ancient than any state or lordship that might be sitting over it at a given time (in other words, peasantries are not invented by lords or states[2], though they, too, are capable of at least partial demographic replenishment and socio-cultural modification through conquests of the *völkerwanderung* type[3] as practised by Turkic as well as Germanic tribes); it evolved slowly in response to various kinds of pressure (including demands from above by incipient or full-fledged exploiting classes for more surplus[4]); it underwent internal differentiation, with the heads of the wealthier households rising to assume leadership of the community, representing it against the lords or sometimes even emerging as village chieftains on their own in relatively 'early' historical spaces from which lordship external to the peasant settlement might yet be missing.[5] Perhaps we might usefully look upon these as potential candidates for ruling class status sent 'up' by village society.

On the other hand, any state-building centre that happened to establish itself in Antiquity or the Middle Ages over the basic substratum represented by categories (c) and (d) could not, given the level of development of the forces of production (including transport and communications technology) available at the time, hope to exercise direct jurisdiction over the extraction and further distribution of peasant surplus in any but the smallest locality; it therefore had to be able sooner or later to undertake fief distribution[6], sending at least some of its original constituents[7] or of its allies[8] 'out' across the face of the land and 'down' into closer contact with local society. Loyal followers that had been rewarded with booty in movables in the past now had to be rewarded with booty in land, and Rent that might have been flowing from the direct producers to any older generation of landlords had to be partially or wholly diverted to servants of the new state in the process. As various authors have noted independently of each other, whether with the Goths and Vandals on Gallo-Roman soil, with the Arabs in Mesopotamia or with the Oghuz in Iran – or for that matter the Mughals in India – the point of origin of all fief systems was the search for a method of 'quartering' or 'garrisoning' a conquering warrior aristocracy and its followers (= an 'army') on the land.[9] But once they received their benefices and were also equipped with the prerogatives necessary for dominating the population and controlling (part of the flow of) the agricultural surplus[10], from mere 'officials' or 'representatives' of the state (which they might well have been especially if their original grants were fiefs-in-salary as in the Ottoman or even in the Carolingian case, and not fiefs-in-gift, as in the case of the relatively inexperienced Merovingians[11]) these fief-holders inevitably began to evolve and acquire some degree of autonomy as notables, magnates or even a hereditary aristocracy effectively wielding at least a share of public power at the provincial level. Alternatively, the centre had to strike some kind of compromise with pre-existing lordship whereby the latter acceded to the imposition of a new set of royal eminent rights from above and hence to the demand to pass on part of their revenue to the state in return for recognition of an irreducible minimum of their traditional status and privileges.

Historically, most cases were a blend of the two: fief-holders and landowners coexisted, either in adjacent spaces of their own or one superimposed on the other, yet never statically but in constant interaction, so that sometimes pre-conquest strata disappeared altogether, the Ottoman *malikane-divani* (half-state, half-estate) system providing fleeting testimony of a time when private freehold had not yet been swallowed up by military fiefs[12], while fief-holders elsewhere took advantage of profligate (Merovingian) or relatively weak (post-Carolingian) royal power to join (or constitute) the ranks of private lords holding only nominally from the king. In still other instances, the state centre sent out not fief-holders but more inspector-like functionaries[13] to encounter, supervise, and receive payment from those local elites that were involved in revenue-sharing arrangements with the king or emperor. And if central power was strong enough, the actual evolutionary process behind the set-up could be inverted and legally redefined so that the state ended up claiming a theoretical right to the entire revenue of the land, of which it pretended to be 'leaving' only a portion in the hands of its 'tax-collectors' at the grassroots level in return for their services and upkeep; these, in turn, might once have been quite powerful on their own, but through integration into the new matrix of social relations it was more like middling types that they ultimately came to appear. Such was the lot of the Ottoman *sipahi*, who retained virtually the entire agricultural surplus of his small *timar*, as well as that of the Indian *zemindar*, who kept only part of his 'taxes' and surrendered the rest under the Mughal *nizamat* – though the one was a petty knight under a strict military fief-system while the other has been conventionally thought of as a 'tax-farmer'. But did the *zemindar* really purchase a tax-farm? At Munich, especially the Indian historians and other Indologists present preferred to speak of 'revenue-sharing' in general [Alam, 1990; Rothermund, 1990]. Now in a way, even a fief system involves sharing revenue, of course, as the derivation of *katia*, *mukataa* and *ikta* from 'cut' or 'slice' in Arabic reveals, and as also indicated by the similarity of the legal fictions applied to the relations of the state centre with *sipahi* and *zemindar*. Nevertheless, it might perhaps have been more precise to restrict the use of this term (that is, revenue-sharing) to the pre-colonial Indian *zemindari* or to those distant Ottoman provinces where for various reasons the *timar* system was not implemented;[14] instead, the pre-conquest land-taxes were collected in collaboration with local elites and part of this revenue was then sent to İstanbul [Özbaran, 1990]. For at the other end of the scale, tax-farming in the strict sense, where a cash payment in advance serves to acquire the right to collect and retain the legally assessed taxes of a certain locality for so many years, also existed in all these societies, as exemplified by the Ottoman *iltizam*.

The point is that there was therefore an entire continuum of coexisting, interpenetrating and complementary forms of tax-farming, revenue-sharing and fief distribution, which under certain conditions[15] were mutually transformable into one another. Furthermore, seen cross-sectionally, they exhibited some common features: the ruling class was never just the centre but was always composed of a 'central' and a 'peripheral' component; the latter was the level where contingents sent 'up' by local society (including local peasant society) met and intermingled with contingents sent 'down' by the royal centre; this basic structure then folded again and again on itself through each successive act of war and conquest, so that like earth layers thrown up by a fault, every medieval ruling class – not as a theoretical abstraction but in its historical reality – was a composite of fragments of different vintage that had been moving around, cutting loose from a defeated locus of power and re-attaching themselves to a victorious one, undergoing cultural and ideological remoulding, emerging transfigured after long hibernations or sometimes completely sinking from sight, thereby also giving rise in its relations with the peasantry to 'the jumbled complexity of legal status' which Marc Bloch [1931: 83] noted, and which to date has not ceased to pose 'fallacies of origin' for excessively legal-minded historians.[16] But whatever its origins and 'mix', once it came into being, the 'peripheral' or 'provincial' wing of this ruling elite was also forever trying, in Muzaffar Alam's [1990] words, to extend its control over (part of) the revenue to the source of revenue, the land itself – and therefore also trying to weaken royal overlordship or to wrest it entirely out of the hands of the most 'statist' faction of the ruling class. Hence, regardless of whether a fief-system or a revenue-sharing arrangement were involved, intra-ruling class conflict (between the fief-distributing centre and the fief-holders, between state and tax-farmers, between the *nizamat* and the *zemindars*) was necessary and inevitable; it was as universal a feature of these Oriental empires as of the Western Middle Ages [Berktay, 1987: 312–14; Berktay, 1990a: 449–51].

ELITE FORMATION

Indeed, it could be said that this was what they all did when they 'governed': basically they 'managed', or tried to manage, the ebb and flow of this internal tension that was part and parcel of the historical dynamics of all traditional agrarian, subject-peasant – I would say feudal – societies. As it arose out of late tribal society, each incipient state-building nucleus of a warrior nobility, whether it had a sizeable religious-ethnic mass following of its own (like the Ottomans), whether it was more 'praetorian' (like the Ghaznevids or the Mughals) or as Bert Fragner [1990] pointed out at Munich more 'tribal' like the Safavids or the Kajars, was faced with the problems of collecting and organising around itself the autochtonous forces of the successively new historical settings that its rapacity and geographical mobility brought it into; of establishing the charismatic or impersonal elements of its rule; of defining or redefining kingship in order to legitimise its hegemony. In short, it had to construct a bureaucratic apparatus, and it had to utilise ideology. For both, external resources were needed: on a material level, it was not easy for purely internal surpluses based only on the slow growth of peasant productivity to provide the money to pay salaries and the firearms to equip troops with; the ranks of counsellors and civil servants had to be replenished periodically with outsiders in a certain process of 'partial reproduction of the ruling class through the state' [Haldon, 1991] if the hold of its own kin-group on the royal line or that of the conquered local elite were to be counterbalanced;[17] neither could the ideology to weld these disparate elements together in statehood be the old customs and traditions of the tribal rank-and-file that was inclined to regard, for example, the Seljukid sultan as, still, only a *primus inter pares* with regard to the rest of the Oghuz clan and tribe chieftains [Köprülü, 1941: 332–3; Berktay, 1990a: 153–4] – resort was therefore had to a new vehicle, usually in the form of a jump to some developed monotheism with its theories of the divine and hence absolute (non-elective, non-accountable) right of kings, which was what High Islam offered to the House of Seljuk and what Christianity offered to eleventh-century Norwegian magnates.[18]

At the Munich Conference, it was in papers on 'elite formation' that various phenomena susceptible to some such generalisation as the above were touched upon. Thus Muzaffar Alam [1990] began with a discussion of the 'integration' of the *zemindari*, a pre-conquest stratum, into the new 'imperial edifice' under the 'protection' of the Mughals. Then Sanjay Subrahmanyam [1990] spoke of 'intra-Asian elite movements', in a theoretical as well as empirical context: pointing out that, although foreign traders in coastal enclaves were sometimes assumed to have always remained as non-participants in the internal affairs of the country in question, this was not the case with the post-fifteenth century diaspora of Persian merchants in the Indian Ocean and their subsequent implantation in Southern India. There their presence, wealth and financial knowhow were immediately tapped by local rulers in furthering processes of state formation, long before they arrived in Northern India and, for the same reasons, came to dominate the Mughal court. Georg Berkemer [1990] then added another dimension with observations on how, among Northern Sircars in the eighteenth century, a major contradiction in 'political development' had been played out in terms of the confrontation between Islam, which became the religious and ideological instrument of consolidating central government, and Hinduism, to which local elites clung in opposing such centralisation. There were, in other words, two different sources from which power was accepted to emanate, and one symbolic form the struggle between the new rulers at the centre and the older local elites took was that of a race to accumulate titles deriving from the one or the other.

All this was extremely interesting both in itself and against the background of medieval, late medieval and early modern Turkish-Islamic history, where examples of a similar as well as a contrasting role for Islam could be found. As already indicated, at the time of the original Oghuz irruption, the Seljukids used Islamic ideology, of which the Iranian 'service aristocracy' were the carriers, to raise themselves far above their tribal followers as Near Eastern autocrats in the traditional Byzantine or Sassanid mould [*Köprülü*, 1938: 63–4; *Berktay*, 1990a: 154]. On the other hand, throughout the fifteenth and sixteenth centuries, the great centralisers of the Ottoman dynasty such as Bayezid I 'the Thunderbolt' (1389–1402), Mehmed II 'the Conqueror' (1451–81) and Selim I 'the Grim' (1512–20) all relied on so-called customary (*örfi*) or customary-sultanic (*örfi-sultani*) law to cut the ground from under the founding aristocracy of the state and the empire, whereas for its part that old Turkish nobility turned to the *Shar'ia* precisely because it provided a bulwark against the cosmopolitanisation of court culture in the hands of Bayezid's Christian advisers, against the rise of the *devşirmes* (the natally deracinated 'slaves of the Porte'), or against the conversion of hereditary patrimonies into land for conditional distribution as service fiefs (that is, *miri* land with its overlordship, or *obereigentum*, concentrated in the hands of the state). Here, then, religious law played the role of a brake on absolutist centralisation, as evidenced by the Islamic reaction under Bayezid II (1481–1512).[19] It was possible, therefore, for the 'same' belief-system in two different historical settings to shoulder quite opposite functions and lead to varying outcomes. Hence, it would seem that this was not so much a matter of the absolute content of this or that (religious) ideology in itself, as of what it came to stand for in combination and contradiction with others in a concrete context.

Yet another point in connection with ideology was the following: for Subrahmanyam, the role played by Persian merchants in Southern India demonstrated the enormous importance of trade in state formation. In Munich, both Alam and Subrahmanyam emphasised 'shop-keeping' as the basic function of the state, and Subrahmanyam maintained that it was from Persian merchants that Southern Indian rulers had learned the art. But was this a logically necessary development – that is to say, would it be only from some merchant class that the top echelon of a military-agrarian elite could receive such expertise? Without disputing either the empirical facts about what actually happened on the subcontinent or the validity of the general proposition concerning trade and state formation,[20] perhaps it was worth noting that contemporary Ottoman authors singled out the *ulema* from the lands of Classical Islam as those that had introduced methods of undertaking systematic surveys (*tahrir*), registering all sources of revenue, building up a tax base, and thereby accumulating immense wealth – practices which could surely come under 'shop-keeping', and which in fact were actually despised as such by the old caste of tribal warleaders who were themselves oriented not towards hoarding largesse but redistributing it to their followers.[21] Persians, again, in the background – though not as merchants but as learned men, counselors, vehicles for the transmission of the state-building ideology of High Islam. It would have been well, at Munich, to have a few papers on ideological 'trade', so to speak, and on the crucial importance of Iran in this regard with respect to both India and the Ottoman Empire, with the Persian language operating a bit like the 'Latin' of this region. And whilst concepts like 'shop-keeping' – and its close kin, the vulgar notion of the bourgeois state as a joint board of directors for the capitalist class – are certainly to be welcomed at a cognitive stage where demystifying the state and its art of government is still the overriding concern, they do run the risk of oversimplification. States are not just about economics, and, historically, not those that only engaged in the relatively mundane business of 'shop-keeping' but those that achieved a more thorough-going dissimulation of the fact through ideology – which, once formed acquires a life of its own – were the more successful empires.

CENTRALISATION AND DECENTRALISATION IN THE IDEOLOGY OF EMPIRE

And indeed, so successful were they at such dissimulation, that it is the 'ideal' dimension of things, in Maurice Godelier's words,[22] which we, too, first encounter through the ideology of the state. For, as Cornell Fleischer [1990] pointed out in Munich for the Ottoman Empire, Bert Fragner [1990] for Iran, and both Muzaffer Alam [1990] and Sanjay Subrahmanyam [1990] for India, what we are faced with in all three cases is essentially a documentation emanating from the state centre itself, from authors that belonged to that 'bureaucratic' core which was always 'more royalist than the king' with whose fortunes its own were very closely allied, even identified, from the beginning. What flowed from their pens, therefore, was a very flattering self-portrait of the central state which (1) deliberately exaggerated its own strength to the point of 'omnipotence'; (2) primarily recorded state activity and also recorded many other kinds of (economic) activity within its redistributionist, provisioning reach as, directly, activities of the state; (3) manifested a profound mistrust of, and inclination to downgrade, all processes and functions that lay outside its scope, including what might be called the private sector; (4) covered entire historical periods like the Ottoman seventeenth to eighteenth centuries in opprobrium for no better reason than that they involved a certain weakening of central government, which was regarded as intrinsically and self-evidently 'bad' [Abou-el-Haj, 1990]; (5) portrayed rival loci of power that rose to the fore in such phases of decentralisation as somehow unworthy, illegitimate usurpers, ruthless, anarchical and avaricious in the extreme – thus the Indian *zemindari* were invariably *fasadi* and *fitnaparvar* for their Mughal overlords: cunning plotters, disrupters of social order, sowers of dissension [Alam, 1990]; (6) cast itself in the role of 'protector' of the peasantry against their predatory encroachments. Ideology, in other words, was also used as a global vocabulary ('economic rights only' vs. additional rights of a political-juridical nature; grants 'conditional on service' vs. life holdings; the 'proposed term' of a tax-farm vs. its 'actual term' [Cızakça, 1990]; possession vs. property; in short: 'public' vs. 'private') and instrument of control over the decentralisation potential inherent in any fief-distribution or tax-farming situation.

Happily, most participants at the Munich Conference may be said to have at least partially converged in sounding warnings from various angles against taking all this at face value. Thus when the present writer, pursuing his attempt at a deconstruction of twentieth-century Turkish historiography, argued that statist-nationalist historians like the late Ömer Lütfi Barkan had departed from Fuat Köprülü's liberal-nationalist approach to commit a double error of 'document fetishism' and 'state fetishism', further magnifying the built-in bias of Ottoman records by projecting onto them the corporatist self-image of the statist, autarkic 1930s reworked as a timeless Ottoman 'golden age' [Berktay, 1990b; also Berktay, 1990a: Ch.III] – while not everyone agreed with the dose of the criticism leveled at Barkan, nevertheless the point seemed to be generally taken that allegations of 'central planning' in the sixteenth century [Barkan, 1937–38: 739–40, 741, 744, 759] were indeed extraordinary and did not necessarily have anything to do with the historical reality of what was, and long remained, very much a pre-capitalist agrarian society.[23] In terms of some of Braudel's [1985: 23–6] generalisations, trade and monetisation, for example, engaged a tiny top stratum of the economy.[24] On that material basis, no 'centralism' was possible in the modern sense, the objective conditions for which arose only during the nineteenth century, when the late-Ottoman central state was created from above in the Tanzimat era [Ortaylı, 1979; Sencer, 1971: 79]. And till then, not only the Mughals [Alam, 1990] and the Kajars [Fragner, 1990] but also the Ottomans were very much aware of the limits to their supposed 'omnipotence', which as a series of Munich papers demonstrated made it impossible for them to rule without the aid and support of local elites whether in Egypt [Özbaran, 1990], Tabriz [Zarinebaf-Shahr, 1990], or Hungary [Veselà, 1990]. During the discussion, it came out that even in the Anatolian and Rumelian heartlands, centralist ideology (to judge from the way imperial emissaries were occasionally prone to be treated by some provincial governors) was not always taken as seriously in daily life as one might conclude purely from the written evidence. As for the state's claim to provide 'protection' and 'justice', this, too, was a rather universal ideological form which simultaneously sought to sanctify existing social hierarchies (for the West: the theory of 'the three orders'; for the East: 'the Cycle of Justice') and to safeguard an average rate of exploitation that would not exhaust the capacity for reproduction of the peasant economy.

Now the state was always blaming local magnates, fief-holders out for self-aggrandisement, and 'privatising' tax-farmers, of course, for transgressing on this average rate and super-exploiting the peasantry; and it is this view of things that has traditionally been taken by the modern literature on the *iltizam* and *malikane* systems of tax-farming in the Ottoman Empire, which in the hands of Barkan [1945, 1964] and İnalcık [1972, 1977] has correlated the growth of large-scale farming with the continuous worsening of the peasant's lot – the whole has been read, in fact, as an extension into Turkey of the East European phenomenon of 'the second serfdom' [Berktay, 1990a: Ch.III]. It appears that the Mughals as well as the Porte were forever talking about economic 'abuse' and 'ruin' as the consequence of the spread of tax-farming [Alam, 1990]. But it was not as if tax-farming developed wholly spontaneously in direct response to market forces; very clearly in the Ottoman case, it was the central state which initiated its expansion from above as a solution to its most pressing problems – and as Ariel Salzmann [1990] argued in Munich, it simply was not true that the state did not know what it was doing when it started converting military fiefs (*tımars*) into tax-farms (*iltizam*) or when it allowed the eighteenth-century transition to tax-farms on a lifetime (*malikane*) basis. Furthermore, any automatic identification of tax-farming with decentralisation would be a mistake, Murat Cızakça [1990] pointed out; his detailed computer analysis of Ottoman records (pertaining only to tax-farms on non-agricultural sources of revenue) seemed to indicate that the state became risk-averse and opted to shift all possible uncertainties onto the shoulders of its tax-farmers when hard pressed by its financial commitments to the military, reversing its stance to rein in on the *mültezims* when it felt such urgent constraints to be relaxing – not drifting blindly, in other words, but making deliberate policy choices, and trying to preserve the flexibility to keep doing so.

To this, it might be added that the financial pressures which compelled the Ottoman Empire, for one, to look for additional sources of cash income, originated within the life-cycle of the state itself. As a relatively uncomplicated organism, the semi-tribal Ottoman principality was 'cheap' to run, and hence it did not need to place an enormous burden on the backs of the direct producers – it was a 'light' state, if indeed it was one. In time, however, it articulated its bureaucratic apparatus, built a huge army, isolated the sultan on a pedestal of his own, surrounded him with the elaborate ritual and magnificence of palace life, and habituated its entire ruling class to a similar and proportionate degree of luxury and ostentation at all levels – which is, again, a universal mode of ideo-political control. All these cost more and more money, and the evolution of Ottoman 'despotism' was therefore a process of *state-deepening* which ultimately came to weigh more and more heavily on the peasantry; then, from the sixteenth century onwards, a quantum jump probably took place in military expenditures when faced with the 'necessity' (rooted in the fact of empire) of waging war over longer distances against European powers that were growing stronger on a capitalist basis. This new material foundation, however, the Ottoman Empire lacked; otherwise put, at a time when absolutism was everywhere seeking to develop more effective taxation,[25] the unproductive consumption of the Ottoman state was making it more top-heavy in a way unwarranted by its mode of production. Like late-Byzantine taxation before it, the oppressiveness of late-Ottoman taxation was a historical product, and to hold the assortment of *mültezims, malikanecis, eşraf* and *ayan* (local notables) solely responsible looks in retrospect rather like an act of Freudian guilt-transfer on central government's part. Hence we simply could not take the word of the state for the peasant's lot [*Alam*, 1990]. I would add: not only for his/her alleged 'misery' under processes of relative decentralisation, but also for his/her alleged 'happiness' [*İnalcık*, 1973: 112] under central government. But such theoretical considerations aside, neither were there firm empirical grounds for presupposing universal mismanagement and super-exploitation by tax-farmers or revenue-sharing provincial elites: on the contrary, for at least part of the early eighteenth century in Eastern India, available data actually hinted at rising peasant yields (and not just price inflation) as the basis of the increase in the amount of revenue turned over to the state by the *zemindars*, again according to Muzaffar Alam [1990]. And the real bleeding white of the Indian peasantry, the doubling of tax revenues within a few years [*Hobsbawm*, 1962: 194–5], took place not under any pre-capitalist revenue-sharing arrangement but through its capitalist transformation under British colonial rule, as Dietmar Rothermund's concluding paper on 'The Mughal Heritage and British Land Revenue Systems' aptly reminded us.

THE QUEST FOR SELF-AWARENESS

Is this, then, to say that the paradigm of 'strong central states' for the Near East and the Indian subcontinent is nothing but a historiographical myth – moreover, that there was absolutely no kernel of truth to the rhetoric of 'ruin' apart from an ideological attempt to keep the process of delegating local powers from getting out of control? No one would wish to go that far; in history as in daily life, there is (usually) no smoke without fire, and as I recall Murat Cızakça perceptively remarking during one Munich debate, behind records emanating from the state and permeated with the world-view of the state, whatever degree of optical magnification or distortion might thereby be introduced, one would still suspect the existence of a state of a particular sort. India, Iran and -probably most of all- the Ottoman Empire did engage in a lot of '(ruling) class reproduction through the state' [*Haldon*, 1991], certainly more than what was going on in the medieval West, though the practice of 'managing the elite' was not unknown there, too, as Mitteis [1975: 22; also *Bloch*, 1928b on the *ministeriales*] has shown. There is, therefore, a real distinction to be drawn between a relatively 'bureaucratic' and a relatively 'aristocratic' legal-political configuration for the ruling class, corresponding to a more prebendal or more patrimonial 'domain', in Eric Wolf's [1966] Weberian terminology, over the fundamental substratum of dependent cultivators. The point is that there are no grounds for absolutising or even fetishising such differences, which need to be pursued in comparative perspective across the full spectrum of all medieval social formations.

This much, most Munich participants would probably have conceded; it was high time that Easternists, too, studied 'their' states calmly, without rhetoric, and 'not as faceless but human', some might have gone on to add. What was significant was that there was no essentialism at the Munich Conference. But how did it come about that so many historians were suddenly agreeing about discounting claims, made by the states in question, for and on behalf of 'strong centralism'? By now we have all read E.H. Carr's *What is History* as a methodological bare minimum; in principle, we all know that writing history is not just about putting down 'the facts' in the one and only way possible – that the historian's work is rooted in the individual and collective present as much as it is in the sources of the past. We are also healthily aware of cases of ideological bias involving historians of other epochs, such as those Ottoman chroniclers that belonged to the imperial bureaucracy. But do we have *self-awareness* – are we capable of maintaining a certain vigilance with respect to our own motivations? 'As we get older, we get honester', goes one Yevtushenko poem. So I felt reason to say in my summing-up at Munich: I have had my reasons for disliking and distrusting states, and one state in particular – what reasons did others have, and why was such a strong 'anti-state' emphasis coming to the surface at this late-twentieth century historical conjuncture? How much of this was the fashion of the times, and would the pendulum swing the other way in the future? To the extent that we persist in posing such questions with respect to ourselves, in deliberately taking our distances *vis-à-vis* our surroundings, and in checking what we are doing not only against the historical evidence but also against historiographical tradition as well as the intellectual stimuli provided by the contemporary world, we stand a chance of becoming better historians.

NOTES

1. On Engels's [1877–78: 195] idea that it was only in Oriental languages that no terminology existed for absolute private property, and the line of thought that AMP theorists have been inclined to base on such errors, see Varga [1967: 102, note 1]. For what Marx and Engels had read and knew of European and Asian history by the middle of the nineteenth century, around the time the *Formen* were written, see Hobsbawm [1964] as well as, more recently, O'Leary [1989]. For a more extended treatment covering various aspects of the proposition in the text, see Berktay [1990a: Ch.IV, especially 314ff.].
2. When Dühring claimed that feudal overlordship of the land had existed from time immemorial on the basis of technical necessity, Engels [1877–78: 195] argued that village communes and individual peasant holdings had existed freely for many

millenia before being brought under aristocratic dominion. In refuting Dühring's notion that it was the aristocracy which had called either slaves and/or serfs into being in order to be able to exploit 'tracts of considerable size', Engels pointed out that 'during the Middle Ages, peasant cultivation was predominant throughout the whole of Europe'.
3. Lucien Musset [1975: 158] mentions for the Germanic tribes that whether these are seen as 'wanderings of the peoples' or as 'barbarian invasions' depends on whether one opts for the German versus the Roman-French view. A similar contrast exists in the case of the migrations of Turkic tribes between Turkish nationalist historiography and the attitude of Arabo-Islamists as well as Byzantine historians.
4. The idea of lordly pressure as a source of gains in peasant productivity has been developed for early medieval Europe by Georges Duby [1974]; it has been partially accepted but also criticised as one-sided by Rodney Hilton [1973a]; instead, Hilton has preferred to conceive of such gains as rooted in a dialectic of lordly oppression and peasant resistance.
5. 'Reasons for inequality among medieval peasants' have been elaborated by Hilton [1978], whose whole argument is predicated on the effective possession by the peasant household of its own small economy – making its partial or total loss, gain or expansion (with or without lordly permission) also possible. Earlier, Postan [1960] had noted the existence of 'charters of villeins', and pointed out how this contradicted previous, legalistic, notions of the supposed inability of 'unfree' peasants to exercise any property rights. Since then, the literature on peasant inheritance customs and village-level land markets has grown considerably, requiring in-depth modification of certain theoretical propositions concerning (West European) feudalism – an overdue revision which most empirical historians are nevertheless reluctant to undertake [Berktay, 1990a: Ch.V, especially 411–12, 429–30ff.]. Both Chris Dyer [1984] and Rodney Hilton [1973b, 1990a, 1990b] have also commented on the leading role of rich peasants within the village community, and the dimensions such leadership assumed in times of revolt or protest. An attempt to set out the multi-tiered structure of feudal land-rights in theoretical form was first made by Takahashi [1952]. For a very professional, empirical medieval historian's informed theorisations about village chieftains as the primordial nucleus, the logically necessary and sufficient kernel, of the lordly class, it is always worth returning to Marc Bloch [1931: 74–6; 1941: 265, 273–4, 279–80, 283, 284, 290].
6. And yet the Roman Empire was able to do without fief distribution from the second or third century onwards, when it was already feudal or becoming feudal by a definition of feudalism based on the prevailing relations of production [Wickham, 1984, 1985]. It could be argued, however, that apart from the exceptional advantages in terms of an initially 'empty' surrounding space as well as ample liquidity (bringing with it the ability to sustain truly salaried central bureaucracies) enjoyed by Mediterranean 'slave-commercial civilisations' [Cameron, 1977: 434] like Greece and Rome in Antiquity, there was even in the latter case a tendency for the state, when finally confronted with increasing pressure from the outside as well as with the collapse of commodity production for relatively large-scale and long-distance markets [Wickham, 1988], to become increasingly unable to rule vast territories without delegating some power to local 'lordly' elites-in-the-making; it was this trend that came to fruition in the barbarian kingdoms after the fall of Rome. As for hypothetical societies of manorial villages initially belonging to individual lords, it might be maintained that as soon as kingship emerges in their interstices, these manors are likely to come under royal eminent rights and to begin to be 'held' in fief from the centre. There is, therefore, some justification for retaining fief distribution as a second and secondary common feature of feudal societies [Berktay, 1990a: 449ff.].
7. Whether for Turks or for Germans: members of the royal retinue, the companions-in-arms, the antrustions initially gathered within the walls of the palace in close attendance at court, often drawn from among the chiefs of other noble clans or tribes accepted to be related to the royal line.

8. For the Germans: vestiges of the Gallo-Roman senatorial class; for the Seljuks in the eleventh century: the Persian 'service aristocracy', in Köprülü's [1981a: 168–9] useful phrase; for the Ottomans in the thirteenth to fifteenth centuries: a similar 'High Islamic' *ulema*, the warrior aristocracies of the other Anatolian principalities, and sections of the Christian nobility of the Balkans.
9. For a treatment of *hospitalitas* which supports this interpretation, where the practice is defined as an involution of the Roman land-tax system that allowed for partial diversion of revenues into the hands of barbarian chieftains, see Goffart [1980]. For the origins and development of Islamic revenue- or land-grants from the first moments of the Arabic invasion of the Near East, and the initial posing of the problem of how to garrison the conquering armies on the land, down to the Seljukid military *ikta*, see Lybyer [1931], Poliak [1939], Köprülü [1938, 1941, 1981a, 1981b], and Cahen [1968].
10. That this, too, was inevitable has been strongly argued by İlber Ortaylı [1978] in Turkey.
11. For a discussion of the difference the degree of experience and statecraft available at the centre can make, see Berktay [1990a: 426–7], where the treatment generalises from the specialised secondary literature dealing with Merovingian, Carolingian and Capetian France, including Marc Bloch [1928a: 52–3], R.H.C. Davis [1970: 116, 140, 142, 297–306], Wallace-Hadrill [1962: 14–19; 1985: 84–5, 106], Fawtier [1960: 60–72], Hallam [1980: 78–98], James [1982: 123–5], and Dunbabin [1985: 44–100, 133–41, 162–222].
12. For an earlier comment on the significance of the *malikane-divani* system, see Berktay [1987: 329, note 31], as well as Barkan's [1939] original contribution plus İslamoğlu-İnan [1987].
13. Like the Mughals' *nizamat*. But other medieval-feudal states were also sending out 'inspectors' all the time: Charlemagne had his *missi dominici*; the Ottomans had their *mehayif müfettişleri* – though they were centuries apart. And the life-cycle of all such measures was similar: pretty soon, the inspectors had to be inspected, as it would turn out that now they were sinking local roots and undertaking 'abuse' in the provinces.
14. Apart from the belt of dependent principalities on the outer fringes of the Ottoman sphere of influence, which, like Moldavia, Wallachia and Bessarabia, only acknowledged the Porte's suzerainty and paid an annual tribute, there were also, within the ring of directly-administered provinces, those which, (a) being further away from İstanbul, (b) not positioned on the northwest-southeast diagonal of the major military campaigns that ran from the Hungarian to the Persian frontier, and (c) strongly held by (non-Turkish) Islamic ruling elites that could not be so easily decapitated, replaced or transformed, were also not reorganised through the *timar* system when they were conquered. Instead, they had a revenue-sharing arrangement with the centre whereby they kept part of their annual tax collections for themselves and sent another part, called the *salyane*, on to the treasury. These '*salyane*-paying provinces' could not function except by leaving local customs untouched and ensuring the collaboration of pre-conquest notables. It is important to emphasise that not only spatial but also military and ideological considerations (receiving and holding *timars* was the ancient birthright of the Turkish warrior nobility that founded the Ottoman state) were involved.
15. These would be, for a transition out of an existing fief system into tax-farming (such as that seen in the central Ottoman provinces from the end of the sixteenth century onwards): the government's thirst for liquidity, the progressive accumulation of merchants' and usurers' capital, and the loosening of the bonds of ideological and political loyalty that had constituted the fabric of the preceding fief system. For a transition into rule by military fiefs (such as that seen in the evolution of the Arabo-Islamic *ikta* out of an initial *katia* form that was more like a tax-farm), the conditions of transformation would be: at least partial decline of any pre-existing cash nexus, the increasing difficulty of calculating and supervising

the relative portions to be retained or forwarded to the centre under revenue-sharing arrangements. For the latter type of transformation, see, again, Lybyer [1931], Poliak [1939], Cahen [1968].

16. For a critique of such legalistic confusions, see Hilton [1976: 14–15]. For Bloch's opposition to "'the developmental fallacy", that is, the confusion between ancestry and explanation', see McLennan [1981: 105–6].

17. 'When examined closely, successful state formation or centralisation in Antiquity and the Middle Ages quite often seems to have involved, the acquisition, frequently through war, of certain external resources or bases of power (plunder, other wealth, slaves, new retinues of armed men, ideological legitimisation) specially available to the state-building centre, which are then brought to bear on the substratum of tribal kinship society out of which that state-building centre is ... trying to emerge, and whose relatively egalitarian traditions keep holding it down. Put the other way round, state formation does not get very far if its incipient vanguard, an embryonic nucleus of an aristocratic elite that has just begun to accumulate wealth and wield power, is thereafter left to confront its own tribal substratum without recourse to any such outside leverage whatsoever' [Berktay, 1990a: 10–11].

18. For information regarding state formation and resistance to it in eleventh century Scandinavia, I am indebted to a paper read at the Birmingham medieval history department by Erik Holst-Andersen (Copenhagen) in 1989. It appears that Norwegian warlords were raiding abroad and then coming back plunder-rich to try and set themselves up as kings; they were also periodically being overthrown and killed because of their violations of notions of tribal rights. It also appears that it was the ideological support provided by Christianity which finally consolidated their position. For information on the similar role played by Christianity in permitting the rise of lordship and kingship in much more isolated Iceland, I am indebted to discussions with Chris Wickham and Andrew Wareham (both of Birmingham).

19. This is an abridged version of the discussion in Berktay [1990a: Ch.1], based on standard accounts such as Halil İnalcık's [1973].

20. For the extent to which trade and other forms of contact with Rome accelerated the accumulation of wealth and consequent social stratification among the Huns, the Visigoths and other 'early Germans', see E.A. Thompson [1948: 171–7; 1965: 1ff., 17–25; 1966: 3–17, 19–21, 32–43] as well as Todd [1972: 14–15; 1975: 16ff., 22–9, 190–93].

21. The *Tevarih-i Al-i Osman*, the chronicle of early Ottoman history penned by Aşıkpaşazade Derviş Ahmed Aşıki from around 1476 onwards, describes the *ulema* as having taught the sultans to construct survey-books, to hoard money and to build up the treasury; this is clearly seen as reprehensible, as a violation of ancient custom. Hence the bitter words Bayezid I – deserted by most of his Turkish vassals – is made to hear in defeat on the battlefield of Ankara (1402): 'You did not dispense with your money. You hoarded it in the treasury ...' [Aşıkpaşazade, Ch.67].

22. Reacting against what he regards as a crude theory of 'reflection', Godelier has recently insisted that to every slice of the 'real' there is also an 'ideal' dimension. So perhaps it was not so ironic that at Munich, too, it should have fallen to the lot of a Marxist to warn against reductionism. I am grateful to Fatmagül Berktay [1990] for an initial discussion of Godelier [1982]; now, also see a fuller treatment in book form [Godelier, 1986].

23. It was, moreover, pointed out that the manner and tone adopted by Barkan in glorifying imperial power, deprecating decentralisation, and assuming the worst for the consequences of the spread of tax-farming, was very much in the tradition in these matters of, for example, Ahmed Cevdet Paşa, the mid-nineteenth century court chronicler (and for some, the standard-bearer of a new historiography – which with his ingrained imperial conservatism he was *not*). This observation

raises the possibility of regarding late Ottoman historiography – itself an extension of imperial court ideology – as a repository of ready-made ideological values and prejudices on which twentieth-century nationalist historians kept drawing in response to the reformulated exigencies of the state. I am grateful to Christoph Neumann (Munich) for the original comment. On Ahmed Cevdet Paşa (and late Ottoman historiography in general), also see three recent articles by Michael Ursinus [1986, 1987, 1988].
24. Interestingly enough, at Munich there was only one paper on trade as such – that by Serap Yılmaz [1990].
25. See Perry Anderson's [1974] discussion.

REFERENCES

Abou-el-Haj, Rifa'at, 1990, 'Efficient Considerations for Theorising Beyond the Nation-State: The Case of Early Modern and Modern Ottoman Society', paper read at the International Symposium on 'The State, Decentralisation and Tax-Farming, 1500–1850: The Ottoman Empire, Iran and India' held at Munich on 2–5 May 1990.

Akarlı, Engin and Cornell Fleischer, 1990, 'Taking Stock of Ottoman History', unpublished discussion paper read at the Rockefeller Foundation Seminar on Ottoman History held at St. Louis, USA, on 12–15 April 1990.

Alam, Muzaffar, 1990, *Zemindari*, Revenue-Farming, and *Nizamat* in Eastern India: A Study of their Interaction with Mughal Central Power in the Early 18th Century', paper read at the International Symposium on 'The State, Decentralisation and Tax-Farming, 1500–1850: The Ottoman Empire, Iran and India' held at Munich on 2–5 May 1990.

Anderson, Perry, 1974, *Lineages of the Absolutist State*, London: New Left Books.

Barkan, Ö.L., 1937–38, 'Osmanlı İmparatorluğunda Çiftçi Sınıfların Hukuki Statüsü' [The Legal Status of the Agrarian Classes in the Ottoman Empire]; in Ö.L. Barkan, *Türkiye'de Toprak Meselesi. Toplu Eserler 1* [The Agrarian Question in Turkey. Collected Works, Volume 1], İstanbul: Gözlem, 1980, pp.725–88.

Barkan, Ö.L., 1939, 'Malikane–Divani Sistemi' [The Half-Estate, Half-State System], in Ö.L. Barkan, *Türkiye'de Toprak Meselesi. Toplu Eserler 1* [The Agrarian Question in Turkey. Collected Works, Volume 1], İstanbul: Gözlem, 1980, pp.151–208.

Barkan, Ö.L., 1939–40, 'XV ve XVI'ncı Asırlarda Osmanlı İmparatorluğunda Toprak İşçiliğinin Organizasyonu Şekilleri' [Forms of Organisation of Agricultural Labour in the Ottoman Empire in the Fifteenth and Sixteenth Centuries], in Ö.L. Barkan, *Türkiye'de Toprak Meselesi. Toplu Eserler 1* [The Agrarian Question in Turkey. Collected Works, Volume 1], İstanbul: Gözlem, 1980, pp.575–716.

Barkan, Ö.L., 1945, 'Çiftlik' [Farm], in Ö.L. Barkan, *Türkiye'de Toprak Meselesi. Toplu Eserler 1* [The Agrarian Question in Turkey. Collected Works, Volume 1], İstanbul: Gözlem, 1980, pp.789–97.

Barkan, Ö.L., 1964, 'Öşür' [Tithe], in Ö.L. Barkan, *Türkiye'de Toprak Meselesi. Toplu Eserler 1* [The Agrarian Question in Turkey. Collected Works, Volume 1], İstanbul: Gözlem, 1980, pp.799–804.

Berkemer, Georg, 1990, 'Elite Formation and Political Development in the 18th Century in the Northern Sircars (Andhra Pradesh/India)', paper read at the International Symposium on 'The State, Decentralisation and Tax-Farming, 1500–1850: The Ottoman Empire, Iran and India' held at Munich on 2–5 May 1990.

Berktay, Fatmagül, 1990, 'Women and Religion: Discourses of Domination and Resistance', unpublished M.A. thesis in Women's Studies, University of York.

Berktay, Halil, 1987, 'The Feudalism Debate: The Turkish End – Is "Tax-vs.-Rent" Necessarily the Product and Sign of a Modal Difference?', *The Journal of Peasant Studies*, Vol.14, No.3, pp.291–333.

Berktay, Halil, 1990a, 'The "Other" Feudalism: A Critique of 20th Century Turkish Historiography and Its Particularisation of Ottoman Society', unpublished Ph.D. thesis in Medieval History, University of Birmingham.'

Berktay, Halil, 1990b, 'Centralisation and Decentralisation in the State-Fetishist Perspective of 20th Century Turkish Historiography', paper read at the International Symposium on 'The State, Decentralisation and Tax-Farming, 1500–1850: The Ottoman Empire, Iran and India' held at Munich on 2–5 May 1990.

Bloch, Marc, 1928a, 'A Contribution Towards a Comparative History of European Societies', originally published in the *Revue de Synthèse Historique*, republished in Marc Bloch, *Land and Work in Medieval Europe. Selected Papers* (translated by J.E. Anderson), London: Routledge & Kegan Paul, 1967, pp.44–81.

Bloch, Marc, 1928b, 'A Problem in Comparative History: The Administrative Classes in France and in Germany', originally published in the *Revue historique du droit français et étranger*, republished in Marc Bloch, *Land and Work in Medieval Europe: Selected Papers* (translated by J.E. Anderson), London: Routledge & Kegan Paul, 1967, pp.82–123.

Bloch, Marc, 1931, *French Rural History: An Essay on Its Basic Characteristics* (translated from the French by Janet Sondheimer), Berkeley CA: University of California Press, 1966.

Bloch, Marc, 1941, 'The Rise of Dependent Cultivation and Seignorial Institutions', in M.M. Postan (ed.), *The Cambridge Economic History of Europe. Volume 1: The Agrarian Life of the Middle Ages*, London and Cambridge: Cambridge University Press (second edition, 1971), pp.235–90.

Braudel, Fernand, 1985, *Civilization and Capitalism, 15th–18th Century. Volume 1: The Structures of Everyday Life. The Limits of the Possible* (translated from the 1979 French original by Sian Reynolds), London: Fontana Press.

Cahen, Claude, 1968, *Pre-Ottoman Turkey* (translated from the French by J. Jones–Williams), New York: Taplinger.

Cameron, Kenneth Neill, 1977, *Humanity and Society: A World History*, New York and London: Monthly Review Press, second edition.

Çizakça, Murat, 1990, 'Ottoman Economy and Society as Reflected by Tax-Farming Records (16th–18th Centuries)', paper read at the International Symposium on 'The State, Decentralisation and Tax-Farming, 1500–1850: The Ottoman Empire, Iran and India' held at Munich on 2–5 May 1990.

Davis, R.H.C., 1970, *A History of Medieval Europe*, London: Longman, revised edition.

Duby, Georges, 1974, *The Early Growth of the European Economy: Warriors and Peasants from the Seventh to the Twelfth Century* (translated from the 1973 French original by Howard B. Clarke), Ithaca and New York: Cornell University Press.

Dunbabin, Jean, 1985, *France in the Making 843–1180*, London and Oxford: Oxford University Press.

Dyer, Christopher, 1984, 'The Social and Economic Background to the Rural Revolt of 1381', in R.H. Hilton and T.H. Aston (eds.) *The English Rising of 1381*, London and Cambridge: Cambridge University Press.

Engels, Friedrich, 1877–78, *Anti-Dühring: Herr Eugen Dühring's Revolution in Science* (translated by Emile Burns); New York: International Publishers, 1976.

Faroqhi, Suraiya, 1988, 'New Approaches to Ottoman History', second draft of a paper read at the International Symposium on 'Legalism and Political Legitimation in the Ottoman Empire and in the Early Turkish Republic, *ca.* 1500 to 1940' held at Bochum on 1–3 December 1988.

Faroqhi, Suraiya, 1991, 'In Search of Ottoman History', paper read at the International Symposium on 'The State, Decentralisation and Tax-Farming, 1500–1850: The Ottoman Empire, Iran and India' held at Munich on 2–5 May 1990, now in *The Journal of Peasant Studies*, this volume.

Fawtier, Robert, 1960, *The Capetian Kings of France: Monarchy and Nation 987–1328* (translated by Lionel Butler and R.J. Adam), London: Macmillan.

Fleischer, Cornell, 1990, 'Centralisation and Decentralisation in Ottoman State Ideology', paper read at the International Symposium on 'The State, Decentralisation and Tax-Farming, 1500–1850: The Ottoman Empire, Iran and India' held at Munich on 2–5 May 1990.
Fragner, Bert, 1990, 'The Myth of a Strong Central State (Particularism and Decentralisation in Pre-Modern Iranian Society)', paper read at the International Symposium on 'The State, Decentralisation and Tax-Farming, 1500–1850: The Ottoman Empire, Iran and India' held at Munich on 2–5 May 1990.
Godelier, Maurice, 1982, 'The Ideal in the Real', in Raphael Samuel and Gareth Stedman Jones (eds.), *Culture, Ideology and Politics*, London: Routledge & Kegan Paul, History Workshop Series, pp.12–38.
Godelier, Maurice, 1986, *The Mental and the Material* (translated from the 1984 French original by Martin Thom) London: Verso.
Goffart, W., 1980, *Barbarians and Romans, AD 418–584: The Techniques of Accomodation*, Princeton, NJ: Princeton University Press.
Haldon, John, 1991, 'State Theory and the Medieval State: Some Comparative Perspectives', *The Journal of Peasant Studies*, this volume.
Hallam, Elizabeth M., 1980, *Capetian France 987–1328*, London: Longman.
Hill, Christopher, 1986, 'Braudel and the State', in *The Collected Essays of Christopher Hill. Volume Three: People and Ideas in 17th Century England*, Brighton: Harvester Press, pp.125–42.
Hilton, R.H., 1973a, 'Warriors and Peasants' [review of Duby 1974], *New Left Review*, No.83, pp.83–94.
Hilton, R.H., 1973b, Bond Men Made Free: *Medieval Peasant Movements and the English Rising of 1381*, New York: Viking Press.
Hilton, R.H., 1976, 'Introduction', in R.H. Hilton (ed.), *The Transition from Feudalism to Capitalism*, London: Verso, pp.9–30.
Hilton, R.H., 1978, 'Reasons for Inequality Among Medieval Peasants', *The Journal of Peasant Studies*, Vol.5, No.3, pp.271–83.
Hilton, R.H., 1990a, 'Seigneurie française et manoir anglais fifty years later', in *Marc Bloch aujourd'hui. Histoire comparée et sciences sociales*, Paris: Éditions de l'École des Hautes Études en Sciences Sociales.
Hilton, R.H., 1990b, *The Change Beyond the Change: A Dream of John Ball*, London: The William Morris Society.
Hobsbawm, E.J., 1962, *The Age of Revolution 1798–1848*, New York and Toronto: Mentor.
Hobsbawm, E.J., 1964, 'Introduction', in Karl Marx, *Pre-Capitalist Economic Formations* (translated by Jack Cohen; ed. E.J. Hobsbawm), London: Lawrence & Wishart, pp.9–65.
İnalcık, Halil, 1972, 'The Ottoman Decline and Its Effects upon the Reaya', in H. Birnbaum and Speros Vryonis, Tr. (eds.), *Aspects of the Balkans: Continuity and Change*, The Hague: Mouton, pp.338–54.
İnalcık, Halil, 1973, *The Ottoman Empire: The Classical Age 1300–1600*, London: Weidenfeld & Nicolson.
İnalcık, Halil, 1977, 'Centralisation and Decentralisation in Ottoman Administration', in T. Naff and R. Owen (eds.), *Studies in Eighteenth Century Islamic History*, Carbondale, IL, pp.27–52.
İslamoğlu, Huricihan and Çağlar Keyder, 1977, 'Agenda for Ottoman History', *Review* (Fernand Braudel Centre, Binghampton), Vol.1, No.1, pp.31–55.
İslamoğlu-İnan, Huricihan, 1987, 'State and Peasants in the Ottoman Empire: A Study of Peasant Economy in North-central Anatolia during the sixteenth century', in H. İslamoğlu-İnan, (ed.), *The Ottoman Empire and the World Economy*, Cambridge: Cambridge University Press, pp.101–59.
James, Edward, 1982, *The Origins of France: From Clovis to the Capetians, 500–1000*, London: Macmillan.
Köprülü, Fuat, 1938, 'Ortazaman Türk Hukuki Müesseseleri: İslam Amme Hukukundan

Ayrı Bir Türk Amme Hukuku Yok mudur?' [Medieval Turkish Legal Institutions: Is There No Turkish Public Law Distinct from Islamic Public Law?], *Belleten* (Ankara), Vol.II, Nos.5–6, pp.39–72.

Köprülü, Fuat, 1941, 'Ortazaman Türk-İslam Feodalizmi' [Medieval Turkish–Islamic Feudalism], *Belleten* (Ankara), Vol.V, No.19, pp.319–34.

Köprülü, Fuat, 1981a, *Bizans Müesseselerinin Osmanlı Müesseselerine Tesiri* [The Influence of Byzantine Institutions on Ottoman Institutions]. İstanbul: Ötüken; reprint of extended essay originally published in 1931.

Köprülü, Fuat, 1981b, *Osmanlı İmparatorluğunun Kuruluşu* [The Origins of the Ottoman Empire], İstanbul: Ötüken; originally published in French; Paris: E. de Boccard, 1935.

Lybyer, A. H., 1931, 'Feudalism – Saracen and Ottoman', *Encyclopaedia of the Social Sciences*, New York: Macmillan, Vol.VI, pp.210–13.

Matuz, Josef, 1990, 'Contributions to the Remittance of the Ottoman Tax-Farming Unit in the 16th Century', paper read at the International Symposium on 'The State, Decentralisation and Tax-Farming, 1500–1850: The Ottoman Empire, Iran and India' held at Munich on 2–5 May 1990.

McLennan, Gregor, 1981, *Marxism and the Methodologies of History*, London: New Left Books.

Mitteis, Heinrich, 1975, *The State in the Middle Ages: A Comparative Constitutional History of Feudal Europe*, (translated from the German by H.F. Orton), Amsterdam and Oxford: North-Holland Medieval Translations, Vol.1.

Murphey, Rhoads, 1990, 'Continuity and Discontinuity in Ottoman Administrative Theory and Practice: An Overview of Post-16th Century Evolutionary Trends in the Ottoman Bureaucracy', paper read at the International Symposium on 'The State, Decentralisation and Tax-Farming, 1500–1850: The Ottoman Empire, Iran and India' held at Munich on 2–5 May 1990.

Musset, Lucien, 1975, *The Germanic Invasions: The Making of Europe AD 400–600* (translated from the 1965 French original by Edward and Columba James), London: Paul Elek.

O'Leary, Brendan, 1989, *The Asiatic Mode of Production*, London: Basil Blackwell.

Ortaylı, İlber, 1978, 'Osmanlı Toprak Düzeninin Kaynakları' [The Origins of the Ottoman Land Tenure System], *Toplum ve Bilim* [Society and Science – İstanbul], No.4, pp.72–7.

Ortaylı, İlber, 1979, *Türkiye İdare Tarihi* [The Administrative History of Turkey], Ankara: TODAİE.

Özbaran, Salih, 1990, '*İltizam* in the Southern Provinces of the Ottoman Empire', paper read at the International Symposium on 'The State, Decentralisation and Tax-Farming, 1500–1850: The Ottoman Empire, Iran and India' held at Munich on 2–5 May 1990.

Poliak, A.N., 1939, *Feudalism in the Middle East: Feudalism in Egypt, Syria, Palestine, and the Lebanon, 1250–1900*, London: The Royal Asiatic Society Prize Publishing Fund.

Postan, M.M., 1960, 'The Charters of the Villeins', in M.M. Postan (ed.), *Essays on Medieval Agriculture and General Problems of the Medieval Economy*, London and Cambridge: Cambridge University Press, pp.107–49.

Rothermund, Dietmar, 1990, 'The Mughal Heritage and British Land Revenue Systems', paper read at the International Symposium on 'The State, Decentralisation and Tax-Farming, 1500–1850: The Ottoman Empire, Iran and India' held at Munich on 2–5 May 1990.

Salzmann, Ariel, 1990, 'Tax-Farming and Usufruct Rights in an 18th Century Ottoman Setting', paper read at the International Symposium on 'The State, Decentralisation and Tax-Farming, 1500–1850: The Ottoman Empire, Iran and India' held at Munich on 2–5 May 1990.

Sencer, Muammer, 1971, *Toprak Ağalığının Kökeni* [The Origins of Landlordism], İstanbul: Tel.

Subrahmanyam, Sanjay, 1990, 'Intra-Asia Elite Movements and Tax-Farmers' Careers in 17th Century Southern India', paper read at the International Symposium on 'The State, Decentralisation and Tax-Farming, 1500-1850: The Ottoman Empire, Iran and India' held at Munich on 2-5 May 1990.
Takahashi, Kohachiro, 1952, 'A Contribution to the Discussion', in R.H.Hilton (ed.), *The Transition from Feudalism to Capitalism*, London: Verso, pp.68-97.
Therborn, Goran, 1978, *What Does The Ruling Class Do When It Rules: State Apparatuses and State Power Under Feudalism, Capitalism and Socialism*, London: New Left Books.
Thompson, E.A., 1948, *A History of Attila and the Huns*, Oxford: Clarendon Press.
Thompson, E.A., 1965, *The Early Germans*, Oxford: Clarendon Press.
Thompson, E.A., 1966, *The Visigoths in the Time of Ulfila*, Oxford: Clarendon Press.
Todd, Malcolm, 1972, *The Barbarians: Goths, Franks and Vandals*. London: Batsford.
Todd, Malcolm, 1975, *The Northern Barbarians 100 BC-AD 300*, London: Basil Blackwell.
Ursinus, Michael, 1986, 'Byzantine History in Late Ottoman Turkish Historiography', *Byzantine and Modern Greek Studies* (Birmingham), No.10, pp.201-223.
Ursinus, Michael, 1987, '"Der schlechteste staat": Ahmed Midhat Efendi (1844-1913) on Byzantine Institutions', *Byzantine and Modern Greek Studies* (Birmingham), No.11, pp.237-43.
Ursinus, Michael, 1988, 'From Süleyman Pasha to Mehmet Fuat Köprülü: Roman and Byzantine History in Late Ottoman Historiography', *Byzantine and Modern Greek Studies* (Birmingham), No.12, pp.305-14.
Varga, Eugene, 1967, 'Sur le "mode de production asiatique"', *Recherches Internationales*, Nos.57-58, pp.98-117.
Veselà, Zdenka, 1990, 'Taxationssystem in den ungarischen Provinzen des Osmanischen Reiches', paper read at the International Symposium on 'The State, Decentralisation and Tax-Farming, 1500-1850: The Ottoman Empire, Iran and India' held at Munich on 2-5 May 1990.
Wallace-Hadrill, J.M., 1962, *The Long-Haired Kings and Other Studies in Frankish History*, London: Methuen.
Wallace-Hadrill, J.M., 1985, *The Barbarian West 400-1000*, London: Basil Blackwell, revised edition.
Wickham, C.J., 1984, 'The Other Transition: From the Ancient World to Feudalism', *Past and Present*, No.103, pp.3-36.
Wickham, C.J., 1985, 'The Uniqueness of the East', *The Journal of Peasant Studies*, Vol.12, Nos.2-3, pp.166-96.
Wickham, C.J., 1988, 'Marx, Sherlock Holmes, and Late Roman Commerce', *The Journal of Roman Studies*, Vol.LXXVII.
Wolf, Eric R., 1966, *Peasants*, Englewood Cliffs, NJ: Prentice-Hall.
Yılmaz, Serap, 1990, 'A propos des relations commerciales entre l'Inde et l'Empire Ottoman dans la second moitié du XVIIIe siècle', paper read at the International Symposium on 'The State, Decentralisation and Tax-Farming, 1500-1850: The Ottoman Empire, Iran and India' held at Munich on 2-5 May 1990.
Zarinebaf-Shahr, Fariba, 1990, 'The Urban Administration of Tabriz in the 18th Century: Persians and Ottomans', paper read at the International Symposium on 'The State, Decentralisation and Tax-Farming, 1500-1850: The Ottoman Empire, Iran and India' held at Munich on 2-5 May 1990.

Abstracts

Introduction
SURAIYA FAROQHI

Debates on the world historical place of the Ottoman Empire in the last few decades have been conducted mainly in Turkey, and largely though not exclusively, in terms of 'feudalism vs. the Asiatic Mode of Production'. This debate cannot be separated from the social and political context in which it was conducted, and the present article attempts to demonstrate these links. Recently, however the terms of the debate have been modified; the Asiatic Mode of Production has receded into the background, while a developing interest in comparative work has furthered the introduction of concepts from European, Chinese and Central Asian history. Ottoman history has become more 'cosmopolitan'.

The Ottoman State and the Question of State Autonomy: Comparative Perspectives
JOHN HALDON

This article examines the nature of the Ottoman state in respect of the question of state autonomy, questions the validity and analytical usefulness of some recent state theorist positions in this regard, and seeks thereby to re-affirm the validity of a historical materialist analysis. It demonstrates that, however independent or autonomous rulers or state elites might be, or be perceived to be, they are inevitably constrained by the structural limitations set upon their freedom of action by the relations of production of the society over which they stand, and more particularly, by the relations of surplus distribution between classes and within the ruling class. In the process of this discussion, the analytical centrality of 'the economic' – the totality of the relations of production in a given social formation – in historical explanation is re-affirmed, and at the same time it is argued that this involves neither a reductionist nor a determinist mode of explanation. Social power, in whatever form it is expressed (economic, ideological, political or military, for example) is a factor of resource control, and the latter is inevitably a configured effect of the structure of the dominant relations of production in a society.

The Search for the Peasant in Western and Turkish History/Historiography
HALIL BERKTAY

Historiography can no longer sustain the naive self-belief of an unreconstructed empiricism in its capacity to arrive automatically at the one and only possible 'truth' by hoarding and quantitatively aggregating all the bits of information contained in supposedly 'neutral' documents. Instead, it has to be able to make up for textual silences or distortions of various kinds; to deconstruct, with the aid of theoretical perspectives that should themselves not be aprioristic but distilled from broader sets of evidence, the built-in biases and deformations that are inevitably imparted to the documentation by the historical circumstances surrounding their birth and the particular point within the hierarchy of a stratified social formation where they originate. For a very long time, history was written only from above; and because the ruling class records on which it was based were generally accepted at face value, it was thought that it had also always been made from the top down. Thus the reality of peasant life and the oppressive nature of serfdom came to penetrate Western medieval history only in the early twentieth century; as for the *raiyyet*, the Ottoman dependent cultivator, he/she has still not been able to assume a significant place and role on the vast stage of Ottoman history. Medieval serfs having kept no comparable accounts for their small economies, early pictures of Western feudalism that were over-reliant on inventories drawn up for the largest ecclesiastical estates tended to exaggerate the scope of the lord's economy and particularly of demesne production based on labour services. The bulk of the documentation for the Ottoman Empire, on the other hand, emanates not from private lordship but from the state, and hence constantly defines the peasant and the peasant holding in terms of legal categories invented by that state, that is, as the basic unit of the tax-system. Western medieval history has succeeded in overcoming its lord-centred approach to serfdom to a large extent, but the document-fetishism of Turkish nationalist historiography continues to complement a state-fetishism that makes it impossible to apprehend the spontaneous socio-economic, class-structured modalities of peasant existence.

Ottoman History by Inner Asian Norms
ISENBIKE TOGAN

The present study compares the principal stages of the state founded by the Mongols in thirteenth and fourteenth-century China and the stages, longer-lasting but in some aspects similar, traversed by the Ottoman state in the six centuries of its existence. The secret of Ottoman flexibility lay in its manner of ordering centre–periphery relations. Power and resources were accumulated at the centre, while in the periphery the central government shared power with local men of nomadic or sedentary background. A novel 'internalist' interpretation is provided for nineteenth-century 'modernisation': New social groups saw in the ideology of modernisation a legitimation of their own demand for a share in political power.

In Search of Ottoman History
SURAIYA FAROQHI

From the beginning of Republican Turkish historiography, the most noted Ottomanist scholars have been aware of European and American work on the mediaeval and early modern history of Europe and have oriented their own research accordingly. In spite of this, comparative research has rarely been undertaken. The present article examines the reasons for this contradictory situation and pinpoints areas in which comparative studies can be particularly fruitful. Focusing on commerce, urban history and the 'Seventeenth

Century Crisis' the author attempts to explain certain remarkable instances of convergence between recent Ottomanist and Europeanist historiography.

Three Empires and the Societies They Governed: Iran, India and the Ottoman Empire
HALIL BERKTAY

Historians of the East are more and more coming to discount the degree of centralism traditionally claimed for or on behalf of the major pre-capitalist polities of their area of study. Such ideas of absolutist omnipotence can be shown to have originated as reflections of the subjective self-consciousness of those sections of the ruling class which were entrenched in – and recast as – the bureaucratic apparatus of the state; it was in their eyes that any decentralising tendencies were automatically construed as 'evil', as so many manifestations of 'corruption' and 'decadence', simply because of the decline of royal power they involved. But was this really always bad for the peasantry, too, as past ideologues of imperial 'justice' have asserted in attacking systems of tax-farming or revenue-sharing and the privatisation dynamics they eventually created? Answers should no longer be based on the aprioristic grounds of a simplistic faith in taking central bureaucracies at their word, a recent conference in Munich may be said to have concluded. And to facilitate empirical research, we also need parallel progress in constructing an overall theory of tax-farming in pre-capitalist agrarian societies, its appearance and disappearance, its modalities of interaction with other forms of surplus management and land tenure.